ISLAND TIMBER

A Social History of the Comox Logging Company
Vancouver Island

Richard Somerset Mackie

Sono
Nis
Press

Victoria, British Columbia, Canada

Canadian Cataloguing in Publication Data

Mackie, Richard, 1957-
   Island timber

   Includes index.
   ISBN 1-55039-101-1

   1. Comox Logging Company—History. 2. Logging—British Columbia—Vancouver Island—History. 3. Forests and forestry—British Columbia—Vancouver Island—History. 4. Vancouver Island (B.C.)—History. I. Title.
SD538.3.C2M33 2000   338.7'63498'097112   C00-910313-9

Sono Nis Press gratefully acknowledges the support of the Canada Council for the Arts and the Province of British Columbia, through the British Columbia Arts Council.

First Printing: November 2000
Second Printing: March 2001

Cover design by Jim Brennan
Page and photo layout design by Jim Bennett
Cartography by Eric Leinberger

Cover photo: Wilmer Gold Collection, 1935, IWA Canada Local 1-80, Duncan, BC — Chris Holmes with Western Red Cedar over 2000 years old at Comox Lake.

Published by
SONO NIS PRESS
PO Box 5550, Stn. B
Victoria, BC v8r 6s4
TEL: (250) 598-7807
http://www.islandnet.com/sononis/
sononis@islandnet.com

Printed and bound in Canada by Friesens.

*I would like to dedicate
my work on this book
to the memory of
Patrick de Fylton Mackie (1922–1999)
and
Allan Cecil Brooks (1926–2000).*

contents

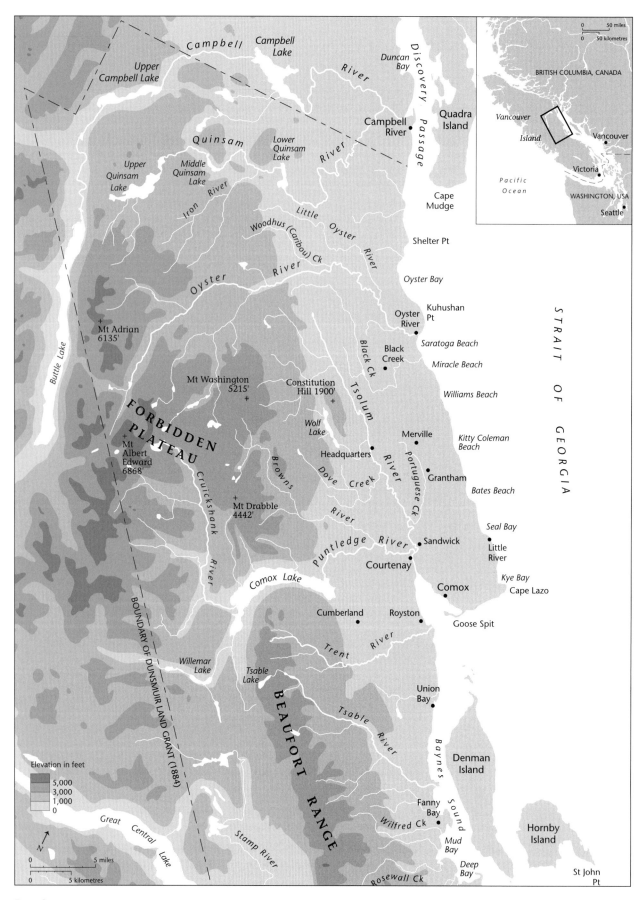

East-Central Vancouver Island

This is a story of long ago,
When I worked for the Comox Logging Co.
The price was seventy-five per M.,
And the quarter to cut was a perfect gem.

—"The Barber Chair Faller"

On the east coast of Vancouver Island, British Columbia, and at the north end of the Strait of Georgia, lies a coastal plain of impressive proportions. Between the Strait and the Vancouver Island Ranges, some two hundred square miles of level gravelly soils stretch from the Tsolum River to Campbell River. From the distance, or from the air, the plain might be mistaken for a continuous old-growth Douglas fir forest, but the communities of Comox and Courtenay, and the rural settlements of Merville, Black Creek, and Oyster River, exist within and around the edges of a second- and third-growth canopy.

In the first half of the twentieth century much of this well-forested and accessible coastal region was owned outright by the Comox Logging and Railway Company. This is a history of that coastal plain during four momentous decades (*c.* 1900–1938) of its existence.

A "logger's Eden" of giant Douglas fir (*Pseudotsuga menziesii*) had developed on the plain since an immense forest fire in 1668. Lumbermen logged these trees on a small scale in the nineteenth century, but it was only after the formation of Comox Logging that the great forest of Comox District began to yield to the crosscut saws of Swedish and Finnish falling gangs. Logs were yarded from the bush by steam skidders and locomotives typical of what historians have called the "glory days" or "heroic era" of logging on the Pacific coast of North America.

Logging, in the popular mind, is about "lumberjacks," that is, fallers and buckers—the men who cut down the big trees of the forest and prepared

them for transport. In reality, fallers and buckers made up only 70 or 80 of Comox Logging's 450 employees. Among the great many other professions and skills required by this "logging" company were timber cruising, surveying, grading, bridge building, saw filing, scaling, rigging, yarding, skidding, loading, hauling, dumping, booming, and towing. Engineers, blacksmiths, mechanics, machinists, welders, train crews, and countless other professional, trade, and labouring professions were needed to keep the company working.

What all workers had in common, directly or indirectly, was an interest in moving logs from the bush to the booming grounds and preparing them for the journey across the Strait to Fraser Mills. At this single large export mill on the Fraser River, the timber was sawn into high-quality, straight-grained lumber and shipped to the markets of Canada and the world. Between 1910 and 1940, Comox Logging prepared an average of 100,000,000 board feet of timber a year. Altogether in these years the company logged about three billion board feet of timber in the Comox District. To put these large figures in perspective, a small house contains about 5,000 board feet. On average, Comox Logging sent enough timber to the mill every year to build 20,000 houses.

Much of this book follows the sequence observed by Comox Logging in rendering an old-growth Douglas fir forest into timber and delivering it to the mill. This is the story of that intricate process, and of a great and fundamental change to the face of the earth—the removal of an ancient forest by human ingenuity and industrial machinery, and subsequent destruction of the remnants by fire. Comox Logging and other Vancouver Island logging companies left behind a vast wasteland of partly burned logging slash which, in 1938, would nourish a fire almost as catastrophic as that of 1668.

But primarily this is the story of the men who earned their living effecting this change to the landscape. Many of them—the Comox Homeguard —grew up on farms in the Comox District; others moved there from Britain, Scandinavia, and elsewhere and married into local farming families. Typically, they alternated seasonally between forest and farm work. *Island Timber* is as much about the men, families, and rural life supported by Comox Logging as about the machines and methods employed by the company. This is a social history both of a logging company and of the communities that provided it with local sources of labour.

This project has challenged and broadened my skills as a writer and historian. My previous books were set in the nineteenth century and based almost entirely on archival documents written by people who had been dead for many years. By contrast, the foundations of this story are interviews with living people—with the actors themselves in this industrial and rural drama.

Since the start of the project late in 1995, I have talked to 150 people who enthusiastically shared their stories about the Comox Logging Company. They lent me books from their sometimes extensive personal libraries, and they retrieved from dusty drawers, basements, and attics old photographs that helped me reconstruct the spatial and occupational contours of this large company. I am grateful to them for allowing me to reproduce their photographs, most of which are published here for the first time.

It was vitally important to meet these men—and their knowledgeable wives—because their opinions and reflections will not be available to future historians. It has been a pleasure and privilege to get to know them, and to be able to contact them when I had a question or wanted to double-check something.

And while *Island Timber* deals mainly with a single company, I hope it also opens a window onto the early history of logging and logging communities elsewhere on the Pacific coast.

A centuries-old Douglas fir forest surrounded the good farmland of the Comox Valley. This photo by Comox photographer Walter Gage shows a wagon road in the valley in about 1910.—COURTENAY & DISTRICT MUSEUM & ARCHIVES, P85-97D

acknowledgements

The inspiration and sponsor of this book was Alice Bullen who, in 1995, applied to the Vancouver Foundation for a grant to write a history of the Comox Logging Company. Alice was then chair of the Filberg Lodge and Park Association of Comox, a non-profit society known for its annual Filberg Festival of the Arts. I would never have written the book without Alice's support and without grants from the Vancouver Foundation and the Filberg Lodge and Park Association. I am grateful to all of them for their patronage—and patience.

Cathy Richardson has been a source of strength and much practical advice since I started the project late in 1995. Our sons Raphael and Rupert were born during the writing of this book, and their older sister Juliet is not much older than the first draft. The love of this family has been a blessing. Greta Richardson has provided frequent and welcome babysitting.

It has been a pleasure to work with the fine editorial, marketing, and design team at Sono Nis Press: Dawn Loewen, Pat Sloan, Heather Keenan, Jim Bennett, Jim Brennan, and Donna Halbert. I will always be grateful to Diane Morriss for her timely support.

Len Todd of Qualicum worked photographic miracles in his small darkroom. Most of the photographic reproductions in this book are Len's work, and I am grateful for his remarkable skill and unflagging interest. My father George Mackie and my cousin Paddy Mackie generously paid part of the cost of the photographs. For their assistance, I am grateful to Cole Harris and Graeme Wynn of the Geography Department at the University of British Columbia, where I benefited from a postdoctoral fellowship from the Social Sciences and Humanities Research Council of Canada in 1998 and 1999. Cole and Graeme's colleague Eric Leinberger transformed my rough sketches into fine cartography.

I also owe distinct thanks to Al Mackie, for always supporting my efforts and for his patient help with a traumatic computer upgrade; to Allan Pritchard, for his enthusiasm, suggestions, and numerous cups of tea; to Jack Hodgins, for his sound advice at a critical moment; to Jeanette Taylor, for her letters and support; to Bob Turner, for pointing me to sources and photographs; to Allan and Betty Brooks, for their hospitality and insight; to Barbara Marriott, Carol Neufeld, and Margo McLoughlin, for tea, pep talks, and introductions; to John Lutz, for encouraging me to talk about this project in the academic setting of the Qualicum History Conference; to Gly Comstock, for providing extracts from his extensive collection of lumber trade journals. For access to early logging maps and other assistance I thank Doug Grant, Dale Harrison, Bill Hembroff, John Jungen, Don McIver, Darrell McQuillan, John Parminter, Norman Sprout, and Gerry Young. For specific documents and references I am very grateful to Jeri Bass, Graham Brazier, Julian Brooks, Maureen Duffus, Bob Griffin, Marguerite Holgate, John Hurley, Rick James, Colin Laroque, Margo McLoughlin, Jeremy Mouat, Brad Morrison, Jamie Morton, John Parminter, Les Pidcock, Fred Rogers, Jill Wade, and Diane Wells.

For work space, answers to research questions, and numerous other matters it is a pleasure to thank Deb

Griffiths, Andrew Ellis, Wendy Fried, Judy Hagen, Catherine Siba, and Pat Trask of the Courtenay Museum; Terry Hale, Linda Hogarth, and Sandra Parrish of the Campbell River Museum; and Barb Lemky of the Cumberland Museum. Martin Gavin and the rest of the staff of the Courtenay branch of the Vancouver Island Regional Library traced books for me, and Lori Sugden of the map library, Geography Department, University of Victoria, provided valuable help.

I must also thank those whose writings on Comox Logging blazed a trail: Harper Baikie, Wallace Baikie, Alex Buckham, Helena Cartwright, Joe Cliffe, Martin Hagarty, Rene Harding, Lyn Henderson, Arthur Hilton, Chris Holmes, Ben Hughes, Dick Isenor and his crew, Rick James, Isabelle Stubbs, and Bob Turner. I am grateful to Lucy Bowdler for permission to reproduce extracts from her interview with Oscar Davies, published in the *Victoria Daily Colonist* in 1969; to Bruce Baikie for permission to use excerpts from Wallace Baikie's *Rolling with the Times*; and to Harper Baikie Jr. for permission to quote from Harper Baikie's *A Boy and His Axe*.

I must also extend my warm thanks to retired employees of Comox Logging, their wives, and their descendants. They welcomed me to their homes, fed me, sometimes boarded me, and helped in countless other ways. Their friendliness, memories, and enthusiasm were inspiring and sustaining during this long project.

A list of all their names can be found at the end of this book, but for specific help with early farming I must thank Bob Cliffe and the late Ralph Harmston; for skid road logging, Eddy Berkeley; for early Courtenay, Bob McPhee, Barbara Marriott, and Ruth Masters; for early Comox, Allan and Betty Brooks, Nancy Brown, and Myrtle Heron; for Headquarters, Walter Anderson, Frank and Ruth Biss, Don and Ruth McIver, Neil and Eleanor Martin, Jack and Dorothy Tukham, and Helen Parkin; for Camp 2 and Oyster River, Margaret Dunn and Herbert Pidcock; for Williams Beach, Bernice James, Mona Law, and Don McIver; for Camp 3, Dick and Eva Bailey, Hi and Mavis Churchill, Frank and Kay Davison, Dick Downey, Myrtle Heron, and George and Amelia Yates; for surveying, the late Bruce King, Darrell McQuillan, and Tony Turner; for steel gangs, Malcolm Carwithen, Mike Majerovich, and Bill Wilson; for falling, Sven Ell and Gunnar Jonsson; for skidders, Hi Churchill, Frank Davison, Walt Edwards, Davey Janes, and Gunnar Jonsson; for the logging railway, Hi Churchill and Beatty Davis; for the boom camp, Ron Bowen, Gloria Draper, the late Donnie Haas, Charlie Nordin Jr. and Fred Thatcher; for towing, the late Harry Nordin and Charlie Nordin Jr.; for loggers' sports, Neil Martin; for the Homeguard seasons, Hi Churchill, the late Stan Hodgins, Davey Janes, and Barbara Marriott.

chapter 1

The Settlers
and Their Farms

HEN THE FIRST COLONISTS ARRIVED AT THE Comox Valley in 1861–1862, they naturally gravitated to an area that accommodated a farming existence—rich alluvial soil along the fertile banks of the Tsolum River and along the lower reaches of the Courtenay and Puntledge rivers. The wharf at Comox, built in 1874, provided the main access to the valley for forty years. By the late nineteenth century, the Comox Valley was known along the coast for its many farms producing a range of dairy products, cereals, feeds, fruits, and vegetables. Later generations of settlers gradually moved from farming to the more lucrative logging industry and formed the essential core of the local woods elite that dominated the Comox Logging & Railway Company for decades.

The fertile soil of the lower Tsolum was the result of a meandering river and First Nations' seasonal burning. The course of the Tsolum River was variable, especially at the mouth where annual floods produced a fertile flood plain, and farther up, a flat, rich lowland remained from the river's meanderings in past centuries. The Comox and Pentlatch peoples of the valley had regularly burned the lower Tsolum region to promote growth of root plants, with the result that the settlers of the 1860s found a rich, almost treeless river valley—a welcome relief from much of the coast of Vancouver Island, where a dense forest came right to the foreshore.

Comox Valley farmer, poet, and historian Eric Duncan recalled the original vegetation in his journals and reports. "There was no natural grass in Comox valley, and the unwooded part was covered with a dense growth of fern, and a tangle of wild rose and berry bushes," he wrote in the 1930s. "The fern grew to a height of five feet, and its roots were a mass of underground ropes, much heavier than those of hops or nettles, making ploughing very difficult, though, as they kept the soil loose and porous, enormous crops of splendid potatoes were raised in early days, and even now it is claimed that Vancouver Island can beat the world in that line."

Almost all of the first settlers were English and Scottish and many names are still familiar in the valley. Among the first families were Beech, Bridges, Carwithen, Cliffe, Duncan, Fitzgerald, Harmston, Machin, McQuillan, Parkin, and Pidcock. Slightly later arrivals from Britain included Anderton, Blackburn, Crockett, Downey, Gage, Hawkins, Marshall, Radford, Rennison, Salmond, Smith, Thomson, and Urquhart. In the 1870s they were joined by newcomers from New Brunswick and Nova Scotia, most of whom had emigrated ten or twenty years before from Scotland and England. They included the Berkeley, Carthew, Casey, Cessford, Crawford, Graham, Grant, Grieve, McDonald, McFarlan, McPhee, Matthewson, and Piercy families. Many had alternated seasonally between farming and logging in the Maritimes, and they continued their way of life in the Comox Valley. Settlers of central Canadian origin included the Hodgins, Janes, McKenzie, and Pritchard families.

Gold Rush hopefuls Sam and Florence Cliffe were among the first families to settle in the valley. Sam Cliffe (1842–1908), a Staffordshire

English Emigrants Wanted

In 1884 the Anglican clergyman in the Comox Valley, Rev. Jules Xavier Willemar, made the following appeal to an English missionary journal, the *Banner of Faith* of the Columbia Mission:

Comox is a small farming settlement on the east coast of Vancouver Island, 125 miles north of Victoria, having a weekly mail communication with that city, and so with the civilised world. The white population—men, women, and children— is about 300, but much scattered. Many of the settlers live in the woods, each family in the centre of a clearing of their own making, which they enlarge year by year.

Though the life of the settlers is one of hard work, it is a free and pleasant one, and they all make a living quite easily. There is room in the Comox Valley for at least 1,000 people, as there is plenty of unoccupied land available for cultivation, and the soil is excellent. We want emigrants to take up the land, and turn our wilderness of forests and swamps into rich farms (swamps here make the best land). The present population is composed of English and Canadian emigrants; the last are of Scotch descent.

I should like to welcome more people from England. If you ever meet with people desirous of making a comfortable home in some colony you might safely recommend Comox as a suitable place.

Steamer Day at the Comox Wharf, c. 1910. Passengers disembark from the CPR steamer *Joan*. The wharf was the lifeline of the Comox Valley from 1874 until the Esquimalt & Nanaimo Railway arrived in Courtenay, four miles away, in 1914.—AUDREY MENZIES

A view of Comox from the wharf, c. 1913. At the left of the wharf is the Elk Hotel, a sportsman's lair with a tennis court in front, and to the right of the wharf is J. B. Holmes' Port Augusta Hotel. Over the next decades, Comox Logging introduced modern industry to this rural community and hundreds of local men went to work in its woods, railway, and boom camp operations.
—GLORIA DRAPER

Horse-drawn farm wagons and passengers leave the CPR steamer *Charmer* at the end of Comox wharf, c. 1920. The wharf provided the means of shipping foodstuffs from the valley.
—WILMA McKENZIE

farmer, left Liverpool for Victoria on the clipper *Silistria* in 1862 along with many other gold seekers from the English midlands, including William and Mary Harmston and their young daughter Florence (1856–1929), and surveyor George Drabble. After ten years prospecting in the Cariboo and around Nanaimo, Sam returned in 1872 to marry Florence—the first marriage among the settlers of the Comox Valley. Sam and Florence bought the Lorne Hotel in Comox and brought up ten children. Their sons Hughie and George Cliffe were prominent with Comox Logging, as were their grandsons Joe and Harold Cliffe. Their daughters and granddaughters married into such prominent logging families as Baikie, McKenzie, Radford, and Thomson.

~

In Britain, land ownership was a privilege beyond the reach of most people. The opportunity in British Columbia to own land was impressive and tempting. Any adult male British subject could acquire 160 acres of unoccupied Crown land for a dollar an acre if he demonstrated a willingness to farm it and make a certain number of improvements—a system known as pre-emption. Most settlers hoped that their land would provide them with at least enough food to subsist.

Settlers fortunate enough to obtain a portion of the Tsolum's fertile alluvial silt only had to clear a mixture of ferns and bramble. No wonder, in a valley dominated by Douglas fir, farmers like Eric Duncan coveted their bottomland. Later settlers occupying the surrounding

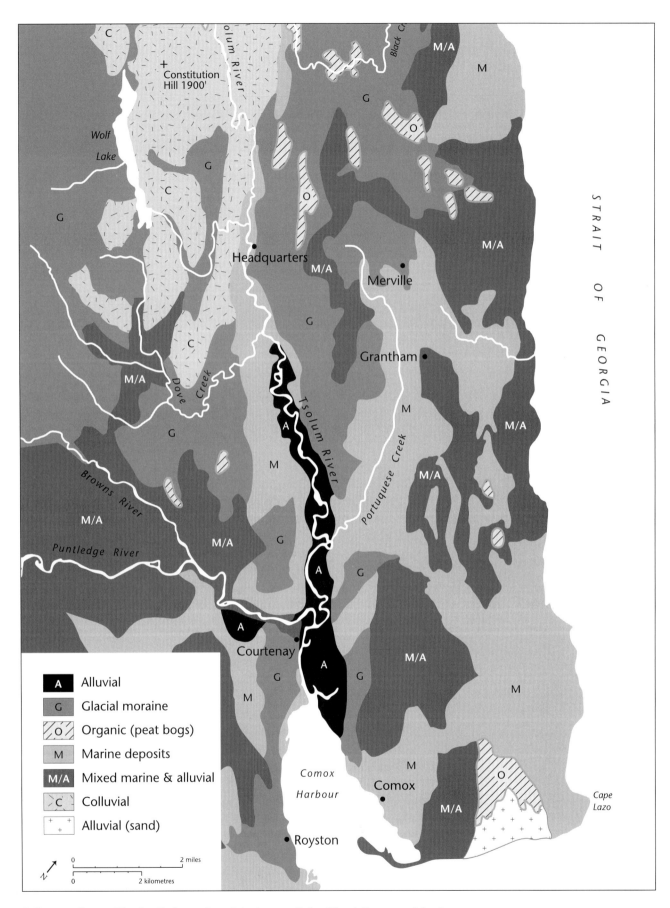

Soil types, Comox District. Redrawn from John Jungen, *Soils of South Vancouver Island*.

The Original Vegetation

James Richardson of the Geological Survey of Canada visited the Comox Valley in 1872:

The surface of this district, which is naturally free from timber, with the exception of single trees and clumps, chiefly of oaks (Quercus garryana), and strips of alder (Alnus oregona) in the bottoms, may be some twelve square miles, the scenery being picturesque and park-like. Its margin is very irregular in shape, and it is surrounded by a growth of very heavy timber, among the trees of which are the Douglas Spruce (Abies douglasii), often attaining two feet [sic] in diameter and 200 feet in height, and in one half of which it is free from branches, and the cedar (Thuja gigantea) often equally large.

The open country, in its natural state, is mostly covered with a growth of ferns, which sometimes attain a height of ten feet, with stems three quarters of an inch in diameter, and roots descending to a depth of three feet. These roots the native Indians prepare in some peculiar way for winter food, and excavate deep trenches to obtain them. The farmers are under the necessity of grubbing up the fern roots before the ground is ready for use, and they are often voluntarily assisted by their pigs in this operation, these animals, it is said, relishing the fern root as food.

forest had to clear their land by arduously cutting trees and burning or blowing stumps before they could plant crops. Most of these trees so laboriously cleared were simply burned as impediments to farming or as fuel, or used to construct log cabins. "A clearing burnt off in September," Duncan wrote, "and sown immediately with timothy or cock's-foot grass among the stumps, will yield so heavily the following summer that the scythe can hardly cut it. If burnt off and not sown it becomes a fearful mass of weeds."

Hay was extremely important as feed for oxen, cattle, and horses, and every farmer had at least a few acres of it. Professor John Macoun noted that the hay was "simply superb," the grasses reaching a height of four or five feet. Horses were known as "hayburners" to the thrifty Comox farmers, and they were indispensable to ploughing and all farming, transport, land clearing, and logging.

The farming country extended to the north, beyond the best land of the lower Tsolum. By 1884, when the Dunsmuir land grant froze the pre-emption process, the best bottomland in the valley had been put to the

Florence Cliffe (née Harmston), the original matriarch of the Cliffe family. She bore fifteen children, of whom ten grew to adulthood, including Lu and Hughie Cliffe of Comox Logging. Florence Harmston was born on the Isle of Man in 1856 and came to the Comox Valley as a girl in 1862. She married Sam Cliffe in 1873 and took over the Lorne Hotel, Comox, in 1883, after growing potatoes for ten years at Maplehurst Farm.
—BOB CLIFFE

Lucius (Lu) and Alice Cliffe at Maplehurst Farm, Sandwick, c. 1914. "Alice Cliffe was a very motherly type, a real matriarch," Tony Turner recalled. Lu Cliffe, a jack of all trades, was a skilled cabinetmaker; dairy farmer; house-, barn-, and boat-builder; sportsman; photographer; watch repairman; and mechanic.
—BOB CLIFFE

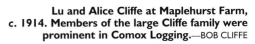

Lu and Alice Cliffe at Maplehurst Farm, c. 1914. Members of the large Cliffe family were prominent in Comox Logging.—BOB CLIFFE

Lu and Alice Cliffe with their son Joe (right, born 1897) and Lu's youngest sister Edith (left), c. 1900. Edith ("Edie") would later marry Comox Logging foreman Clay Walsh (often pronounced "Welsh"), and Joe Cliffe would become a high rigger and foreman for Comox Logging.—NANCY BROWN AND MYRA BAIKIE

Alice Marshall came to the valley from Manchester, England, as a schoolteacher and married Lu Cliffe, son of 1860s immigrants, in 1896. Here, she feeds wheat to her chickens from an empty Swift's Premium Lard pail, c. 1910. Comox Harbour is in the distance.—BOB CLIFFE

Alice Cliffe and her six children at Maplehurst Farm, c. 1914. Left to right: Harold, Florence, Percy, Joe, Walter, and Roy. Harold and Joe Cliffe would both work for Comox Logging for many years. Logging technology came and went, but nineteenth-century families like the Cliffes adapted to change and showed a remarkable persistence. Walter Gage photo.
—NANCY BROWN AND MYRA BAIKIE

Roy Cliffe (1903–1992) and dog at Maplehurst Farm at Sandwick, near Courtenay, 1943. Bob Filberg photo.
—FILBERG LODGE & PARK ASSOCIATION

plough and smaller, more marginal farms were being hacked out of the forest all the way up the "Colonization Road" past Grantham, Black Creek, and toward Campbell River. Here, the land was less fertile than on the lower Tsolum, consisting of marine deposits and glacial moraine. Later known as "Merville soil," it was heavily treed, swampy in places and, when cleared and drained, best suited for grazing and growing hay. Farming families of note here were Sackville, Blackburn, Hanham, and Hodgins.

Most settlers practised mixed farming; that is, they grew crops and raised livestock. Before the opening of the Union Mine (later the Cumberland Mines) by Robert Dunsmuir in 1888, they sold their produce, often with difficulty, in Victoria, Nanaimo, New Westminster, and the logging settlements along Burrard Inlet. However, the new colliery provided a market for dairy and poultry products: milk, cream, butter, cheese, eggs, and chicken. Eric Duncan remembered selling a ton of potatoes to lumberman Robert Grant of Cumberland. "Money may be scarce in the valley," Grant told him, "but there is lots of it here," and he counted out twenty one-dollar bills.

As well in 1888, the Courtenay townsite was surveyed. This would become the main town and service centre in the valley, terminus of the E & N Railway, and a second important market for valley farmers. A fall fair—hosted by the Comox Agricultural and Industrial Association—

Eric Duncan, Farmer and Poet

Eric Duncan was a Shetland Islander and nineteenth-century survival who looked on the twentieth century with deep suspicion.

Into the 1940s he remained true to the rural values of 1870s. Motor cars were the bane of his existence. Once, some friends in a car stopped him as he was bustling along the road heading out of downtown Courtenay. "Would you like a ride home?" they asked him. "No thanks," he replied, "I'm in a hurry."

He held thrift, oats, and potatoes in equally high esteem. He defended his early rising by saying "The morning hour has gold in its mouth." He always gave two sacks of oatmeal to the annual Community Chest drive. Others gave homemade jams or treats, but Duncan thought that the needy could eat oats if they were so destitute.

He considered potatoes "a universal blessing":

The foolish notion that they are too fattening is refuted by the fact that they are a mainstay of the populations of Ireland and Shetland, where fat people are curiosities.

Nature faithfully furnishes the provision suited to the different latitudes and their differing inhabitants. We cannot grow California oranges and lemons, but neither can they grow our apples and potatoes. Just compare a Comox Gravenstein with one of theirs.

Duncan's keen sense of place, and his skill with words, resulted in two books of rural poetry.

Eric Duncan in front of St. Andrew's Anglican Church at Sandwick, near Courtenay, 1942. Duncan, who arrived from the Shetland Islands in 1877, spent his career extolling the rural virtues of the Comox Valley in his verse and historical writing. Bob Filberg photo.—FILBERG LODGE & PARK ASSOCIATION

Maude McKenzie (*née* Cliffe) and her sons Bill and Jack at the McKenzie Farm, Torrence Road, Comox, c. 1914. Both Bill and Jack would have notable careers with Comox Logging. Walter Gage photo.—WILMA McKENZIE

was begun in Courtenay in 1893. Harvesting, threshing, and barn-building were often community efforts; a spirit of cooperation united these rural families, just as it would their children who worked for Comox Logging.

Central to the rural economy was the Comox Creamery, established in Courtenay in 1901, which shipped dairy products to cities and settlements all along the Strait of Georgia. The creamery gained a well-earned reputation for quality, and by 1903 dairying was well on its way to becoming the principal industry in the Comox Valley. "Before everything else a farmhand must be a good milker," Eric Duncan wrote in that year. "The favourite cattle, in their order, are the dairy short-horns—Jerseys, Holsteins, and Ayrshires." The bulk of the grain grown in the valley was fed to livestock, while baking flour was imported from Manitoba.

By 1900, the valley was inhabited by an interrelated population supported by farming and logging. Most settlers were farmers, some were loggers, and many—especially the younger men—were both. Farming was still more important than logging as a means of livelihood, but logging was catching up fast. Comox essayist Dora Crawford caught this tension in 1897 when she wrote: "About one half of the district is open land, or covered with light timber, and well adapted for agricultural purposes; the soil being principally vegetable or sandy loam, and the remainder is covered with a heavy growth of fir, spruce, and cedar, the cutting down of which furnishes a great number of men

Maude Victoria McKenzie

Second daughter of Sam and Florence Cliffe, Maude Cliffe was born on Queen Victoria's birthday and took her name. In 1895 she married John (Big Jack) McKenzie, a logger from Bruce County, Ontario. After running a livery business they bought a sixty-five-acre dairy farm on Torrence Road, Comox. Their sons Bill and Big Jack McKenzie were important members of Comox Logging between the wars.

"Maude McKenzie could do anything at all, just anything at all," her niece Margaret Smith said. "She was a wonderful cook, she could drive horses—she drove one of the first automobiles." She was strong enough to carry a large sack of grain tucked under each arm.

She had mixed feelings about the Canadian and British navy sailors who visited Comox Harbour. If she liked them she cooked dinner for them, but if they persisted in stealing her apples she didn't hesitate to fire a warning blast from her shotgun in the direction of the orchard.

employment during the summer months." Similarly, in 1903 Eric Duncan noted that "settlers without capital often work part of the year in the camps." Later, Duncan lamented the detrimental effect of logging's high wages on the rural economy.

In 1910, the five largest and most productive farms in the lower valley were those of Alex Urquhart (now Farquharson's Farm), Byron Crawford, Thomas Cairns, Willie Robb, and Sam Piercy. Other farms along the road to Campbell River belonged to George Grieve, William Halliday, and William Beech. Leo Anderton of Comox, who then divided his time between farms and logging camps, recalled that in 1908 he pitched hay for Byron Crawford for $2.00 a day with board, considerably more than Crawford's general farm workers, who were paid between $.75 and $1.25 a day.

Whatever their occupation, the landowners kept their land, and families stayed on. Sons of men who farmed in the 1870s were logging in the 1920s. Intermarriage between the first colonists and later arrivals was inevitable and soon almost everyone in the valley was related through blood or marriage. Close ties were formed well before the logging era. The Comox Logging Company was later called a "family company," sometimes disparagingly—but its workforce originated in the reality of a small valley community bounded by the sea and

A Cliffe and McKenzie family group at the McKenzie Farm, Torrence Road, Comox, c. 1914, looking south with the Beaufort Range in the background. Walter Gage photo.—WILMA McKENZIE

Harvesting hay in the Comox Valley, c. 1914. Oxen and horses, then necessary for transport and logging, consumed large quantities of hay.
—BRITISH COLUMBIA ARCHIVES, B-07290

The Seasons in the Comox Valley

In 1903 Eric Duncan recorded the seasonal rounds of his farm on the Tsolum River:

Very often the plough is at work every month of the winter, though nothing is gained by putting in seed before April. Haying generally begins about the 20th of June, and harvesting about the 1st of August; but the weather can never be absolutely depended on, and sometimes it pays to postpone haying till the middle of July; and then the hoe is busy, for the moisture helps the weeds as well as the pasture amazingly.

Potatoes are dug in October, and it is well to have turnips and beets under cover by the middle of November, as after that the alternate rain and frost make them nasty to handle and spoils their keeping qualities. Sown grasses of all kinds, but especially clovers, thrive wonderfully; in fact, the white clover is spreading everywhere, covering the roadsides and making itself a kind of nuisance in gardens and hay-fields. I am sorry to say the weeds of civilisation are getting here at last.

Big Jack McKenzie with his horses King and Jerry at McKenzie's farm on Torrence Road, Comox, 1943. John McKenzie worked his way west from an Ontario farm in the 1880s, reaching British Columbia in 1887 with a CPR construction crew. In his retirement, McKenzie rented himself and his horses out for clearing land, ploughing, mowing hay, hauling logs for firewood, and other rural necessities. Bob Filberg photo.
—FILBERG LODGE & PARK ASSOCIATION

Eric Duncan's Rural Poems: a Sample

From "The Tsolum River" (1881)

Now the farmer yokes his oxen
And commences to his ploughing.
Throws the precious seeds in handfuls;
Harrows it beneath the surface,
In the joyful expectation
Of a fair and bounteous harvest.

. . . .

Then the farmer toils in earnest,
Working late and working early;
Gathering in the gladsome harvest,
Lest the falling showers should harm it,
Lest the pouring rain should spoil it.

From "An Ox Song" (1896)

Does he slacken? Weeds in turnips,
Fern among the grain,
Outspread hay, and dark clouds gathering,
Spur him on again.

mountains. The twentieth-century dynasties of Comox Logging—the families of Berkeley, Blackburn, Cliffe, Grant, Grieve, Harmston, Janes, McQuillan, Machin, Parkin, Piercy, and others—all began as farmers, and some of them returned to the land when the forests were no more. In the twentieth century they formed an informal logging elite based on kinship, pride, longevity, and a general sense of landedness. Such men were known as the Comox "Homeguards."

Ploughing on the Comox waterfront, February 1925, with the Beaufort Range in the distance and short-billed gulls enjoying the freshly turned soil. Mack Laing photo.—BRITISH COLUMBIA ARCHIVES, I-51807

Except in the lush and clear valley bottoms, Comox settlers had to remove and burn trees and stumps from their pre-emptions. Englishman John Blackburn came to the Comox Valley in 1894 after marrying Ada Throup, who was from a prominent farming family in Sooke. Here, John and Ada Blackburn pose with their horse team and an impressive pile of roots and stumps at their farm at Grantham, c.1910.—FRED BLACKBURN

Left to right: John Blackburn, Austin Blackburn, an unidentified man, and a team of "hayburners" haying at the Blackburn farm, 1910. In 1916, John Blackburn sold his "farm timber" (like that in the distance) to Comox Logging for $350, and his son Austin and grandsons Fred and Gordon all went to work for the company.—FRED BLACKBURN

A noteworthy victory over nature: John and Austin Blackburn bring in the hay harvest at the Blackburn farm, 1910. Hay was the most important crop of this marginal land, for it fed horses and cattle—vital for transport, land clearing, and dairying.—FRED BLACKBURN

George Grieve, who had arrived from New Brunswick in 1874, operated a steam threshing machine which made the annual rounds of valley farms. Grieve designed this machine and built wooden patterns for the bearings and shafts which were sent to Victoria to be moulded in iron. "Many an autumn," Duncan wrote, "the well-known whistle was heard as it made its rounds, danced after by successive generations of boys." Walter Gage photo, c. 1905.—AUDREY MENZIES

The Courtenay Fall Fair, *c.* 1910. At first the Fall Fair, which met annually in Lewis Park, Courtenay, was largely an agricultural meeting. Loggers' sports were not prominent until the late 1920s. "Nearly as far back as I can remember we Denman Islanders would make our annual trip to Courtenay to attend the Fall Fair," Wallace Baikie wrote. "We would go to Comox on the *Rex*, Alby Graham's boat. My dad and other farmers and loggers usually were contestants in the Tug of War. My uncles would be displaying their apples and vegetables. The ladies would be interested in flowers and cooking, etc. We kids would get into races." Walter Gage photo.—BABS HIND

The fourth generation in the Comox Valley: Cliffe Midwinter, Florence Stewart's son, in 1943 at Maplehurst Farm. Bob Filberg photo.
—FILBERG LODGE & PARK ASSOCIATION

Vegetarian Diet

Eric Duncan died in 1944 at the age of 85. Before his death he revealed the secret of good health:

Every morning I divide a quart of fresh milk into three parts, and my unvarying daily diet, to which I always come with a hearty appetite, is as follows:

Breakfast: boiled oatmeal porridge, one third quart milk, one raw apple.

Midday meal: (as I have no time then to cook) whole wheat bread and butter, one third quart milk and an apple.

Supper: potatoes boiled with carrots, or onions, one third quart milk, one apple.

I do not drink the milk separately. I sip it along with other food. You will notice that I have butter only once a day. Some have advised me to use eggs but I do not find them necessary. Being a farmer and doing a farmer's work I am sure of good clean milk.

I do not alter one iota for holidays. Why should a man punish his stomach because it is Christmas? Surely he can have peace and goodwill and generosity in his heart without that.

Now I do not say that my style of living would be suitable for everybody, but I do say that great quantities of meat, pudding, pie and pastry as well as the fancy drinks, tea, coffee, etc., could be cut from the average person's diet without doing him the least harm.—COMOX DISTRICT FREE PRESS, 1967

24

Looking west across the Urquhart Farm to Courtenay, with the Forbidden Plateau behind, 1912. "The valley is acknowledged to be the largest continuous stretch of good agricultural land on Vancouver Island, and is mainly occupied with dairying," wrote Eric Duncan in 1916. The Urquhart dairy farm occupied the rich soil at the mouth of the Courtenay River. It was the home of Alexander and Margaret Urquhart, from Inverness, Scotland, who in a single year sold 17,000 pounds of butter from this farm. Walter Gage photo.—BRITISH COLUMBIA ARCHIVES, G-02555

Folk Cures

Sam Cliffe and Eric Duncan, Comox Valley settlers of the 1870s, recorded a number of home remedies for ailments and afflictions.

Cliffe's colonial diary contains a variety of practical recipes and instructions: "To Preserve Skins," "To Make Gunpowder," "For Wasp or Scorpion Stings," "For Body Lice," and "To Preserve Meat," among others.

Similarly, Eric Duncan wrote a number of recipes in the inside front cover of his Bible: "To Cure Corns," "Healing Liniment," "For Rheumatism," "For a Cold or a Cough," and "Ant Cure," which was: "Pour ounce or two of bisulphide of carbon into holes." He also suggested the following important medicinal preparation:

Liniment for Rusty Nail Wounds: 2 oz alcohol, 2 oz oil of origanum, 1/2 ounce tincture of camphor. Saturate piece of soft cotton cloth, and bind on wound. Renew every two hours till relieved. Good for any flesh wound on man or beast and every family should keep a bottle of it.

Duncan was skeptical of at least one remedy he copied into his Bible—a "Cancer Cure." "According to this prescription," he wrote, "52 drops of carbolic acid were to be mixed with 4 ounces of glycerine, and then a tablespoonful of this mixture was diluted in a tumbler of water. A tablespoon of the resulting dilution was to be taken three times a day."

Jack Crockett, the unofficial "Mayor of Grantham," in 1943. An Ulster Protestant, John Crockett arrived in the Comox Valley in 1899 at the age of twenty-two. After a short career as a teamster, he and his wife Winnifred Gabriel established a thriving farm on Headquarters Road where they and their many children produced potatoes, milk, and cream for Comox Logging camps. Bob Filberg photo.—FILBERG LODGE & PARK ASSOCIATION

chapter 2

Logging the Rivers and Shoreline

You see, in those days it was very hard to handle logs outside of the water. You had to get them in the water. That was the only way you could take them any distance.

—JOE CLIFFE, July 1980

HE RICH SOIL OF THE LOWER TSOLUM RIVER VALLEY was of limited extent, and by the 1870s the best land in the Comox District had been taken up. However, what were inadequate conditions for farming were superb for timber. The entire coastal plain bounded by Campbell River, the Vancouver Island mountains, Comox Lake, and the Strait of Georgia was covered by massive stands of Douglas fir, western red cedar, and hemlock. American-born logger Bob Filberg, who came to the Comox Valley in 1909, recalled, "This was the Garden of Eden for loggers . . . almost solid fir, flat terrain, dense stands, five-foot fir on the stump."

In August 1668, a devastating fire swept Vancouver Island, consuming most of the forested plain between Comox and Campbell River. In the pre-contact era, such fires seem to have occurred at intervals of 150 to 350 years, and this regular fire regime favoured the growth of the shade-intolerant and fire-resistant Douglas fir. Young Douglas fir seedlings quickly colonize a burned area, and mature trees develop a very thick, protective bark. Surveyors and loggers constantly found charred bark and fire scars on old trees, and scorch marks can still be seen on old Douglas firs at Miracle Beach Park and Cathedral Grove Park near Parksville. By the late nineteenth century, there were immense Douglas fir stands of uniform age and excellence—the logger's Eden described by Filberg.

Inconveniently, before the twentieth century the great Douglas fir forests were too large and too distant from the shoreline and major rivers for transport to the great sawmills of the south coast. Indeed, getting timber to the water was the greatest problem facing early loggers, who usually cut trees on the coastline and lower stretches of the major rivers emptying into the Strait of Georgia.

An Anglican clergyman's son inaugurated the logging industry in the Comox Valley. In 1877, after fifteen years of farming, Reginald Pidcock

This ancient Douglas fir was growing two miles from Comox when Mack Laing photographed Cecil "Cougar" Smith sitting at its base in May 1943. The thick, fire-resistant bark of a tree like this could keep a kitchen wood stove warm all night long. "The bark resembles cork," wrote surveyor J. D. Pemberton, "is often eight or nine inches thick, and makes a capital fire." Such bark gave great comfort to the many people who scavenged it from logging shows for domestic use. Mack Laing photo.
—BRITISH COLUMBIA ARCHIVES, I-51817

opened a sawmill on the bank of the Courtenay River in what is now downtown Courtenay. Up until then, settlers either imported their building lumber from south coast sawmills, or lived in simply constructed log cabins.

When Pidcock opened his mill in 1877, the Comox District had only fifty-nine householders, of whom forty-four were farmers; the rest were labourers, carpenters, and blacksmiths. This was a farming district with some logging on the edges, but many embarked on local logging careers by working for Pidcock or supplying him with timber from their own 160-acre properties. These included Joe Fitzgerald, Willie Harmston, William Duncan, Joe Grieve, Archie Pritchard, and two of the Smith brothers of Black Creek.

In 1885, Pidcock sold the mill to three brothers originally from the Scottish Highlands: Alex, John, and Harry Urquhart, who remodelled it into a steam-propelled plant. In the 1890s they awarded the timber supply contract to the firm of Smith & McKenzie—Horace Smith and

Big Jack McKenzie of Comox. Smith & McKenzie provided the Urquharts with enough timber from the Courtenay area to keep the mill running.

~

The first logging camp in Comox District was opened by John Berkeley, an English-born New Brunswicker. Under contract to Victoria lumberman William Sayward, Berkeley and a dozen men launched an oxen-logging operation in 1877 at the mouth of Dove Creek, where it flows into the Tsolum River. Expecting to be able to get their logs to the ocean, they skidded their logs into the Tsolum, but ran into major troubles when they tried to float the massive bucked logs down the river. The logs, five to six feet across, were too large and too heavy for river driving. Not only did they run aground everywhere, they also amassed in midstream into formidable log jams.

Among Berkeley's successors was Archie (James Archibald) Pritchard. In 1882, he established an oxen-logging camp on the Trent River and logged on the coastline between there and Buckley Bay. Archie's descendants recalled that he greased his skid roads with dogfish oil traded from Qualicum Joe. He cut his own boomsticks, and his timber buyers hired the Hudson's Bay Company's old steamship *Beaver*, then converted to a tug, to tow the logs to market. Pritchard and his gang camped right on the beach and returned to Comox only on Sundays, often walking all the way around the bay to get there. They lived in a tent set up on a rough platform of boards, with a second piece of canvas for a fly, and the wolves howled in the woods behind them at night.

Other local loggers included the McFarlans and Grahams of Denman Island, all Maritimers, who supplied cedar shingles (later called shakes)

Archie Pritchard

An early logger of Comox District, Archie Pritchard was born in 1852 at North Wakefield in the Gatineau area of Quebec, immediately north of Ottawa, into a family that had arrived from northern Ireland two generations earlier.

In 1871, at the age of nineteen, Archie came to British Columbia. Family tradition has it that he spent his first winter in British Columbia splitting cedar shakes at Hastings, Burrard Inlet, the future site of Vancouver. Later in the decade he lived and logged at Oyster Harbour, now Ladysmith. His name first appears in the Comox records in March 1882, when Reginald Pidcock sent him a shipment of lumber.

At a time when many newcomers married into Comox Valley families, Archie Pritchard bucked the trend by bringing his childhood sweetheart, Maggie Cameron, out from Quebec to Comox.

In his old age he enlisted his sons' help in clearing a large farm in Comox. His grandson Gordon Pritchard recalls that the old Gatineau logger was "pretty strict" but let down his guard on at least one occasion. When he found his boys playing poker one Sunday, he said, "Poker, eh? That's a good game," and sat down and played a hand with them.

He died in St. Joseph's Hospital, Comox, in 1919. His sons John and Walter Pritchard both worked for Comox Logging.

Vancouver Island forest fires, c. 1550–1650. Redrawn from a map in R. L. Schmidt, "The Silvics and Plant Geography of the Genus *Abies*."

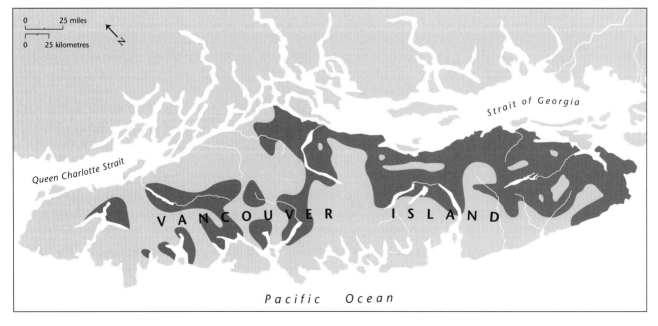

Engraving of Reginald Pidcock's sawmill on the Courtenay River, c. 1877–1878. Powered by a turbine-driven water wheel of 45 h.p., it was fed with Douglas fir logs from Pidcock's own land and later with logs from other settlers, who floated them down to the mill or dragged them with oxen over skid roads. "The little waterpower sawmill was jammed into the bush on the river bank," Eric Duncan wrote. "It had just been built (1877) by a young, well-educated Englishman, who had got the settlers' help to dig a two mile ditch to a creek which he had found back in the woods. When I came, he was cutting only rough lumber, and it was not till later that he got out a planer from England around the Horn."
—COLUMBIA MISSION, *ANNUAL REPORT* (LONDON: 1878)

for the valley's log cabins. They cut and shaped their shingles with a froe and "draw-knife" (spokeshave). For their efforts they were known as the "woodpeckers." The Smith family of Black Creek also produced cedar shingles for commercial sale in the 1880s. Harry and Walter Piercy, cousins from New Brunswick, opened a logging camp just south of Union Bay in the early 1880s, and two eastern Canadians named Cunliffe and Harding, with a crew of fifteen to twenty men, logged in 1883 at Williams Beach, north of Comox. In 1885 Charlie Brown, an Englishman, and Billy Pollock, from Maine, logged in the Dove Creek area for Croft & Angus of Chemainus. Another local logger was Charlie Rabson, who logged on the Tsolum River and around Courtenay with Harry Piercy as his foreman.

The major lumber company in the Comox District before 1900 was King & Casey. These partners specialized in cutting and booming timber for the big southern mills. Lewis Casey, the senior partner, was from Nova Scotia; Michael King, from Michigan, cruised timber and prospected. Described by Rene Harding as "tall and handsome, likable and efficient," King married Mary Cowie of Fanny Bay, while Lewis Casey married Jennie Creech of Comox. Mike's brother Jim King was also an expert woodsman, timber cruiser, and prospector. King & Casey logged around Comox and from their camp at Dove Creek horse-logged up the Tsolum River in the 1880s. They drove their logs down the river in the spring and fall freshets and sold them to Andrew Haslam, a Nanaimo lumberman and politician. They also established a farm base

Merchants, farmers, and loggers on the verandah of the Elk Hotel, Comox, c. 1890. At the far right is Lewis Casey's brother Jim. Next to him, with his hand on a double-bitted axe, is Big Jack McKenzie Sr., who was then working for King & Casey. E. C. Brooks photo.
—MYRTLE HERON

Lumberman Archie Pritchard (1852–1919) and his wife Maggie Cameron, who died in childbirth in 1895 at the age of 31.—ALLAN PRITCHARD

Big Jack McKenzie

An early logger with connections to the Urquharts' mill was John "Jack" McKenzie, born on a farm in Uptergrove, Ontario, in 1863.

McKenzie logged in Minnesota before working on CPR railway construction in the Rockies in 1887. Three years later he and Percy Smith were logging around Quadra Island for King & Casey. "A man named Jack Mackenzie [*sic*] working in Duncan Bay fell off his chopping board and cut himself badly," wrote Campbell River settler Fred Nunns in November 1891. "A steamer called for him and took him to Nanaimo."

He moved to Comox in 1892 and married Maude Cliffe a few years later. Big Jack logged for the Urquharts' mill, opened a livery service, and finally bought a farm.

When he got his first car, McKenzie instinctively cried "Whoa!" when he wanted it to stop. Big Jack McKenzie died in 1958 at the age of ninety-five.

Oxen logging teams, skid road, and crew, somewhere in the Comox Valley, c. 1900.—COURTENAY & DISTRICT MUSEUM & ARCHIVES, P200-1252

at Comox where they grew produce for their camps, stored hay for their livestock, and kept their oxen, horses, barn, and orchard.

King & Casey hired many early settlers, both in the woods and on the farm. Their stockman was Syd Rabson and their mail boy was Lu Cliffe, who picked up their mail twice a month from the steamer at Comox and took it down to their Dove Creek camp on his pony. "He got $1.50 for the job and thought it was big money," Joe Fitzgerald recalled. By 1890 King & Casey, owing to the scarcity of accessible shoreline timber in the Comox area, had moved the centre of their logging operations to the Quadra Island and Campbell River area. In these northern regions and islands they could still log along the coastline and fell their logs right into the water, or build short skid roads down to the water.

⁓

All these early loggers used skid logging—yarding over forest roads surfaced with small logs laid horizontally about ten feet apart over which oxen or horses pulled logs. At one logging show in the Courtenay area, Lance Berkeley (1888–1943), John Berkeley's son, was hired to grease the skids on the way to the water and to rake away dirt and debris left by the horses and logs on the way back. Lance was also in charge of the little sled or "boat" that was drawn behind the team. It held supplies like the rigging, brooms, grease bucket, axes for limbing and sniping, and the "dogs," which were U-shaped, spiked bars driven into log butts for pulling logs along the ground. Grease for the logs was all-important.

At that time, commercial oil and grease were scarce and expensive, and rendering grease was a smelly, tedious operation. Lard, dogfish oil, fish oil, bear fat, pig fat—in fact anything that was handy on the farm or woods and that might help logs slide along skids—was rendered outside in barrels.

It was quite a job to build a skid road, according to Eddy Berkeley. "You had to dig the bed logs into the ground a little to keep them stable. You didn't want them to roll as you dragged logs over them. This was called 'finding their ride.' For the logs to ride smoothly, you had to snipe them at one end with a sharp axe. You couldn't have too many curves in skid roads, and the road had to be reasonably level, though you could pull logs slightly uphill if you had to." Logs were tipped onto the rollway (the main skidway) with a Gilchrist jack—sometimes called a "Killchrist" jack for its tendency to slip. The skidway was like a railway: there was a main branch and minor branches.

Fallers always "high stumped" their trees in the skid road era. There were two good reasons for leaving high stumps, as Eustace Smith recalled: "One was to get above the deposits of pitch often found in big trees, and another was to avoid having a log with a flaring butt that would make it difficult to run over the skids."

The arrival of the steam donkey engine in the Comox Valley in the first decade of the century marked the end of logging with oxen and horses, and marked the introduction of ground yarding. The donkey engine took the place of oxen and horses in logging operations; it was considered a very strong animal surrogate able to yard, or pull, the heavy logs for great distances. "As a young boy I became very interested in these small machines," recalled Joe Cliffe (born 1897). "We thought they were tremendous because they could pretty easily pull a fair-sized log through the woods, breaking small saplings as it came to the landing." Logging operators could now do away with skid roads, for the engines were powerful enough to yard the logs across the ground. But the problem with ground yarding, according to Cliffe, was that "the logs were always hanging up—especially when they logged without lift . . . you were lucky if your log went a hundred feet without hanging up, especially at first when you had changed roads and were starting a new road. Your road got like a big ditch. . . ." However, these engines were such an improvement upon previous systems that everyone wanted one, for example, Howard McFarlan on Denman Island and George Doane in Comox.

∽

In the 1870s and 1880s, the magnificent forests of the Comox District came to the notice of mill owners on the south coast. At first, mills at Burrard Inlet, New Westminster, Chemainus, and Victoria were supplied with local timber, but when such stocks ran out, logging capital migrated northward—up the Strait of Georgia. In the late nineteenth century, the southern sawmills began to buy or lease large tracts of timber all over the coast, including the Comox District. By the 1890s, most timber cut in the Comox area was destined for the big export mills on the south coast of British Columbia—only a little for the Urquharts' mill. Much of this northern timber was provided by the

Eustace Smith, Skid Greaser

Eustace Smith (1876–1964) recalled that he went to work at age fourteen greasing skids on the original Courtenay townsite for his brother Horace Smith and Big Jack McKenzie:

Our little operation there was typical of many on the coast at that time, for most of the logging camps were small affairs. The motive power was provided by horses or oxen. Only the very best timber was taken out. Falling had to be done so that the logs could be got to the skid-roads with a minimum of trouble. Jacks were used to get them into position for the animals to haul them. Logs had to be barked, at least on one side, and the front ends "sniped" to make riding easier and to prevent the timber catching on the skids. The skid-roads were laid out with the greatest care and required skill to so arrange them that they would have just the proper degree of incline to facilitate the movement of the logs. As the horses or oxen were tugging at their loads a man or boy went just ahead with a pail of grease or oil and smeared it in the hollow, or depression chopped out of the skid as a track. In some cases a piece of hardwood would be inlaid in this depression, which was then called a "glut."

Big Jack was a powerful man and proud of his prowess as a logger. Typical of the times was a remark I heard him make one day; "I would not put an axe into a tree for less than sixty dollars a month!" He was a top woodsman and he wanted top wages, and sixty a month was just that.
—McKELVIE, "THE 'S' SIGN"

A horse team belonging to lumbermen ▶
Grant & Mounce yarding a log down
a skid road to their Cumberland sawmill,
c. 1910. The coal-mining town of
Cumberland (previously known as Union)
was built with lumber from this mill.
—GERRY GRANT

Fred Swan and his horse-logging crew, c. 1905. The horse team has just yarded a turn of logs over the skid road to the log dump. Horses had replaced most oxen-logging teams in the Comox Valley by 1905. Walter Gage photo.—COURTENAY & DISTRICT MUSEUM & ARCHIVES, D-523C

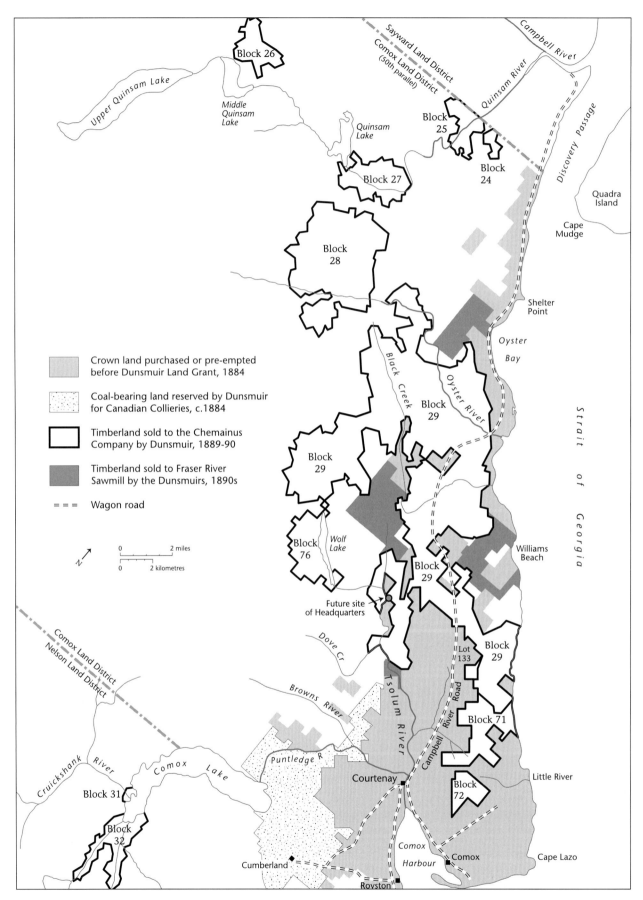

Comox Land District, 1900. Redrawn from a map in the possession of Bill Hembroff.

Lu Cliffe in later life, c. 1938. Bob Filberg photo.—FILBERG LODGE & PARK ASSOCIATION

Lucius Cliffe, Craftsman

Born in Comox in 1873, the eldest child of Florence Harmston and Cariboo miner Sam Cliffe, Lu Cliffe was considered the first non-native boy born on Vancouver Island north of Nanaimo.

Lu was mail boy for loggers King & Casey and later worked for the Dunsmuirs as payroll escort between Comox and Cumberland. He helped build the Comox Dyke in 1895, and the following year he married Alice Marshall, a teacher from England. They inherited "Maplehurst," a 96-acre farm at Mission Hill, from Lu's uncle Willie Harmston.

At Maplehurst, he cleared the remaining land and went into dairy farming on a large scale. He cut barn timbers on the Tsolum, squared them with a broad axe, and skidded them home with horses. His grandson Bob Cliffe recalled that he also supervised barn-raising bees. "Barn raising was a big event in those days!" He cut all the timbers by hand, raised the timbers with horses, and finally roofed the new barn. He also built houses, boats, and furniture, and did everything from cabinet work to splitting his own shakes.

"Uncle Lu was a great person," his niece Margaret Smith said, "and he was a good-looking man!" Like all the Cliffes he was a keen Mason, and he is widely regarded as the originator of the Cliffe family's inventiveness. He died in 1947. His sons Joe and Harold Cliffe became managers with Comox Logging.

small logging operators and handloggers on the north end of the Strait of Georgia. Many logs, Eustace Smith recalled, "were produced by handloggers scattered throughout the coast, wherever there was good holding ground to make up booms. These small operators were mostly financed by the mills who supplied provisions, tools, boom chains, etc., and also sent a tug to tow the booms when made up, with the understanding that the logs were delivered to the mill financing the operation." The local demand for labour grew, putting pressure directly on the men who farmed in the valley, and particularly on their sons, to work in the woods.

The small logging operations were replaced in the early 1900s by the larger operations of the southern mills, which had acquired tens of thousands of acres of inland timber in the Comox District. Their properties were obtained in the wake of the Esquimalt and Nanaimo Land Grant of 1884, when the provincial government granted coal magnate Robert Dunsmuir a massive tract of heavily forested land. Dunsmuir, in return, pledged to build a railway between Victoria and Duncan Bay just north of Campbell River. He and his son James looked upon the property as a source of ready real estate capital, and lumber entrepreneurs were among the eager buyers. Indeed, the Dunsmuirs' enormous private fiefdom spawned several smaller ones, in the form of profitable logging companies that purchased timber blocks from the Dunsmuirs.

One such company was the Victoria Lumber & Manufacturing Company, formed in 1889 when Wisconsin lumberman John Humbird purchased the Croft & Angus timberlands and mill in Chemainus from the Dunsmuirs. Humbird agreed to build a large new export mill at Chemainus in return for the right to purchase one hundred thousand acres, at five dollars an acre, of prime timber from the Chemainus and Nanaimo valleys and from the watershed of the rivers that drain into Comox Harbour. Loggers knew this company (whose timber holdings would later be acquired by Comox Logging) as the "Chemainus Company," "Chemainus Timber," or simply as "The Chemainus." Such names are still used by men whose fathers or grandfathers worked for the company a hundred years ago.

The Chemainus Company's holdings were selected in 1889–1890 by timber cruisers Joe Hooker and Joshua Marshall, who staked 51,623 acres (almost 81 square miles) of level timberland. "In all cases where these big blocks were secured," timber cruiser Eustace Smith wrote, "the areas selected were picked for heavy stands per acre, with a preponderance of fir, which was the only timber considered of value." The land was selected with a view to driving logs down the Tsolum, or down the swift Puntledge River from Comox Lake to Comox Harbour, and towing them to the mill at Chemainus. The properties bore some two billion feet of high-grade timber, the largest of them Block 29 which, at 31,036 acres (48 square miles), extended in a jagged fashion from the Puntledge River to the drainage of the Campbell River. Retired surveyor Tony Turner recalled that Block 29 was "irregularly shaped. Whoever laid it out followed the best timber—most of Block 29 was flat like this table." It included all or part of the Bates Beach, Dove Creek, Headquarters, Black Creek, Merville, and Oyster River areas.

Howard McFarlan, a Maritimer, ran a family operation in 1905–1906 at Henry Bay, Denman Island, across from Comox. His logging equipment included a donkey engine, a team of six horses, and a crew of twelve men and one boy. Note the two-drum donkey engine, the crosscut falling saw glistening with oil, and the inclusion of an entire family—babies, dogs, and all. Skid greaser George Cliffe of Comox is sitting in the bottom centre of the photo with a dog on his lap. Francklyn photo.—INEZ CLIFFE

McFarlan's six-horse team has just yarded a log down a skid road from the forest to the dump, where the log is poised for tipping onto the beach. Francklyn photo.—INEZ CLIFFE

Joe Fitzgerald rolling a log off the landing at Howard McFarlan's camp at Henry Bay, Denman Island, c. 1906. Born in Australia in 1862, Fitzgerald came to the Comox Valley as a boy. He became the first timber cruiser in the district and later the grand old man of local logging circles. Here, he demonstrates the use of a Gilchrist jack. Francklyn photo.
—INEZ CLIFFE

McFarlan's logs on the beach at Henry Bay beneath the log dump. The boy at the far left is skid greaser George Cliffe (1892–1973) of Comox, who became a loading engineer on Comox Logging's big steam skidders between the wars. Francklyn photo.—PHYLLIS CURRIE

Until about 1900, the Chemainus Company extensively logged its southern properties on the Chemainus and Nanaimo rivers, but after the turn of the century the company focused on its Comox holdings. Joe Cliffe recalled: "By this time, at Chemainus, they had logged back all around their mill, and they were looking for easier logs. You see, back then the towing was really cheap." Between 1903 and 1910, the Chemainus Company built up three distinct going concerns—a fledgling railway show at Little River, a woods camp on the Tsolum River, and another camp on the Puntledge River.

~

In 1901 the Chemainus Company engaged two American loggers remembered only as Allan and South to build a logging railway five miles north of Comox at the mouth of Little River. They brought in a locomotive from Chemainus—the first in the Comox District and the first anywhere north of Nanaimo—to haul their logs to Little River. "This little engine ran on rails made of six-inch poles which were laid parallel with the skid road," wrote Comox historian Rene Harding. "Its wheels were hollowed for this purpose. The logs were dragged behind." The locie had concave wheels—that is, they were shaped like the rim of a wheel with no tire—and ran on wooden, not steel, rails. The train dumped its logs from a wharf at the site of the present Powell River ferry landing at Little River. Allan & South went broke several years later, and Lyman Hart and Tom Bambrick took over the primitive railway. They replaced the wooden poles with steel rails, brought in a wood-burning Shay locomotive, dumped from the same wharf at Little River, and logged on contract to the Brunette Sawmill Company at Sapperton, near New Westminster, until 1910.

Among the men who worked at Little River during this period were Arthur Knight, Leo and Joe Anderton, Harry Vogel, Clay Walsh, Stan

Hughie Cliffe's Precocious Career

One of ten children of Sam and Florence Cliffe, Hughie (Samuel Hughes) Cliffe was born in Comox in 1889. According to his daughter Lorna, there were too many children in the Cliffe family so Hughie was "farmed out" as a blacksmith's assistant in North Vancouver. He started greasing skids with tallow at the age of ten on a Vancouver skid road.

He learned how to run a donkey engine and returned to Comox in about 1905 to work for George Doane, but spent much of his youth in coastal logging camps. In the First World War he logged timber for wooden ships, and he joined Comox Logging in the 1920s as foreman at the Royston boom camp.

As a boy and young man Hughie Cliffe knew many of the eccentric loggers of the coast, including Chin Whisker Anderson, a "progressive logging operator of the day," who introduced "such small, but much appreciated luxuries as a small enamel pot for placement under bunks in bunkhouses."

Another of Hughie Cliffe's friends was "Step-and-a-half Phelps," who ran a tight camp at Port McNeill. He got his nickname from a badly set broken leg which forced him to take an extra half step with every stride. His motto was "Up the Hill or Down the Channel."

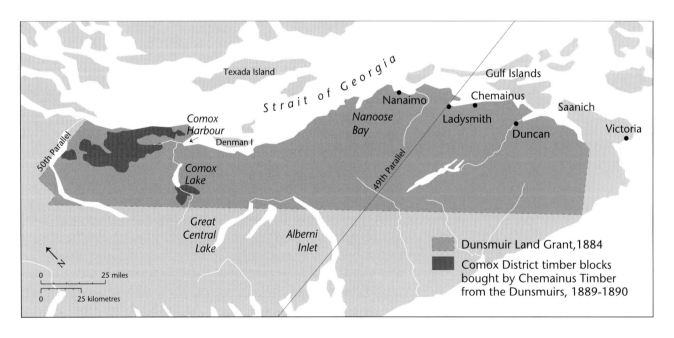

The Dunsmuir Land Grant, 1884.

George Doane's operation somewhere on Comox Harbour, c. 1905. A crew of eleven, including a line horse and line horse boy, are shown in front of an early donkey engine. "The horse is a line horse, which used to drag empty cable back into the woods," wrote an early logger. "They were used before haulback was invented. Such horses could walk on logs and loved chewing tobacco. They had caulks on their shoes and were part of the crew." Most of the men are holding double-bitted axes, but the third man from the left is holding a spud for barking trees. The youthful engineer standing in front of the boiler is Hughie Cliffe. Walter Gage photo.—WILMA MCKENZIE

Gage, Albert Grant (of the Comox Grants), and Albert's young son Arthur (Butch) Grant (born 1894), who greased skids. The crew of their Shay locie included Dave Thomas (engineer), Ed Small, Billy Miller, and Bob Martin. Both Clay Walsh and Butch Grant later became foremen with Comox Logging. Leo Anderton recalled Little River fifty years later: "I started out as a loader and then went from loader to swamper and then from swamper to rigging slinger and then when I was slinging rigging I got $4.00 a day, and a hook tender for $5.00 a day. And that was the two highest paid men in the woods. And the rest of the men got from $2.75 to $3.50 a day."

～

The Chemainus Company's attempt to cut valuable timber on the banks of the Tsolum and Puntledge rivers without resorting to railway logging was a brave effort, but a spectacular failure. It was an example of the rash and uninformed application of eastern logging practices (for smaller trees) to the very different conditions on Vancouver Island. Around 1905 the Chemainus Company employed King & Casey to log on the Tsolum River near the future site of the model town Headquarters—six miles up the Tsolum River from Courtenay. Their plan was as follows: donkey engines would yard logs over skid roads to

Buckers W. Mullen and J. Swan tackle a large Douglas fir at George Doane's camp on Denman Island in 1907. Nellie Holmes photo.
—COURTENAY & DISTRICT MUSEUM & ARCHIVES, D-677

The Brunette Company's Shay dumping logs on the wharf at Little River, c. 1907. Walter Gage photo.—WILMA MCKENZIE ▶

George Doane had a skid road and horse team operation between Point Holmes and the booming grounds in Comox Bay. In 1905 he installed a donkey engine on a rock pile on the Croteau Beach mud flats, where he also boomed his logs from around Comox Harbour. Shown here is Doane's "steam pot" on its artificial reef. Walter Gage photo.—BABS HIND

The Brunette Sawmill Company's new forty-ton, wood-burning Shay locie crossing a muddy wagon road at the site of the Comox airport, c. 1907. This engine is almost new: the boiler jacket and cylinder jackets are still gleaming. Left to right: Ed Small, Dave Thomas, and Billy Miller. Walter Gage photo.—FILBERG LODGE & PARK ASSOCIATION, BILL HIND DONATION

the Tsolum River near its confluence with Wolf Creek. A dam placed on the outlet of Wolf Lake would provide enough water to float the logs down the Tsolum to Comox Harbour.

The first part of the plan worked well. Mike King brought two donkey engines into Courtenay on scows. The donkeys were taken to pieces, loaded on wagons, and reassembled at the future site of Headquarters. Other logging machinery was taken up the river on horse-drawn wagons. Logging started in the spring, and manager Lewis Casey and his men logged for the entire summer. They cut at least fifteen million feet of very fine timber from a region that produced up to five hundred thousand board feet per acre. They sniped the timber and yarded it by donkey engine over skid roads to the banks of the Tsolum, where they stored it until the rainy season.

The next part of the plan failed miserably. When the rains came in the fall they pushed the logs in the river and opened the Wolf Lake dam so that a tremendous flood swept down the valley. The flood swept the logs down through the Comox Valley, leaving them stranded on the riverbanks and mired in farmers' fields; the logs blocked the river in several places, interfered with the salmon runs, and even altered the course of the river.

This was an emergency. Millions of feet of large, heavy, and valuable timber obstructed the river. Logging historian Bob Swanson wrote that the Tsolum was "plumb full of Douglas Fir" for six miles up from Courtenay. Bob McQuillan, who farmed at Dove Creek, worked his horse teams for two whole seasons pushing the logs back in the river, and Joe Thomson, who ran the Chemainus Company's boom in the mouth of the Courtenay River, gathered and boomed the logs that got that far. Local loggers, remembering John Berkeley's failed drive on the same river in the 1870s, blamed the situation on John Humbird, the American owner of the Chemainus Company. Swanson recorded that the decision to drive logs down the Tsolum was made by Humbird himself: "It was a sweet mess, and no wonder the coast loggers thought Old Humbird, the big shot at Chemainus, was out of his mind when he'd ordered the river filled with logs and forbade the building of a skid road along its banks."

Humbird sent for an experienced colleague from Wisconsin to solve the problem. Mathias (Matt) Hemmingsen, born in Norway in 1876, had been working for logging companies since he was fourteen and was an expert horse and sled logger, river driver, and general lumberman. By 1894, aged eighteen, he was foreman of a Wisconsin camp owned by Humbird and the Weyerhaeuser family, and by 1905, not yet thirty, he was already a superintendent. Forty years later Hemmingsen recalled his instructions from Humbird:

Here's what I want you to do: you logged the cheapest logs ever to be sent down White River. Now, when this drive is finished, Hemmingsen, I want you to go out west to a place called British Columbia and be logging superintendent at Chemainus. They log a lot differently out there than they do here—but sit on a stump for two or three weeks until you learn how it's done and then fly at her—but get logs—that's all I want.

On his arrival Hemmingsen went right to the Tsolum River where, his son John (now eighty-five) said, "a very poor management decision" had been made, namely Humbird's decision to adopt the Wisconsin system of river driving. Bob Swanson recorded Hemmingsen's arrival:

At Black's Hiring Office, Vancouver

Bob Martin, for many years head brakeman and conductor on Comox Logging's main-line train, started his Comox career at Little River in 1906.

From Gabriola Island, Martin was descended from a Cowichan woman and Jonathan Martin of the Hudson's Bay Company.

Martin started at the age of fourteen as a hooktender with the Shawnigan Lake Lumber Company, and by 1906 he was locie foreman. In that year, according to his son Neil, he was down at Black's Hiring office in Vancouver. Tom Bambrick came up and asked him, "Would you like to come to Comox?" Martin agreed, and then asked, "I have a rigging slinger with me—can I bring him up?" Bambrick answered, "No—there's quite a lot of farm boys up there looking for work." It turned out that Martin's friend was Leo Anderton, a Comox "farm boy" whose family farm was on the Little River Road. Bambrick hired both men.

His boss at Shawnigan wrote in 1906 that Martin had been with the company for several years, "during which time he fired the locomotive six months or more, and proved in this as well as other work in the camp a valuable trustworthy man."

Martin followed the lead of many other logging newcomers by marrying a local girl, in this case Archie Pritchard's daughter Mildred.

Puntledge River Driving

The twenty-acre property of Courtenay environmentalist and historian Ruth Masters includes the site of Archie Pritchard's Puntledge River logging show. When Ruth was a girl, three shacks still remained from Pritchard's camp.

At the edge of a hundred-foot bank, a veritable cliff above the noisy Puntledge River, runs an old skid road. Distinct grooves mark exactly where log skids ten feet apart were dug into the forest floor almost a hundred years ago. At the top of the cliff is a trough four or five feet deep, left when logs were skidded from the bush and down the steep bank into the Puntledge. A donkey engine was placed directly across the river from the chute, and logs were yarded out of the woods, over the bank, and into the river.

When Ruth was a girl, the forests around her house were full of big old-growth stumps. Her English father dug them out by hand, "back-breaking labour," Ruth said, or he blew them up with blasting powder. For years she found strands of cable while working around the property.

And so Matt Hemmingsen landed on Vancouver Island on June 2, 1906, to find the Tsolum River plugged with fifteen million feet of timber. He sized up the situation with a practised eye. Then he carefully blasted the rock bends out of the river and, with the fall floods, the drive started. Matt rode the last big blue butt right into Courtenay. The booming ground was filled with logs six tiers deep and a million and a half feet went out to sea.

John Hemmingsen said that the first thing his father did was clear out the rocks and debris which were obstructing the Tsolum River. Then, with the help of Lewis Casey, he dammed the little streams going into the main river. With the Tsolum clear of obstacles, he let the water out of the dams. "He was lucky there was enough rain and water." After this expensive failure, no more river driving was attempted.

Matt Hemmingsen also had to clear log jams from river drives on the Puntledge River. The Puntledge is a swift and powerful river, of ideal proportions for an eastern log drive, but it also contains sections too shallow for the large logs of the west coast. Veteran logger Archie Pritchard, the Puntledge camp manager, had the unenviable task of driving first-growth logs down the swift river. Grandson Allan Pritchard said that the Puntledge River drive was a "fiasco" and that such log drives were "plainly impossible."

~

The Chemainus Company had not been alone in staking a claim to the Douglas fir forests north of Courtenay. In the late 1880s Quebec

Nellie Holmes of Comox took this photo of logs being dumped into the Strait of Georgia at Allan & South's camp, Little River, 1905.—COURTENAY & DISTRICT MUSEUM & ARCHIVES, D-677

lumbermen James Maclaren and Frank Ross acquired one hundred thousand acres of Dunsmuir's grant, as well as timberland in the lower Fraser Valley, on the east coast of Vancouver Island, on Quadra Island, and at Duncan Bay north of Campbell River. They contracted with King & Casey to log on the Campbell River. Maclaren and Ross established two large sawmills on the Lower Mainland: the Barnet mill east of Vancouver, intended for production of lumber to be shipped to the Prairies, and Fraser Mills near New Westminster, which made its first water borne shipment in 1891.

Fraser Mills' first years of operation were plagued with difficulty and it was shut down in 1893 and remained closed for some years. In 1902, Maclaren and Ross sold Fraser Mills and their Comox Valley timber limits to Seattle lumberman Lester David, who set up a new company called Fraser River Saw Mills. David re-opened Fraser Mills in March 1903, upgraded and modernized, after almost ten years of inactivity.

David also set up a logging camp on the lower Tsolum River. Leo Anderton recalled that it was "on the river bank just below the old Duncan store. And Arthur Radford was superintendent of the camp." A native of Devon, England, Radford had come to the Comox Valley in about 1890 and married Florence, the oldest daughter of Sam and Florence Cliffe.

Lester David owned enough timber to keep Fraser Mills busy for many years. As well as the properties originally acquired by Maclaren and Ross, David controlled an additional 6,077 acres which stretched in isolated blocks from Dove Creek, Tsolum River, Black Creek, and Oyster Bay to the Strait of Georgia. David, according to Major Hilton of Comox Logging, was also adept at "rounding up timber belonging to farmers" in the Comox Valley. A settler might cultivate only part of his 160-acre pre-emption, leaving much of his valuable farm timber undisturbed and impossible to conceal from the covetous eyes of logging companies.

David also made tentative plans to log by rail on his Comox District timber, but his undoing was his attempt to buy Chemainus Timber's 52,000 acres north of Courtenay. He bought an option for this property but unluckily was unable to arrange the finances. In 1907, having overextended himself, he sold a controlling interest in Fraser River Saw Mills to a syndicate of wealthy capitalists headed by A. D. McRae and A. D. Davidson of Winnipeg. Both were Ontarians who had made millions in the United States selling appropriated Cree and Assiniboine land to American farmers. For $750,000 they got David's six thousand acres in Comox, along with Fraser River Saw Mills, the Anacortes Lumber & Box Company, and some timber on the Lower Mainland. Most importantly, McRae and his associates also inherited David's option on the Chemainus Company's prized 52,000 acres of timberland between Courtenay and the Quinsam River.

McRae and his associates formed the Fraser River Lumber Company in 1908 to log their newly acquired island timber and to export lumber from Fraser Mills. Fraser River Lumber continued Lester David's policy of rounding up farm timber from Comox Valley farmers. It also planned to carry out David's former plan—to transport logs by rail from the woods to Comox Harbour and boom and tow them to the renovated Fraser

Joe Thomson, Chemainus Boom Man

Born in about 1878, Joe Thomson worked as a young man for a fowl dressing plant in his native England.

At the turn of the century he went to the United States and ran a fly-by-night business presenting one-night picture shows in small towns, until he and his partner went broke in Walla Walla, Washington.

He came to Comox early in the century and oxen- and horse-logged with Tom Piercy on Denman, with Archie Pritchard at Fanny Bay, and for Andrew Haslam at Duncan Bay. He also cruised timber with Joe Hooker and Joe Fitzgerald. On one notable occasion he and his friend Cecil Smith performed a "typical logger's trick" by blowing eight hundred dollars in a spree at the Elk Hotel in Comox. He settled down in 1908 when he married Myra Cliffe, sister of Lu and Hughie. In the First World War he cut trench timbers at a sawmill in France with the Canadian Forestry Corps.

Thomson was fond of pointing out that he, Tim Paterson and Reid Good of Comox Logging, along with Jesus Christ, all celebrated their birthday on the same day.

Historian Helen Mitchell fondly recalled the "fascinating manner in which he recounted his adventures, liberally sprinkled with profanity and unflattering epithets."

Lester David's logging crew near the lower Tsolum River, 1906 or 1907. Standing at the far left is camp superintendent Arthur Radford (1868–1952). Walter Gage photo.—NANCY BROWN AND MYRA BAIKIE

Mills. "It will be realized that railway grades could only be successfully operated where there was a reasonable terrain," Eustace Smith recalled, and McRae had the ideal timber property for railway logging. "As the good timber is fast receding from the beach," observed the *Victoria Daily Colonist* in April 1905, "the day is not far distant when the saw log hauling of the coast will be entirely a railroading operation." Anxious not to be left behind, in 1909 Fraser River Lumber began construction of a logging railway from the mouth of the Tsolum to Dove Creek.

In 1909 Fraser River Lumber established a railway logging subsidiary named the Comox & Campbell Lake Tramway Company. The name is itself significant: it announced that the ambitious parent company planned to log by rail between the Comox Valley and Campbell Lake, pieces of which area they already owned. The company built a railway slipway on the Tsolum north of Lewis Park to unload locies and machinery from scows or rafts that had been brought up the Courtenay River on the high tide.

In preparation for railway logging, Fraser River Lumber hired men experienced with railway layout, construction, and operation, including its first superintendent, an American named Jim McGuigan. A young man from Gabriola Island, Bob Martin, previously of Hart & Bambrick, was hired in June 1909 as fireman and conductor; he was joined in the fall of 1909 by a surveyor named Evans and his young American assistant Bob Filberg. Years later Filberg was fond of recollecting that Martin was "the only man around who came here before I did." Late in 1908, Fraser River Lumber also hired Arthur Mansfield Hilton, a footloose adventurer straight from the frontiers of the British Empire, to work in accounting at Fraser Mills.

How Alexander McRae Got His Money

Born in Middlesex County, Ontario, in 1874, Alexander Duncan McRae moved to Minnesota aged nineteen to join a bank formed by a family friend, A. D. Davidson, according to historian R. W. Aldred.

Davidson and McRae developed an interest in vacant land between Regina and Saskatoon which had been surrendered by the Cree and Assiniboine people to the Canadian government in Treaty 4 of 1874. In 1890, the government granted 840,000 acres of Treaty 4 land to the Qu'Appelle, Long Lake & Saskatchewan Railway.

In 1902 Davidson and McRae formed the Saskatchewan Valley Land Company and bought the railway company's land grant for $1.53 an acre and an additional 250,000 acres of Treaty 4 land from the federal government for $1.00 an acre. As well, in 1903 they were appointed land agents to William Mackenzie and Donald Mann's Great Northern Railway

After a huge advertising campaign in 1902 and 1903, Davidson and McRae sold the Treaty 4 land to American farmers for between $2.25 and $12.00 an acre. Some fifty thousand people settled in Saskatchewan under Davidson and McRae's colonization scheme. Both men became millionaires.

McRae later said, "On the sale of 5,500,000 acres we netted about $9,000,000 . . . that is where I got my money."

Major Arthur Mansfield Hilton seated in an undercut soon after his arrival in the Comox Valley, about 1912. In 1908, on landing work at Fraser Mills, this imperial adventurer wrote in his diary a Latin motto—*Ubi boni, ibi patria*—and its translation: "Wherever my welfare is secured, there is my fatherland." Hilton would be associated with Comox Logging until 1920. Leonard Frank photo.
—BRITISH COLUMBIA ARCHIVES, 90167

Major Hilton
and the Margins of Empire

Major Arthur Hilton was intimately connected with Comox Logging's early years. Born in England in 1872, he ran away from school to join the Royal Navy when he was thirteen. His parents bought him out of the navy, but to thwart them he joined the Royal Army Service Corps before he even got home. Later he attended the South Kensington School of Art, obtained a certificate in elementary machine construction, and rejoined the Imperial Army as a clerk, serving in Ireland, England, Bermuda, and South Africa. Eventually he was promoted to staff sergeant-major.

Hilton left the British Army in 1906, aged thirty-four, and emigrated to the United States. In the space of two years he worked for a logging company at Port Orchard in Puget Sound, for a Seattle-based shipping company, and in the office of a cannery in Alaska. Many years later Hilton told Comox historian Rene Harding that there was "quite a story" behind his hiring by the Fraser River Lumber Company in 1908. He had just returned to Seattle from a trip to the Bering Sea when the secretary of the lumber company, aware that Hilton had worked briefly as a bookkeeper and log scaler at Port Orchard, "advised him that a logging manager was wanted for the biggest logging company in the British Empire."

"Oh, hell!" said he. "What do I know about logging, I was just a little microbe in a little logging camp." "Hell nothing!" answered the secretary. "Don't tell them what you don't know in this country—tell them what you do!" His friend took it upon himself to send a telegram to Fraser Mills in Major Hilton's name, to which he got a reply and a request to attend their office . . . and that is how he got the job as assistant manager.

In 1908, Hilton was responsible for Fraser River Lumber's accounting systems at Fraser Mills, and was also chief draftsman at the company's machine shops. His diaries show that with his first earnings he invested in South African mines: 1,000 shares in the Schuller Diamond Mines, 200 shares in Birthday & Pew Gold Mining Company Ltd, and 100 shares in both Saxon Gold Mines and West Rand Proprietary. Eventually he was promoted to Comox Logging's office manager at Headquarters. He died in 1958.

~

When Fraser Mills was rebuilt again in 1908, it required two hundred men to remove the old machinery and install new sawing and planing machines. "It will require over twenty cars to transport the order from the factories and foundries in the east to the coast," a journalist reported. Master sawyer J. P. McBane cut the first lumber early in 1909. In July 1909 alone the mill sent over 175 railcars of lumber to the Prairies, and another nine million feet went out by ship. At this time the "Circle F" insignia was adopted on the company's locies, ship funnels, log stamps, letterhead, and elsewhere. It stood for Fraser River Lumber Company rather than Fraser Mills, or Filberg, as some have thought.

McRae and his associates vastly enlarged their timber holdings in February 1910 when they exercised their option to buy Chemainus Timber's 52,000 acres between Comox Lake and Campbell River. The purchase price was $3,500,000 cash for what one commentator called "one of the largest blocks of timber in Canada." H. R. MacMillan, who later worked for the Chemainus Company, estimated that the acreage contained as much as two billion board feet of timber. The high price is an indication of the booming British Columbia economy in 1910, of the high quality of timber on the low-lying coastal plain, and of its unparalleled potential for railway logging. People connected with the Chemainus Company later regretted the 1910 sale, which lost so much accessible timber to a rival company. John Hemmingsen (a former director of MacMillan Bloedel) said that the Chemainus Company made a "major mistake" in selling their Comox District timber.

McRae's large purchase led him to the edge of insolvency and forced him to sell a controlling interest in Fraser River Lumber to railway magnates Sir William Mackenzie and Sir Donald Mann, who in 1909 had embarked on the construction of a third transcontinental railway, the Great Northern, into British Columbia. These men tapped great reserves of central Canadian and British capital through board member and London financier Robert Horne-Payne. In March 1910, Fraser River Lumber ceased to exist when McRae and his new associates formed a new company to embrace the enormous acquired assets which included mills, tugs, timberland and leases, and railways. Known as the Canadian Western Lumber Company, it was capitalized at $15,500,000. Its formation signalled the end of the coastline logging era. The best of the accessible timber on the shoreline and major rivers had been cut, and the great forests of Comox District were owned by a single large Canadian company that planned to extend railway logging into the inland logger's Eden between Courtenay and Campbell River.

Canadian Western was the largest lumber company in British Columbia and one of the largest business enterprises in the province. This new firm inherited a strong position on coastal British Columbia. On the mainland, it owned Fraser Mills, the largest sawmill in the British Empire and the second largest in the world; and on Vancouver Island, it controlled one of the largest stretches of Douglas fir forest on the west coast of North America. On Vancouver Island, the new company logged through one of its subsidiaries, the Comox Logging & Railway Company ("Comox Logging")—a name and a company that endured for half a century.

An up-to-date logging railway was an essential part of Canadian Western's plan for logging the Douglas fir forests of Comox District. Pictured here is Comox Logging's One-Spot, a wood-burning Baldwin engine built in 1909. Behind it are the tents of an early logging camp. Leonard Frank photo, c. 1912.—VANCOUVER PUBLIC LIBRARY, 6044

Some of the original management of Comox Logging pose for photographer Leonard Frank, in 1912. Left to right: Mr. Hogg (railway section foreman), Jim McGuigan (logging superintendent), and Arthur Hilton (office manager). Leonard Frank photo.—BRITISH COLUMBIA ARCHIVES, 90185.

James McCormack

An important figure in Comox Logging history, James McCormack was born in 1859 on Prince Edward Island into a family that had come originally from the Isle of Skye in the Scottish Highlands.

At about age twenty McCormack migrated to Rock Creek, Minnesota, where he entered the lumber trade. By the time he was thirty, he had managed a company there for the Weyerhaeuser family.

He married in the United States and had four children before returning to Canada in 1907 to manage the Columbia River Lumber Company at Golden. "Old J. D. McCormack," recalled Joe Cliffe. "When he got there he thought the timber was pretty nice, just as good as Michigan. So he thought, 'This is it!' He found out later the timber was better on the coast."

He moved to the coast in 1910, became vice-president of Canadian Western two years later, and helped start St. Joseph's Hospital in Comox in 1914. He made regular inspections of the company's subsidiary at Comox until his death in Vancouver in 1935.

James McCormack's daughter Florence (born 1895) married Bob Filberg, and his niece Ruth McCormack married Charlie McIver of Headquarters.

chapter 3

*It was amazing
the country that was
logged the hard way.*

—JOE CLIFFE, July 1980

Full Steam: 1910–1914

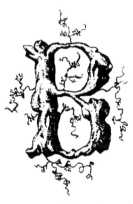ETWEEN ITS FORMATION IN 1910 AND THE outbreak of the First World War, Canadian Western spent well over a million dollars enlarging and modernizing operations for its subsidiary Comox Logging. Alexander McRae and his wealthy colleagues were determined to make their large investment yield a profitable return. Everything depended on bringing their immense capital and modern technology to bear on their sixty thousand acres of level Douglas fir forest north of Courtenay. Modern technology meant steam power: steam-powered donkeys and skidders, steam locies, a steam-powered "humdirgen" to dump the logs in the sea at Royston, steam tugs to tow them to the Fraser River and, on the mainland, steam-powered trains to haul the lumber to the hungry market of the Canadian Prairies.

In Block 29, over thirty thousand acres, Canadian Western owned perhaps the richest timber on the British Columbia coast, but only an expensive logging railway could make it accessible. The river and shore-line era had passed, and the logging company was poised to move into its spacious interior domain. McRae lent Canadian Western a million dollars of his personal fortune to pay for the necessary expansion which, in addition to equipment, included extensive trackage, the railway depot and model town of Headquarters, advance logging camps in Block 29, a new log dump and booming ground at Royston, and capable managers.

Canadian Western's original Vancouver management of March 1910 consisted of Colonel A. D. Davidson, president; Alexander McRae, vice-president and managing director; and James McCormack, secretary and assistant treasurer; but by 1912, Davidson had stepped aside, McRae was president, and James McCormack was vice-president. On the Island, Jim McGuigan was logging superintendent and Arthur Hilton was office manager at Headquarters. These men had been attracted to British Columbia by the unprecedented prosperity of the tenure of Premier

Comox Logging's first log dump was on the Tsolum River at Cooper's Corner (previously Duncan's Corner) at Sandwick, half a mile upstream from Courtenay. The railway ran down the west side of the Tsolum to the Puntledge Indian Reserve, part of which was leased for the construction of a log dump, cookhouse, and other buildings. The logs were then driven down the river into Comox Harbour, where they were made up into booms off the Comox Dyke. The Fraser River Lumber Company had started railway logging here late in 1909. In this 1911 photo, the company's wood-burning engine, the Number One or "One-Spot," pushes a load of sniped logs into the dump. Walter Gage photo.
—BABS HIND

Engineer Davie Thomas watches the train crew tip a flatcar load into the Tsolum at Cooper's Corner, c. 1911. "The output of the camps," wrote an early visitor, "was loaded daily on the flat cars and taken to Courtenay. The line ran to a pier which was slightly canted. Blocks were removed from the logs which were mechanically rolled into the mouth of the river." This "Prairie" type Baldwin was a standard short-line locie. Wood served as the original fuel, but in 1911 the railway was connected with Canadian Collieries' line between Union Bay and Cumberland, and the engines were gradually converted to burn coal. Still later they were converted to burn oil.
—BRITISH COLUMBIA ARCHIVES, 90141

The Grading Camp at McQuillan's Crossing

In a 1957 interview, timberman Pete McLoughlin recalled the origins of Comox Logging's first railway grading camp on Harry McQuillan's property:

In 1909 the late . . . AD McRae dickered with Mr McQuillan on the Plateau Road . . . for a piece of land and a bit of timber [Section 74]. Now, the final outcome of this transaction was, he paid $1,500 for a stand of timber which was then known as Cowie's Crossing.

Now the first camp of the Comox Logging and Railway Company was established there and it was a grading camp. And the McQuillan farm supplied them with milk and eggs and butter, etc., and they also supplied them with a load of straw—the cost was $2 by the way. And that straw made the first bunks for Comox loggers and they made up their bunks from that.

And the camp was one that didn't last too long because they were on the move all the time.

But the first logs that were hauled from there were hauled by the late Mr Bob McQuillan . . . by horses and they were taken to the Sandwick corner and I think one can still see the remains of the first dump—log dump—there, and the price was $2.50 per thousand. They were hauled over the skid roads by horses.

50

Lords and Ladies and Christ Everything

J. D. McCormack attracted British capital into the Canadian Western Lumber Company, and just before the First World War, Canadian Western was owned by about four thousand British investors. Among the larger shareholders were about twenty people with titles. "At one time it was almost all owned by the Brits—Lords and Ladies and Christ Everything," said Howard McQuinn, son of Camp 3 foreman Jack McQuinn.

A group of major shareholders toured Comox Logging's woods operations in the 1920s. Howard McQuinn recalled that they were given a big supper at the cookhouse when the regular camp dinner had been cleared away. Howard was stunned to see some of the shareholders wearing short pants. He'd never seen adults wearing shorts. He and his friends found this very funny.

The shareholders ate in total silence. "There was no noise from the cookhouse—everyone was so busy eating."

Richard McBride (1903–1915), when immigration reached record levels and the province's natural resources invited outside capital.

In the spring of 1910, at the time of the takeover, Comox Logging's railway network was in its infancy. A single locomotive did all the work, though others were on order. The company was still buying "farm timber" from local farmers on the outskirts of Courtenay and had not yet reached its own valuable timber in Block 29.

One of the farmers on Dove Creek was Ulsterman Harry McQuillan, who owned two sections not far from downtown Courtenay, at the corner of the Plateau and Dove Creek roads. McQuillan benefited from being adjacent to Comox Logging's main line right-of-way leading to Block 29. He had pre-empted the lot thirty years before and ran a profitable farm at McQuillan's Crossing, but he also had a good deal of old-growth timber that he did not intend to cut himself. In 1906 he had sold the timber on Section 75 to Lester David. For a time, Comox Logging's railway ended at "McQuillan's Crossing," where the company built a grading camp at what was briefly the end of steel. Harry McQuillan's son Bob—later a rigger with Comox Logging—got his first job delivering milk to the camp.

In March 1910, Comox Logging's main camp was still on the lower Tsolum at Cooper's Corner, Sandwick. However, the site was now

In the middle is James McCormack, vice-president of the Canadian Western Lumber Company, on a tour of Comox Logging's new railway operations in 1912. To his right is Jim McGuigan, logging superintendent of Comox Logging, and to his left is skidder expert Pete Crane. Leonard Frank photo.—BRITISH COLUMBIA ARCHIVES, 90181

mainly a log dump and terminus for McRae's logging railway. There were no roads in, so the camp could only be reached by boat, scow, or raft. The railway, according to Major Hilton, "ran down opposite Cooper's Corner where they also had a cookhouse. Mrs. Faber used to be the cook. Her husband [Fred Faber] worked on the boom. Boom men and others used to cross the river by a boat which was hanging to a wire rope stretched across the river." Barbara Marriott (*née* Duncan, born 1906) remembered crossing the river with her mother to visit the Dalrymples, who later ran the cookhouse. "They had a cookhouse on the other side," said Rene and Bob Harding. "If they wanted to cross they had a rowboat and a cable to go to the cookhouse. You could holler—you could almost speak to them. Or just jump in the boat and pull, though it might be convenient if you waited till high tide."

The Tsolum log dump was soon found to be inadequate for the quantity and size of the timber being cut. Ralph Harmston recalled that with increased production, log jams were "really messy" at Sandwick, and that crews spent more time getting logs from the river to the booming grounds in the bay than into the river in the first place. "More and more and more wood was coming in, and it jammed more often." This location was abandoned in 1912 and the operation moved to the south side of Comox Harbour, four miles away at Royston. The new dump and booming facility meant the construction of a bridge (the Condensory Bridge) over the Puntledge River, the extension of the railway through Courtenay (right past the loggers' favourite watering hole, the Riverside Hotel), and the purchase of five acres of land at Royston. The first load of logs was taken to the new dump on March 1, 1911, and the dump remained in constant use for the next forty years.

Locie engineer Jack Carthew, who dumped the first logs at Royston in March 1911, recalled that "they used the same small engine that the Chemainus had used for a short time, then they started with some switch engines in the woods. They would make up twenty loads of logs at a siding near the Condensory Road past the bridge, and then I would haul them to Royston."

Mile by mile, the railway was extended up the Tsolum River valley toward Block 29. Wooden ties for the new railway were supplied by Dan Kilpatrick, who had bought Pidcock's old Courtenay sawmill from the Urquhart brothers. Steel rails were brought to Comox on a tramp steamer, loaded onto scows, towed across to Royston on the company's original tug *Lythia*, and unloaded there at a special temporary wharf. The company had seventeen miles of railway early in 1911 and seventy miles two years later. New spur lines were constantly built, both into the company's timber and into farm timber. About twenty-five miles of new track were laid every year and old spur lines were constantly closed, their rails taken up and recycled.

A large workforce resulted: six hundred men early in 1911, seven hundred in June 1913. These men had to be housed. The Tsolum log dump and the grading camp at McQuillan's Crossing lodged a few men, but most stayed in bunkhouses at the numerous temporary camps built in the company's first few years of operation. Between 1910 and 1912, nine different camps were built—Camps 1 to 9—which moved from location to location as required. For instance, in 1911, eight camps were

Extending the Grade

In 1980, Joe Cliffe recalled Comox Logging's first advances into the timber north of Courtenay:

The first I remember of Comox coming here was they brought scows on the high tide right up into the little river—the Tsolum—and unloaded them on the point, you see, between the two rivers. And they started making grades, railroad grades. They took off there on a curve and went up and hit the old Northern Pacific Railroad survey, the one that was supposed to go across Seymour Narrows and up Bute Inlet all the way to the Cariboo.

So Comox just went up and hooked onto that and all the survey work was done because it went clear through to Seymour Narrows, and you couldn't get a better grade than a railroad grade main line. . . . They logged of course as they went up the road. I'd say maybe a year and a half they dumped logs into the Tsolum River at the mouth, and boomed the logs there, then towed them down to the beach area and tied them up down in front of the Indian ranch.

Soon after that they found that if they were going to be any kind of an outfit they would have to get a bigger place to dump the logs, so then they started to put the railroad right through from the Condensory, which wasn't there then of course, right down to Royston . . . and that put them right into business, although it cost a lot of money.

Getting away from the Farms

In 1980, Joe Cliffe recalled that Comox Logging's first major camp was Camp 7:

And the first logging camp built by Comox was at Burns Road [Camp 7]—where they crossed Burns Road and—incidentally, that was right on the back end of Parkins' property. Bob Parkin was married by this time and he had a piece of property and a home right there by the camp.

From there they logged all around Dove Creek way, and down around Browns River back of a few farms, then widened out all the way up, got away from the farmers, up around above Headquarters, from there to Oyster River—in fact, further than that—but that was the end of the timber block property.

open, three the next year, and seven in 1913, to log the scattered farm timber. These portable camps, with their cookhouses, bunkhouses, and married men's houses, were moved frequently on skids and flatcars.

The main camp between 1910 and 1912 was Camp 7, situated at "Parkin's Crossing" on the corner of the Dove Creek Road and Burns Road about a mile north of McQuillan's Crossing. The camp occupied part of Isaac (Ike) Parkin's 300-acre Tsolum riverfront property. Camp 7 had the advantage of being directly on the main line between the new dump at Royston and the timber, and it served as a base for logging Parkin's farm timber and surrounding properties. There was also a school at Camp 7, known as Nikrap (Parkin spelled backward), which opened in 1910 and counted among its pupils members of the McGuigan and Hogg families.

Camp 7 was also the site of a great innovation in the coastal logging industry: the institution of monthly pay. Comox Logging's early workforce included many transient loggers engaged through the hiring halls of Vancouver. "In those days," historian Ben Hughes wrote, "it was said that every camp had three crews: one coming, one going, and one on the job." Usually, men were paid when they quit, when they felt "stakey," or at the end of the season. "Prior to 1910," Major Hilton recalled, "men were not paid until they quit, when they would take their

The Three-Spot locie backs a long load onto the wharf at Royston, c. 1912. The company hired Gillie Brothers of New Westminster to drive pilings, build a wharf for log dumping, and lay out rafting pockets at its spacious new booming grounds. Note the long timber sticks occupying the first two flatcars. At the right are the company's cookhouse and bunkhouse. By the spring of 1913, Comox Logging had a fleet of 100 flatcars. Fully laden logging trains became part of everyday life in the Comox Valley. "Every hour or so," wrote a 1913 visitor, "a long train of logs, containing sticks great both as length and diameter, is run through the town to the booming grounds on Comox Bay." Leonard Frank photo.
—MARGARET SMITH

53

Buoyant booms in the rafting pockets at the end of the wharf at Royston, 1919. A lone figure, probably a scaler, stands among the massive logs. In the distance are the cliffs at Point Holmes, near Comox, which extend down to Goose Spit.—MONA LAW

Comox Logging's One-Spot on the trestle at Cooper's Corner, c. 1911. The arrival of this locie two years before had pitted the canny American loggers against the dubious farming folk of the Comox Valley. The *Comox Argus* recalled in 1953 that "the greatest triumph" of superintendent Jim McGuigan came when he brought the One-Spot up the Courtenay River on a barge: "All the farmers laughed at the fool logger who thought he could get a locie under the bridge. He pulled the smoke stack down and pulled the plug in the scow and allowed the barge and the locie to sink to the bottom. He took a line down to the bend in the river to a giant fir and hauled on the barge at the bottom of the river pulling her under the bridge. Then he pumped the barge dry and put in the plug and raised her, and when the farmers came back the next day to jeer the trick had been done."—BRITISH COLUMBIA ARCHIVES, 90140

Comox Logging's steam shovel and steel gang laying ties and steel through Courtenay in 1910 or 1911, when the company's right-of-way was extended to Royston. The steam shovel was also used to grade Union Street, Courtenay's main street.—COURTENAY & DISTRICT MUSEUM & ARCHIVES, P200-116

Comox Logging's Three-Spot pulls a load to the log dump at Royston, fall 1911. Engines always ran backwards to the log dump, a safety measure to reduce stress on the boiler. The bridge shown here crossed the Puntledge just above the present Condensory Bridge. This postcard, addressed to Miss Jean Menzies of The Manse, Sandwick, March 29, 1912, reads: "Dear Jean, I suppose you see the train with the logs like this picture sometimes as you go to school. With love, Madeline."—AUDREY MENZIES

The Origin of the Temporary Camps

Joe Cliffe explained the preponderance of short-lived logging camps in the lower Tsolum area:

When they were logging out from Headquarters, there were a couple of places they had to log on a certain date, you see, so they had little temporary camps. In order to get these logs, they put out little spur railroads as fast as they could, and got the timber down on them and never hauled. They just had to cut the timber.

The timber was all felled for about two years before it was ever logged. They couldn't get roads into it that fast. The fallers could walk in a couple of miles, you see, and fall this timber. They were good blocks and they didn't want to lose it.

The wharf at Royston after the August 1, 1912 accident. The pilings at the right show very little cross-bracing, a possible cause of the accident.—FILBERG LODGE & PARK ASSOCIATION, JACK CARTHEW DONATION

The wreck of the Three-Spot at Royston, August 1, 1912. Walter Gage photo.—BABS HIND

A Spill in the Chuck

A notable accident occurred on August 1, 1912, involving Comox Logging's big new main-line locie, the Three-Spot—the largest engine on Vancouver Island and the "elite of logging locies." Manned by engineer Pa Dixon and brakeman Buster Brown, the Three-Spot toppled the Royston wharf and crashed into the mud flats of Comox Harbour.

The accident occurred when the log unloader broke its driving chain while moving swifters on the boom. When the Three-Spot came in to move the disabled unloader, the trestle started to sway and then collapsed, sending locie, crew, and unloader into the saltchuck.

"Loco 3 & unloader precipitated into bay at 2 p.m. this day," Major Hilton noted in his diary. "Dixon broken leg below knee. Brown bruised & cut face." Dixon grabbed hold of a large plank and paddled ashore. "Saw Dixon in hospital," Hilton wrote two weeks later, "progressing favourably."

Salvage companies wanted too much to raise the locie, so Jim McGuigan laid a line down to the stranded locie, brought in two scows, trussed the Three-Spot to the scows with a cable, raised her as the tide came in, towed her into the beach, placed rails under her, and lowered her onto the track as the tide went out. None the worse for wear, the engine served continuously until it was scrapped in 1944.

The Three-Spot halfway out the Royston log dump, ready to drop its load of logs, c. 1912. This locie arrived in the fall of 1911. At the left is a pile of logs dropped previously. Boomsticks are lying on the mud flats in the foreground. **Walter Gage photo.**—BABS HIND

Flatcars stacked with old-growth timber await dumping on the trestle leading to the log dump at Royston, c. 1912. **Leonard Frank photo.**—BRITISH COLUMBIA ARCHIVES, B-08339

The **Three-Spot**, Comox Logging's main-line locie, at a railway crossing in about 1912. Among the early train engineers (known as "hoggers") were Dave Thomas, Pa Dixon, Jack Carthew, Fred Smith, Tom Kennedy, and Harry Duff; train crews included Spike Maloney, conductor Bob Martin, brakemen Buster Brown and Jack Hawthorne, and the fireman affectionately known as Shorty the Gink. Among the crew members shown here are **Pa Dixon, Bob Martin, and "Old Man" McGregor. Leonard Frank photo.**—BRITISH COLUMBIA ARCHIVES, 90182

Pierre Colet's Vanilla Extract

According to Oscar Davies, who was storekeeper at Camp 9,

Pierre Colet, our cook, made the best hotcakes in B.C., and his beefsteaks were always just right, but something about him was bothering me. He was ordering far too many bottles of vanilla and lemon extract, both expensive items.

It was my job to keep the cost of the meals at 30 cents a day so I called in the bullcook and asked him about the extract. Somewhat reluctantly the man told me enough for me to realize that Pierre was making a drink from the extract, to which he added vinegar, baking soda and water. The next day Pierre's order came in with four more bottles of extract. I promptly crossed them off the list. When his order arrived with no extract, he came hammering at my door at 11 p.m., screaming for it. This continued for three nights.

Meanwhile an old friend of mine had arrived at the camp and was bunking in with me. "What's all this about?" he asked when Pierre arrived on his nightly caper.

"He's drunk on a concoction of extract," I explained. "He'll soon go off to bed."

But Dick, a tough Yorkshireman, was in dire need of sleep. He went out to advise Pierre to go to bed. For his trouble he received curses and uncomplimentary remarks about Englishmen so my friend waded into Pierre and beat him up. That ended my nightly visits from Pierre.

◀ **A Comox Logging train with sniped logs pauses at a logging camp, c. 1912. The locie steams away in the distance. Sniping (bevelling or cutting around one end of a log with an axe to prevent hang-ups) indicates that these logs were still yarded out of the woods by donkey engine. It may seem odd to see sniped logs on flatcars in 1912 photographs, but they reveal that these logs came not from Comox Logging's new skidder show but from its older, donkey-engine, ground-yarding, parbuckle-loading show. Sniped logs finally disappear from photographs when logs were "flown" or dragged through the air by Lidgerwood skidders.**—MARGARET SMITH

pay to Vancouver and go on a traditional binge." The change resulted from a showdown between Hilton and Otto Fechner, proprietor of the Riverside Hotel in Courtenay. Fechner had developed the habit of advancing money to loggers. Hilton, a conscientious manager accustomed to British Army regime and economy, refused to allow Fechner to serve as the company's unofficial banker and instituted a regular monthly payment plan, as described by historian Rene Harding:

When Major Hilton started in the logging camp they didn't have a regular payroll. Men used to work until they felt stakey then they would come and ask for their time, quit, spend all their money—come back, often picking up the old rags they had thrown away, and start all over again.

It was around 1909 or 10, when the Major went up to old Camp 7, headquarters in those days, and told the time-keeper to make up the time for everybody. He was astounded, and wondered if the company was going to close the camps.

"No," said he, "pay them up to the end of the month."

The crew was accordingly gathered in. They wondered what was up, thinking the outfit was closing down.

"No," he told them, "you're going to get this every month."

It was a system which was copied by all other logging camps on the coast, and proved most satisfactory.

On this first occasion he was asked to withhold some five or six thousand dollars from different men, which, it was explained, was payable to the owner of the Riverside Hotel, O. H. Fechner, he having advanced them money on the strength of a time cheque issued by the timekeeper.

Major Hilton gave him cheques for these amounts and told him to advise Fechner that in future a man who earned the money would be the one to receive it and any advance he might make would be at his own risk.

Camp 1 was set up in about 1910, three miles north of Camp 7, in Crockett's field at the corner of Headquarters and Smith roads. (It was not the first Camp 1; camps were highly mobile and their numbers were recycled.) In 1915, Camp 1 was moved to the Coleman Road east of Merville, and at the end of the war it was moved to a location behind Miracle Beach.

A rare first-hand account of life at one of Comox Logging's nine early camps has survived in the reminiscences of a timekeeper named Oscar Davies, who came to work at Camp 9 in 1911. Many years later Davies recalled the details of his winter's work in an interview with Mills & Boon writer Lucy Bowdler of Nanaimo. A bank accountant in Vancouver, Davies answered an advertisement for a timekeeper and storekeeper at Camp 9, not far north of newly built Headquarters. He was interviewed, quit his old job, accepted the new one, and took the CPR boat to Comox, all on the same day:

At Comox, a horse-drawn wagon was waiting to take me to Courtenay, from whence I used shank's mare along the logging railway to what was referred to as Headquarters Camp, a few miles inland. There I was given full instructions regarding my dual job at the new camp, by the office manager.

Number Nine Camp was brand new, the junior employee who accompanied me to it informed me. A clearing for the camp had been made and the railway was already running to it. At the moment, accommodation was only temporary, of course, and simply consisted of two large marquees, or field tents. One was bunkhouse for 24 men; the other that place without which no camp could function—the cookhouse.

I smiled when I heard that the name of the head man of the camp construction gang was Carpenter and I soon learned, when the timber arrived, that his men were real handymen. A large bunkhouse to sleep about 90 men was started, then a cookhouse, an office and store for me with sleeping accommodation attached as well as a filer's shed, and so on. Also on hand was a team of fallers and buckers who came to clear places for the various foremen. The homes and families of the latter would be transported to our camp by the railway before the actual logging commenced.

An early crew of Comox Logging, probably at Camp 7, c. 1911. The man with the axe is faller Walter Brown, and Hughie Cliffe is standing fourth from right.—MYRA BAIKIE AND NANCY BROWN

The cookhouse at Camp 7, Parkins Crossing, Dove Creek, c. 1912. Notice the main-line tracks, water tower with spout for filling locies, the triangular dinner gong hanging in front, and a circular, hand-cranked whetstone for sharpening axes.
—BRITISH COLUMBIA ARCHIVES, 90145

In all probability this is Camp 2 in its original location "just outside Headquarters" near Sprout's farm, c. 1914. In the foreground is the water tower for filling locie boilers and behind are the cookhouse and managers' and married men's houses.—MARGARET SMITH

A close-up of the foremen's house at Camp 2 , c. 1914. The spartan furnishings include two tin water buckets and an enamel jug on an upended crate, a small table with an enamel wash bowl, and two double-bitted axes to cut firewood. Seated to the right of the door is Clay Walsh, a logger from Chatham, New Brunswick, who met Edith ("Edie") Cliffe at her family's Lorne Hotel and married her in 1915. Clay Walsh went on to work as a Comox Logging foreman for many years. —MARGARET SMITH

Soon afterwards, Davies continued, the whole area was enveloped in a heavy snowstorm that lasted for four days. The cook tent collapsed, burying the contents under a weight of snow; the railway to newly opened Headquarters was blocked; and a shipment of meat was unable to get through to Camp 9. Pierre Colet, the cook, and the enterprising loggers showed great resourcefulness:

We found that the only meat we had with which to feed twenty-four men, was bacon! Lovely with eggs, for breakfast, but to keep hard-working men going? The prospect laid me low. But again I was to discover that a crisis was simply a challenge to those loggers. They formed a hunting party and set off for the woods. To my amazement they returned triumphantly with two bucks and the jaunty promise of more where those came, should the need arise.

We had a supply of flour but only the bunkhouse heater to cook it on. Pierre, our cook, worked frantically to produce flapjacks in lieu of bread, venison steaks, bacon and the occasional chipmunk for one of them men who relished this particular delicacy. This went on for six days so it was small wonder that when a train finally got through with supplies it was greeted with sustained cheers. I'm sure the loudest of all came from Pierre!

Although it was now November, Davies continued, logging commenced:

Loggers were arriving now and the foremen began to sort out their gangs. The timber cruiser, who planned the order in which the giant firs and cedars were to be felled, gave his instructions to the foreman faller. The expert tree climber [high rigger] scaled a tall fir, chopped off the top and erected what was called a "flying machine" which would hoist the logs into the air, after which the donkey engine pulled them to the loading platform alongside the railway.

The tree climber was paid $4.25 for his day's work. The bucker, who trimmed the trees and sawed them into logs, received $3.25 for his day. The railway gang, comprised of eight Italians under a Cornish foreman, each received $2.50 per day. All the men were charged 90 cents a day for good, substantial meals.

Usually this heterogeneous assortment of men got along very well together. It is an indisputable fact that the fallers, who worked in pairs, there being no machine sawing in those days, actually competed to see which crew could fell the most trees a day.

Everything the loggers needed was stocked in my store, i.e., all necessary clothing; underwear, shirts, socks, boots, tobacco, snuff and cigars. The Swedes were my best customers for the snuff, often buying twelve boxes at one time.

The Saturday following pay day fell into a set pattern, when a party of six men would be formed to take the handpumped trolley down the railway to the saloon at Courtenay. Orders from the men were taken for their month's supply of Scotch, rye, gin, etc.

Davies remembered a Swede named Ole Olson who gave him his grandfather's gold watch and a wad of bills for safekeeping when he suspected he might have "one hell of a night." He leaned toward Davies confidentially and said, "She's going to be one hell of a night, and I no vant to shoot somebody tomorrow morning—so you keep for me!" In the spring of 1912, Davies continued,

We now had over a hundred men in the camp and I found it an interesting study in human nature to observe how they spent the long winter evenings. Many played poker, of course, as long as their money lasted. Among these was a man who was said to have been a dealer in a San Francisco gambling joint. He nearly always won, probably because he had an uncanny sense of knowing when he had a losing hand.

There were of course the usual group who never tired of living in the past. They told and re-told their experiences in the "good old days." They often produced much laughter as they competed for the tallest, most exaggerated whoppers! And, strange as it may seem, there were some who passed all their leisure hours with poetry books.

These small, early camps were eclipsed in importance by Headquarters Camp, the jewel in the crown of Comox Logging's woods operations, the departure point to the timber heartland, and the base

Trains in the Backyard

Born in 1907, the eldest of ten children, Edith McNish (*née* Crockett) was a small child when Comox Logging's Camp 1 was built on the Crockett family's 160-acre farm at the corner of Smith and Headquarters roads. She can remember the big bunkhouse, cookhouse, and the timekeeper's office. At one time, she said, there were more men at Camp 1 than in the whole of Courtenay. She can also remember the men and packhorses leaving Camp 1 to build the new base, Headquarters, in 1911.

As a girl Edith heard Comox Logging trains coming from Courtenay every morning. They would stop at the different farms to pick up loggers on their way to the woods and camps.

Edith and her siblings turned out to welcome the arrival of the first E & N train to Courtenay in 1914, but she and her brothers and sisters "didn't think much of it" because they were used to seeing bigger trains "right in their backyard."

Edith also recalled that Comox Logging dug a well at the camp as a source of water for its locies. The concrete cribbing from the well is still visible in the field.

Several members of the Crockett family were later associated with Comox Logging, including Edith's brother John, whistlepunk on a skidder crew, and sister Barbara, housekeeper at Filberg House for many years.

The cooks outside the cookhouse door at Camp 2, c. 1914. Several of Comox Logging's early cooks were French-Canadian, among them Pierre Colet and F. Drapeau.—MARGARET SMITH

Unidentified blacksmiths at a Comox Logging camp, c. 1912—possibly Camp 1 or Camp 7. The men are working on a pair of skidder tongs. Leonard Frank photo.—VANCOUVER PUBLIC LIBRARY, 6070

camp for the assault on the forest to the north, opened in 1911. It was a permanent settlement, quite unlike the collection of moveable bunkhouses, houses, and filers' shacks typical of temporary camps, and it would remain Comox Logging's base until 1958.

≈

Comox Logging's original logging ventures featured both traditional ground yarding and primitive highlead logging. In 1910, logging was still done with skid roads, logs were laboriously sniped for ground transport by small donkey engines, and loading them onto flatcars was achieved by means of platforms and parbuckles. The parbuckle loading system was a method in which donkey operators combined their engines' brute power with cables, blocks (pulleys), parbuckle slings, and loading platforms. Simple ground yarding was insufficient to load flatcars; what was needed was some way of lifting the logs onto the flatcars. Lift or "highlead" could be achieved by attaching a block to a tree, stretching a cable between the donkey, block, and log, and parbuckling the log from a loading platform onto the flatcar. In this way, parbuckle slings, which had been used in shipping for two hundred years, were effectively adapted to steam logging, and donkey engines took turns yarding and loading logs. This method made valuable use of highlead and maximum use of a steam donkey's power.

One disadvantage of parbuckle loading was that large logs still could only be rolled into position on flatcars. They could not be lifted bodily and positioned exactly where they were wanted, and only a tier or two of logs could be loaded onto a flatcar. "They only had a very small load, you know. They seldom had a second tier unless the logs were very small. If they were big, they put a couple on and let it go," Joe Cliffe recalled. Another disadvantage was that a loading platform ("landing," "bed," or "rollway") had to be built next to the railway track. Moreover, the donkey could do only one thing at a time: it could either yard logs from the forest or load them onto a flatcar. Both took time and labour.

Early highlead methods led directly to the invention of what was known as "aerial logging." In about 1910, machinery manufacturers in Louisiana capitalized on the power of steam and the potential of highlead to devise a machine that could aerially yard and load at the same time—the massive two-engine, steam-powered Lidgerwood flying machines with a daily capacity to yard and load 125,000 board feet of logs. Comox Logging's parbuckle loading system had used minimal highlead in the form of raised gin poles or blocks attached to nearby trees, but the new method called for a standing tree to be topped at 100 or 120 feet, secured with guylines, and used for both yarding and loading. Logs were yarded through the air and loaded onto flatcars with cumbersome, 120-pound tongs. The sole business of the twenty-two-man skidder crew was moving logs—yarding them from the bush and loading them securely onto flatcars.

In 1911 Comox Logging got its first Lidgerwoods. These state-of-the-art machines were the first in British Columbia and among the first on the entire west coast of North America. The wharves and docks at Royston had not yet been completed, Joe Cliffe recalled, and the skidders were brought up the Courtenay River on scows and unloaded at Cooper's Corner slip.

The Origins of Highlead Yarding

In their later years, Eustace Smith and Joe Cliffe recalled the transition from ground to highlead yarding.

Smith: *Around 1907, a new method of logging was introduced, which was a change from ground yarding to loading-out points, to high lead; this consisted of a spar tree rigged up with heavy yarding blocks placed at a high level, guyed for the heavy strain. In this way the nose of the log was lifted clear and would ride over all obstructions without being held up en route, which so often happened with ground yarding through logged over areas.*

Cliffe: *The ground yarding system lasted until about 1910. Some bright and brave young logger, by nailing cleats on the side of tree, was able to hang a block or pulley up the tree with a couple of guy-lines spiked to stumps. By threading the main line through the pulley he was able to increase the amount of logs per day with less hard work.*

This was a great improvement, and in no time at all it was used all over the coast. . . . The whole idea of getting the yarding line up as high as possible was to get the nose of the log up above the windfalls and rubbish. Stumps were cut too high in those days so logs had to come around them not over them as can be done today.

The Latest Wrinkle

Comox Logging's revolutionary Lidgerwood "flying machines" were state of the art in 1913, when journalist H. D. Forde wrote the following description:

Flying machines, the latest wrinkle in the logging industry, cost in the neighbourhood of $16,000 apiece, and have an average capacity of yarding up out of the bush and loading twenty-five cars of logs per day. As each carload of logs averages 5,000 feet, it requires no vast stretch of one's imagination to grasp that a grand total of 125,000 feet of logs has not only been hauled out of the bush, but at the same time has been loaded on cars by one machine. . . . The "Flying Machine" is one of the most modern methods of hauling logs and loading them on a train.

Comox Logging employed two forms of parbuckle loading in 1912. In the first, shown here, a thirty-foot gin pole, resembling a short telephone pole, was raised across the track from the loading platform and secured by three guylines attached to stumps. The top of the pole hung over an empty flatcar, and a line ran from the donkey engine to a loading block (pulley) fastened at the top of the pole. The pole and block then provided enough highlead to parbuckle the logs onto waiting flatcars. "They used a little short gin pole and rolled the logs up," recalled Joe Cliffe. "They built all this expensive decking to the height of the car then more or less rolled the logs onto the car." Leonard Frank photo.
—BRITISH COLUMBIA ARCHIVES, 90174

The second method was the same as the first except that the block was attached to a live tree, rather than to an improvised pole. A cable from the donkey engine extended to a loading block secured forty or fifty feet up the tree which, as in the first system, was located on the far side of the railway tracks and directly over the loading platform. This height, combined with the donkey's brute power, provided the lift required to roll the logs onto the flatcars. Leonard Frank photo, 1912.—BRITISH COLUMBIA ARCHIVES, 90173

Comox Logging donkey engine and crew, possibly based at Camp 7, c. 1911. Standing at the left is Hughie Cliffe (1889–1964), who much later ran Comox Logging's boom camp at Royston. The man seated at the lower right is holding an empty bottle, perhaps hoping that it will refill itself.—LORNA CLIFFE

Aerial logging. The "flying machine," wrote a visitor in 1913, "is one of the most modern methods of hauling logs and loading them on a train." The skidder yards a log into the landing by means of a cable threaded up to blocks, skyline, and carriage. The loading crew, below, awaits the log's arrival. Leonard Frank photo, 1912.
—BRITISH COLUMBIA ARCHIVES, 90164

Comox Logging's Two-Spot engine, known as "the deuce" (at right), hauls out a load of logs while the skidder (centre) yards a log to the landing pile. Leonard Frank photo, 1912.—BRITISH COLUMBIA ARCHIVES, B-08340

Donkey Engine Evolution

Donkey engines did all the work for Comox Logging until the first Lidgerwood skidders arrived. Years later, Bob Filberg was asked what kind of donkey engines were in use on coastal British Columbia when he came in 1909.

From 1900, he said, the standard machines on the whole Pacific coast were 9 × 10 donkeys—"little two-drum machines" consisting of a haul-in drum and a haulback drum, but they had been getting "larger and larger, and faster and more powerful" since the turn of the century.

"Steam donkeys logged the timber from stump to railroad," Filberg recalled. "It was a short railroad haul to mill or tidewater—the terrain was mostly valleys, the stand of timber heavy. . . . Donkeys were two-drum yarders with a spool for loading. . . . A donkey with a heavy sled weighed less than fifty tons." A line horse pulled the heavy yarding line from the donkey out to the timber.

In 1905 a reporter noted that oxen had disappeared from the Vancouver Island woods, horses were scarce, and "large donkey engines by their whistle, smoke and jets of steam, tell of the camps away back in the woods, where Douglas firs are reeled in one, two, and three thousand feet along the skid roads."

Big Jack McKenzie Jr., Comox Logging high rigger, on his way up a back spar to rig it with guylines, blocks, lagging, and tackle. The rigging crew waits below to lend assistance. Skidder logging was impossible without fully-rigged spar trees. Vincent Russell photo, c. 1914.—MARGARET SMITH

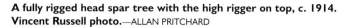

A fully rigged head spar tree with the high rigger on top, c. 1914. **Vincent Russell photo.**—ALLAN PRITCHARD

An enlargement, showing the high rigger giving a thumbs-up gesture. "This is a spar tree," Walter Pritchard wrote on the back of this photo. "The head rigger is on top. He sets the rigging and oversees the logging." What Pritchard didn't say was that high riggers specialized in performing tricks while 120 feet up. Some were fond of handstands, some performed little dances, and some were given to urinating on the skidder crew below. One rigger claimed to be able to throw his hat in the air, skim down the tree, and catch his hat before it reached the ground. **Vincent Russell photo.**—ALLAN PRITCHARD

Joe Cliffe and the First Skidders

Many years later, Joe Cliffe recalled that the first Lidgerwoods arrived in 1911 soon after the completion of the booming grounds at Royston:

And soon after that they got the skidders. I guess they had that in mind. They got the skidders, six of them, which was the biggest accumulation of skidders on the west coast. I have been in all the camps in Washington and Oregon and nobody had that many skidders. Quite a few camps had two or three, but Comox had six. They were twice as expensive as the donkey engines, more complicated and an awful lot more rigging. It was all aerial logging: no fooling around dragging logs. . . .

With all that stuff I guess the million dollars was used and that put them into business in a big way. They must have had quite a crew on making roads because even in a straight line it's at least eight miles to Headquarters [from Royston]. . . . They expanded very quick once they got out in the open. You see, they had to log the back end of farms and bits of timber for about two miles out of Courtenay. Then they were able to put in branches and get more machines working.

Enlargement of photo on opposite page showing the skidder with a sparkcatcher on the chimney, indicating that they are working in hot weather. Vincent Russell photo, c. 1914.—ALLAN PRITCHARD

A pile of logs (right) has been yarded into the skidder landing in preparation for loading onto empty flatcars. The skidder crew and loading crew wait while the Lidgerwood idles. Leonard Frank photo, 1912.—BRITISH COLUMBIA ARCHIVES, 90186

An early photograph (c. 1917) showing the two skidder engineers or "levermen" at work: at the front is the loading leverman and, behind, in his accustomed place near the boiler, is the yarding leverman. This skidder had not yet been converted to crude oil: note the pile of wood behind and the fireman peering at the camera.
—AUDREY MENZIES

"Riding the tongs" above a skidder setting, c. 1917. The high rigger climbs the tree (right) while two riggers ride the yarding and loading tongs. Above them is a mass of carriages, blocks, and rigging. By the 1930s this sort of work was uncommon, and major alterations were made to the rigging only after the rigging had been lowered. "There's people all over the tree!" exclaimed Davey Janes, who started on a skidder crew in the 1920s. "It's a bloody circus!"—AUDREY MENZIES

Logs going up the jackladder at Fraser Mills,
c. 1912.—BRITISH COLUMBIA ARCHIVES, B-08353

◀ Taken at the same time as the images
opposite, this photo shows the high rigger
making his way up the head spar tree
while the loading and yarding levermen wait
on the skidder below. Visible on the base of
the tree is the blazed *X*, a signal to the fallers
to leave this tree standing as a spar tree.
—AUDREY MENZIES

Fraser Mills, c. 1912, on the Fraser River above New Westminster. "It was a good place for a sawmill," Joe Cliffe asserted,
"because sea-going boats liked to come up and put a week in there in fresh water to clean the hull while they were loading."
At right is the jackladder that led into the mill; at left a sailing vessel takes on a load of lumber. Logs were stored here and
upstream in fresh water safe from the ravages of teredo worms. **Broadbridge-Bullen photo.**—BRITISH COLUMBIA ARCHIVES, 90148

At first, Lidgerwoods went by a number of creative names: "cable-way skidders," "cable-way system," "overhead cable machines," "overhead rigs," and most dramatically, "flying machines," so-called because they caused logs to "fly" from where they were cut to where they were loaded onto flatcars. The various names reflected the aerial nature of this new technology, a radical departure from the ground-yarding methods previously employed. Skidders were first used about four miles north of Courtenay on the Dove Creek Road, as Jack Carthew recalled: "Then, up past Parkin's Crossing, they brought in skidders, and that was the beginning of overhead logging in the area. It was the summer of 1911. They logged all around Dove Creek with those machines."

Comox Logging soon mastered skidder logging, bought additional skidders, and entirely abandoned ground yarding and parbuckle loading. By 1914 the company had four of the machines; by 1917, six. In the 1920s, the company attached two skidders to each of the three main camps north of Headquarters—Camps 1, 2, and 3. The company's method was to push the railway and skidders into the jagged corners of Block 29 and to move its three main logging camps accordingly.

∾

Expansion continued on other fronts. In 1911, three large, steel ocean-going tugs were ordered from English shipyards for the purpose of towing booms from Royston to the Fraser River. Previously, the company had hired tugboats from other companies to perform this service. Built to Canadian Western's specifications at shipyards at Newcastle-on-Tyne, the 125-foot *Dreadful* came around the Horn and arrived at the mill in August 1912. The largest steel tug on the Pacific coast, she was sent on her sea trials to Prince Rupert in September with the company brass on board, and shortly afterwards made her maiden forty-hour trip from Comox to Fraser Mills with 1.5 million board feet of lumber. The other two ocean-going tugs, the *Fearful* and the *Cheerful*, were both eighty-five feet. The *Joyful*, sixty feet, specialized in towing booms from Royston across to Comox Logging's tie-up in the shelter of Comox Spit. The *Joyful* arrived in the fall of 1912, replacing Captain Swallow's little tug *Shuswap*.

∾

Canadian Western's goal after 1910 was to make Fraser Mills independent of all other lumber producers by logging its own land and buying as little timber as possible on the open market. The mill reached new levels of productivity under mill manager W. E. Rogers and sales manager Henry Mackin. In 1911, for example, the mill was open 310 days of the year, cut 350,000 board feet every ten-hour shift, and added a night shift. The May 1911 shipment of 12.7 million feet was a record for any sawmill in British Columbia. But Canadian Western still had to buy one-third of its timber on the open market simply to keep the mill busy, and it was almost twice as expensive to buy other producers' timber as to cut it on Block 29 and ship it to the mill. In 1911, Canadian Western's directors hoped that the "cable-way system" of logging would speed output production, and with skidders in use, output at the mill went from 109 million feet in 1911 to 170 million the next year—enough to build 34,000 small houses.

Master Sawyer at Fraser Mills

In 1925, J. P. McBane, formerly master sawyer at Fraser Mills, recalled that

This was a brand new plant and I had the honour of cutting the first log there [in 1909]. The plant had a capacity of 350,000 feet of lumber daily.

Fraser Mills, being close to Vancouver, was also a sort of show place and it was here that all the visiting dignitaries were taken to see how lumbering in the Northwest is carried on. The Duke of Connaught, brother to the late King Edward, was one of our visitors. He seemed to take a great deal of interest in the head saws and asked many questions about the mechanism.

Just before the war, in 1914, the Duke and Duchess of Sutherland, then on a tour of Canada, came out to see us cut logs. We had other callers, too, among them a whole flock of the Canadian Newspaper Association. They were the boys who could ask the questions. I sawed lumber in the Fraser plant until 1917, eight years.

Saw filers with large band saw at Fraser Mills, c. 1912.
—BRITISH COLUMBIA ARCHIVES, F-2270

The townsite known as Millside or Maillardville at Fraser Mills, with the mill in the distance, c. 1912.—BRITISH COLUMBIA ARCHIVES, B-08381

But this was not just a sawmill. Fraser Mills was also equipped to turn the mill's lumber into specialized house-building materials, among them shingles, doors, and window frames. In 1910, the sash and door factory churned out 1,000 doors a day; a separate cedar mill cut 150,000 feet a day; and two years later the shingle mill could produce 600,000 shingles in a ten-hour shift. In 1913 British Columbia's first plywood plant was opened at the mill.

Exports boomed. Stocks between forty and sixty million board feet were always on hand. In 1912, eighty per cent of total output was sent by rail to feed the building boom on the Canadian Prairies. The prairie market seemed insatiable; the company owned 154 retail lumberyards throughout western Canada in 1911 and nearly 200 a year later. McRae and Davidson fed the prairie settlement boom they had helped create.

Ten per cent of the output was shipped to Australia and South Africa, and the final ten per cent was sold in British Columbia. Vancouver was built with Vancouver Island lumber, as Joe Cliffe recalled: "Everything cut went into Vancouver mills. I guess Vancouver don't know it, but the whole coast of British Columbia built Vancouver."

The mill had a very large workforce of 877 men in 1913. A few years earlier, to overcome a shortage of skilled labour and to avoid hiring Oriental labour, Davidson had "induced" the population of a small French-Canadian lumbering village to travel west in a colonization scheme reminiscent of his and McRae's prairie settlement scheme of the previous decade. In 1909, the 110 workmen and their families arrived in a special thirteen-car train of the CPR. The company sold them half-acre lots and house lumber at very reasonable terms. The mill soon supported a community of four thousand workers and their families. Known originally as Millside, the town assumed the name Maillardville with the immigration from Quebec. The company also negotiated the immigration of fifty families from Malta to work at Fraser Mills. They arrived early in 1913. Other mill workers in that year included 168 East Indians, 57 Japanese, 29 Chinese, and many eastern Europeans.

≈

By 1914, Comox Logging had assumed the shape it would retain for most of its existence. The last years of the McBride era in British Columbia had witnessed the expansion of Comox Logging and its parent company Canadian Western. Fraser Mills had been enlarged and, on the Island, logging had been expanded to reduce the company's dependency on expensive logs bought on the open market. The company had left the farm timber behind and moved into the rich timber of Block 29, buying a logging railway and a fleet of locomotives and building nine logging camps as it progressed. Comox Logging also invested in four efficient new Lidgerwood "flying machines" with impressive logging capacity. Outside experts like Jim McGuigan and Arthur Hilton had been hired, but more importantly, men from local farms were flocking to work for the industrial giant in their midst.

chapter 4

*I'm longing to go back
to my little Comox shack
with the chickens
and the ducks and the door*

—from "My Little Comox Shack,"
a song by Bessie Vessey, 1927

Making
the Homeguard

RITISH COLUMBIA LOGGING HISTORIES TEND TO
emphasize the transiency and distant origins of the
workforce. At first glance, the sources for the Comox
Logging Company support this. In 1910, the company
needed hundreds of trained and knowledgeable men
almost overnight to run its extended operations and
its nine camps, and many of these men were found in
the hiring halls of Vancouver. Timekeeper Oscar
Davies, for example, recalled the "heterogeneous assortment" of a
hundred men at Camp 9 in 1911, which included a French-Canadian
cook, a Yorkshireman, a gambler from San Francisco, at least one
Swedish faller, and, on the steel gang, a Cornish foreman, eight Italians,
and an Australian socialist.

While such hirings were considerable, Comox Logging also had a long
tradition of recruiting local men. In 1910, the company found it could
exploit the skills and resources of several generations of lumbering in the
Comox District. Men from this farming community had, in fact, logged
in the valley since the 1870s. Members of the Berkeley, Cliffe, Fitzgerald,
Grant, McKenzie, Piercy, Pritchard, and Smith families had worked for a
number of local logging outfits, including King & Casey, Chemainus
Timber, and Fraser River Lumber. Members of other farming families,
such as Duncan, Grieve, Harmston, McQuillan, and Parkin, joined
Comox Logging in the early decades of the century.

The amalgamated company of 1910 inherited a diverse workforce
from its predecessors: men who had worked for the Fraser River Lumber
Company, like Arthur Hilton, Bob Martin, and Bob Filberg; men who
were transferred from Canadian Western's subsidiary at Golden (the
Columbia River Lumber Company), like builder Bill Haggarty and
engineer Harry Shepherd; men who had worked for McFarlan on
Denman Island, like George Cliffe and Joe Fitzgerald; who had worked
for the Chemainus Company, like Joe Thomson; for George Doane

Many Comox Logging employees joined the 102nd Battalion ("Warden's Warriors") in the First World War. Big Jack McKenzie Sr., then over fifty years old, is standing at the rear of this group, in the doorway. Walter Gage photo, *c. 1916.*—WILMA McKENZIE

The 102nd Battalion preparing to board the CPR's *Princess Charlotte*, June 10, 1916. This photo was taken from an upstairs window of the Elk Hotel, Comox. Walter Gage photo.
—AUDREY MENZIES

in Comox, like Hughie Cliffe; and for Hart & Bambrick at Little River, like Clay Walsh and Butch Grant. "Many of the present employees of the Comox Logging and Railway Company were employed by that Company when operations were started," wrote a *Comox Argus* reporter in 1940. "The people of this community have been intimately connected with the logging industry for a long period, and have seen logging developed from ox teams to the fast, powerful equipment used in logging today." The celebrated Comox Homeguard originated well before 1910.

Despite the presence of these men and others, and the continuity they lent, the company's new railways and logging facilities also required highly trained workers of every description. In the space between 1910 and the start of the First World War, Americans were hired in two key areas: management and skidder technology. The company hired a capable managerial corps including James McNaughton, Tom McLarty, and Clay Walsh who, like McCormack, tended to be Canadians with experience in American logging. The most notable of the Americans to arrive in the early years were logging engineer Bob Filberg; Louisiana skidder expert Jay Baptist; snub-nosed tough guy Jack McQuinn and his brother-in-law from the Willamette Valley, faller Lilburn Hunt; camp foreman Len Harding; locie engineer Shorty Miner; and engineer, hotel proprietor, and baseball enthusiast R. B. ("Pa") Dixon. "A whole raft of them [Americans] came here at the same time," Hunt's son Bob said. Lilburn Hunt was "just a logger going around the countryside from camp to camp" when he first came to Comox in 1909. Loggers like Hunt and McQuinn "just made the rounds, those guys. My old man was the same. If they woke up and the hotcakes weren't right, they'd throw them on the floor and move on to another camp." After 1916, when Filberg married McCormack's daughter and secured a managerial position with the company, he hired many of his old American friends. "When Filberg took over the outfit he went down there and got that bunch," Bob Hunt said.

Even in 1910 the accessible lowland Douglas fir forests of Washington and Oregon had been largely eradicated, the result of sixty years of continuous logging. A glut of skilled labour on the American market combined with lucrative offers of work in British Columbia drew loggers over the border. The prosperity that, in Canada, accompanied the end of the Edwardian era and welcomed the reign of King George V in 1910 lasted only for a few years. The bubble burst with the depression of 1913 and the outbreak of the First World War in August 1914.

～

The war had a devastating impact on the Comox Valley. Logging, like farming, was considered an essential service in wartime, but many men left those occupations to go to war. For the first year of the war, eligible men left the valley to enlist in regiments based in Nanaimo, Victoria, or Vancouver. But in November 1915 the Comox-based 102nd Battalion of the Canadian Infantry Division—known as the North British Columbians and "Warden's Warriors"—came into being. The battalion originated in the House of Commons in Ottawa, when a Member of Parliament challenged the member for Comox-Atlin, Henry Clements, "to produce a unit from his barren constituency."

Sandwick Cousins Die in France

Robbie Duncan (born 1894) and his cousin Charlie Duncan (born 1895) died on the same day in France in 1918. They were unusual cousins: Charlie was born Charles Pritchard, son of Archie, but his mother Maggie died in childbirth. He was adopted by Robbie's uncle Eric Duncan and his wife Anna.

The *Record of Service* of the University of British Columbia includes both men:

Robert George Duncan. *He enlisted with the 102nd Battalion in January, 1916, crossing to England in June. He proceeded to France with that regiment in August, and served with them in all their engagements till the time of his death. He was mortally wounded on September 27, 1918, and died the following day. He had been promoted to Sergeant, and was awarded the Military Medal shortly before his death.*

Charles Andrew Duncan. *He enlisted with the 196th Western Universities Battalion as a private in March, 1916, proceeding to England with that unit in November. He went to France with a draft to the 46th Battalion in Feb., 1917, serving through the engagements at Vimy Ridge and Passchendaele, and being twice wounded, the second time so severely as to be invalided in September, 1918. Lieutenant Duncan was killed at Canal du Nord, in front of Cambrai, on September 28, 1918, while leading his platoon into action. He was buried at Quarry Wood Cemetery, near Bourlon village.*

Robbie Duncan's brother Johnny (1896–1976) became a well-known surveyor with Comox Logging.

Men joined up throughout the Comox-Atlin constituency, especially in the prosperous Comox Valley and the islands and coast to the north. They trained on the Comox Spit and were sent briefly to England and then on to Belgium in August 1916. They went into battle immediately at St. Eloi near the Ypres salient. Six men were killed and twelve wounded on the first day. In the next two years the battalion fought at numerous battles including the Somme, Vimy Ridge, and Passchendaele. There was an overall mortality rate of twenty-eight per cent—almost every family in Comox District was affected—and the battalion was combined with one from Ontario. The simple war memorial next to the post office in Comox is dedicated to the memory of the 676 men who died with the 102nd, but their names are not listed.

After the war, Hilton tried to rehire as many original employees as possible. In January 1919, for example, Frank Irwin wanted his old job as bookkeeper. "I was in the company's employ during the summer of 1914," he wrote, "and left early in August of that year to enlist in the Canadian Expeditionary Force with which I went overseas. I served with the 7th Batn. in France, having recently returned, and have been honourably discharged. I held various ranks from private to Co'y Sergeant Major." Hilton hired him.

≈

Before 1920, two classes of Comox Logging employees emerged: a stable and privileged minority—a kind of aristocracy of tradesmen and foremen at Headquarters and the camps, many of them with local connections—and a transient population of loggers hired in Vancouver. Most of the management, office staff, engineers, surveyors, foremen, train crews, tradesmen, and other skilled workers were permanent employees of the company, living at Headquarters or at their Homeguard farms in the valley. At the same time, the company employed a good many short-term employees: the fallers, buckers, riggers, chokermen, and some members of the skidding crews, as well as the steel gangs and section gangs. At first, these men came from the hiring halls and agencies of Vancouver, and they tended to be "foreigners," that is, recent immigrants from Europe.

After 1921, local farm men and boys were given preference over outside men. Howard McQuinn related that his father Jack, who came from a farm in Oregon, was the first to man a skidder with a local crew. Filberg, who had been made logging superintendent recently, said to him, "For Christ's sake, leave them alone, they don't know anything!" Filberg was content to hire loggers in Vancouver: he would contact Black's Agency and ask for a hookerman or ten chokermen. Such workers, however, weren't always reliable, so McQuinn ignored Filberg and trained a crew of local men. They learned quickly and when the camps closed down in the fire season or in the winter "they just went home." They were also available for work at a moment's notice.

It became company policy to train and retain local men, and by the 1920s stability was Comox Logging's hallmark. Work and wages lured Comox Valley farmers into the woods, and the company hired largely in the valley. "Even if they were from Courtenay," Frank Davison said, "they were country people. There were no city slickers in Comox Logging."

Les Marshall and Ambrose Morris Go to War

According to Mona Law, her father Les Marshall (1896–1986), a Comox logging faller, used to tell the story of how he and his friend Ambrose Morris went to war. In 1916 Les was ploughing on Berkeley Grieve's farm when Ambrose came to see him. He was going to Nanaimo to join up, but he didn't want to go by himself; he wanted Les to go with him.

Les objected. "I've promised Berkeley Grieve that I'll finish the ploughing and I don't want to go back on my word," he said. Ambrose then offered to help him finish the ploughing, and Les agreed. Ambrose brought over another team of horses and the two men worked all night to get the job done. The moonlight assisted them, and the next day they went to Nanaimo.

In England they were assigned to different regiments and lost contact. Later, some time in 1917, Les was sent to the front lines to make sure his regiment's trenches connected properly with those of the neighbouring regiment. When doing this, he met Ambrose manning the other regiment's machine gun emplacement far out on the zig-zag front lines. The friends were delighted to see each other, but their time together was short. Les had gone only a short way back down the trench when he heard a "whiz-bang" (trench mortar) land behind him. He ran back to find that the mortar had killed Ambrose instantly.

The 102nd Battalion leaving Comox, June 10, 1916. This photo was taken from the upstairs verandah of the Lorne Hotel. One of the two boys running beside the soldiers is Wallace Baikie, age fourteen. Baikie recalled: "On arriving at the spit we could see the men marching off. A half a dozen of us left the boat and caught up with the soldiers. We ran along, visiting the ones we knew until we got to the Comox wharf. Everybody was held up until the soldiers boarded the ship and then we were allowed out on the wharf. It sure was an experience seeing all those men all over the ship and up in the rigging. There was a sad little group left when the boat pulled away." Walter Gage photo.—AUDREY MENZIES

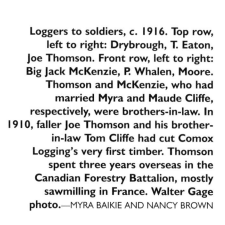

Loggers to soldiers, c. 1916. Top row, left to right: Drybrough, T. Eaton, Joe Thomson. Front row, left to right: Big Jack McKenzie, P. Whalen, Moore. Thomson and McKenzie, who had married Myra and Maude Cliffe, respectively, were brothers-in-law. In 1910, faller Joe Thomson and his brother-in-law Tom Cliffe had cut Comox Logging's very first timber. Thomson spent three years overseas in the Canadian Forestry Battalion, mostly sawmilling in France. Walter Gage photo.—MYRA BAIKIE AND NANCY BROWN

Bruce King of Ladysmith concurred. "In Courtenay they could pick up the whole crew locally. They didn't need bunkhouses because they all bought acreages; a lot of them had farms. In peak periods they might hire in Vancouver, but it was a Homeguard company. The advantage was they always had a crew. In bad times with layoffs they could always get them: there was the basis of a crew there always."

But Filberg certainly had a point. Farmers did not become good loggers overnight, and at first they were unfamiliar with advanced aerial logging methods. Gordon Pritchard (1892–1988) recalled that when Comox Logging started, some local people weren't alert enough: "They were farmers who didn't appreciate the dangers." Perhaps predictably, "farmer" became a term of derision in the woods. According to Ralph Harmston, "There was a favourite saying in the woods: if something didn't go right you'd say, 'Come on, you farmer!'" Still, farmers were versatile, adaptable workers familiar with machinery of all kinds and accustomed to logging their "farm timber," if only for firewood.

The local hiring policy pursued by McQuinn and Filberg did not prevail generally on the British Columbia coast, where whole crews were hired at the Vancouver agencies. The verses of celebrated logger-poet Bob Swanson, for example, describe remote north-coastal logging camps accessible only by Union Steamships and inhabited by transient, hard-drinking, bachelor loggers known as bush apes: "So back to the jungle you're heading once more/ To the bush where the tame-apes roam. . . . Money when saved is a worry, so never your pleasure deprive/ Live for today and be happy, tomorrow may never arrive."

Comox Valley men who logged elsewhere tended to notice the differences. Davey Janes, who worked for Campbell River Timber between the wars, recalled that all the fellows there came from Vancouver. The superintendent was said to be an SOB; depending on how he felt in the morning he might fire an entire crew and hire a new one from Vancouver. There was always a crew working, a crew coming, and a crew going. Davey heard of one superintendent at Campbell River whose "crew met him in Vancouver and beat the hell out of him—walked on his face. This is the gospel truth."

∾

Of course, there were as many daughters as sons on Comox District farms, and the Cliffe and Pritchard daughters, for example, married loggers from outside the district. Maude, Edith, and Myra Cliffe married John McKenzie from Ontario, Clay Walsh from New Brunswick, and Joe Thomson from England respectively, while Mildred Pritchard married Bob Martin from Gabriola Island, and so on. A family tree showing the connections between different Comox Logging employees would be exceptionally complex. For a start, the Cliffe and Harmston families have been related since 1873—before a single tree destined for a sawmill was cut in the Comox Valley.

There were good reasons for transient loggers to put down roots in the valley: Major Hilton's 1910 policy of issuing monthly paycheques, which invited permanence; the presence of farmers' eligible daughters; and the opportunity to buy farms and settle down. The valley had many attractions that, for example, Hastings Sawmill's isolated camp at Rock

The Making of the Homeguard

We were at Headquarters when the loggers came back to work that spring [1921]. They brought them up from Courtenay by train, fed them their lunch and took them on to camp afterwards. There must have been two or three hundred of them who had wintered in Vancouver and come up to Comox by special boat. I don't recall the Company moving the men in that manner after that time.

Bob Filberg, about that time, realized (I heard him say it) that the company was going to be there for a long time and he was interested in establishing a permanent crew all down the line and not having to bring in so many of his crew from Vancouver. From that time on local boys had a preference.

Bob was always encouraging and advising his men to get a hold of a piece of land and build a home, which a lot of them did. The soldier settlement at Merville turned out to be a good source of manpower; these fellows could work their land and also get a job with the Comox. This increased as the families started to grow up and look for work. From that time on the number of local men increased. When the company started logging on the Bevan sidehill and on the Comox Lake they took on quite a few Cumberland boys. Again when the Mennonite settlement came into the Black Creek area, another group of potential loggers became available, especially the younger generation. It was just a few years until all of the personnel of the Comox Logging were local residents.—Wallace Baikie, Rolling with the Times

Bay completely lacked, and after 1921 stability was the norm. Even relative newcomers, like Swedish and Finnish fallers, bought land and married locally. John Holmes estimated that by the 1930s, half of Comox Logging's employees came from farms in the valley.

Wherever it operated, Comox Logging carried a certain rural mystique. Retired loggers remember Comox as a family company or a Homeguard company, meaning that company employees were drawn from the tightly knit and interrelated farming families of the Comox Valley. The term "family company," according to Stan Hodgins (1914–1998), referred especially to families like the Grants and the Janes, whose sons became foremen, skidder engineers, and locie engineers while maintaining farms in the valley. "Call them Homeguards or family," Stan said. The men who worked for Comox Logging were "pretty well all from here," Stan continued. "Homeguards, they used to call them," as opposed to workers who stayed in bunkhouses at remote logging camps. "If you were just staying in a bunkhouse, you could just jump in a boat and go to Vancouver and go to another camp." According to Davey Janes, Comox Logging hired from an agency only if men were not available locally. The company's Homeguard tradition produced a novel feature of logging camp life: married men's housing as well as bunkhouses for the single men.

The Cliffes, capable Homeguard family of Comox—and of Comox Logging, c. 1930. Top row, left to right: Joe, Walter, Roy, Percy, Harold. Front row, left to right: Alice, Lu, Florence. "The Cliffe boys were gorgeous-looking people," recalled Florence Cooper (*née* Olson), "handsome and personable." Charles Sillence photo.—LORNA CLIFFE

Most farm incomes were too meagre to support large families. Davey Janes' father had a farm of eighty or ninety acres, and he sold cream to the creamery, but Davey and his older brothers went into logging. "There was no money in farming in those days—goodness' sakes!" Davey Janes did not believe that farm work clashed with woods work; he said that "farming was nothing" and that the Homeguards' farms were mostly small affairs. Davey's brother Norman Janes bought a dairy farm in 1935 but, Norman's daughter recalled, "his woods wages provided the money for the purchase of the farm, not the other way around. He had to get up in the morning at 5:00 a.m. to milk the cows, and then he'd go logging." He later went into beef cattle which didn't take as much looking after.

Stan Hodgins, raised on a farm in Merville, worked in the woods because there was no other work. "There might be a little work in haying time," but milking cows was the only permanent work, and it didn't appeal to farm boys who could get good money in the woods and whose agility and brawn were needed there. Ralph Harmston said that his father, Toynbee Harmston, farmed on the lower road "till he pretty near starved to death. Farming was pretty tough." Dairy farmers sold their cream to the Comox Creamery, and some sold bottled milk in Courtenay, but the market was saturated for dairy products (the valley accommodated 2,750 milking cows in 1921). In the 1930s Ralph took turnips and a ton of potatoes into Cumberland and sold them for a dollar a sack, but it wasn't much, and "by the time you'd paid for the seed in the ground, there was very little profit. You'd sell your spuds, sure; but after that what do you sell?"

One of the few Courtenay farmers to make an income solely from farming was an Englishman named Francis Bullock, a neighbour of the Berkeleys, who sold poultry, cream, and seven varieties of apples. He stored the apples in the shed part of the barn: he laid down some straw, put a layer of apples on top, some straw on top of them, then another layer of apples, and so on. The animals below kept the apples just warm enough not to freeze. Once or twice a week he took a load of chickens and apples into town.

It was hard to avoid working in the woods. Most able-bodied men over about sixteen years of age went to work for Comox Logging. As Jim Muckle remarked, "The company was the only real employer" in the valley. It employed between four and five hundred men in the 1920s, most of whom lived in the camps or in Courtenay, Comox, Merville, Bevan, and Cumberland.

The Homeguards kept their farms despite the attractions of logging. "They called them the Comox Logging farmers, you know. All those guys in Courtenay all owned a farm," said Bruce King. Larry Lehtonen noted that land taxes were low in those days and besides, "When you're brought up on the land, it's hard to let the land go." The great advantage of owning a farm was that it provided a place to return when the woods were closed.

In those days, Bob Harding recalled, even if you worked for Comox Logging you didn't work steady. There was no such thing as unemployment insurance, and you had money only when you worked. In the fire season they'd shut down; if there was too much snow they'd

Homeguards' Cradle

Local boys found summer work with Comox Logging when as young as fourteen or fifteen, and many quit school when permanent woods work arose.

"Farming," Barbara Marriott said, "was a real gamble. So a farm boy would go and get a job in the woods. Any boy in grade seven who knew he wouldn't pass grade eight could get a job in the woods as a whistlepunk and could say to his teacher, 'I'm making more money than you are!' and they'd be self-sufficient."

A Courtenay Homeguard who wishes to remain anonymous said that, years later, after Crown Zellerbach's purchase of Comox Logging, a Vancouver manager complained, "Why do so many of you Comox guys have such a lot of seniority? You must have started as babies!" It was true; this Homeguard had started work at fifteen.

Wallace Baikie recalled, "Many young fellows, as soon as they could get out of going to school, would get hired on with the company, which substantiates Bob Filberg's idea that the company did not have to hire men out of Vancouver when they could hire and train local boys."

The Teachers and the Homeguards

Homeguards seemed especially attracted to young teachers sent to the many schools in the valley and in the logging camps. Eric Duncan noticed this trend at the turn of the century:

All through the country districts the Government maintains free schools three miles apart wherever there are a dozen children of school age. . . . Teaching is naturally with most girls only a prelude to marriage; but this never diminishes the supply, for the examination board lets them in faster than the clergyman lets them out.

Cliffe family matriarch Alice Cliffe (née Marshall) came to the valley as a teacher, and among the other members of the Cliffe family who married teachers were Roy, Harold, Hughie, Percy, and Edgar Cliffe. Others to marry teachers included Lewis Biss, John Crockett, Norman Janes, Bill McKenzie, and Harry Radford. Many valley women became teachers, including Florence Cliffe; the two Duncan girls, Barbara and Margaret; and Edith Crockett.

The aftermath of the great Merville fire of July 1922. **Mack Laing photo.**—BRITISH COLUMBIA ARCHIVES, I-51800

Land clearing: Mack Laing of Comox uses a peavey to stoke a stump fire at Brooklyn Creek, Comox, April 1928. "Clear your land with labour of hand and dynamite, spend four or five hundred dollars an acre on it, drag out the old stumps and the network of roots and underbrush—still the forest is watching. Go away for five years and it will march in again. Some day, when men grow tired, it will reclaim every inch of this coast," wrote journalist Bruce Hutchison. **Mack Laing photo.**
—BRITISH COLUMBIA ARCHIVES, 96668

shut down; if the markets collapsed they'd shut down. "So a lot of the fellows would buy some land, often from the company, and start a stump ranch with cows and chickens and a garden. If you were out of a job you were out of a job, period; you had to have some way of surviving the low spots. That's why they became farmers. With the exception of the farms on the dyke road, there were very few farms of any consequence in the district, but lots of stump ranches."

~

One local source of logging labour was the controversial settlement at Merville, seven miles north of Courtenay. It was founded in 1919, settled by returning soldiers, and probably named for a village in France (Merville-au-bois) where the soldiers had been in battle; but in reality Merville was Comox Logging's bastard son, conceived amid the stumps and slash of Block 29. For $70,000, the provincial Land Settlement Board bought 14,000 acres of recently logged-over land in Block 29 from the Comox Logging Company, as the *Comox Argus* noted in May 1919:

Some fourteen thousand acres purchased from the Canadian Western Lumber Company for the low price of five dollars an acre, have been set aside. Camps have been erected, comfortable, sanitary camps. Logging grades are being cleared of old ties, levelled and utilized as splendid wagon and automobile roads. Men and teams are rapidly changing the face of the country and clearing machinery is being rushed to its destination. Present plans are said to provide for the subdividing of the tract into farms averaging 80 acres in extent, although opinions are expressed as to the advisability of limiting the farms to a smaller acreage so fertile is the soil and so great the promise of intensive farming.

Before 1920, a total of 279 families came to Merville, but not all stayed. There were problems: some of the soldier settlers "didn't know a cow from a horse or a shovel from a hoe," as Stan Hanham put it; more importantly, the land was nowhere near as fertile as promoted. "The Merville settlement was a terrible thing," Norman Sprout said, "a good example of what not to do." The land had supported some of the finest Douglas fir forests ever logged, but as Dick Isenor described, "their stumps were like huge molars with the roots penetrating deep into the gravel and sand to the hardpan beneath. They did not pull easily." The Merville Settlers' Association bought a donkey engine which went from farm to farm pulling stumps and yarding the debris into huge piles, which were then burned. But these slash fires destroyed the soil beneath them, leaving huge and sterile "clinkers" of useless ground. Then, in 1922, much of slash-covered Merville was destroyed by a great fire that started in logging operations in the Campbell River area. Almost fifty settlers lost everything.

Most of the settlers left Merville after the fire, and few who stayed could make their living entirely from farming. Among the Merville vets who worked for Comox Logging were Jack Armstrong, Jack Clifford, Eric Flinton, Jack Frazer, Tommy Mitchell, James Sedgewick, Peter Sprout, Timothy Wasilieff, and Fred White. Many other Merville settlers or their sons worked for Comox Logging, including brothers Cyril, Charlie, and Stan Hodgins. (Stan was the father of novelist Jack Hodgins, whose historical novel *Broken Ground* [1998] takes the reader from the craters of the Western Front to those of the Soldier Settlement.) These settlers ran "stump ranches" featuring a cow, chickens for eggs and poultry, and endless firewood for their stoves.

No Money in Farming

Farming did not contribute much to a Homeguard household's income; most valley residents relied heavily on income from Comox Logging.

One example was Lance Berkeley, who had forty-eight acres on what is now Twenty-ninth Street in Courtenay. He and his family cleared the land into a ten-acre field, a five-acre field, and a grazing ground that was part clear and part bush. Between the wars they milked from six to ten cows and sold the cream to the Comox Creamery. But Lance Berkeley used to half-joke that he "worked for Comox Logging to keep the farm going!"

Fred and Gord Blackburn recalled that their Blackburn and Janes grandfathers "came here to farm . . . they came for the same reason," but "in those days they never made a living out of farming," and their sons had to work in the woods to keep the farm. Fred and Gord lived on ten acres on Cumberland Road when their father worked at Comox Lake, but the family didn't sell any food from the property. They ate everything they grew. "It was for us."

Fred (Siegfried) Erickson

A "Swede-Finn" from Finland, Fred Erickson started working as a hand faller out of Headquarters in 1927 and stayed with Comox Logging for the rest of his career. His wife Emilia was also a Swede-Finn, and the couple had three boys, Harry, David and Frank.

Fred felled trees out of Headquarters and Camp 3 six days a week, but his passion was his dairy farm on what is now the Island Highway, one kilometre north of Merville. The highway was then a dirt track through logging slash at what his son Harry called "the end of civilization."

Among the Ericksons' friends were Fred Dahl, Uno and Esther Forsman, Nestor Hagg, and fallers named Nurmi, Wirta, and Jylha, who helped at work bees on the Erickson farm. Fred, who was very musical and a great dancer, helped arrange the big "Swede dances" at the Merville Hall.

In the 1938 fire, Fred stayed on the dairy farm and put all the family's valuables down the well. The fire missed the farm.

Some of the Finnish and Swedish fallers brought wives with them from Scandinavia. Emilia Erickson, who came from Finland to join her husband, is shown here at her first house in Merville in 1930. She and her husband had a dairy farm here, one kilometre north of the present Merville Post Office. Fred Erickson photo.—HARRY ERICKSON

Fred Erickson and his two-year-old son Harry in front of their house in Merville, 1931. Emilia Erickson photo.
—HARRY ERICKSON

Fred and Emilia Erickson's new barn at their Merville dairy farm, 1932 or 1933. "Comox Logging was sometimes referred to as a family company," Barbara Marriott explained, "because they all knew each other and most had lived locally, and the Swedes and Finns followed suit with the others. The fact they had land helped stability." Emilia Erickson photo.—HARRY ERICKSON

Many Finnish and Swedish employees of Comox Logging bought logged and burned-over land in Merville and, through communal effort, formed small farms. One of them was Fred (Siegfried) Erickson. Pictured here is a work bee for Erickson's new chicken house in 1933. Among those shown are Esther and Uno Forsman, Fred Erickson (with dog), Harry Erickson (the boy at the front with the bottle), and Finns named Nurmi, Wirta, and Jylha. Note the burned logging slash and snags in the background, reminders of the 1922 fire. The dirt track in the background became the Island Highway, with Campbell River to the left. Emilia Erickson photo.—HARRY ERICKSON

The view up Union Street from the corner of Isabel Street, Courtenay, on July 1, 1927, showing the Dominion Day Parade. Walter Montgomery photo.—BRITISH COLUMBIA ARCHIVES, F-08673

Booming Courtenay in about 1920, looking down Union Street to the Courtenay River Bridge, now the Fifth Street Bridge. The unofficial bar of the Comox Logging Company, the Riverside Hotel, built in about 1890, is at the top left. "Saturday nights in Courtenay were wild," recalled Don McIver. "There'd be fights. It was the one night a week when the drinkers could really drink." Proprietor of the hotel was Pa Dixon, a retired locie engineer with Comox Logging. "The first storey of the Riverside Hotel was open," remembered Beatty Davis, "and on that porch was a whole stuffed elk, and every once in a while the guys would climb up there on its back!" Later, in the evening, they gathered outside the hotel to watch the day's last trainload of logs—their handiwork—roll through town to the booming grounds. The McPhee Block is the large low building in the centre of the image, and the Courtenay Hotel is visible at the edge of the fields in the distance. The tracks of the Comox Logging Company can be seen directly beneath the Riverside. "They [loggers] came in and blew their money locally," recalled Barbara Marriott, "spent it in local businesses . . . the money stayed in the local economy."—AUDREY MENZIES

Among the larger farmers was Peter Sprout, originally from Lethbridge, Alberta, who had been wounded at Vimy Ridge in 1917 and invalided home. He and his wife Jennie Brown, a war bride, worked hard to establish a dairy farm among the six-foot stumps of their 140-acre property. Sprout worked occasionally as a blacksmith's helper at Headquarters.

The Settlement Board also bought stray pieces of land, including several large farms dating from the late-nineteenth-century wave of settlement, and subdivided them for returned soldiers. As Eric Duncan recalled, sixty-year-old Alexander Ledingham of Merville "sold his cleared and valuable farm to the Soldier Settlement Board (who placed four families on it) and bought a lot and log cabin in Courtenay." The board bought Adam McKelvie's farm at Dove Creek and divided it between ten returned soldiers, and also bought five hundred acres of logged and unoccupied land at Dove Creek. One of the Dove Creek soldiers was Ron Williamson's grandfather, who used to say "he was glad Comox Logging logged the timber so that he could start a farm." Another of the "Empire settlers" of Dove Creek was blacksmith Arthur Harrington Gray from Derbyshire, whose sons joined Comox Logging.

The Mennonite community at Black Creek provided a source of labour for Comox Logging in the 1930s similar to that provided by Merville in the 1920s. Davey Janes recalled that Comox Logging was "really lucky" to have these men. Religious refugees from Czarist Russia, the Mennonites began to arrive in 1932 from the Prairies and bought what Stan Hodgins described as the poorest land between Courtenay and Campbell River. After the fiasco at Merville, no one wanted logged-off, stump-covered land, and real estate agents like George Bates sold it to the newcomers for as little as five dollars an acre. "The Mennonites had to pick lots of rocks," Hodgins said, "but they grew some good crops."

"It's wonderful what they did," Rene Harding recalled. They drained the swamps between Black Creek's stony ridges and grew fine crops of strawberries, raspberries, and black currants; and their horse teams with wagonloads of firewood were a common sight in Courtenay. Eleanor Keller and Bob Cliffe said that the Mennonites were so desperate for work during the Depression that they urged Jack McQuinn to hire two of them for the price of one. Quite a few worked in the bush, including the Klassen, Enns, and Schulz families. The women stayed at home pulling stumps and running the farms.

Typical of the Black Creek Mennonites was Henry Schulz, born in Siberia in 1911. When he was fifteen, Schulz immigrated to a Mennonite farming community in Saskatchewan, and in 1932 moved with his parents to a hundred acres of logged-over land at Black Creek, where they built a barn and bought a cow, pig, and chickens. His father Peter Schulz wrote an article for a Mennonite newspaper "telling about this wonderful place where the air was so clean, the scenery so beautiful, and the land so cheap. . . . We found things much more interesting than looking at snow dunes in Siberia, or sandstorms in Saskatchewan," Henry Schulz recalled. Two years later Henry got a job with the Comox Logging steel gang.

≈

From Ypres to Merville

Born in Spain in 1891, Chris (Cedric Chrishop) Holmes was educated at an English boarding school while his father, a civil engineer, worked for the Port Authority in Rangoon, Burma.

Holmes came to Canada in about 1909 to visit his uncle, a doctor in Ontario who soon afterwards moved to Victoria. Chris played soccer for a time and then visited the Comox Valley. There he got a job as a carpenter at one of Comox Logging's early camps in the Kitty Coleman area. He had never handled a hammer or a saw before.

Upon the declaration of war, Chris and a friend went right down to Victoria to enlist as privates in the Canadian Expeditionary Force. Chris was badly gassed at Ypres in 1915 and, when he recovered, was transferred to the East Surrey Regiment as an instructional officer. He met his wife Mary Osborne in England; they returned to Canada with their daughter Patricia, and took up land at the Merville Soldier Settlement. Disappointed with the "awful mess of stumps" at Merville, Chris and Mary moved in 1920 to a farm on Headquarters Road, where they ran Jersey cattle and brought up Patricia and her younger brother John.

"He farmed at first, of course, like all good Englishmen," said John Holmes, but he could not make a living at it. "The problem on the farm was the same one that is still ongoing," said daughter Patricia Williams; "expenses have a way of exceeding income, especially on small, new farms where there aren't enough working family members to cope with everything that has to be done." Chris then "decided to do something constructive": logging.

Chris Holmes worked first near Campbell River with International Timber before rejoining Comox Logging in about 1928 as scaler, watchman, timekeeper, storekeeper, and eventually office manager at Headquarters. He retired in 1958 and took a keen interest in the history of Comox Logging before his death in 1974.

▶ Tranquil Comox was overlooked during Courtenay's railway and logging boom. This aerial view of the eastern waterfront of Comox, 1938, shows the nut farm and waterfront house of naturalist Mack Laing at bottom right. In the middle of the waterfront is Bob and Flossie Filberg's estate and their house known as "Grancuna." Back from the waterfront is a rural landscape with the Pritchard farm in the middle distance. Bob Filberg photo.—FILBERG LODGE & PARK ASSOCIATION

A Skunk Cabbage Bouquet

Ruth Masters lives on twenty acres of second-growth forest on the Powerhouse Road, Courtenay, logged at the turn of the twentieth century by Archie Pritchard for the Chemainus Company.

Ruth's father William Masters immigrated to Canada from England in 1902, settling first on a farm in Saskatchewan. After serving in the First World War, he brought his wife Jessie (a war bride) back to the farm, but "her nose froze," and before the winter was over the couple moved to the English-like climate of Vancouver Island.

Mr. Masters looked first at Soldier Settlement land at Merville but, horrified at its poor quality, bought the land above the Puntledge River and moved his wife into an old logger's cottage there.

The first thing Mr. Masters did was go out and gather some "beautiful lilies" for his wife, only to find that they were foul-smelling skunk cabbage. In the following years he dug and blasted out eighty-five old-growth stumps and tried to recreate England, planting a garden and orchard with hawthorn and ivy, as well as Baldwin, Grime's Golden, and Russet apples.

"Dad tried for subsistence," Ruth said. "It was just survival. We were churchmouse poor. Mice didn't have much to come and go on in our house!" Ruth's brother Bill later worked as a chokerman for Comox Logging.

Looking down Union Street from the corner of Judson Street, Courtenay, c. 1940. Union Street, the busiest street in the main service centre of the Comox Valley, was a hive of activity on weekends.—HUGH HILTON

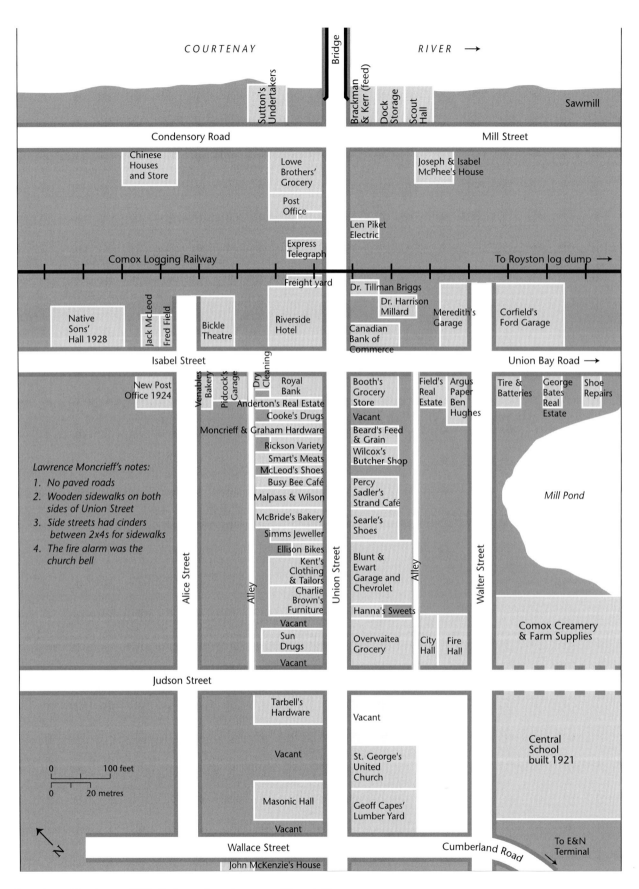

Downtown Courtenay, 1924. Redrawn from Lawrence Moncrieff's map of his *Victoria Colonist* delivery route, 1924.

Poppies and Foxhounds

Dairy farmer Arthur Smith of Beaver Meadows came from a labouring family in Leicestershire. When he was a boy, the landowners' horses and hounds chased foxes through the fields of poppies he was weeding, trampling the crop.

At the turn of the century Arthur immigrated to Saskatchewan where, as a carpenter, he built part of North Battleford using red-hot nails in the freezing winter. His son Sid was born there in 1909. Arthur had another five sons and a daughter.

Arthur Smith brought his family to Comox in 1918, first to the Cairns farm on the Dyke, and then to a 600-acre farm at Beaver Meadows on Little River Road, which he bought from the Soldier Settlement Board. He and his sons turned it into a successful dairy farm. "We cleared it up," Sid Smith recalled. "Some of the stumps took thirty sticks of powder! You'd do a bunch and then run from one to the other, and by the time you finished running, the first would be going off! The best time to blow stumps was in the wintertime when there was water in the holes: the water made a cushion, and it made a better job of blowing the stumps." Little River itself originates on this large farm.

Sid met Clay Walsh's daughter Margaret in 1935 when he was working as a herdsman and she was working on the McKenzie farm in Comox. They were married in 1947 and lived at Beaver Meadows farm until Margaret's death in 1999. Arthur Smith, who lived to be 95, used to come over in his old age to weed Margaret's poppies.

All this rural activity swelled the size of Courtenay and benefited the merchants. Just before the First World War, Comox Logging's monthly payroll was $40,000. Employees could cash or deposit their monthly paycheques only at the bank in Courtenay. The town also became more accessible: a passable road had finally reached Courtenay from Parksville in 1906; Comox Logging's railway to Royston was completed in 1911; and the E & N Railway made its way to Courtenay in 1914. Between the wars Courtenay grew as a service and manufacturing centre, with a creamery and condensory, garages, banks, hardware stores, a lumberyard, feed outlets, a theatre, churches, Masonic hall, city hall, and numerous stores from jewellers to grocers.

An early promotional tract noted that "to Courtenay merchants, the week after pay day is the week of the month." Saturday was a half day of work for many, and in the afternoon a great many loggers and their families would descend on Courtenay from the camps to do their shopping and visiting. Myrtle Heron remembered going into Courtenay from Comox in the 1930s with her grandmother Maude McKenzie (née Cliffe), who "knew everyone" in Courtenay. To Myrtle's embarrassment, her grandmother "would be talking to everyone and even had conversations with people across the street!" Union Street (now Fifth Street) thronged with loggers, married and unmarried. They might go to a movie, and after 1928 there was always a Saturday night dance at the Native Sons' Hall, which had a "beautiful dance floor," Barbara Marriott recalled, made of maple. The floor, mounted on large springs, undulated gently to the beat of the music. Many loggers met their wives—local women—at these dances.

Comox, meanwhile, had been eclipsed in importance with the arrival of roads and railways at Courtenay and urban and commercial growth there, though the Royal Canadian Navy and the British West Indies fleet continued to patronize sheltered Comox Harbour. Many young Homeguard families from Comox—Cliffe, Grant, Hawkins, and McKenzie, to name a few—went to work and live in the logging camps to the north, while Comox retained the navy and hospital and preserved its quiet, pastoral reputation. Among the liveliest Comox businesses were two venerable hotel-pubs, Dusty d'Esterre's Elk Hotel and the Lorne Hotel (the latter also known as "Cap's" after its owner, Great War veteran Captain Maurice Fairburn). Comox also had the CPR's Coastal Steamship Service, which remained a favourite means of travelling between the Comox Valley and Victoria, Vancouver, and Nanaimo until the 1940s. But this was mainly for passenger travel; freight was generally sent by railway to Courtenay. Even the mail came by train after the 1920s, and Edgar Cliffe (1896–1954), owner of the Tyee Freight Service, met the train every day in Courtenay and took a load of merchandise to Comox.

People who grew up in Comox between the wars recall a sleepy village in which cows from the Comox Peninsula wandered at random, keeping the grass down and tinkling their bovine bells. One cow walked right into someone's kitchen, and a girl who sleepwalked awoke with cow dung on her feet. Simple wire loop fences, painted white, were put up solely to keep the cows out.

Residents recall the "McKenzies' cows" and the "Hawkins' cows" with affection. Creatures of habit, they would wander over to Allan and

Quiet, residential Comox from Comox Harbour, 1939, a commercial backwater to thriving Courtenay. In the distance are (left to right) the United Church, post office, George Ellis's Bay Store, the Ellis house, and (far right) the home of Anglo-Irish eccentric Dusty d'Esterre. The field was part of the family farm of Comox Logging's locie engineer Jack Carthew, who ran sheep there. Brant geese dot the foreground. Mack Laing photo.—BRITISH COLUMBIA ARCHIVES, I-51812

Marjorie Brooks's house at 10:00 a.m. on their diurnal circuit, and they'd pass by again before dark on their way home, bells tinkling. In fact you could tell the time of day by the cows' whereabouts. The Elk Hotel capitalized on Comox's pastoral reputation by selling little Swiss-style souvenir cowbells with a copper plate attached reading "Elk Hotel Comox VI." (The "Comox VI" post office address, dating from colonial days, was used until the 1940s. VI, of course, stood for Vancouver Island, but Betty Brooks [*née* Hatfield] finally started using "BC" when one of her letters was sent to the Virgin Islands by mistake.)

Meanwhile, in the bush to the north of Comox and Courtenay, Comox Logging was furiously building camps and laying track as the company laid siege to the timber wealth of Block 29. The base of this onslaught was the railway and logging hub known as Headquarters—a model camp and a model town driving the economic engine of the Comox Valley.

chapter 5

Headquarters

Headquarters was a model town. It was set up beautifully.

—MABEL CLIFFE (*née* Olson)

Logging superintendent Bob Filberg with his son Robert and daughter Mary on the boardwalk outside the Filberg house at Headquarters, c. 1927. John Tukham photo.—JACK TUKHAM

FOR ALMOST FIFTY YEARS FROM ITS OPENING ON THE upper Tsolum River in 1911, Headquarters served as the centre of Comox Logging's extended operations north of Courtenay. The company's administrative headquarters, it was also the base of railway and logging equipment maintenance, and a fully serviced community complete with store, post office, hotel, and dance hall. It was staffed by managers, engineers, and tradesmen, some of them from Homeguard farming families in the Comox Valley. It contained comfortable houses for the company's white-collar workers as well as for tradesmen connected with its railway system and machinery repairs. Headquarters was not a logging camp but a company town and a tradesman's paradise, a place of industry on the southern edge of Block 29, and in its permanency quite distinct from the moveable camps to the north.

Chief of the office and clerical staff was Major Arthur Hilton, imperial adventurer, who took up residence at Headquarters in 1911. In that year, aged almost forty, he married Elizabeth McClintock, with whom he had three children. Hilton's early diaries show him as a conscientious and hard-working office manager. His policy of monthly payments was adopted by other logging companies on the Pacific coast. Not only did he manage the office, he was also postmaster and in charge of accounting and of purchases—everything from potatoes to locomotives. He also had the awful responsibility of arranging and attending, on the company's behalf, funerals for loggers killed in the woods.

Hilton was assisted by an office staff consisting of timekeeper, bookkeeper, and pay master John Tukham; timekeeper Milton Campbell; storekeeper Andy Hough; and storekeepers/accountants Charlie McIver and Lewis Biss. Born in Estonia in 1891, John Tukham came to Canada before the First World War, changed his name from

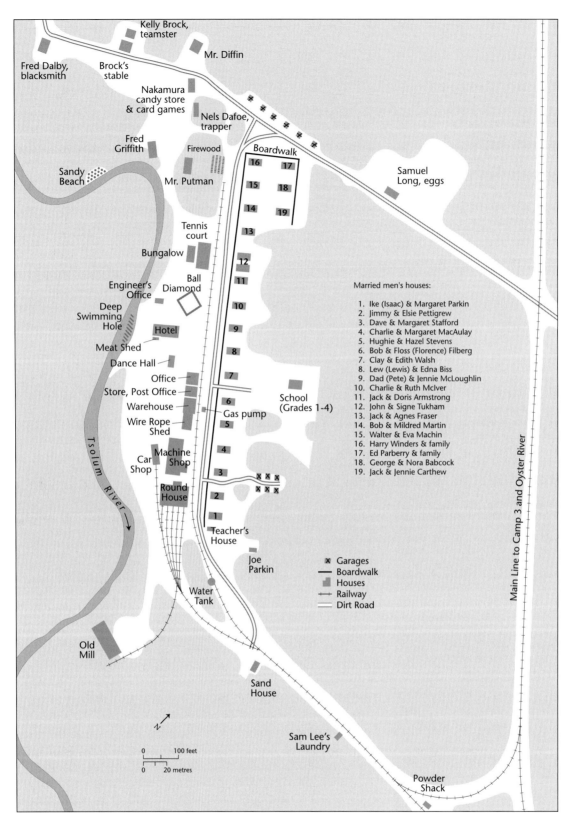

Headquarters, 1926. Redrawn from a map by Neil Martin and from aerial photographs provided by Don McIver.

Married men's houses:

1. Ike (Isaac) & Margaret Parkin
2. Jimmy & Elsie Pettigrew
3. Dave & Margaret Stafford
4. Charlie & Margaret MacAulay
5. Hughie & Hazel Stevens
6. Bob & Floss (Florence) Filberg
7. Clay & Edith Walsh
8. Lew (Lewis) & Edna Biss
9. Dad (Pete) & Jennie McLoughlin
10. Charlie & Ruth McIver
11. Jack & Doris Armstrong
12. John & Signe Tukham
13. Jack & Agnes Fraser
14. Bob & Mildred Martin
15. Walter & Eva Machin
16. Harry Winders & family
17. Ed Parberry & family
18. George & Nora Babcock
19. Jack & Jennie Carthew

Garages ✕
Boardwalk ▬
Houses ■
Railway ┼┼┼
Dirt Road ═

Lewis Biss:
From the Cotswolds to Merville

Born in the Cotswold Hills of Gloucestershire, England, in 1892, Lewis Biss left school at the age of fourteen to apprentice in a solicitor's office. He tired of this and looked for a more practical vocation, which led him to become indentured to a cabinet maker. Still restless, he emigrated to Canada in 1912, following his parents and other family members. He made his way across the country by working at harvesting jobs in Ontario and on the Prairies, ending up at his uncles' farm near Langley, British Columbia.

In 1914, Lew Biss, his father, and his brother joined up (they were known as the "Langley Lads") and Lew fought at Ypres and elsewhere. Miraculously, all three survived the war. After the war Lew and his brother Jack moved to Merville under the Soldier Settlement scheme, but his brother soon returned to the mainland. Lew's son Frank said that his father "fought it out and developed a little plot of land" on what is now Kono Road, where he grew fine vegetables and discovered an abiding love of gardening. But this was not enough to make a living and, like many Merville settlers, he gravitated into Headquarters' employment orbit. In 1920 he was hired as boilermaker's helper and a few years later became assistant to blacksmith Fred Dalby.

His career was furthered in 1922, when he married Headquarters school-teacher Edna Ferries. In 1924 Lew moved his family, which now included two boys, from his Soldier Settlement "ranch" near Merville to House No. 8 at Headquarters, to be closer to his work. By now, said Frank Biss, "he knew there was something better to do than swing a sledgehammer for a living," so he took a correspondence course in accounting and became storekeeper at Headquarters. He did all the ordering for the cookhouses and camps at Bevan, Camp 3, Oyster River, and elsewhere.

Lew was an entertaining pianist, playing in a Headquarters trio with John Tukham (violin) and Earl Stafford (sax). He also played with a much better band, called "Les Moody's Imperial Foot-warmers," at dances from Fanny Bay to Cape Mudge. In July 1936 he moved to Ladysmith as timekeeper; later, he became pay master there. Lewis Biss died in Ladysmith in 1955.

Juhkam to Tukham, and joined the Canadian Army in the war. As timekeeper he kept track of men's hours and determined the amount of their paycheques. In 1922 he married Signe Anderson, daughter of Fred Anderson, the Swedish welder at Headquarters. Charlie McIver, born on Prince Edward Island in 1891, quit rural school teaching there, came west, trained in accounting, and became chief accountant at Headquarters. He married Ruth McCormack, J. D. McCormack's niece.

In 1920, Bob Filberg took over as chief of the Headquarters office. He was in many ways Hilton's opposite. While Hilton had wandered through the military outposts of the British Empire, Filberg had wandered through the logging camps of the far western American frontier, and his career resembles a morality lesson distilled from the works of Horatio Alger, Samuel Smiles, and Norman Rockwell. Despite their differences, both Hilton and Filberg were self-made and shared a common background of youthful independence and struggle.

When Major Hilton was working as a "little microbe in a logging camp" at Port Orchard, Washington, Bob Filberg was working as a line horse boy at a logging camp on the opposite side of Puget Sound. Fraser River Lumber hired him in 1909 as surveyor's assistant, and he progressed from there to marrying the boss's daughter in 1916. After 1920 Bob Filberg was the big wheel at Headquarters. He and his wife Floss had two children, Mary and Robert Jr. (Robert was also known as Rob, Bud, and Buddy).

~

The railway was at the centre of life in Headquarters. Foreman of the entire locomotive end of operations was Clay Walsh, and the engineer and crew of the company's main-line train also had houses at Headquarters: Jack Carthew (locie engineer), Bob Martin (head brakeman), Harry Winders (second brakeman), Joe Parkin (fireman), and Jack Armstrong (fireman). Bob Martin told historian Ben Hughes that he used to be at work at six in the morning and he sometimes wouldn't be back until two the following morning. He also noted that the railway was a vital link with civilization: "Those were the days when steam was always kept up in the old One-Spot so that, if any sudden illness or accident befell anyone at Headquarters the patient could be taken out to hospital, as the only road led through swamp that was often flooded in the spring or winter and the only access to the outside world was by the logging railway."

While the hotel at Headquarters housed many temporary workers who stayed for a season or two before moving to the woods camps or leaving the district, the town's tradesmen and Homeguard train crews gave the settlement a good deal of stability and permanence. Men like Carthew, Martin, and Armstrong were known for their local connections and their extraordinary longevity with the company. Carthew and Martin unloaded the first load of logs at Royston in 1911, and the last in 1953. Both men had deep roots in the Comox Valley. Carthew, the son of a local carpenter originally from Nova Scotia, owned a sheep farm on the Comox waterfront, and Martin was married to Mildred Pritchard. Jack Armstrong, an exceptionally tall (six feet, six inches) and powerful man, was known for his ability to lift locie wheels

The first people to occupy a house at Headquarters were office manager Arthur Hilton and his new bride Elizabeth McClintock, shown here on the steps of their house in 1911. All three of their children were born before the Hiltons left Headquarters in 1920. —HUGH HILTON

Headquarters in 1912, known at first as ▶ Fraserville. When Headquarters was new, the company was still logging to the south of the settlement, and the town was for a time on the logging frontier. In the distance is the original, uncut forest. At the far left, on the bank of the Tsolum River, is the tent camp dating from the construction of the town. This early photo, taken from the roof of the sawmill that never sawed, shows the three main areas of Headquarters: roundhouse and machine shop, hotel, and residential section. The Three-Spot and a Heisler locie (the Four-Spot or Five-Spot) wait outside the roundhouse. Stumps and piles of slash cover the whole townsite. Each newly built house has a woodshed and an outhouse behind it, but the houses still lack both shade and lawns. All the buildings were painted white with a uniform green trim.
—RALPH HARMSTON AND AUDREY MENZIES

The Hiltons' dining room at Headquarters, c. 1914.—HUGH HILTON

Bob Filberg, Surveyor's Helper

Born in Denver, Colorado, on June 13, 1892, Bob Filberg was the only child of a Swedish tailor and army deserter named Adolf Filberg and of Lizzie Degnan, a "tailoress" of "pure Irish" ancestry from New York. The family moved to Seattle in 1900, and two years later Adolf lost his way in the Alaskan wilderness and froze to death.

In 1906, fatherless Bob Filberg got a job driving a line horse for the Pendleton Lumber Company at Fur, near Mt. Vernon. In the next few years he worked at Milketo, Washington, and at Seqiew, on the Olympic Peninsula.

He came to Canada in the spring of 1909 on a survey gang for the Anderson Logging Company at Union Bay, nine miles south of Courtenay, and worked briefly the same summer for the International Timber Company at Campbell River. He joined a Fraser River Lumber survey crew in the fall of 1909, at the age of 17, and spent the winter laying out logging railways and bridges outside Courtenay.

After a stint in Golden he returned to Seattle and studied engineering at the university prior to 1914. "He also joined a boxing club in Seattle," Joe Cliffe recalled, "and became a better than average lightweight boxer." He then returned to Comox as engineer in charge of Comox Logging's railway and track building. Promotion was rapid after his 1916 marriage to Florence (Floss), the daughter of his boss J. D. McCormack, who appointed him superintendent in 1919 when Jim McGuigan quit. "You can have the job for a year," he told Filberg, "providing you make some improvements."

Headquarters in 1920

Wallace Baikie, who worked as a surveyor's assistant and scaler for Comox Logging from 1920 to 1927, recalled in *Rolling with the Times* the community on the Tsolum River:

Headquarters was quite a little settlement. It had a large building housing the several offices, store, warehouse and storage space. Next was the machine shop, a round house and car maintenance shop. Then they had a dance hall or recreation building, also the bungalow where the office staff slept and the hotel . . . where the single men lived.

There were about forty married men's houses [in the general Headquarters area] and a school, all across the track from the other main buildings. The steel gang worked out of this head quarters and the large sidings where the mainline engine (the Three Spot) made up its train. They also had a tennis court. A long board walk ran all the way down in front of the first row of married men's houses. There were also settlers in that area who worked for the company and took part in the social life. The Saturday night dances would draw people from the whole area. They even had their own orchestra; Lewis Biss piano, Jack Martin fiddle, and one of the Parkin kids or Pete McLaughlin [sic] on the drums.

in the machine shop. These men hauled flatcars of logs from different sidings and camps down to Royston.

Headquarters was also the base of the steel gang, run for most of the interwar years by a feisty, cigar-smoking French Canadian named Joe Asselin. The steel gang, which undertook railway construction, was a heterogeneous group made up of between fifteen and thirty recently arrived immigrants from northern and eastern Europe. Related to the steel gang was the section gang or crew, which kept the railway grades in good repair. Between the wars the foreman of the section gang, known as the section boss, was an Irishman named Fred Griffith, who lived on the Tsolum near Headquarters on a small farm with a splendid vegetable garden. "He grew the biggest carrots you ever saw," recalled Don McIver.

The roundhouse was used for the repair and maintenance of locomotives. It contained five stalls where locies were repaired, overhauled, or simply stored when not in use. At first, the company's fleet of flatcars was repaired in the roundhouse, but soon a car shop was built especially for the repair and maintenance of flatcars, which were subject to a tremendous amount of wear and tear, particularly when being loaded with logs at the skidder settings. (Flatcars were sometimes broken when large logs were dropped on them by inexperienced loading engineers.) "It was heavy work in the car shop," Frank Davison recalled. "They had to drill holes to put bolts through on flatcars. There was lots of woodwork."

Foreman and head carpenter of the car shop was Charlie MacAulay. He had a talented staff that included carpenters Ike Parkin, John (Jack) Fraser, Frank Murtsell, and timberman Peter McLoughlin. With ten children, Ike Parkin of Dove Creek had the second-largest family at Headquarters (George Babcock had twelve children). Descended from the Malpass family of Nanaimo, the Parkins had been on Vancouver Island since the early 1850s. McLoughlin, born in Ireland in 1897, grew up in England and came to Canada as a young man. He joined the car shop crew after working as a brakeman. Pete McLoughlin was known for a long wedding story that ended, "The bride has lovely teeth—both of them!" He was known as "Dad" or "Pa" McLoughlin; his wife Jennie was known as "Ma." His brother Johnny McLoughlin married Ike Parkin's sister Margaret and became a locie engineer and track foreman. Among Pete McLoughlin's children was Peter Jr., who became a timekeeper with Comox Logging.

Near the roundhouse was the machine shop. Foreman of the machine shop was Dave Stafford, from Phoenix, British Columbia, a considerate man who went around whistling all the time to give his staff full warning that he was coming. He was known for his kindness to the schoolchildren of Headquarters, for whom he made hoops, playground slides, customized whistles, bracelets, and kaleidoscopes.

The machine shop was the core, the heart, of Comox Logging's entire woods operation. It was manned by blacksmiths, boilermakers, mechanics, machinists, lathe hands, welders, and general handymen. In 1935, equipment in the machine shop included three lathes and two forges, as well as a planer, shaper, wheel pass, wheel borer, electric welding outfit, and a powerful air hammer for pounding and shaping hot steel. It was a hive of activity; a centre of industry, expertise, innovation,

Major Hilton and his office staff at Headquarters, c. 1914. Front row, left to right: John McGarry, Charlie McIver, Arthur Hilton, Milton Campbell, John Tukham, unknown. Standing behind: unknown. McIver and Campbell were old friends from Prince Edward Island, while Tukham was from Estonia. Vincent Russell photo.—HUGH HILTON

Four men with a brand-new Marion grade shovel, *c.* 1925. Left to right: timekeeper John Tukham, unidentified shovel operator, storekeeper Lewis Biss, and steel gang boss Joe Asselin. **John Tukham photo.**—JACK TUKHAM

Up but Not Running

The massive cement walls of a sawmill at Headquarters, now covered with graffiti and littered with the detritus of teenage parties, still stand in the bush above the Tsolum River. A favourite story in the Comox Valley is that the company agreed to build the mill in return for certain logging concessions from the provincial government, but the government neglected to include the words "and operate" in the agreement—so the company built the mill but never switched it on.

What is known for certain is that Comox Logging built this "rough timber mill" with a capacity of some 75,000 feet of lumber a day in 1912–1913. Its intended purpose was to cut the smaller logs from the company's timber limits since "many of these are lost when subjected to the big tow to Fraser Mills" (*Telephone Talk*, 1913).

"There was a sawmill built at Headquarters and that sawmill never turned a wheel," recalled Peter McLoughlin Sr. "It even had the kindling in the fire boxes of the boilers to start. But it never did turn a wheel. They abandoned it—they dammed the river there—they abandoned the whole deal; they never worked it at all. It later got into the hands of Major Hilton. He bought most of the parts from there. But the cement building itself—it still stands." The mill may well have been a victim of the 1913 recession.

Hilton used the parts to build a mill in Courtenay, but it burned down a few years later.

Inside the office at Headquarters, *c.* 1914. Left to right: unknown (seated), Charlie McIver and Milton Campbell (against wall), unknown, Arthur Hilton. It was in this room that most of the records of the Comox Logging Company were produced and stored. Vincent Russell photo.—MARGARET SMITH

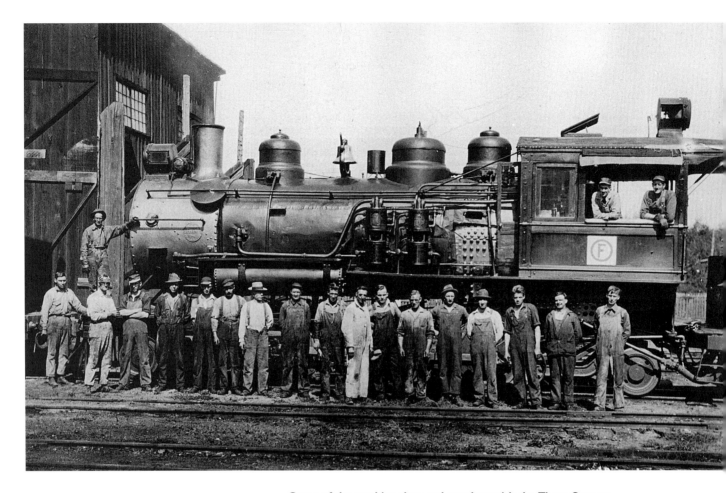

Crews of the machine shop and car shop with the Three-Spot at Headquarters, 1927. The Three-Spot had just been serviced when this photo was taken. According to machinist Walter Anderson, an internal overhaul was done every five years. It could take a month to take the boiler and tubes out, right down to the frames, and wait for the provincial boiler inspector, Robert Swanson, to come and inspect it. Left to right: Bob Martin, head brakeman; Harry Winders, second brakeman (with hand on train); Walter Machin, handyman; Fred Dalby, blacksmith; George Babcock, boilermaker; Pete Sprout, blacksmith's helper; Bob Millan, clean-up guy; Pete McLoughlin Sr., timberman in car shop; Fred Anderson Sr., welder; Bill Rourke, shop worker; Ed Parberry, gas mechanic; Cecil Stafford, machinist; Jimmy Pettigrew, foreman; Frank Murtsell, car-knocker (carpenter); Jack Fraser, car-knocker; Walter Anderson, handyman and mechanic; P. Morgan, oiler and handyman; Charlie MacAulay, car shop foreman. In cab: Jack Carthew, engineer; and Jack Armstrong, fireman. Walter Montgomery photo.
—CUMBERLAND MUSEUM & ARCHIVES

Jack Carthew, locie engineer, with the Eleven-Spot or Sixteen-Spot, c. 1940. Typical of the Comox Homeguard, Carthew ran a sheep farm in Comox and, with the exception of a few years at Powell River, spent his entire career with Comox Logging. Bob Filberg photo.
—FILBERG LODGE & PARK ASSOCIATION

George Babcock, Boilermaker

Born in Collingwood, Ontario, George Babcock was nine months old when his mother died. As a young man he apprenticed as a boilermaker in Regina, where he met his wife, Nora, a nurse from Port Elgin, Ontario. Their twelve children—seven girls and five boys—were born between 1914 and 1933.

The Babcocks moved to the coast, hoping a change in climate would benefit George's weak lungs. They reached Headquarters from Fraser Mills in 1920. Daughter Helen (born 1914) recalled that when George crawled into locie and skidder boilers to replace the rivets, he'd get so hot they'd have to hose him down with cold water. He worked at nights.

In 1933 he built a two-storey house for his family on Fitzgerald Road near Headquarters. They'd been in the house for a week when George Babcock caught pneumonia while digging the well. According to Helen, he had tried to dig out a big rock lodged in the blue clay at the bottom of the well. He'd dig on one side, and the rock would roll into the hole he'd made. He never got the rock out, but caught a chill trying. He died soon afterwards in the Comox Hospital, at the age of forty-three, leaving behind his twelve children, the youngest of whom was three months old. "The well was cursed," said Helen. "My mum was up top pulling the blue clay up in buckets, by the bucketful. It never did clear! The well stayed like that. The water was the rottenest water I ever had to deal with."

Five or six years later the house burned down on a hot day while Nora Babcock was away. "Everything was thrown into that well—bedsteads and everything." The Babcocks moved away soon after.

and specialized industrial trades. It was at the shop where tongs, marlinspikes, and many other tools and devices were made for use in the bush; where donkey engines, skidders, and gas shovels were repaired and overhauled; and where new parts were forged and tooled to fit. Shop workers, for example, fitted yarders with new skids for woods work. "They had the choice of the best timber," Davey Janes said, and the skids had very little taper to them. One of the sleighmakers was Fred Erickson of Merville, formerly a faller out of Headquarters and Camp 3. His son Harry recalled that Douglas fir was the strongest wood for sleighs, and that his father also made hayrack booms for skidders at the Headquarters shop, from only the choicest timber. When work was slack he maintained the boardwalks. It was also at the shop where Dave Stafford invented a log dumper known as the "humdirgen" for use at Royston.

Headquarters' main blacksmith of the 1930s was Hughie McKenzie, formerly of Camp 2. He and his wife Birdie (*née* Banks) often won the Saturday night waltz competition at Headquarters. Son of Courtenay blacksmith and mayor Johnny McKenzie, Hughie was fired when he started to make logging tongs on the side, and he subsequently opened a machine shop in Courtenay. Merville settlers Peter Sprout and Lewis Biss worked as blacksmith's helpers to McKenzie and later to fellow blacksmith Fritz Johansen Dalby.

Fritz Dalby, known as "Fred," was born in Oslo, Norway, in 1899. After a short time in the United States he came to Canada, working briefly at Camp 3 before moving to Headquarters with his wife Anna. He specialized in making perfectly balanced sets of tongs for grappling and lifting logs on skidder settings. "My dad made those tongs so balanced that they could be thrown and they'd hook on," his son Ralph said. Dalby also turned wheels for locies, and made chisels, hammers, marlinspikes, and smaller hand tongs for use in forges.

Headquarters' boilermakers spent their time with steam-powered locies, skidders, and donkeys. This was exacting and demanding work. Ike Parkin's son Norm started working as a boy of thirteen at Headquarters in the summer of 1917. Dave Stafford and his colleagues built a tin sleeve to slide Norm in and out of a locie boiler, and his job was to chip off the boiler accretions with a hammer and chisel. When interviewed in 1984, Norm Parkin said that he had suffered from claustrophobia ever since.

In the 1920s, George Babcock was the boilermaker at Headquarters. After his death from pneumonia in 1933 he was succeeded by Tommy Crowther, who also worked in the store at Headquarters. Crowther's assistant was Eddy Murtsell, son of car-knocker Frank Murtsell. Young Eddy had been working as a chokerman at Cowichan Lake, but the safety record was poor there and his mother talked to Bob Filberg, who said, "Bring him up here and we'll put him in the shop." He started in November 1934, aged twenty, as boilermaker's helper, rebuilding skidders in the Headquarters shop. Crowther was very fussy and slow, Murtsell recalled, but as Dave Stafford said, "When he's finished with it you can bet your ass it's perfect!" Welders Swan (Sven) Peterson, Fred Anderson, and Charlie Olson were also essential to the operation.

Henry Parkin ran Headquarters' small but growing gasoline engine repair shop; Ed Parberry was gas mechanic; and the machinists and

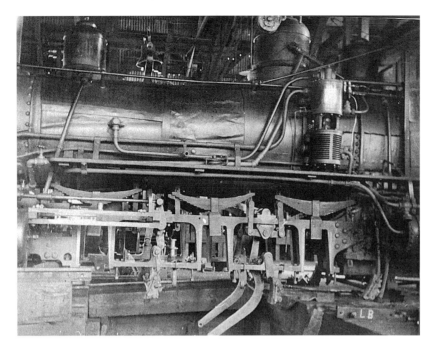

Servicing the One-Spot in the roundhouse, c. 1935. This was known as "tearing down a locie" by the shop crew. "They've dropped the drivers and they're working on the running gear," said Walter Anderson of this photo.
—WALTER ANDERSON

Homeguard Joe Parkin, one of a large farming family at Dove Creek, standing in front of the Eleven-Spot or Sixteen-Spot, c. 1940. Bob Filberg photo.—FILBERG LODGE & PARK ASSOCIATION

Inside the machine shop, c. 1914. Vincent Russell photo.—BRITISH COLUMBIA ARCHIVES, 90180

Inside the machine shop, c. 1914. At left a donkey on a sleigh has been brought in on a flatcar for servicing and new sleighs. At right is the powerful air hammer with a forge beside it and a pipe to take away the smoke. Vincent Russell photo.—BRITISH COLUMBIA ARCHIVES, 90151

Ike (Isaac) Parkin (1875–1960) worked in the car shop, where he fixed flatcars. He was also head carpenter in charge of building sleighs for donkey engines. He ended his career as flagman at Courtenay Crossing, succeeding Jack Hawthorne. Bob Filberg photo, 1943.—FILBERG LODGE & PARK ASSOCIATION

A man named Michel (right) at the air hammer in the Headquarters machine shop, c. 1914. "The steel had to be hot first," Walter Anderson recalled, "and then they'd pound it out." Vincent Russell photo.—BRITISH COLUMBIA ARCHIVES, 90177

Aleda Murtsell and friends, c. 1924. Left to right: Aleda Murtsell holding Fred Tukham; John Murphy (postmaster at Headquarters); and Signe Tukham holding her son Jackie. John Tukham photo.—JACK TUKHAM

Jimmy Pettigrew, Headquarters machinist and shop foreman, in 1944. Pettigrew served his apprenticeship at the Victoria Machinery Depot, worked on CPR boats as Junior Engineer, and was initially recruited by Bob Filberg because he was a very good baseball player. He specialized in repairing locies and skidders. Bob Filberg photo.—FILBERG LODGE & PARK ASSOCIATION

Single life in a company town. This photo was taken by John Tukham in the winter of 1927–1928. Walter Anderson wrote, "The camp was closed down for too much snow. Fred Dalby the blacksmith in the shop & his wife owned 2 houses further up the river—one big house & one small one. They lived in the big one, and we rented the small one until the camp opened again." Pictured here are (left to right): Helmer, Gunnar Johnston, Fred Anderson Jr., Walter Anderson.—JACK TUKHAM

◀ The Chinese cooks at Headquarters, c. 1925. John Tukham is at the back wearing a flat cap. Several of Comox Logging's early cooks were French Canadian, but they were replaced in 1921 by Chinese cooks. "The Chinese cooks were brought in to replace the white cooks," Wallace Baikie recalled. "Apparently with prohibition in force, the white cooks were more interested in making moonshine than they were in cooking, so the management decided to make a change."—JACK TUKHAM

Oswald Harmston, foreman at Comox Lake, 1938. He is standing next to one of Comox Logging's little speeders. Bob Filberg photo.
—FILBERG LODGE & PARK ASSOCIATION

lathe-hands included locie expert and later shop foreman Jim Pettigrew, Dave Stafford's son Cecil, and Fred Anderson's son Walter. Walter came from Sweden at the age of seventeen to work at Headquarters in 1924. After a few months on the section gang and the steel gang, Walter became a lathe-hand and machinist in the shop. He ended up as head mechanic in the 1950s. Notable for his size-fourteen feet, Walter Anderson was known as "Boots." He still lives on his beef farm on the Tsolum River Road.

The shop also employed Walter Machin, who was from an old Comox Valley farming family. He was described variously as a jack of all trades, roustabout, and handyman. He painted buildings, fixed the wooden sidewalks, and laid firebricks in the locies. An "old Scotchman" named Bob Millan was the clean-up guy, and P. Morgan was locie oiler and handyman. Others who worked in the machine shop at different times were Max Adamscheck, Dick Emblem, and Larry "Young Sailor" Lehtonen (son of Finnish high rigger Sailor Lehtonen).

Larry Lehtonen started working at Headquarters in December 1937, at the age of sixteen, as a machinist's helper. It was tough to get jobs then, but Larry recalled that he went to master mechanic Stafford and asked for a job. "Are you a mechanic?" Stafford asked. "We're only hiring a mechanic." But Stafford employed him anyway, and the job lasted over forty years. Eventually he replaced Stafford as shop foreman. "I always wanted to be in the shops, like someone wants a violin. That was my violin," Larry said. Great ingenuity and resourcefulness were required. "We could make almost anything at the machine shop," he said. "So many problems came up and you'd find an answer. There was no time to contact the manufacturer. If it broke down they wanted it fixed like yesterday. When you have a good crew—good men—you can fix almost anything, as long as you have a positive attitude!"

≈

Life existed outside the machine shop at Headquarters. Beyond the shop were the warehouse, store, post office, and company offices, all of them long, flat buildings built beside the railway (unlike those at the camps, Headquarters' buildings were all constructed on site). In front of all the buildings was a landing where the trains coming from the bush or from Courtenay dropped men off. Near the warehouse was the "line shed," the shed for storing lines (logging cable), and next to the tracks in the middle of Headquarters was the speeder house where a gas pump was later installed.

Everyone bought their groceries at the store because, in 1911, cars were scarce and it wasn't possible to drive to Courtenay for groceries. Instead, people placed orders with merchants in Courtenay, and the goods were brought in by boxcar. People from as far away as Camp 3 charged for their food at the Headquarters store.

The main building beyond the office was the hotel, which housed unmarried men who worked at the machine and car shops, on steel and section gangs, and on the logging crews based out of Headquarters. The hotel doubled as "cookhouse," and there workers and visitors alike were well fed. Jack Beadnell (born 1913) accompanied his father, the federal fisheries inspector, when he visited Headquarters to monitor salmon

Headquarters and the Fire of 1925

The fire that destroyed Camp 3 came close to Headquarters, as the *Comox Argus* reported on August 13, 1925:

All the 40 families that make their home at Headquarters were sent out by train or cars to safety. Then the men who were left behind set themselves down to fight the fire. Members of the Courtenay fire brigade went out to assist and a dozen streams of water were kept going to wet down the roofs of all the buildings of the little town. At one time about ten o'clock on Sunday afternoon [August 9] the situation looked desperate. A hot, whistling wind full of flying embers was not more than half a mile off and blowing direct on the town. Then a change of wind similar to that which sealed the fate of Camp 3 saved that of Headquarters. The wind shifted and took the wall of flame more towards Merville and the fight was won for the day.

Ralph Dalby said that his father Fred Dalby, Headquarters blacksmith, dug trenches and lowered his tool chests into them as the fire approached. He buried his precious tools in case the fire reached the town, but then the wind changed and the town was spared.

"The children and their families were evacuated to Courtenay and the surrounding area," teacher Nellie Cartwright recalled. "Helen Babcock remembers that she saw her first dry cereal during her enforced stay at the Courtenay Hotel."

runs in rivers within the company's timber limits. Jack can still remember the marvellous meals at the Headquarters hotel. The hotel steward was G. A. (Jack) Martin, who had previously run the Elk Hotel in Comox, and who was in charge of all Comox Logging's cookhouses. He was known for his excellent coffee, the secret of which was adding whole eggs, shell and all.

Martin was also in charge of the kitchen staff. Most of the white cooks employed by Comox Logging were laid off en masse in the spring of 1921 and replaced by Chinese cooks, because the white cooks were making illicit liquor during BC's brief prohibition era. Headquarters' time book for 1921–1922 shows that, in the summer of 1921, F. Drapeau remained in charge, but he was gone by October. Among the eight Chinese cooks at the hotel in 1921–1922 were Jung Kim Chong, Gam Wong, Chong Wing Quong, Wong Peck, and Lou Zee Lue. Kwong Toy and Ching Ling were bedmakers at the hotel. Several of the cooks stayed in the Comox District: Charlie Leung later ran the Royal Café in Courtenay, and Sam Lee became Filberg's cook.

The Chinese cooks were unfailingly kind to the children of Headquarters. Neil Martin recalled that the cooks worked at the back of the hotel, and "the boys would go back there and ask, 'Any pie, Cook?' And if he had any, he'd come out and give you a chunk of raisin pie." Eddy Murtsell added that the Chinese cooks would first make them do a chore, for example, shake out some old flour sacks, before giving them a piece of pie.

Next to the hotel was the dance hall, built around 1920, where dances were held every Saturday night and where badminton, whist, and a game called "500" were played. It was also the venue for school concerts, and on occasion, the hall doubled as bunkhouse for overflow logging crews when there was no room in the hotel.

Beyond the hotel was a bungalow for important guests and unmarried white-collar employees. Guests included "big shots," surveyors, and visiting auditors from Vancouver. It had four bedrooms, a large living room, and a lovely garden. It burned down in the late 1920s or early 1930s and was not rebuilt.

Attached to the bungalow was a tennis court which, Peter McLoughlin recalled, was at first levelled with cinders, and later surfaced with two-by-fours on edge (or two-by-sixes, depending whom you ask), which made for a wonderful deck. It was not an ideal surface, however, because when the two-by-fours started to rot they were replaced with new ones, making for an uneven surface that sent balls careening in the wrong direction. Nearby was a baseball diamond where the boys of Headquarters played against the shop crew.

Next to the river was the engineer's office, in reality a shack right on the bank above the Tsolum. This was the working domain of Hughie Stevens, Comox Logging's chief engineer and surveyor, who lived with his wife Hazel and two sons on the front street at Headquarters. In the early 1920s Stevens' little office also provided temporary accommodation for his assistants Alec Tilleard and Wallace Baikie.

Housing was provided for families of nineteen key managers, tradesmen, and main-line locie crew. The first six houses were larger than the other thirteen; they had six rooms each while the rest had only

Frank Murtsell, Car-Knocker

Frank Murtsell was learning forestry in Sweden when he decided, in around 1910, to come to British Columbia and study silviculture methods. His son Eddy said that they laughed at Frank on the coast of British Columbia. "Look at all the timber!" they said. "We don't have to plant any!"

Work was abundant, and Murtsell was put in charge of a grading crew laying steel between Courtenay and Headquarters. This was in about 1911, when Comox Logging was still dumping logs at Cooper's Corner.

Murtsell was joined by his fiancée Aleda from Sweden, and the newlyweds' first home was a tent with a wooden floor at Headquarters. A bear once tried to join them in the tent. Eddy was born in Courtenay in 1914.

Frank Murtsell later put his carpentering skills to work in the car shop at Headquarters as a "car-knocker" (flatcar repairer), and he also built donkey sleds. He was a conscientious carpenter. His wife used to say that he put temporary constructions together so solidly that it was hard to take them apart. "He made sure it was all very skookum," Eddy remarked.

The bungalow at Headquarters, next to the tennis courts. Right, an unidentified tennis couple, c. 1925. "That was a dandy court!" commented Barbara Marriott. John Tukham photos.—JACK TUKHAM

The Headquarters Hotel with some rural visitors, c. 1930. Some of the cows at Headquarters wandered all the way from Merville. One night, unable to sleep because of cow bells, brakeman Norman Battersby went out and pulled the bells off the offending cows. Chris Holmes photo.—JOHN HOLMES

The Wrong Side of the Tracks

Children were not allowed to cross the railway tracks into the industrial region of the settlement; they were expected to stay on the house side of the tracks.

When they were about eight or ten, Frank Biss, Don McIver, and some friends decided to test this rule. Don McIver was a daredevil and came up the track planning to cross. Filberg saw him and said, "You come over here and I'll take you to the woodshed and I'll cut your ears off!" Don crossed over anyway, so Filberg took him to the woodshed and closed the door. The other boys heard screams followed by a loud WHUMP! But McIver came out with his ears on. For dramatic effect Filberg had hit or thrown something violently. "We never went near the tracks again," Frank Biss said.

Jack and Fred Tukham on the Malahat Drive, *c.* 1938.

Signe Tukham (*née* Anderson) with her sons Jack (left) and Fred fishing at the Wolf Creek dam, *c.* 1928. Born in 1900, Signe left Sweden in 1920 to visit her father Fred, welder at Headquarters. She worked for two years as a nanny for the Filbergs before marrying John Tukham. Fred was born in 1923 and Jack the following year.

John Tukham photos.—JACK TUKHAM

Four children at the east end of the Headquarters boardwalk, *c.* 1912. The row of identical houses and the lack of lawns and gardens mark this instant company town.

four rooms. The houses were the handiwork of carpenter Walter Rigler and his gang. All the houses, Eddy Murtsell recalled, had rustic siding on the outside, painted or papered lathe and plaster on the inside, no insulation, and wiring for overhead lighting only. At first, there were no sockets to plug appliances into, so families like the Murtsells wired in some outlets themselves. Electricity came in through Merville. The rent was ten dollars a month, which included electricity. All houses featured ventilators above the windows and, in these pre-refrigeration days, "meat safes" on the back porch. In the early days, naturally, toilets were outside. Initially the houses were exposed to sun and rain, and people took to planting hops outside as a quick source of summer shade. Lawns, fruit trees, hedges, and gardens soon enlivened the barren landscape. Lewis Biss, for example, planted a laurel hedge in front of his house. A boardwalk ran by the houses (and along the length of the town), and picket fences were soon added, largely to keep cows out of people's gardens. Cows, some of them from as far away as Merville, wandered through Headquarters in the 1940s, as they did through Comox. By the 1920s a second-growth forest enveloped the town, hiding the old-growth stumps around the houses.

Fresh water was brought to town in reinforced wooden pipes from Wolf Creek, which had been dammed at its mouth. Some was piped for domestic use and some was stored in a water tank standing on poles beside the railroad tracks to the south of town. Steam locies stopped beneath the tank to fill their thirsty boilers. The Wolf Lake reservoir became a popular spot for evening fly fishing.

"Headquarters," said Margaret Smith, "was a good place for kids, a nice, compact place." Neil Martin described it as a "a wonderful place for boys." The Tsolum River, which meandered through the forest to the west of town, was a big part of this childhood paradise. One ideal play area was a sandy beach to the north of town, near a spot where the blue clay banks of the Tsolum were exposed. The river was deep in spots, and young children had to stay in the shallows and avoid the old mill, which was out of bounds. Older children, however, frequented the deep swimming hole beneath the hotel. When the boys came up from swimming at this hole, they would sun themselves on the corrugated tin roof of the lean-to behind the surveyors' shack. Eventually, when plumbing was installed at Headquarters, children were forbidden from playing in the Tsolum downstream from the mill because the town's sewage was dumped right into the river.

The boys of Headquarters also played and foraged in the forests surrounding the town. Like teenagers throughout the Comox Valley, they harvested cascara bark, which flourished along the river banks where it was moist. Frank Biss and Neil Martin were told to leave a strip of bark at least as wide as one-third of the trunk's circumference, so the tree would survive and regenerate the bark. This they did fastidiously. Then they dried the harvested bark in the sun, took it to Courtenay, and sold it for manufacture into a laxative. They were always disappointed at how little it weighed after it dried, and how little they got for it.

All the houses in Headquarters had wood stoves. Firewood was supplied by a teamster named Kelly Brock. The company brought in "cull logs" (damaged or undersize) from Royston, and dumped them

Walter Rigler, Carpenter

The carpenter at Headquarters was a man named Walter Rigler, whom Neil Martin remembered as an active man. "Old Filberg wouldn't have any lazy lump at that time when men were a dime a dozen!"

Nonetheless, Rigler was out of work in the Depression when low demand for lumber meant layoffs. A source who preferred not to be identified told a story about Rigler during these lean times:

Rigler was a builder, an Englishman, who kept bees and flowers. He was a nice gentle fellow and very religious. In the Depression he was out of work, and one day he was in his garden tending his flowers. His wife, who was also religious, was saying, "Walter, you've got to get some work!" He was out there mucking with his flowers and his wife just blasted him! And Walter said what he always did, which was, "When God is ready he will send me some work. God will find me some work when God is ready." But his wife said, "But you need to get some work now!" To get away from his wife's hectoring he walked around to the front of the house and there was Bob Filberg coming through the gate. He said, "Walter, we're building a little place up at Comox Lake and we have a little job for you."

Headquarters' Dance Hall

Timberman Peter McLoughlin recalled:

They had a dance hall . . . they had dances every Saturday night, and at one time every other Saturday night, and whist drives every other Wednesday night. And as I say they had their own community club and they were quite popular, these dances, because they were a little bit out of the way and in the thirties quite a few people had cars and so it wasn't any effort to get out of town [Courtenay] that distance.

Teacher Nellie Cartwright remembered that Headquarters' active social life centred around the dance hall:

I remember the strawberry socials held there and in the bungalow in late June. The dance hall was well used for badminton, school concerts, and almost every Saturday night dance they had a prize waltz. This was usually won by . . . Birdie and Hughie McKenzie. School picnics were held on the bank of the Tsolum River near the swimming hole which was between the bungalow and the hotel.

There was no church at Headquarters and Roman Catholic families like the Filbergs, McIvers, MacAulays, and McLoughlins drove down to Comox for Mass every Sunday.

off the flatcars at the very end of the spur beyond the tennis court, where Kelly Brock bucked them with a Wee McGregor and split the rounds into firewood. With his horse and wagon, he delivered wood and bark to the houses and woodsheds of Headquarters. People were especially fond of the thick old-growth Douglas fir bark, which lasted the whole night, leaving embers that could be rekindled for the morning fire.

In the mid-1930s Bob Biss and Fred Tukham, young entrepreneurs, decided to provide a little competition for Brock. They formed what they grandly called the Headquarters Wood and Bark Company and hired their younger brothers Frank Biss and Jack Tukham as assistants. At first, Frank Biss related, they found trees that were down, sawed them up with buck saws, carted the wood into town in wagons, and sold the wood "up and down Headquarters street to the housewives." But it was hard work, and Fred Tukham, who had a quick mind, decided they should poach the bark supply of the main-line train crew. Brakemen Bob Martin and Norman Battersby used to stop the train at the Headquarters siding, about a mile from town, knock off every bit of loose bark into the ditch, and hire Kelly Brock to cart it home for them. So young Bob and Fred got hold of a little railway pushcart and took it along the tracks to the siding, which meant pulling a hand-operated railway switch on the way. After school they'd go out and salvage Martin and Battersby's bark and bring it in close to Headquarters. They'd push the cart out of the way, hide it in the bush, put the bark into their wagons, and sell the bark to the housewives for "five cents here and ten cents there." As Frank Biss described, "Fred was the promoter, my brother was the operator, and we two youngest were the workhorses."

They assumed that the slow adults knew nothing of their act of petty theft, but their get-rich scheme was foiled when word got out that the Three-Spot had gone off the track half a mile out of Headquarters. The four boys could hear the roar of the steam locie as the men tried to get it back on the track. They were hanging over the fence by their houses, pretending not to know anything, when locie engineer Jack Carthew walked past. When he reached the boys he said quietly, "I know who didn't throw the switch right," and kept on walking. The boys had thrown the switch to get the pushcart down the siding, but they didn't quite get the bar down into its locked position, and the vibration of the main-line locie had shaken it loose. The incident ended there, as did the Headquarters Wood and Bark Company.

School, of course, was inescapable. Headquarters children went to grades one through four at the camp school, which opened in temporary quarters in the fall of 1911 with children named Butler, Dixon, Hogg, King, McGuigan, and Parkin in attendance. Later, families who lived and farmed across the Tsolum, like the Fitzgeralds and Murtsells, also sent their children to the school, and other children walked down the tracks from the Dove Creek area.

"One hazard of employing young lady teachers for the school," wrote schoolteacher Helena (Nellie) Cartwright, "was that they soon married and became ineligible for teaching." Ten teachers came and went at Headquarters school between 1911 and 1920; several married local men. The only male teacher, Harry Smith, died of the Spanish influenza in

111

1918. Many children were taught by Miss Nellie Cartwright (1905–1995), who arrived at Headquarters from the Tsolum School in 1931 and managed to stay single. She recalled that the company charged her ten dollars a month for rent, a fee that included firewood.

Children were bused to Tsolum School for grades five through twelve. Bus driver "Old Man Blakeley" came into Headquarters to pick up the kids, who enjoyed sitting next to him on his lunch bucket and watching as the bus made its way through the countryside. Blakeley himself lived with his family of daughters on a little farm right on the corner of Kitty Coleman Road and the highway.

Nellie Cartwright recalled the children's joy when the Headquarters school was closed for an entire week during the great snow of January 1935. "Snow started falling on Sunday and kept falling for the week, gradually covering fence wire after fence wire until five foot fences had disappeared. It was not until the next Sunday that anyone was able to leave or enter Headquarters."

According to Neil Martin, a fatal accident was averted during the great snowfall by Hazel Stevens, who lived across from the warehouse. She looked out of the window and saw blacksmith Joe Butchers making his way through the snow to the machine shop, which bore a heavy load of snow on its corrugated roof. She happened to look out again just as the snow let go and slid off the roof. Hazel realized Joe was either in the shop or buried under a crippling weight of snow. She alerted Dave Stafford. "Old Stafford was pretty smart," Neil Martin recalled. "He got out a long pole and probed around and found Butchers, and they got him out still living. Butchers was a great old guy!" Eddy Murtsell, who helped push the snow off the roundhouse roof with planks, remembered that the piles of snow were still there in July.

Some employees, like Joe Fitzgerald and Fred Dalby, lived on farms near Headquarters. Sam Lee's laundry was on the outskirts of town, as were Kono the dressmaker's farm and Nakamura's store, which sold ice cream, candy, and card games to children, and where loggers played a game called "punchboard." A community known as "Lapland" or "Finland" developed nearby. Many district farmers found good markets supplying a range of produce to the town. Before his death in 1919, veteran logger Archie Pritchard drove his buggy up to Headquarters with loads of vegetables and apples from his farm in Comox. Others did the same, and farmers within range of the logging camps provided food directly to the hotel and to resident families. Among those who provided food to the town were old Joe Hodgins, who sold beef from his farm at Merville, and the Crockett and Sprout families, who delivered cream-rich Jersey milk to Headquarters households.

Beyond the model town were Comox Logging's outlying camps, consisting of moveable houses and shacks that could be picked up and hauled away on a flatcar at a moment's notice—a far cry from Headquarters' comforting permanence.

A Headquarters Boyhood

Born in 1920, son of a Headquarters blacksmith, Ralph Dalby went to grades one through four at Headquarters school, where his teacher was Nellie Cartwright. Later he went to Tsolum school.

Ralph recalled that Headquarters families would go up the tracks into logged-off areas in search of blackberries. Engineer Shorty Miner would take them in his locie. "Boy, oh boy! We'd fill washtubs full!"

Countless grouse lived in the burned-over logging slash. Blue grouse would sit defiantly on stumps, but the willow grouse would fly up into trees and sit there. Ralph and the other boys hunted them all with slingshots made by slipping a rubber tube over a Y-fork. Ralph got to be so good at it that he could hit the grouse right in the head.

He had an extensive paper route as a kid, delivering *The Province* for ten dollars a month. He had to ride his bike all the way to Courtenay every morning for the papers, and customers along his twenty-mile tour included the Crocketts, Walter Anderson, and Bob Filberg. For pocket money he babysat the slightly younger McIver and Tukham boys.

Ralph was sixteen when his father was transferred to Comox Logging's new Ladysmith division, and within a year he was working in the sawmill at Chemainus.

Headquarters school, 1934. Back row, left to right: Don McIver, Keith Stevens, Roy Dalby, Frank Biss, Jack Tukham, Willie Dafoe, Robert Stevens, Miss Marguerite McKee (teacher). Front row, left to right: Jean McIver, Evelyn Fletcher, Gracie Babcock, Charles Lyons, Norman Sprout, Ella Hugo, Toshi Takata, Elva Babcock.—JACK TUKHAM

Playing a game called "heading downriver" at Headquarters, c. 1929. In their canoe from front to back are Bob Biss, Fred Tukham, Jack Tukham, Howard Babcock, Keith Stevens, and Frank Biss.—FRANK BISS

chapter 6

The Outer Camps

One of the worst worries a logging manager can have is hot dry long summers. In such conditions everything in the woods will burn—felled and bucked timber, bridges, machinery and even the camp you live in.

—JOE CLIFFE,
"The Filberg I Knew"

N ITS FIRST FEW YEARS OF EXISTENCE, COMOX LOGGING operated nine camps within ten miles of Courtenay. There was a good reason for this. The company was still logging isolated patches of farm timber, and each patch needed its own camp, no matter how small and temporary.

By 1914, however, the company had used up the patches of farm timber on the lower Tsolum and moved into the 60,000-acre vastness of Block 29 and beyond. The land was divided into three areas, each serviced by a camp and two Lidgerwood skidders. The three camps bore the functional names Camp 1, Camp 2, and Camp 3.

These woods camps had much in common. Indeed, their parts (bunkhouses, cookhouses, married men's houses, sheds) were interchangeable. Readily portable, they could be moved at a moment's notice on the company's flatcars. "They'd move the whole camp and still call it by its old name," Davey Janes explained. In the early 1920s, Wallace Baikie wrote, Comox Logging "never worked too far from camp. They logged out two or three miles, then moved the camp." Camp 3, the most permanent of them, lasted for less than twenty years in the same place—in sharp contrast to Headquarters, which survived, and thrived, for close to fifty years. They fizzled out one by one as accessible timber was cut: Camp 1 closed in 1921, Camp 2 in 1926, and Camp 3 in 1942. Two other camps—4 and 5—were both short-lived, and logged most of the area that became Merville just prior to and during the First World War. Camp 4 was situated at what is now the corner of Merville Road and the west side of the Island Highway. After the war it was taken over by the Soldier Settlement Board. Camp 5, open from about 1914 to 1916, was a mile and a half down Williams Beach Road on what became Reid's Farm.

These outer camps were on the frontiers of the company's operations. They housed men trained in different aspects of railway and skidder logging: surveyors, steel gangs, fallers, buckers, skidder

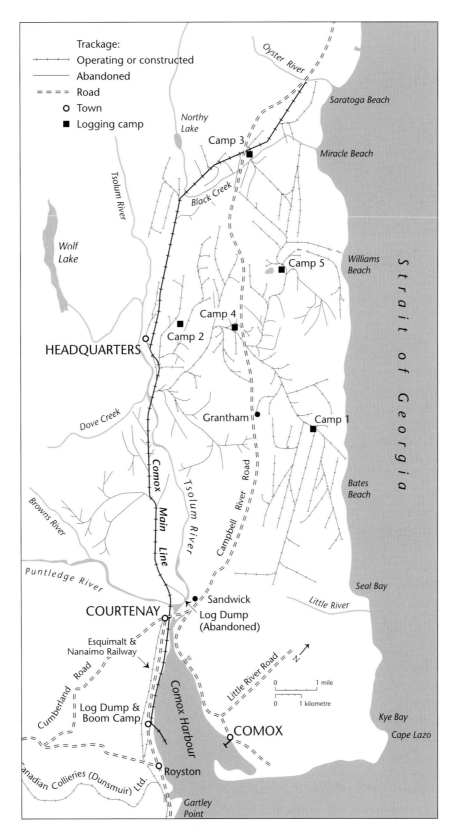

Comox Logging railways and camps, 1917. Redrawn from a map by Robert Turner in his book *Logging by Rail*.

levermen, high riggers, hookers, chokermen, and many others. Residents of the camps were loggers, not tradesmen. They were closer to logging than Headquarters, which, comparatively, was in civilization, a mere eight miles from Courtenay. The outer camps had blacksmiths and filing sheds, but nothing like the industrial base of Headquarters or its accumulated technical skill. They were isolated outstations of Headquarters and depended on the base camp for supplies and repairs. Even Camp 3 had no road connection to start, and of all the camps only it ever had electricity. Set in the middle of logging slash, the camps were also more exposed and vulnerable to fire.

The outer camps also housed a great many men from Europe—the Swedish and Finnish falling and bucking crews and the cosmopolitan grading crews and steel gangs. Unmarried for the most part, these men lived in the camps' bunkhouses. Many of them—especially the Swedes and Finns—later married local women, left the bunkhouses, and bought small farms in the valley.

Still, the outer camps remained predominantly Homeguard, because the married men's houses were inhabited in large part by men and families from the Comox Valley. Many workers at Camps 1, 2, and 3 in the interwar years came from nineteenth-century farming families of the valley. The Baikie, Beech, Berkeley, Blackburn, Cliffe, Downey, Grant, Grieve, Harmston, Hawkins, McKenzie, McQuillan, Parkin, Piercy, Pritchard, and Radford families were represented among the foremen, skidder crews, and yarder crews. The same can be said for the slightly later arrivals—the early twentieth-century farming families like

Stan Hanham, Farmer

Six-year-old Stan Hanham immigrated to Canada from England on a troop ship in 1917 with his mother and sister. His father had died in the war, and his mother decided to join her sister in Vancouver.

Through mutual acquaintances, Mrs. Hanham heard about recently widowed Grantham farmer John Blackburn, who was in need of a housekeeper. Mrs. Hanham and her children arrived at Grantham in March 1918, and by the year's end she and Blackburn were engaged to be married.

As a boy, Stan watched trainloads of logs coming up the railway, from as far away as Bates Beach. Later, his stepfather John Blackburn took up the ties on what became Kitty Coleman Road.

Stan wrote and passed his grade eight exams in 1927. His contemporaries at Tsolum School were Stan Hodgins and Davey Janes. "Everybody went to work for Comox Logging," Stan recalled. Filberg, whom he met on the street in Courtenay, said, "Just go and see the camp boss at Headquarters." John Blackburn gave him the choice of staying on the farm or working in the woods. "At that time they were paying four dollars a day to go—and most boys went." Stan began setting chokers in the fall of 1928.

Stan Hanham now lives in retirement in Comox.

A Comox Logging Heisler locie—either the Four-Spot or the Five-Spot—at Camp 1, Kitty Coleman Road, c. 1916. Camp 1 was "on the track and could be moved," Norm Parkin recalled.—AUDREY MENZIES

Engineer Johnny McLoughlin at the controls of Comox Logging's Shay locie, the Six-Spot, 1916. These small geared locies were ideal for short-hauling and switch-work along sometimes steep branch lines. Switch engines like this did the hard work of hauling flatcars in and out of skidder settings.—AUDREY MENZIES

Bailey, Gray, Hodgins, and Janes. Some of these families contributed three, four, or five sons to the company's workforce.

By contrast, Headquarters had its Homeguard representatives of the Carthew, Cliffe, Machin, Parkin, and Pritchard families, but they never dominated Headquarters in the way they dominated the married contingent of the outer camps. These camps had, therefore, quite different personalities from that of Headquarters. As Homeguard camps they were extensions of the farming communities of the valley, and there, the Homeguards adapted themselves to the new logging economy.

∽

The original site of Camp 1 after 1910 was Crockett's field on Headquarters Road, south of Headquarters; in 1915 it moved into Block 29 near the present junction of Coleman and Hardy roads, east of Merville. Between 1916 and 1918, Camp 1 logged part of the region that became Merville from its Coleman Road base, and also logged farm timber. Farmers like John Blackburn, Alex Salmond, Alexander Ledingham, and Frederick Janes benefited from the sale of their timber to the company. For example, Blackburn, who had moved to Grantham in 1894, negotiated with Major Hilton in 1916 for the sale of one hundred acres of farm timber, for which he received five hundred dollars.

John Blackburn's stepson Stan Hanham remembered how John used to load his sleigh with straw on Saturday nights and pack about twenty Camp 1 fellows—cooks and falling crews—down to the Courtenay

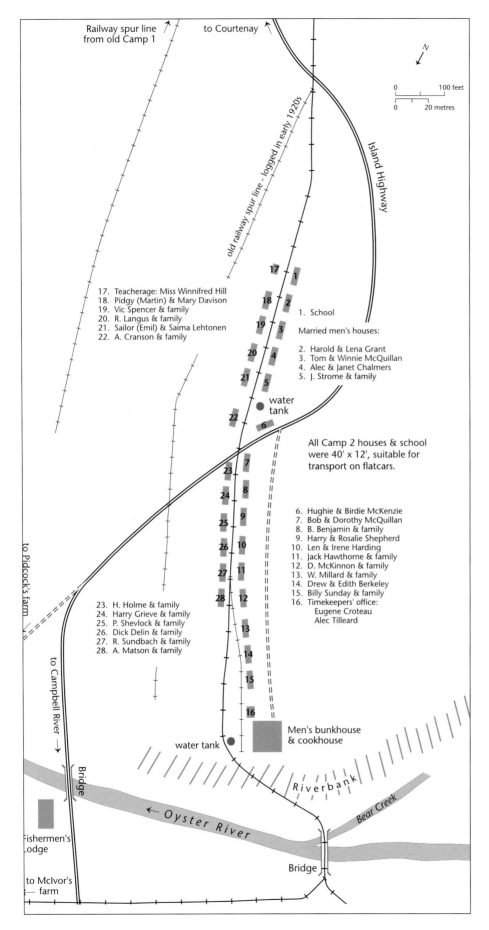

Railway spur line from old Camp 1

to Courtenay

Island Highway

old railway spur line - logged in early 1920s

0 — 100 feet
0 — 20 metres

17. Teacherage: Miss Winnifred Hill
18. Pidgy (Martin) & Mary Davison
19. Vic Spencer & family
20. R. Langus & family
21. Sailor (Emil) & Saima Lehtonen
22. A. Cranson & family

17
18
19
20
21
22

1
2
3
4
5
6

1. School

Married men's houses:

2. Harold & Lena Grant
3. Tom & Winnie McQuillan
4. Alec & Janet Chalmers
5. J. Strome & family

water tank

All Camp 2 houses & school were 40' x 12', suitable for transport on flatcars.

7
8
9
10
11
12
13
14
15
16

23
24
25
26
27
28

6. Hughie & Birdie McKenzie
7. Bob & Dorothy McQuillan
8. B. Benjamin & family
9. Harry & Rosalie Shepherd
10. Len & Irene Harding
11. Jack Hawthorne & family
12. D. McKinnon & family
13. W. Millard & family
14. Drew & Edith Berkeley
15. Billy Sunday & family
16. Timekeepers' office:
      Eugene Croteau
      Alec Tilleard

23. H. Holme & family
24. Harry Grieve & family
25. P. Shevlock & family
26. Dick Delin & family
27. R. Sundbach & family
28. A. Matson & family

to Pidcock's farm

to Campbell River →

water tank

Men's bunkhouse & cookhouse

Riverbank

Bear Creek

Bridge

← Oyster River

Fishermen's Lodge

to McIvor's farm

Bridge

From Maple Syrup to Clam Chowder

One man who left a permanent mark on the Comox Valley was Eugene Croteau, son of a wine merchant near Montreal. Croteau joined Comox Logging after prospecting at Rossland, and by the 1920s he had settled down as a log scaler and timekeeper at Camps 2 and 3. This guileless man was fond of cards, but he was no match for the card sharks at Camp 2 and preferred the more civilized company of the Smiths and Pidcocks at Oyster River.

Once, Cecil and Mary Smith asked him to say grace at one of their children's birthday parties. He said, "Oh Lord, come down through the roof and bless this food—I'll pay for the shingles!" "Mother nearly had a fit," the Smiths' daughter Margaret Dunn recalled.

Starting in the 1920s, Croteau spent all his spare time hunting and prospecting in the mountains above the Comox Valley, and he was among the first to open the area to recreational use. He kept horses at Comox and established a camp, known as Croteau's Camp, next to Croteau Lake on the Forbidden Plateau.

At his retirement house on the Comox waterfront, this old bachelor became famous for his clam chowder, cake doughnuts, and maple syrup sent to him every year by his family in Quebec. Every New Year he visited Allan and Marjorie Brooks's place at Comox wearing a cravat and sporting a large gold nugget from his prospecting days. He was quite deaf and he talked non-stop.

Camp 2, Oyster River, 1924. Redrawn from maps by Herbert Pidcock and Robert Pidcock.

Hotel. One Sunday morning he found a full bottle of whisky among the hay. According to Stan, Blackburn also supplied milk to a temporary Comox Logging grading camp in what became Merville:

> It was a tent camp with over thirty men, mostly northern Europeans. Some of the men would come down to the farm in the evening and buy fresh milk to drink. They would say, "This isn't the same milk that you sent to the cookhouse," which was ten gallons a day. Dad assured them it was, so they watched him milk and take it to the camp and put it down the well to keep it cool. . . . A couple of the men got up hourly and watched the cook go to the well and skim the cream off and add water to the can! The recipients were the wives of the two bosses.

From December 1918 until the fall of 1921, Camp 1 was in its final location, described by oldtimers as "back of Miracle Beach," or "into Miracle Beach," in Block 29. The best account of this last Camp 1 comes from Wallace Baikie. Baikie, at the age of nineteen, worked as a scaler at the camp in the final few months of its existence—the spring and summer of 1921. It was "getting pretty well logged out; we only had two or three four-man gangs to look after." The camp foreman was an American named Charlie Renecker who had worked in the woods near Seattle. "Charlie was the Camp Boss," Baikie recalled. "They called him 'Bull of the Woods.' . . . Charlie was married and living in camp. Mrs. Renneker [*sic*] was an American and they eventually split up. I would say that probably he would be a hard man to live with." Renecker was known for his home brew called "Near Beer."

Others at Camp 1 included Major Clark (timekeeper), Harry Shepherd (yarding engineer), Len Spencer (locie engineer), Emil "Sailor" Lehtonen (rigger), Toynbee Harmston (skidder man), and an old bull bucker named Clarence McCormack.

Major Clark, who shared the office and commissary building with Baikie, was also a devotee of Near Beer: "The Major had a sideline going, selling Near Beer to the loggers," Baikie wrote. "Prohibition was still in force and it was interesting watching those Finns consuming great quantities of that two percent beer. The major sold it over the counter at the Commissary. One night two big Finn fellows had a bet going, who could drink a quart fastest without taking the bottle away from his mouth. The major was to be the judge. It turned out to be a draw so they immediately drank the second quart in record time. What capacity!"

Nobody, Baikie continued, packed a lunch in those days, preferring the abundant cooked meals back at the camp kitchen: "When noon time came the locomotive with a couple of flat cars would be waiting, pick up the different groups as it came along and wheel us into camp. The dinner bell would be ringing and we would charge in, eat our meal in fifteen minutes and the locomotive would be whistling to take us back out by one o'clock. They did that for years."

Camp 1 was closed in the fall of 1921, and over the next year the camp's men, families, and buildings were moved to Camp 2 or 3.

≈

Between 1918 and its closure in 1926, Camp 2 was perched on Comox Logging's main line, just over a mile up the Oyster River from the Strait of Georgia and eighteen and a half miles from the Royston boom camp. It was on the south side of the Oyster near the present highway bridge

A Blast from a Steam Pipe

Train crews were not above teaching a lesson to boys who stood too close to the railway track. Robert Pidcock, who grew up at Camp 2 in the early 1920s, recalled the following incident:

> Our playground was between the school and the railway tracks. . . . The locomotives were hauling loads of logs past the school several times a day. The oldest of us boys used to stand so close to the tracks when the train went by that we could almost touch the train.
>
> One day, when the 7 Spot locomotive was coming back with a string of empty cars, we were as usual standing very close to the tracks. The train crew had hooked up a hose to the steam pipe. Just before the train arrived at our spot, they turned the steam on. The steam had had time to cool before the train reached us, but we were thoroughly soaked. What a scare! We ran away like scared Jack Rabbits!
>
> I'm certain that if we could have looked back, we would have seen the train crew laughing and enjoying the scene at our expense. One thing for certain: we never stood close to any of the passing trains again.
> —"Record of Teachers at Oyster River School, 1922-33"

Comox Logging's safety committee at Camp 2, c. 1927. Left to right: Alex Kapella (section crew), Bob McQuillan (grade crew), Harold Grant (assistant foreman), Len Harding (foreman), Alec Tilleard (scaler), Frank Helman (bucker).—NAN McPHEE

Eugene Croteau, shown here as a retiree in 1929, helps neighbour Mack Laing clear land for a new road. He is drilling a hole in a stump for dynamite. Mack Laing photo.—BRITISH COLUMBIA ARCHIVES, I-51819

A Lidgerwood skidder working out of Camp 2, Oyster River, c. 1918. The stack of firewood at the right reveals that this skidder has not yet been converted to crude oil. These Camp 2 men would have patronized the beer parlour at Fisherman's Lodge on the Oyster River, run by Jim English and later by Big Jim and Ma Taylor.

—CUMBERLAND MUSEUM, C-150-16

and what is now Catherwood Road. The camp was moved there after being destroyed by fire at its earlier location near Sprout's farm, north of Headquarters. ("Fire at Camp 2," wrote Major Hilton in his diary on July 2, 1918. "Wiped it out completely. Men women & children to Hqs.")

Camp 2 was run by a young American named Len Harding, a protege of Bob Filberg's and formerly a skidder engineer based at Headquarters. Harding was an avid hunter and fisherman who had gained experience logging at Sedro Wooley, Washington. Like most foremen in the 1920s and 1930s, he was adamantly anti-union. He was apparently "a heller with the women"—a trait he shared with his boss Bob Filberg. Harding's side-push was Harold Grant, a Comox Homeguard who died young of pneumonia.

Others at the camp in the early 1920s were timekeepers Pete McLoughlin Jr. (who went out with schoolteacher Madge Daniels) and Buck Tilton; scalers Alec Tilleard and Eugene Croteau; section boss Bill Shevlock and his side-push Alex Kapella; high riggers Big Jack McKenzie Jr. and Sailor Lehtonen and their wives Ella and Saima; bull buckers Fred Braker and Wallace Baikie; loading levermen Vic Morrall and George Cliffe; yarding levermen Bill Myers and Harry Shepherd; brakemen Harry Grieve and Bob Hildebrand; blacksmith Hughie McKenzie; rigger Drew Berkeley and his wife Edith (whose twin daughters Bernice and Beryl were born at Camp 2); faller Austin Blackburn and his wife Marjorie Janes; and the families of Tom and Winnie McQuillan, Bob and Dorothy McQuillan, Alec and Janet Chalmers, and Pidgy (Martin) and Mary Davison. Other married men included Dick Delin, Jack Hawthorne, and Billy Sunday.

Timekeeper Buck Tilton, who shared the office building with Wallace Baikie, also brewed Near Beer. One Sunday the men in camp bought a barrel of beer and rolled it out in the yard and drank the whole lot. Apparently, the foremen at Camp 2 also "liked to drink and have parties," as Howard McQuinn put it. As a result, productivity at the camp never reached that of Camp 3, although there was much competition between the two.

~

A mile from Camp 2 was a small and friendly settlement at the mouth of Oyster River. Here, the famous cougar hunter Cecil Smith and his wife Mary (*née* Pidcock) had a productive farm where they brought up their five children. Their daughter Margaret Dunn recalled that this beautiful farm bordered Oyster River on the north and the Strait of Georgia to the east. Their house was on a knoll, and to get to the beach you'd go through the fields, across the creek, and through a narrow strip of timber. Smith, a "marvellous farmer," raised pigs for the company and delivered milk and vegetables to Camp 2, accessible by a dirt road up the Oyster River. Although she was only eight, Margaret did a grown-up's work on the farm. Her father would take her up to Camp 2 in his Model T touring car, which served as delivery van.

The sounds and hazards of Comox Logging were never far away from the Smith farm. One afternoon they heard the sound of a skidder

Austin Blackburn leaves the farm

Son of Merville farmers John and Ada Blackburn, and stepbrother of Stan Hanham, Austin Blackburn was born in Victoria in 1891 and moved with his parents to Merville when he was three.

Blackburn was working on his father's farm when a fellow from a Comox Logging survey gang came along and told him that their chainman had been injured, and that if he wanted a job he'd better come along. He went along. His first day with Comox Logging was August 2, 1920.

Austin Blackburn never returned to the farm, working instead as a faller at Camps 2 and 3 and later running the crew boat on Comox Lake. A good musician, he played the harmonica, guitar, and accordion at barn dances in Merville. Later he bought a farm on the outskirts of Courtenay.

John Tukham labelled this photo "Camp 3 Chopsuey feast 1920." It is the only known photo of the inside of a Comox Logging cookhouse before the 1930s. Clockwise from left: unknown woman, Charlie MacAulay, Charlie McIver, Jack McQuinn (head of table), unknown, Hughie Stevens, Goldie McQuinn, and four unknown visitors at right. John Tukham photo.—JACK TUKHAM

Feeding Camp 2

In 1922, Cecil "Cougar" Smith handed over his farm at Oyster River to his brother-in-law Will Pidcock. Son of Reginald and Alice Pidcock, Will Pidcock was born at his father's sawmill in Courtenay in 1874 and grew up at Fort Rupert, Alert Bay, and Quathiaski Cove, where his father was an Indian Agent and sawmill operator.

After marrying Mary Holmes, the Quathiaski school teacher, Pidcock moved to Victoria in 1908 to manage the historic Craigflower Farm. In 1922 the Pidcocks moved to the farm at the mouth of Oyster River, as son Herbert recalled:

The farm ran from the highway on the west side down the Oyster River to the ocean on the north and had a mile of sandy beach on the east. There was around thirty acres of cleared land where Will grew grain and vegetables. He also ran a dairy (with around thirty cows) as he supplied milk and cream to the families and cookhouse of the Comox Logging Company at Camp 2. This camp was just over a mile from the farm and the children went to school in a bunkhouse supplied by the Comox Logging Co. Will also got swill from the cookhouse for feed for his pigs. He also supplied vegetables to the families.

A Schoolboy at Camp 2

Son of Will and Mary Pidcock, Herbert Pidcock was born in Victoria in 1915, attended Craigflower School, and, at the age of seven, moved with his family to Oyster River, just after the 1922 Merville fire.

From 1922 until 1926 Herbert went to the Camp 2 school, which was an old bunkhouse painted red. The school was portable; it was propped up on a set of yarder skids upon which cribbing, made of railway ties, came to the height of a child. A set of solid steps led from the ground to the front door past the skids and all the cribbing. The logging trains passed by only fifty or sixty feet away, but they were so frequent that the boys thought nothing of them.

Among the other children at the school were the Sundbach and Benjamin children and Georgia Ployart, who rode her horse to school from a neighbouring farm. Herbert, by contrast, walked over a mile to and from school, sometimes accompanied by Winnifred Hill or Madge Daniels, the Camp 2 teachers, who boarded with his parents.

whistle blowing incessantly. They thought a logger must have been seriously injured or killed, when in fact a tree limb had fallen across the whistle lever. The whistle kept going and going until the steam finally ran out. "It was an eerie sound," Margaret remembered. The 1922 Merville fire came close to their barn, and a desperate gang of men came through cutting snags to slow the progress of the fire. "I can still see them lying on the floor getting a few hours' sleep." At the time of the Merville fire, Cecil's brother Horace happened to be at Oyster River helping with some ploughing. Horace returned to find his own farm at Merville destroyed. The chickens were "frizzled," Margaret recalled, still standing up where the fire had overtaken them, and his cows' hooves were so badly burned that he had to destroy the poor animals.

The lack of a school at Oyster River prompted the Smiths to move to Comox in 1922, where Cecil was appointed a government cougar hunter—earning his well-known moniker "Cougar Smith." Margaret, who was then ten, had never been to school, but she regretted the move to Comox because her father loved the farm. As it turned out, they needn't have moved—a school opened at Camp 2 the very next year.

The new tenant of the farm at Oyster River was Mary Smith's brother Will Pidcock, his wife Mary (*née* Holmes), and their six children. Will and Mary Pidcock continued to supply Camp 2 with milk, cream, and vegetables.

Until the late 1920s, the Smith and Pidcock families hosted Comox Logging's annual picnic on their farm's beach at the mouth of Oyster River. The Pidcocks charged fifty cents a car, and people came from Headquarters and all the camps. What is now gravel was then a beach of pure white sand. Known at first simply as Oyster River Beach, it was developed into a resort between the wars and renamed "Saratoga Beach" by the new American owner.

Among the competitions were races (for boys and girls sixteen and under), a pie-eating contest (boys only), high jump, tug-of-war (men's and women's), and the ladies' nail-driving contest (held for women only because it was assumed that all red-blooded men could drive a straight nail).

The Oyster River picnic also featured traditional loggers' sports. Among these were tree-climbing, falling, bucking, cable-splicing, and log-rolling, but the event also included rope-climbing for the benefit of the riggers. Herbert Pidcock (Will and Mary's son) recalled that rope-climbing took place at a huge fir at the edge of the field. This tree was six feet at the base. The loggers tied a heavy hemp rope to a limb fifty or sixty feet up the tree and competed to see who could climb the rope the fastest and ring a bell at the top.

The food was marvellous: the Chinese cooks would be there with a big fire and they'd cook lunch and dinner, with hot dogs and hamburgers available all day long. Everything was free to company employees.

Herbert Pidcock, at the age of ten, witnessed the dismantling of Camp 2 in 1926. The bunkhouses were moved onto flatcars; even the cookhouse was taken apart and taken away. The camp was moved to

Comox Logging's new operations at Bevan and Comox Lake and in 1928, the picnic was moved to a more central location at Lewis Park in Courtenay.

~

With Camp 2 gone, Camp 3 became the main camp north of Headquarters. Originally, in 1914, Camp 3 was situated west of Dove Creek Road, but over the winter of 1917–1918 it was moved to Black Creek, south of Oyster River, where it was rebuilt on the west side of the Island Highway across from what is now the PetroCanada station. In 1922 it moved to its final location near Northy Lake.

Burned in 1922, partly burned in 1923, razed to the ground in 1925, and threatened in the 1938 fire, Camp 3 was the most fire-prone of all camps. "They were burnt out nearly every year or so," Bernice James recalled. Despite the hazard, Camp 3 took on a settled aspect after 1925, and like Headquarters it became a community of families: Homeguard families moved there, other loggers married local women, children were born, schools were built. With its dominant Homeguard element, the camp was part of the social fabric of the valley.

Bob Filberg, however, had a preference for American foremen, and the boss of Camp 3, Jack (John Grover) McQuinn, was an American (as were Renecker of Camp 1 and Harding of Camp 2). But all three men, like Filberg himself, settled in Canada. Jack "Greasy" McQuinn, in fact, became a legendary figure in British Columbia coastal logging. Born in 1892 on a farm near Fossil, Oregon, he went to work in the woods as a whistlepunk at the age of twelve, and before he was nineteen he had worked in many logging camps, including the one at Pysht, where he first met Bob Filberg, and at Comox, where he worked briefly for Fraser River Lumber.

Hired by Comox Logging, McQuinn proved himself so valuable that he replaced Clay Walsh as assistant superintendent in the early 1920s and spent the rest of his career with Comox Logging. Camp 3 was McQuinn's particular bailiwick, and it was here, between his arrival in 1919 and his departure for Ladysmith in 1936, that McQuinn ran day-to-day logging operations. "You couldn't argue with or oppose McQuinn," said one source. "He was a very powerful figure. He did most of the hiring and firing."

McQuinn's capable side-push was Homeguard and former head rigger Bob "Scratchy" Grant of Comox, son of a Nova Scotian farmer and brother of Butch and Mack Grant. Scratchy Grant took over as woods foreman of Camp 3 when McQuinn moved to Ladysmith.

In June 1918, 107 men and 10 women lived at Jack McQuinn's Camp 3; about half of the names were Finnish, Swedish, or Russian—fallers, buckers, and grade crews—reflecting wartime hiring policies. Among the schoolchildren at the camp school (known as McGuigan's) were Sybil, Johnny, and Howard McQuinn; Grace and Dodie Cowie; and Joy and Doris McKenzie.

In the summer of 1922, the company moved Camp 3 to a new location twelve miles up the Island Highway from Courtenay, north of Northy Lake and half a mile east of Black Creek. The new camp would provide access to the uncut timber of the upper Oyster River and the

The 1922 Fire at Camp 3

The men were working out in the Black Creek area and the train crew could see this fire coming. They rushed back to the old camp, picked up the women, kids, and men that happened to be around, loaded them on flat cars and got them out of there in the nick of time. Some of the men wouldn't come and spent the night in wells and in Black Creek.

This fire had started up in the International Timber works and was fanned up with a north-west wind that afternoon. It came down across the Oyster River and between Camp 2 and the new Camp 3 and on down to Merville, burning out fifty or sixty settlers. One boy [Jack Clifford] lost his life. The velocity of that fire must have increased as it travelled towards Merville, as that ridge just north of Merville had been logged several years before and was coming up in a fine crop of second growth fir. Those little trees were flattened to the ground, blackened and stripped of all foliage.

The fire had started ten or twelve miles north of the Oyster and came down through the standing timber, crowning in places and jumping from snag to snag until it got into some of the Camp 2 fell and bucked timber which gave it more momentum as it carried on towards Merville. It missed the new Camp 3 by half a mile. We could hear the roar and see the flames in the standing timber as it passed by.—Wallace Baikie, *Rolling with the Times*

Goldie McQuinn, Camp 3 Matriarch

Of Dutch-American and Oregon pioneer descent, Goldie Fredenburg of Marcola, Oregon, married Jack McQuinn in 1910. She gave birth to no fewer than eleven children, some on each side of the international border.

Born in 1893, Goldie lived to the age of 100—long enough to see one of her grandsons recite a poem, "Goldie the Oldie," at a family gathering in the 1980s. It begins:

*Gramma Goldie, young and free
    Born in 1893,
Enjoyed her youth but blew it when,
    She married John in 1910.
Married John from town of Fossil
    Had a family quite colossal.*

—Thomas O'Brennan, *Our Branch of the Tree*

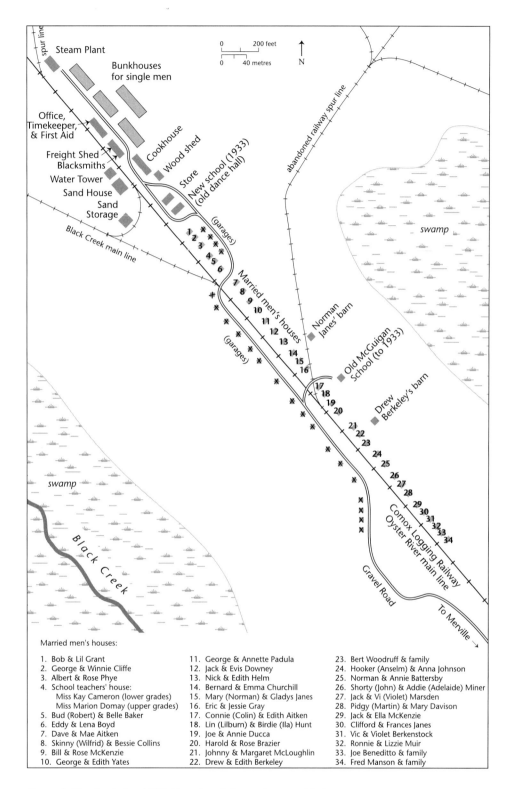

Married men's houses:

1. Bob & Lil Grant
2. George & Winnie Cliffe
3. Albert & Rose Phye
4. School teachers' house:
   Miss Kay Cameron (lower grades)
   Miss Marion Domay (upper grades)
5. Bud (Robert) & Belle Baker
6. Eddy & Lena Boyd
7. Dave & Mae Aitken
8. Skinny (Wilfrid) & Bessie Collins
9. Bill & Rose McKenzie
10. George & Edith Yates

11. George & Annette Padula
12. Jack & Evis Downey
13. Nick & Edith Helm
14. Bernard & Emma Churchill
15. Mary (Norman) & Gladys Janes
16. Eric & Jessie Gray
17. Connie (Colin) & Edith Aitken
18. Lin (Lilburn) & Birdie (Ila) Hunt
19. Joe & Annie Ducca
20. Harold & Rose Brazier
21. Johnny & Margaret McLoughlin
22. Drew & Edith Berkeley

23. Bert Woodruff & family
24. Hooker (Anselm) & Anna Johnson
25. Norman & Annie Battersby
26. Shorty (John) & Addie (Adelaide) Miner
27. Jack & Vi (Violet) Marsden
28. Pidgy (Martin) & Mary Davison
29. Jack & Ella McKenzie
30. Clifford & Frances Janes
31. Vic & Violet Berkenstock
32. Ronnie & Lizzie Muir
33. Joe Beneditto & family
34. Fred Manson & family

Camp 3, Northy Lake, 1936. Based on information provided by Dick Downey, Lois Shopland, and Frank Davison.

Mack Laing of Comox took this photo of smouldering logging slash after the great Merville fire of 1922. The stump is Douglas fir and the bent saplings are willow. "So eager have been the gale-driven flames," Laing wrote, "that they warped the green saplings as they rushed through this logged off land but left for more fuel downstream before consuming them."—BRITISH COLUMBIA ARCHIVES, I-51798

Austin Blackburn and his daughter Evelyn on the porch of the Blackburn house at Camp 3, c. 1923.—FRED BLACKBURN

northern timber blocks. Workers had just moved the cookhouse, bunkhouses, and logging equipment to this new location when "Old Camp 3" (the remains of the camp at the previous location) was completely destroyed in the great Merville fire of July 6, 1922. Women and children were evacuated by train, leaving the married men's houses, the school, and several cars to be consumed in the inferno. (Later, whenever Austin Blackburn drove up the Island Highway, he'd point at the remains of a burned-out car and say, "There's my car!" to his children.)

Construction of the new camp continued and was going full swing over the winter of 1922–1923. A number of rather battered married men's houses had been brought in on skids along with fifteen or twenty eight-man, wood-heated bunkhouses when, in 1923, a brush fire got out of hand and destroyed six houses at the camp.

Then, only two years later, in August 1925, Camp 3 was completely destroyed by fire. The fire started at Skidder 6, working near the camp, and soon spread to the camp. Bunkhouses and the cookhouse were destroyed, along with the office, storehouse, blacksmith's shop, filing house, and pumphouse. Mechanic Ed Parberry heroically saved all but one of the thirty-two cars in camp at the time of the fire by tearing off the instrument panels, hot-wiring the engines, and sending them down the road with anyone who was available. "If he had waited until the keys were forthcoming," the *Comox Argus* noted, "the cars would have been a heap of twisted metal now."

Many other stories of this catastrophe have survived. Myrtle Heron (*née* McKenzie) was a year old at the time of the fire. Her mother Ella ran out of her house with Myrtle and her baby clothes, and left everything else behind, including a precious ruby ring (a gift from husband Big Jack McKenzie Jr.) hanging on a nail on the wall. George and Winnie Cliffe lost all their possessions in this fire, including their wedding presents. Butch (Arthur) and Decie Grant also lost everything. Their son John said that behind the camp was a swamp, and when the fire was approaching Butch tied the family cow up in the swamp. Then the train came and took everyone away to Headquarters along with whatever belongings they could carry. The cow survived.

One of the most dramatic fire stories comes from Bernice James, whose father Bud Baker was a locie engineer at Camp 3. Bernice was four years old at the time. Her mother Belle, who was eight or nine months pregnant, was peeling apples for a pie when they heard the locie whistle. They had all been taught that a long whistle meant trouble, so Bernice asked, "Is that a bad whistle?" Her mother answered, "Yes," and got her bundled up and ready to go. Then they heard Bernice's dad coming down the tracks on an engine, hollering at the Cliffes, McQuinns, and other families to get out. When he reached his own house, he bellowed, "Get Bernice and get the hell out—we're being burned out!"

Goldie McQuinn came right over in her car and picked up Bernice, Belle, and the midwife Winnie Cliffe. They shared the car with the McQuinn children (Sybil, Howard, Pearl, Dorothy, Bernice, and Ila) along with Goldie McQuinn's sister-in-law Birdie Hunt, for a total of eleven in the car. "All I can remember is the dogs howling," Bernice

Jimmy McIvor of Oyster River

An old Highlander (or Cape Breton Scot, depending on the source), Jimmy McIvor lived on the north side of Oyster River at the river's mouth. He had been shipwrecked there in the 1880s when he was a young fellow. Margaret Dunn (*née* Smith) recalled that he was "a great big man and kindness itself."

"McIvor's log cabin was constructed of axe-cut timber, with a clay mixture between its squared-off logs," wrote Rubina Twigg. "A mounted elk rack hung above the door." "The McIvor," as he called himself, made his own clothes out of gunny sacks. He got butter and eggs from Mary Smith, but generally he did not eat well: his tea was so strong and black that visitors could hardly swallow it, and he used to tie a rope around his stomach to ease his indigestion.

He refused to sell his farm timber to Comox Logging, as Arthur Mayse wrote: "McIvor had told us how once when cash was scarce and expenses heavy, he had decided to sell some of the timber off his wooded acres. A deal was made. The loggers moved in. But McIvor didn't cotton to the way they were knocking down trees—his trees—indiscriminately with their steam-powered steel lines. He ordered them off the land. . . ."

McIvor earned his income from road and bridge maintenance and from selling beef in the Comox Valley. Stan Hanham recalled seeing McIvor making his way down into Merville from Oyster River in about 1918. "I remember seeing him in his wagon going to Cumberland with a couple of dead beef with all eight legs sticking straight up in the air." A character from another century, he died in about 1940, and his cattle turned feral.

Evelyn Blackburn and her mother Marjorie on the steps of the Blackburn house at Camp 3, c. 1923, in the middle of vast Block 29. Notice the ever-present stumps, tar paper roof, cedar kindling blocks outside the front gate, railway tracks at the front door, and the two long poles for pushing bark off rail cars.
—FRED BLACKBURN

An unidentified family at Camp 3, c. 1923. The house has been mounted on an old set of cold decker skids for easy transport. Camp 3 houses, Barbara Marriott recalled, were small and simple. "They were not elegant, but boy, were they ever clean!"—FRED BLACKBURN

School and Playtime at Camp 3

Jean Feely (*née* Baikie) described what life was like in Camp 3 when she was a six-year-old girl, in 1922:

Located at the far end of the camp, barely forty feet from the main railway line which carried logs to the Royston booming grounds, the school building was a typical logging camp bunkhouse, long and narrow so it could be moved from place to place by train if the need existed. The outside was board and batten while the inside consisted of painted shiplap. The heater was located at one end of the building and three loosely fitted windows rattled whenever the wind blew. There was no electric light and the teacher had to bring her own gas light to the dim quarters.

The tops of the stumps were a wonderful place to play, they were nice and flat, a little pitchy if we weren't careful. One of the scores of entertainments was sitting on the stump and counting the loaded railway cars going by. The huge logs were really a wonderful sight. At the end of the cars was a caboose, on which the mail used to come into the camp. Another pastime was whipping soap suds. We would scrounge bits of soap and beat them until it stood up in peaks. Then we would add beet juice or other colouring until it turned out into beautiful fluffy peaks. It was a lot cleaner than mud pies!—Isenor et al., *For Our Children*

Camp 3 was an isolated place in the early 1920s, accessible by several gas speeders powered by Model A Ford engines. Among the passengers on this speeder—fallers going to Courtenay on their day off, c. 1925—are Fred Dahl, Nestor Hagg, and Mr. Dahlberg. "There wasn't a road into camp at that time," Wallace Baikie wrote. "You had to leave your car out three miles and walk down to camp on the ties. If you went out for an evening you could borrow a hand car." Fred Erickson photo.
—HARRY ERICKSON

The "Deuce" (Two-Spot) and a gang of men pull a new house into place during the reconstruction of Camp 3 in 1925.
—EVELYN HARDY AND FRED BLACKBURN

**Log-rolling contest at the Oyster River
picnic, c. 1925.**—BERNICE JAMES

**The ladies' nail-driving contest at the annual company picnic, Oyster River, c. 1925. The
1925 champions were Birdie Hunt, Aleda Murtsell and Miss N. McNeill.**—JACK TUKHAM

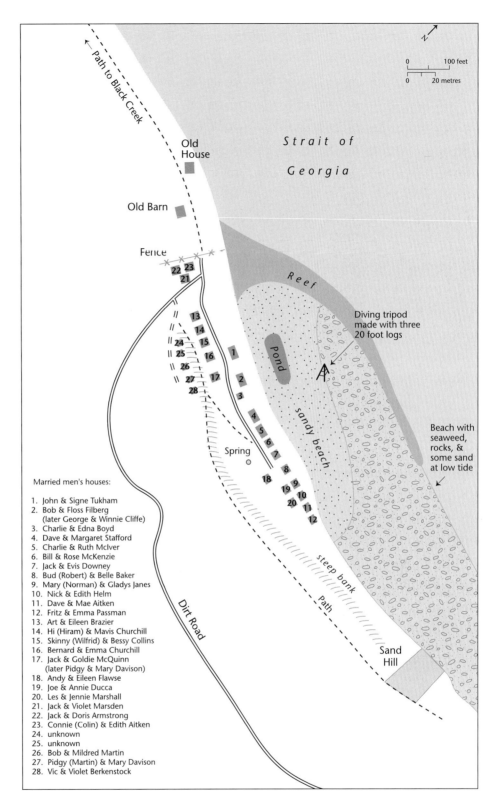

Married men's houses:

1. John & Signe Tukham
2. Bob & Floss Filberg
   (later George & Winnie Cliffe)
3. Charlie & Edna Boyd
4. Dave & Margaret Stafford
5. Charlie & Ruth McIver
6. Bill & Rose McKenzie
7. Jack & Evis Downey
8. Bud (Robert) & Belle Baker
9. Mary (Norman) & Gladys Janes
10. Nick & Edith Helm
11. Dave & Mae Aitken
12. Fritz & Emma Passman
13. Art & Eileen Brazier
14. Hi (Hiram) & Mavis Churchill
15. Skinny (Wilfrid) & Bessy Collins
16. Bernard & Emma Churchill
17. Jack & Goldie McQuinn
    (later Pidgy & Mary Davison)
18. Andy & Eileen Flawse
19. Joe & Annie Ducca
20. Les & Jennie Marshall
21. Jack & Violet Marsden
22. Jack & Doris Armstrong
23. Connie (Colin) & Edith Aitken
24. unknown
25. unknown
26. Bob & Mildred Martin
27. Pidgy (Martin) & Mary Davison
28. Vic & Violet Berkenstock

Williams Beach, 1936. Redrawn from maps by Don McIver and Frank Davison.

Children at Williams Beach, c. 1930. The destructive forest fires of the 1920s prompted Comox Logging to evacuate logging camp families to the seaside every summer. Bob Filberg's big waterfront house is behind. John Tukham photo.—JACK TUKHAM

recalled. "Some dogs were tied up and couldn't get free—we just had to get right out." They escaped from the camp, and Goldie dropped the children at "Grannie and Grandpa Cliffe's" (Lu and Alice's) farm at Mission Hill. Belle was told, "You're staying here till you have that baby!" Lu and Alice's daughter Florence Stewart daringly returned in her car to the camp before it burned and put Bernice's dad's guns and all her mother's crystal wedding presents down the well. They survived, but nothing else did.

Belle Baker's baby was born at the Cliffe farmhouse August 29, 1925—nine-pound Roberta, a sister for Bernice.

≈

After the 1925 destruction of Camp 3—the third serious fire in four years—and the harrowing escape of the women and children, many children and families moved to the safety of Williams Beach for up to two months during the summer fire season. Bob Filberg had bought an old picnic property at Williams Beach and turned it into an unofficial company resort. He hired carpenters to put up some two-by-four and two-by-six cabin frames in a couple of rows along the beach, then he brought in some lumber and shakes and invited men from Headquarters and Camp 3 to build their own summer cottages. "If you want to put up a summer house, I'll give you the lumber," he said.

Many Homeguard employees took advantage of his offer and spent their time off building at Williams Beach. Old Jim Sedgewick, a retired

Hazards of the Oyster River Picnic

Comox Logging's picnics at Oyster River were an annual highlight for everyone in the extended company family. "Bob Filberg had a good time at his first Company picnic," wrote Wallace Baikie. "His main pastime all day was to see how much ice cream he could stuff into the kids. He claimed one little girl ate twenty-five cones."

Announcers were Walter Woodhus of Oyster River and John Tukham of Headquarters, who ran the events and loved using a big bullhorn. Baikie, who placed third in the high jump in 1921, recorded that "John Tukham with his broken English was the announcer and blurted out loud and clear over the horn, 'First prize, Harold Grant; Second, Bob Grant; and Vallace Baikie, tird.'" Tukham announced his "tird" prizes year after year. "The kids went ape!" Bernice James recalled.

Baikie also described a hazardous sport at the 1921 picnic:

Someone had brought this big ball of iron or steel with a hole in it to attach a six foot piece of rope. Filberg probably had it made up in the machine shop. The contest was to see who could throw it the furthest. One big fellow wanted to try his luck. He took the rope and ball and began hopping around in a circle until he lost his direction and let the ball go sailing right over the spectators. There was a bad scramble and luckily it landed without hitting anybody. That was the last time that the loggers were allowed to try that sport.

The 1927 Picnic

A correspondent for *Canadian Forest & Outdoors* visited Comox Logging's annual picnic at Oyster River in August 1927:

The logging company provides prizes. Very handsome ones indeed, since about a thousand dollars is expended in prizes alone. They also provide two excellent meals during the day, setting up species of open air cafeteria, from which everyone may carry away a loaded tray free of any charge. . . . The Comox does the thing in style.

At perhaps ten o'clock of the appointed morning picnickers commence to collect along the sandy beach. The logging folk are used to early rising hours. They want their fun to commence good and early and they want plenty of action, too.

Here you will see them gathering more than three hundred strong. Such a wide diversity of nationality and type. Husky Swedes with their blond headed families, dark-skinned Italians groomed for the occasion. Canadians, Englishmen or an occasional happy-go-lucky Yankee.

They are all alert, eager for any amusement which may present itself. A hard-working, hard-playing crowd demanding entertainment from the word go. Consequently the sports commence early, usually with the stereotyped racing, long jumps, hammer-throwing, etc. . . .

bunkmaker from a skidder setting, spent a year cutting cedar shakes, and the men did their own roofing.

Filberg's offer was open only to married men and their families, and it was an unwritten rule that those who didn't go to the beach every year lost this perk. Among the men whose families spent summers at Williams Beach were Connie (Colin) Aikman, Dave Aitken, Jack Armstrong, Bud Baker, Vic Berkenstock, Austin Blackburn, Charlie Boyd, Art Brazier, Bernard Churchill, Hi Churchill, George Cliffe, Wilfred "Skinny" Collins, Martin "Pidgy" (or "Pitchy") Davison, Jack Downey, Joe Ducca, Bob Filberg, Andy Flawse, Nick Helm, Norman "Mary" Janes, Charlie McIver, Bill McKenzie, Jack McQuinn, Jack Marsden, Les Marshall, Bob Martin, Jim Mathers, Fritz Passman, Dave Stafford, and John Tukham. Some families also stayed in tents.

Williams Beach was a great place for children. One of the Cliffe clan, Captain Tom Cliffe, was skipper of a CPR ship that passed up and down the Strait of Georgia in front of the beach. Bernice James (*née* Baker) remembered that the kids would get bulrushes, dip them in coal oil, and hold them up at night as torches. They would run up and down the

Homeguards at play: George Cliffe, Belle Baker, and Rose McKenzie at Williams Beach, c. 1930. George Cliffe was in the prime of a long career as a loading leverman.—BERNICE JAMES

Alec Tilleard in his later years (1938) at Comox. Bob Filberg photo.
—FILBERG LODGE & PARK ASSOCIATION

Singing in the Woods

Scaler, timekeeper, tenor, trapper, Englishman, and returned soldier Alec Tilleard first appears in the Comox Logging records in 1920 as surveyor Hughie Stevens' assistant at Headquarters.

In 1922, Tilleard took on a scaling job at Camp 2. "This was his choice," according to Wallace Baikie, "as he was having trouble keeping up to Stevens in the woods and he preferred being more or less his own boss on the scaling job." He trapped illegally, selling his hides, mostly beaver, to a friend in Victoria. He remained at Camp 2 until it closed in 1926.

Tilleard was a regular visitor to the Smith-Pidcock farm at Oyster River in the 1930s. "He had a magnificent tenor voice," Margaret Dunn (née Smith) recalled. "I can hear him now going home!"

After scaling logs on the Royston boom for many years, Tilleard retired to Comox, where, Tony Turner said, he built a "very nice house." He continued to sing in church and in Charles Sillence's Courtenay Choir. Bruce King first met "the old time water scaler" in 1935 at Comox: "He had a great baritone voice, and his sister was a concert pianist. He made the 'Queen's Mead' out of honey. Prior to that he'd been a woods scaler. You could hear him singing in the woods—everywhere."

beach and "Uncle Tom" would oblige them by blowing the whistle on his ship. Many families dug clams and hunted ducks and deer on and around the beach.

After the war, Filberg, who held the property in his own name, sold the property as a tourist resort, complete with the cottages built by his workers.

∽

After the 1925 fire Comox Logging rebuilt Camp 3 on the same site. Bill Haggarty, the company's master carpenter, was in charge of construction of this up-to-date "model camp." In only three or four months Haggarty built an entirely new camp, including a large cookhouse; four steam-heated bunkhouses with washrooms, toilets and drying facilities; and twenty-five married men's houses. The married

Master carpenter Bill Haggarty (shown here in 1940) was an "up-the-creeker" from the Ottawa Valley and a fiddler known for his jigs and reels. "My father was originally a wheelwright in Ontario," his son Colton wrote, "but by the turn of the century wheels were going out of fashion, so dad came west and became a millwright, then a contractor." He moved to British Columbia in 1910 and worked at Canadian Western's subsidiary in Golden before coming to the Comox Valley. Among his projects were Camp 3; the Native Sons' Hall and the Roman Catholic Church in Courtenay; the weather station at Cape Lazo; and Bob Filberg's house on the Comox waterfront. "Bill Haggarty was a great talker and a good listener," Wallace Baikie wrote. "I can see him standing with his head cocked to one side when some problem had to be discussed." **Bob Filberg photo.**—FILBERG LODGE & PARK ASSOCIATION

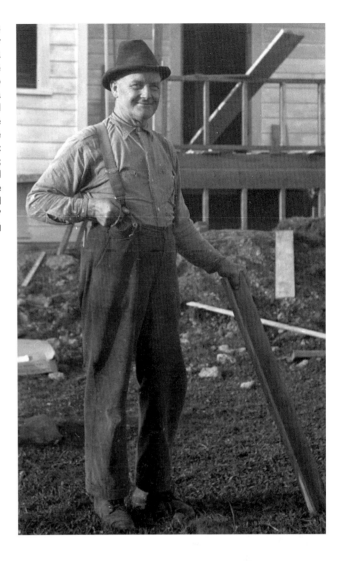

Williams Beach had been a popular summer retreat for the Comox Homeguard since 1914. Here, faller Austin Blackburn of Camp 3 supervises his nephew Davey Janes (left) and his daughter Evelyn Blackburn, c. 1923. Only five years later young Davey would be working as a whistlepunk for Comox Logging.—FRED BLACKBURN

Mary and Bud Filberg at Williams Beach, 1932. Bob Filberg photo.—FILBERG LODGE & PARK ASSOCIATION

men's houses were stained with brown paint thinned with the mixture of diesel oil and fuel oil that Comox Logging burned in its locies. All Camp 3 buildings were finished with a distinctive vertical board-and-batten siding made of rough cedar boards.

The southern end of the camp was residential, with the married men's houses, garages, and the camp school. The northern end of camp was the administrative, maintenance, and industrial area, with the office, filers' and blacksmiths' sheds, bunkhouses, cookhouses, store, community hall, sandhouse, and water tower.

The camp stretched half a mile along the tracks. By 1925 a road, known at first as the Camp 3 road, had been extended to the camp, which meant that men living nearby could drive to work, pooling and picking up five or six men on the way. Davey Janes had such an arrangement in the late 1920s. Indeed, Neil Martin explained that the name "Camp 3" is a bit misleading because not everyone who worked there actually lived at the camp. The road served to connect the camp with the larger rural community to the south.

Until 1933 the camp school was behind the married men's houses, but afterwards it took over the community/dance hall located at the north end of the camp. The school retained the name McGuigan's School, after Comox Logging's first superintendent. Children attended early grades at the school before being bused to Tsolum School. Among the schoolteachers were Molly Akerman, Rose Baikie (Wallace's sister), Kay Cameron, Marion Domay, Bernadette MacAulay, and Mr. Duncan. As was the case at Headquarters, female teachers generally married local men: Rose Baikie, for instance, married Bill McKenzie; Molly Akerman went out with Joe Cliffe. They were well-paid: Rose Baikie made $960 in 1922–1923. The teacher lived in the "schoolmarm's cabin" next to McQuinn's cabin, where she could be kept safe from the predatory single men of the camp.

In the 1920s Camp 3 experienced something of a population explosion, four boys being born there in 1926 alone. By the 1930s it had a population of about three hundred. Preschools had not yet been invented, and children played on stumps in their parents' fenced yards. In the 1930s, the camp's only two babysitters were Eva Manson and Evie Aitken, who charged thirty-five cents a night.

The four large bunkhouses lodged unmarried men from the grading, section, skidder, and train crews, as well as young, mainly Scandinavian fallers and buckers. "They were big long buildings," Hi Churchill recalled. "There were twenty-four beds in each half of a bunkhouse; same in the other half." Single Homeguards stayed in the bunkhouses before moving into the married men's houses farther down the tracks, and dozens of Swedish and Finnish fallers stayed there before buying their stump ranches in Merville. The camp's night watchman and "hostler" George Yates made sure that the steam-heated bunkhouses were kept warm. The fallers and buckers also needed abundant hot water to wash the tree pitch and saw lubricating oil from their hands. An array of twenty-two pipes ran from Yates's steam plant into every bunkhouse, and Hi Churchill, who bunked there in 1930, recalled that the pipes would crack and bang when the steam came through, and he had to move his bed to avoid the condensation dripping from the

The 1925 Fire

The *Comox Argus* reported that on August 8, 1925, Camp 3 was destroyed by fire:

At ten o'clock in the morning No. 6 skidder was working about 1,500 feet from Camp 3. A wire cable from the spar tree broke, and breaking, coiled around a cedar snag. At once the air was full of sparks and flame and the tree was alight. But the crew had been prepared for just such an emergency and five minutes after the outbreak had the hose from the locomotive playing on the fire. But under the urge of a strong wind nothing could hold the flames and they spread with irresistible rapidity. It was at once seen that Camp 3 was in danger. . . .

When the wind changed it blew the smoke into the eyes of the army of firefighters and half suffocated them. Before this it had been seen that the situation was pretty desperate and all the women and children had been sent out either by car or by train to Headquarters so that the attention of the men would not be distracted by thoughts of the safety of their families.

Then the fire jumped to the roof of the first house—the McQuinns—and it went up as if a lighted torch had been dropped on it from an aeroplane. Almost at once other houses were ablaze and there was nothing further to do but to make good the escape of the men working and abandon the camp to fate.

ceiling. "They had a piece of canvas to pull over them so you wouldn't get wet from the steam dripping!"

The bunkhouses had a sitting room in the middle and a table where the guys played cards. Boarders also had access to a pool hall and recreation room that was run, in 1924, by Jeff Hannah, and a store, run at first by Andy Flawse, who lived with his family in the back of the store. Flawse had a car that he used as a taxi, and he'd make liquor runs into Courtenay. "When a guy in a bunkhouse wanted a bottle, [Andy] would go and get it," remembered Dick Bailey. Joe Ducca later took over the store.

Families at the camp also shopped at the store, as Eva Bailey (*née* Manson) recalled. "There was a grocery store at Camp 3. If you had no money, you'd go and charge it up and you'd pay it off bit by bit." Merville storekeeper Mel Saunders supplied groceries to the camp, as did several Courtenay merchants, including Malpass & Wilson and the Lowe Brothers' Chinese store. "I liked them [Lowe Brothers]. You paid your bill by the month and they'd put a bag of candy in with your groceries." Freddie Parkin, who had taken over Eric Duncan's grocery store and post office at Sandwick, delivered groceries and mail along the road as far as Camp 3. He took weekly orders, and "sometimes Freddie would let us go along for a ride in the truck," Barbara Marriott (*née* Duncan) remembered.

Like the others, Camp 3 was supplied by local farms, but on a smaller scale owing to its greater isolation. Affectionately remembered are Mr. Grieve, who brought green apples in his car and sold them by the box, and Bob Woods from Mission Hill, who delivered fresh milk.

Camp residents aimed for self-sufficiency in the Depression years, and many planted fruit trees and cleared enough land for flower and vegetable gardens in this fire-devastated region. "Lots of people had chickens out the back," recalled Frank Davison, "and lots had little vegetable gardens and grew vegetables." In true Homeguard fashion, two men at the camp, Norman Janes and Drew Berkeley, put up small garage-like barns fifty or sixty feet behind their houses for their cows and chickens. Pear trees and Russet apple trees, as well as foxgloves and introduced vines, still thrive at the overgrown site of the camp. Big Jack McKenzie Jr. planted foxglove from seeds provided by his wife, Ella Hawkins from Comox. Their daughter Myrtle Heron thought her mother might also have planted the Scotch broom that still flourishes at the camp. "She was great for planting all kinds of things."

⁓

For the unmarried men of Camp 3, "room" meant a bunkhouse and "board" meant the cookhouse, which offered substantial breakfasts, box lunches, and dinners for a dollar a day in the 1930s. "The bunkhouse fellows, when they came in on a crummy, all they were interested in was the cookhouse," said Jimmy Weir, who lived at the camp from 1926 to 1928. "You'd see them on the cookhouse steps waiting for the cookhouse to open. They just sat and waited. But they earned it and they were big eaters, the fallers and buckers."

For many newcomers from Europe, the Camp 3 cookhouse was a place to learn basic English. Hi Churchill remembered Croatians who couldn't speak enough English to ask their neighbours to pass the food,

Miss Bernadette MacAulay's first class, Camp 3, 1930. Top row, left to right: Bernice Baker, Frank Davison, Cecil "Buster" Yates, Fred Manson, Georgia Ployart, Miss MacAulay, Vera Miner, George "Pat" Cliffe, Jim Miner, Thelma Miner. Middle row, left to right: Ruby Woodruff, Pauline Downey, Beverly Flawse, Bernice Berkeley, Beryl Berkeley, Jean Marsden, Lois Janes, Bobbe Baker, Myrtle McKenzie. Front row: George Yates, Eugene Helm, Jack Downey Jr., Elmer Helm, Fred Yates. After this photo was taken, Frank Davison went home to his mother and said, "I know I took a good picture, Mum." "How do you know that?" she asked. "Because I was standing right next to Bernice Baker!" he said. The camp school closed in 1941. Walter Montgomery photo.—DICK DOWNEY

Bernice Baker (aged five) and Bobbe Baker (aged one), in front of the Bakers' house, Camp 3, c. 1926. Notice the hops growing against the house for shade.—BERNICE JAMES

Bernice Baker sitting on the well in front of the Bakers' brand-new house at Camp 3, *c.* 1925. When he was five or six years old, Pat Cliffe said to Bernice Baker, "I don't think I can ever marry you." Bernice asked, "Why not?" and Pat said, "Because your dad's a Liberal and mine's a Conservative."—BERNICE JAMES

Evelyn Blackburn (at right) with a friend on a Douglas fir stump outside the Blackburn house at Camp 3, *c.* 1923, with fire-scorched snags behind. Myrtle Heron (*née* McKenzie) recalled the "broken stump" in the schoolyard at Camp 3. She fell on it, gashing her hand badly, and her mother rushed her to Dr. Briggs in Courtenay, but all he did was put a tape on it. She still has the scar on her hand.—EVELYN HARDY AND FRED BLACKBURN

Wilma McKenzie, daughter of Bill McKenzie and Rose Baikie, on a snowy day at Camp 3, *c.* 1933, with the McKenzie house behind.—NANCY BROWN

Bert (Albert) Woodruff (left), locie fireman, and John "Shorty" Miner, locie engineer, in the cab of the Seven-Spot, 1938. Shorty Miner was a good-natured man who always played Santa at the Camp 3 Christmas concerts. Born in Plattsburgh, New York, Miner grew up in Missouri and moved to British Columbia before the First World War. He worked in Vancouver and Ladysmith (where he met and married a granddaughter of Chief Capilano) before becoming a steam shovel operator in the early days of Comox Logging. Bob Filberg photo.—FILBERG LODGE & PARK ASSOCIATION

The steam-heated bunkhouses for single men at Camp 3, c. 1929, looking north. This photo was taken for his family in Germany by a young German faller named Otto Richter. "The bunkhouses were an improvement on the old wood stove eight-man buildings but with twenty men in each wing there wasn't much privacy, especially if you had some heavy snorers in the crowd," wrote Wallace Baikie. The bunkhouses were off limits to children.—ELEANOR KELLER

Robert Stonehouse Baker of Camp 3, also known as "Bud" or "Bob." Born in 1898 at Brechin, Nanaimo, the son of a farmer who had worked for Henry "Squire" Bullock on Saltspring Island, Bud Baker grew up in Nanaimo and Cumberland. His best friend Joe Cliffe got him a job as a high rigger with Comox Logging in 1918, and a few years later he got his engineer's ticket. He worked as a fireman and as an engineer on locies and cold deckers. Bob Filberg photo.—FILBERG LODGE & PARK ASSOCIATION

Car-knocker Joe Sampson next to his little shack at Black Creek, c. 1925.—JACK TUKHAM

Brakeman Reg Churchill at Camp 3, c. 1928. Churchill came west with his mother and brothers from Yarmouth, Nova Scotia, after his father's death in the 1919 flu epidemic. He worked in the woods, as a brakeman at Comox Lake, and later moved to Cranbrook.—WALLY CHURCHILL

141

"so they just ate whatever they could grab. Slowly they learned to say 'Pass the . . .' and they gradually got enough to eat."

For breakfast, Jimmy Weir recalled, the Chinese cooks specialized in a stack of pancakes with two fried eggs slapped between each pancake. For lunch, they prepared the huge sandwiches which junior members of the skidder crews carried to work. Many men didn't like the company's policy of hiring Chinese workers, but Jack McQuinn was very fussy and he wanted the best cooks, who tended to be Chinese. When the camps closed these workers went to Vancouver. At Christmas, according to one foreman's descendant, "Jack would send them some of his own money as an advance." When the cooks returned from the winter layoff, they brought presents for the bosses' children—on one occasion a crate of firecrackers for the boys. Children loved their great big sugar cookies.

Dick Bailey (who worked as chaser and head loader) and his wife Eva recalled that the quality of life at the camp was "marvellous" owing to the nearby resources of the surrounding logged-off and burned-over country. In the Depression era people at the camp were self-sufficient. Unlike Headquarters, the camp had few year-round occupations, and people relied more on the blackberries, deer, and grouse that proliferated along with fireweed in the clear-cuts.

Originally, residents paid six dollars rent per month to the company, but this was raised to fifteen dollars when electricity reached the camp in about 1935. Rent included free firewood and Douglas fir bark from the skidder settings. Dick Bailey recalled that the section crews would gather the bark up and stack five or six feet of it on a flatcar, then dump it in front of the Camp 3 houses. "They used to roll in a three-foot sawlog and a load of bark every fall," said Wallace Churchill (born 1929), a boy at the camp in the 1930s, "and the guy would come with the Wee McGregor. The sawlog would be a real peeler. The guy with the old McGregor sawed it into blocks and he'd even wedge it, and then I had to split it and stack it in the woodshed." Bark burned splendidly in the simple kitchen wood stoves that heated the camp's houses, but the stoves lacked temperature gauges, "so you'd put your hand in the oven to see if the heat was OK," said Eva Bailey.

≈

Most men at Camp 3 were involved directly with logging or the railway. There were only a few white-collar jobs, the most important being surveyor, timekeeper, and scaler.

Hughie Stevens and Tony Turner, based at Headquarters, were the surveyors. Stevens' disgruntled assistant at Camp 3 between 1922 and 1927 was Wallace Baikie, who was piqued because he had to perform many unrelated tasks, some of them quite mundane. In addition to his official job as surveyor's assistant, Baikie also worked as scaler, cruiser, grass seeder, painter, and overseer of the tie-cutting and telephone pole operations. He also found time to run an illegal trapline on Black Creek with scaler Alec Tilleard of Camp 2. "Tilleard supplied the traps, I looked after my area and he took my skins. This was all done on the quiet." In the fall of 1922 Baikie made sixty dollars from the trapline.

Timekeepers at Camp 3 kept track of employees' working hours and notified Tukham and McIver at Headquarters, who then issued monthly cheques. Eugene Croteau, Eric Flinton, and Jimmy Sheasgreen (the last another of Filberg's proteges) worked as Camp 3 timekeepers over the years.

Scalers measured the amount of timber that the fallers and buckers cut in the woods. They calculated by the thousand feet and added up the totals at day's end. One scaler was John Pritchard (1891–1972), a son of early logger Archie Pritchard and formerly a faller. John Pritchard lived on his family farm on what is now Pritchard Road, Comox, and commuted to Camp 3. A typically versatile Homeguard, he raised cattle and grew hay, and was adept at splitting cedar, shaking roofs, making fences, cutting glass for windows, and plumbing. He was also in demand as a digger of wells. "He had lots of capacities," said his nephew Allan Pritchard. Other scalers at the camp included Wallace Baikie, Norman Parkin, and Eric Flinton.

~

A fatal accident took place near Camp 3 in August 1920. The Four-Spot's boiler blew up and landed six car lengths down the track. Engineer Sam Willoughby and fireman Frank Davison (born 1899) were killed but the brakeman, Wilbur Watson, survived. The story goes that Davison was counting ten-dollar bills at the time of the explosion, and people were picking up bills like confetti as they rained from the sky. Joe Cliffe described the scene in a later article: "It was about nine in the morning after the July 1st celebrations. No. 4 had just succeeded in pulling a string of empty cars up a long 3% grade, and as the engine levelled out at the top of the grade, the water on the top of the fire box suddenly became less than normal causing the boiler water to vapourize completely, causing the rivets in the boiler to all let go, causing a terrible explosion. The writer [i.e., Joe himself] visited the site of the accident a few hours later. The explosion was terrible, tearing the boiler plate into shreds like paper. The boiler was blown about seventy feet straight down the track landing on its front end between the rails. The cab was blown to shreds and the wheels stayed on the track at the site of the explosion. The locomotive was burning coal, the heavy grates were broken in many pieces and driven into the ties and road bed. The power of steam was well displayed."
—FILBERG LODGE & PARK ASSOCIATION, BOB BERKELEY DONATION

Railway construction and maintenance was a large part of Comox Logging's operation, and Camp 3 was home to a grading crew. An Italian named George Padula was grading foreman, and the resident shovel operator was Tom McQuillan. Also attached to the camp were section gangs who maintained the company's northern tracks and kept them in repair. Bill Eastman's bridge-building crew, who worked in tandem with the grading crew, also stayed at the camp for long periods.

Camp 3 boasted a large contingent of railway personnel, necessary because Comox Logging had up to half a dozen engines running at any time as far north as Quinsam River. Camp 3 remained the railway base for these distant operations until its closure in 1942. Locie engineers resident at the camp before that date included Bernard Churchill, Joe Ducca, Johnny McLoughlin, John "Shorty" Miner, Fred Smith, Len Spencer, Sam Willoughby, and Bert Woodruff. Bud Baker, Frank Davison, and John Miner (Shorty's son) worked as firemen. Brakemen who lived at the camp included Reg Churchill, Martin "Pidgy" Davison, Dick Delin, and Wilbur Watson. They operated the company's switch trains rather than the Headquarters-based main-line locie.

Connected to Camp 3 was a shack at the Black Creek siding where, in 1924, car-knocker Joe Sampson and his helper Albert Phye repaired and greased flatcars. If something was wrong with a flatcar, or if it needed oiling, the brakeman wrote the problem on the side of the car with chalk and left it at a siding for the car-knocker to fix. Cars with serious problems were taken to Headquarters for repair. Sampson, who had albino colouring, lived in a shack with a barrel to catch the rainwater. "Mostly he worked at a siding someplace," Hi Churchill said. "He had a little shack with material in it for repairing things." By the 1930s Phye had taken over from Sampson.

~

Other professions related directly to falling and skidder logging. Blacksmiths at Camp 3 included Bert Mansfield, Hughie McKenzie, and Jake Roloff, whose helper was a German named T. F. Tinga. They forged such items as tongs and made minor repairs to logging and railway equipment. Sawfiler for much of the camp's existence was Jabe (Jabez) Day, formerly a bucker, who like Baikie and Tilleard kept a winter trapline along Black Creek. Among the camp's fallers in 1924 were Austin Blackburn, Lin Hunt, Fred Manson, Les Marshall, and two sets of brothers, Charlie and Olson Widen and Bill and Sid Woods.

Most of the married men's houses at Camp 3 were inhabited by the crews of the two skidders (Skidder 5 and Skidder 6) attached to Camp 3—some fifty men in all—or by the six- or seven-man cold decker crews. Prominent on these logging crews were members of the Comox Homeguard, especially the Berkeley, Cliffe, Grant, Janes, and McKenzie families, who were considered typical of this woods elite. Skidder and yarder engineers Connie (Colin) Aitken, Dave Aitken, Bud Baker, George Cliffe, Ray Dawson, Reid Good, Arthur "Butch" Grant, Mack Grant, Clifford Janes, Bill McKenzie, and Bob Piercy lived at the camp, as did head riggers Drew Berkeley, Jack Downey, Norman "Mary" Janes, and Big Jack McKenzie Jr. Married men's houses at Camp 3 were also rented by riggers Eddy Boyd, Ronnie Muir, Fritz Passman, and George

Courtney Ingram, Blacksmith and Car-Knocker

Born in Devon, England, in 1892, Courtney Ingram trained as a blacksmith before immigrating to Canada in 1913. He worked for his blacksmith uncle in Alberta before coming to British Columbia the following year to work on the construction of the Vedder Canal near Chilliwack. After that, he worked briefly as a blacksmith for a logging company near Powell River before joining the Royal Canadian Horse Artillery in 1914. He spent four years on the Western Front, seeing action at the Second Battle of Ypres and at the Somme, and was twice wounded and badly gassed.

After the war, he returned to British Columbia and to Stokes Logging near Powell River before joining Comox Logging in about 1920. Soon afterwards he married Lucy Davis, from the large Davis family of Union Bay. After working as a blacksmith he was made a car-knocker at Oyster River, fixing skeleton cars and doing minor repairs to all running stock. Four years in the trenches of Flanders and northern France had left him partly deaf, and he walked with a limp from a leg wound.

In the early 1930s, when he was ten, Bill Hembroff spent a couple of days with his "Uncle Court" in his spartan but comfortable little cabin on the main line at the edge of the Oyster River, several miles north of Camp 3. One of Courtney's tasks was to pump water up into a water tower for Comox Logging's engines. He usually pumped the water at night. He took Bill out picking blackberries on nearby ground "that had just been logged off a couple of years before."

Courtney Ingram was later transferred to Comox Lake and Ladysmith, where he retired. He died in 1977.

Leaving Camp 3

The company charged $1.00 a day for room and board at the Camp 3 bunkhouses, and some Swedish employees opted to buy small farms in nearby Merville and commute to work. Gunnar Jonsson, for example, arrived from Sweden in 1930 and worked as a rigger for $4.00 a day, but wages went as low as $2.50 a day in the Depression, and "if you stayed in the bunkhouse they charged a dollar a day with grub and all." After a few months in the bunkhouse, Jonsson bought some land in Merville and married a neighbour's daughter (Jennie Goodsell) soon afterwards:

I worked for fourteen years altogether with Comox Logging out of Camp 3, but I didn't live there. I bought a place on Kitty Coleman Road—after World War I they divided up the area and sold it because they wanted to get the returned men out of the cities, Vancouver and Victoria, and into the country. At first I was in a bunkhouse in Camp 3 for a few months, and then Mrs. Patterson at Kitty Coleman took me in for several months. In this time, thirty-one acres at Coleman Road came for sale for three hundred dollars! . . . I had twenty years to pay for it. This was 1931.

The house had burned down; the bed springs were still laying there in a heap, and there was only an eighteen-by-twenty chicken house with a wire front. I wanted to build a house, but the fellows said, "Why don't you fix up the chicken house? You could shingle it, put in some windows and a floor." So I did it, and when I got married I lived there for the first two or three years. I met my wife living next door. This was sixty-three years ago!

Super; by head loaders Dick Bailey, Ernie Collins, Wilfred "Skinny" Collins, Eric Gray, Aly (Aloyleus) Helm, and Jack Mitchell; and by hookers Nick Helm and Anselm "Hooker" Johnson. Also, Camp 3 was the base of a rigging crew known as the "flying corps." In the early 1920s it was led by Norman Janes and Jack Downey, but Drew Berkeley (1896–1942) took over when Janes and Downey were assigned as head riggers to Skidders 5 and 6. Other members of the rig-up donkey included, at different times, Joe Cliffe, Bob "Scratchy" Grant, John Marsden, Dave Pattison, and Slats Robertson.

Between the wars, Camps 1, 2, and 3 provided loggers with a community and social domain, places with family houses and schools on the southern edge of unlogged territory. The company also provided perks like the loggers' sports at Oyster River and the summer resort at Williams Beach. For married men, these remote logging camps offered an alternative to solitary bunkhouse life, and the presence of women and children probably made these communities more pleasant. But primarily these portable outer camps were highly effective work stations for achieving a radical change in the Vancouver Island landscape: the removal of 60,000 acres of Douglas fir forest covering Blocks 25 to 29 between the Tsolum River and Campbell Lake.

Comox Logging's skilled work crews logged this region by means of a well-rehearsed procedure. First to the enter the forest and lay the groundwork for logging were the cruisers, surveyors, grading crews, and steel gangs.

One of the Americans to start working for Comox Logging before 1920 was Jack "Greasy" McQuinn, skidder expert and later foreman at Camp 3. "By God, they were loggers!" recalled Jack Beadnell of Americans like McQuinn. His men had great respect for him because he had come up through the ranks. He was known as a great storyteller, "prone to exaggerating a good story to make it better," as his grandson Thomas O'Brennan wrote. Once, while walking along a log to work, McQuinn saw a bear at the other end of the log. He kept walking until the bear wisely stepped off the log. "Grandpa tipped his hat and said, 'Good morning,' and went on his way." This photo was taken by Bob Filberg on the Comox golf course in 1943.—FILBERG LODGE & PARK ASSOCIATION

145

chapter 7

Preparing the Ground

We often started at five or six o'clock in the morning and seldom finished before the summer dusk was making work difficult. We struggled through undergrowth where bushes and ferns were in some cases as high as our heads.

—HUGH KEENLEYSIDE,
timber cruiser

IMAGINE A STRETCH OF COUNTRY THAT HAD NEVER BEEN logged: a continuous old-growth forest interrupted only by streams, swamps, and the occasional hunting trail or cart track. Comox Logging's magnificent property—this "logger's Eden" north of Courtenay, carved from the 1884 Dunsmuir land grant—was one such place.

"The road up from Comox," wrote Campbell River historian Helen Mitchell, "was little more than a widened trail, a long exhausting day's ride by horse and buggy. In those days travellers sometimes broke the journey half way with an overnight stop at Walter Woodhus' roadhouse at Salmon Point. There was no bridge over the Oyster River; pedestrians crossed by means of a hewn log, while horse-drawn vehicles forded the stream at its shallowest point."

This wilderness soon changed dramatically. In the 1920s and 1930s, with impressive efficiency, Comox Logging systematically cut its 60,000 acres of timber (Blocks 24 through 29) between the Tsolum and Quinsam rivers. But logging did not just happen: much painstaking preparation came first, sometimes years in advance of the time trees actually began to fall.

The first Comox Logging representatives to enter a block were the timber cruisers, who determined the character of the timber and assessed its total value. By custom they divided the company's property into 160-acre squares called "forties"—so called because each forty measured forty by forty chains. (A chain was a linked metal surveying instrument sixty-six feet in length.) They ran four "cruise lines" through each forty which enabled them to assess about twenty per cent of all the trees.

They then produced a cruise map of their survey, 400 feet to the inch and with 25-foot contours. The map showed swamps and ridges; indicated whether the block was well or poorly timbered; and specified various features of the trees, including their age, size, and frequency of

A section of the road to Campbell River, Oyster River area, c. 1912. Walter Gage photo.—COURTENAY & DISTRICT MUSEUM & ARCHIVES, D6386

Making fortunes in timber: timber cruiser Eustace Smith (left) with Bob Filberg, c. 1935.
—FILBERG LODGE & PARK ASSOCIATION

Eustace Smith, Timber Cruiser

The Comox Valley produced British Columbia's best-known timber cruiser of the first half of the twentieth century.

Born in England in 1876, Eustace Smith came to Black Creek when he was eleven and was put to work right away cutting shingles by hand at his older brother Horace's stump ranch. He married Letitia Mathers in 1900 and took up land in Beaver Cove. To support his family, Smith worked as a handlogger in Mackenzie Sound, Alert Bay, and Port Neville. In 1905, after an infant son and daughter died, he and his wife abandoned the farm and moved to Vancouver. There Eustace set up as a timber cruiser, with his offices in the Standard Bank building.

"There's hardly a piece of timber on the coast that I can't tell you something about," Eustace Smith claimed in 1948. His signature was a ten-inch-high S blazed into the corner trees on each lot or block he surveyed. "You could always tell his corner posts by an S about a foot high," Tony Turner said. "He had a little pocket axe, a hatchet, and he whipped it out, and whip-whip-whip"—he had made his mark.

Eustace later claimed that his knowledgeable advice made many fortunes in the British Columbia lumber industry. He died in Vancouver in 1964.

snags, dead tops, butt rot, and other defects. Listed on the side of every map was the forty's estimated total quantity of timber, along with the amount for each species, measured by feet board measure (FBM).

"If the cruisers were any good they did a good job of the contour map," said retired surveyor Tony Turner. Cruise map information was used by company managers in deciding when a property should be cut: for example, if it contained a good deal of cedar, and the market price of cedar was low, they might decide to postpone cutting until the price had improved.

In 1948, timber cruiser Eustace Smith described his training and methods as follows:

Setting up camp at the area to be cruised is the first step. Then a control point is established, usually a surveyed corner post of the property. The cruiser must know timber. To hold down a job of this sort it is helpful to have had initial training as a scaler in the woods. This gets his mind set on sizes and qualities—two of the most important items on the report sheet. Accessibility of the logging ground is shown by the contour maps and is a vital part of the cruiser's work.

The essential knowledge of a timber cruiser may be summarized as follows: before qualifying he must join a crew, first as compassman whose duties are to carry the compass and measure the distances in chains along a base line. He learns to mark a point every ten chains with a picket. He has to run a true line from the starting point to the boundary of the area being cruised using a base line as a check on the accuracy of his courses and measurements.

When the cruise is finished, the report should form the preliminary plan of operation, well conceived and detailed; very different from an early cruiser's partly intuitive assessment. Consequently today's cruiser takes more responsibility. Instead of "I guess this tract will cut out six million feet," his statement may read "I feel I can recommend the purchase as a safe investment."

Comox Logging also hired Vancouver partners Hal Gardiner and Ted Nairn for timber cruising. Together they cruised nearly all of Comox Logging's E & N lands in the Comox Valley, Ladysmith, and Nanaimo Lakes areas. "They were an interesting couple of guys," Tony Turner recalled. Eccentrically, for their evening tent work they preferred "a six-candle candelabra—six candles in a stick in a row—and refused to use a Coleman lantern which would have been a hundred per cent better." Despite this, Turner said, "their cruise maps were very good, very accurate—their contours were bang on."

After the cruisers finished their work, they passed along their maps and calculations to the company's logging engineers, based at Headquarters. These men (loosely known as "surveyors") planned in advance the whole logging operation.

Although they based their maps on the timber cruisers' maps, the surveyors also did much detailed field work of their own, chopping brush and traversing swamps, creeks, and ridges. They determined the logging railway's best route through the forest and around natural features like rivers, swamps, or hills; and they found the best locations for bridges and skidder settings.

The setting was the basic unit of skidder logging: the stage upon which it took place. It comprised a block of timber fifty to eighty acres in size and straddling a railway spur line. Settings did not correspond to the cruisers' forties, which simply gave the engineers an idea of where the good timber was. Surveyors determined the size and shape of settings based on a number of considerations, including topography, the yarding capacity of the skidder, and property boundaries.

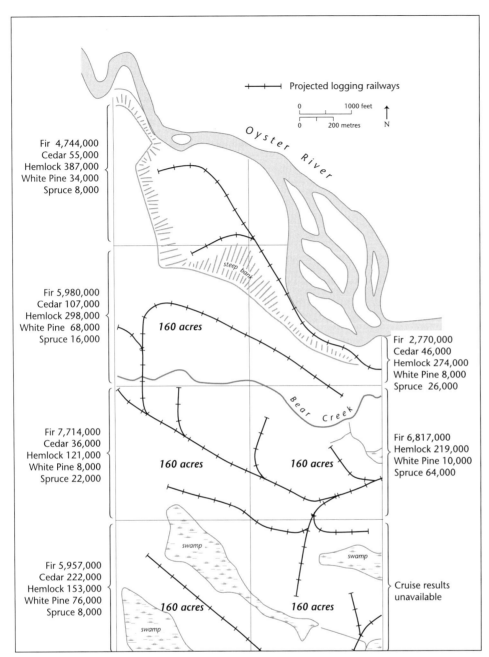

0   1000 feet
0   200 metres
N

Oyster River

Fir 4,744,000
Cedar 55,000
Hemlock 387,000
White Pine 34,000
Spruce 8,000

steep bank

Fir 5,980,000
Cedar 107,000
Hemlock 298,000
White Pine 68,000
Spruce 16,000

160 acres

Fir 2,770,000
Cedar 46,000
Hemlock 274,000
White Pine 8,000
Spruce 26,000

Bear Creek

Fir 7,714,000
Cedar 36,000
Hemlock 121,000
White Pine 8,000
Spruce 22,000

160 acres

160 acres

Fir 6,817,000
Hemlock 219,000
White Pine 10,000
Spruce 64,000

Fir 5,957,000
Cedar 222,000
Hemlock 153,000
White Pine 76,000
Spruce 8,000

swamp

swamp

160 acres

160 acres

swamp

Cruise results
unavailable

Comox Logging map of timber cruise results and projected railways, Oyster River, c. 1921, redrawn from a map at the TimberWest office, Courtenay. Douglas fir comprised at least ninety per cent of the original forest in Comox District.

Hughie Stevens and five assistants built these cabins on ▶
Cariboo (Woodhus) Creek in 1924, as Comox Logging
prepared to log Block 28 on the far side of Oyster River. "We
decided to build a cabin in the centre of the block," Wallace
Baikie recalled. "This we did. We cut poles and split shakes
for the walls, roof, and floors, and made bunks out of the
same material. The only things we had to pack in were the
nails, cookstove, stove pipe, and cooking utensils. . . . The
cabin was built on Cariboo Creek, so we were close to fresh
water, and in a stand of tall fir timber." Mack Laing photo,
1925.—BRITISH COLUMBIA ARCHIVES, I-51806

The view here was owned outright by Comox Logging. Shown is the Black Creek bridge on what is now the Island Highway between Courtenay and Campbell River, 1918. Davey Janes recalled that "it was like looking down a hole in the timber." This tunnel-like road wound through the old-growth forest of Block 29. By 1938 this forest had been converted to slash, snags, and saplings.—COURTENAY & DISTRICT MUSEUM & ARCHIVES, D-638c

Every setting was divided into four quarters. With an axe, the surveyors blazed a line of trees around the setting and between each quarter so that the fallers would recognize their quarters and know where to cut. "What took the most time was chopping out the cross-section lines," recalled former engineer Tony Turner. The surveyors also marked several spar trees in each setting with a double cut in the shape of a cross, so that the fallers would leave them. These spar trees were vital for skidder cables and rigging—vital, in other words, for aerial logging.

Comox Logging's engineers were, consecutively, Charlie Armstrong, Bob Filberg, Hughie Stevens, Johnny Duncan, and Tony Turner. They had their own office and a privileged, professional position in the company. They also tended to be keen sportsmen, taking advantage of the abundant game in the regions slated for logging. Johnny Duncan, for example, taught Tony Turner the art of fly fishing in the Oyster River—world famous for its salmon and steelhead.

A young man from Denman Island named Wallace Baikie got his first job with Comox Logging in the fall of 1920 as axeman on the survey crew. He helped Hughie Stevens lay out railway grades in Comox Logging's Block 28 beyond the Oyster River, as recorded in his recollections:

> H. E. Stevens and his helper Alec Tilleard had been the survey crew before I was taken on as an axeman. My salary was seventy-five dollars a month, and my board. We worked six days a week and in all weather but we had a certain amount of office work, plotting and drafting etc. which we could do on the stormy days. My job as axeman was that I had to be the head man, out in front, keeping on line and doing a lot of axe work. Stevens used a staff compass mostly. He used only a transit and large level on bridge work. For woods work, a compass and a hand level was all that was needed on logging grades. Stevens' theory was that, what possible difference does it make after running a mile or so of survey line, if you are out five or six feet either way; or after running hand levels over that same distance if you have an error of one foot up or down. What difference does it make to a temporary grade or branch line; you are not going to get any more or cheaper logs. I have seen the grading foreman with Stevens' OK, swing a grade a few feet to miss a row of big stumps just to save powder and work. As long as it was gradual, the loci and cars would run just the same.
>
> A three man crew can run a lot of line in a day, particularly if they have a good axeman. The secret is to keep on line and not to wander off line cutting down trees and brush unnecessarily. The axeman has to brave the crabapple swamps and wade around in a foot of water (just part of the job). In those days we wore Stanfield underwear, usually woolen pants and a mackinaw coat. Stevens wore a cruiser jacket and cruiser boots. I just wore ordinary logger boots, and made no attempts to keep my feet dry.

After their field work was completed, the surveyors produced their own 400:1 topographic maps on heavy brown paper three feet wide, using a T-square and protractor. From the maps they prepared a master plan showing the logging railway, skidder setting numbers, branch line numbers, and other features. They laid out railways about 2000 feet apart to accommodate the Lidgerwood skidders' 1100-foot cable length. The engineers then prepared two tracings of the plan in different colours: one for the grade foreman and one for the logging foreman. The area was now ready for the grading crew and steel gang.

≈

The grading crew, mostly recent arrivals from Europe, had the most physically demanding work in a largely manual profession. Their job was to clear the railway right-of-way sixty to eighty feet wide. This

The Contents of Eustace Smith's Pack

In 1948, still working at the age of seventy-two, timber cruiser Eustace Smith had completed about six hundred surveys on the coast and in the interior of British Columbia. He told a reporter from *Forest and Mill* that he carried a tent, fly, axe, aluminum cooking utensils, a sleeping bag, and "a balanced diet of good staple food" for his cruising camp:

Eustace Smith gives an example of what can be accomplished in the culinary arts. Preparing for a cruise he takes sufficient for a two- or three-week stretch. With the aid of a reflector he makes his own bread, and carries side bacon, dried beans and fruit, powdered milk, rice, rolled oats, butter in cans, jam, tea, coffee, flour and baking soda. Much of this food, small in original content, bulks up when prepared. His equipment includes light fishing tackle but he rarely carries a gun. Not only does it interfere with his work but the steel affects the accuracy of the compass.

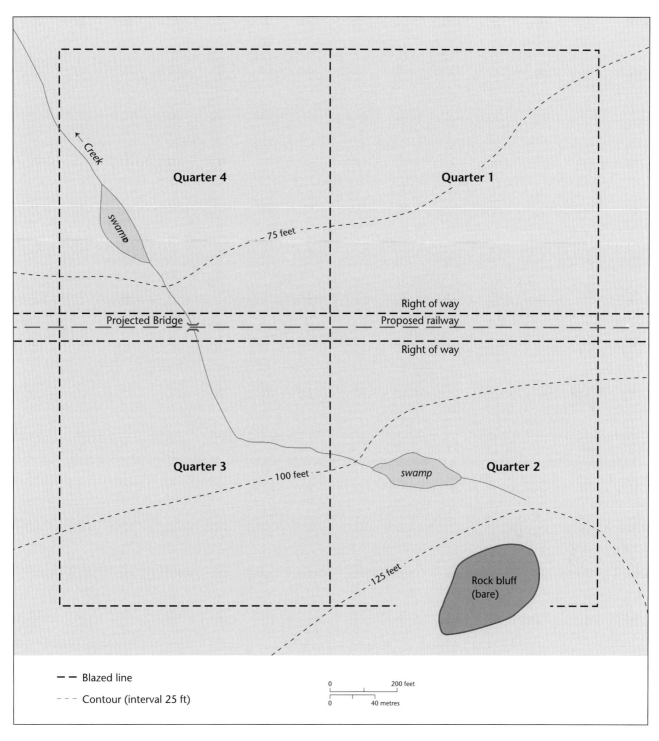

Quarter 4

Quarter 1

Creek

swamp

75 feet

Right of way

Projected Bridge

Proposed railway

Right of way

Quarter 3

Quarter 2

100 feet

swamp

125 feet

Rock bluff
(bare)

— — Blazed line

- - - Contour (interval 25 ft)

0   200 feet

0   40 metres

A basic skidder setting, showing blazed sixteen-acre quarters and railway right-of-way.

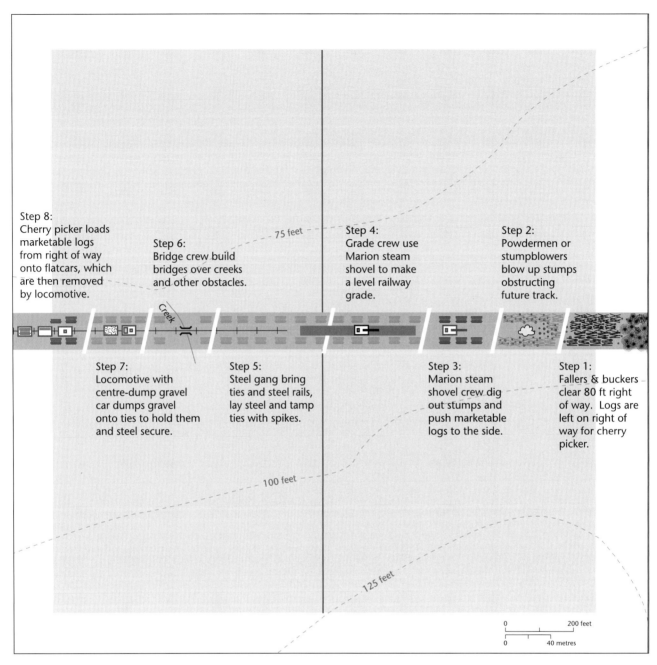

Step 8:
Cherry picker loads marketable logs from right of way onto flatcars, which are then removed by locomotive.

Step 6:
Bridge crew build bridges over creeks and other obstacles.

75 feet

Step 4:
Grade crew use Marion steam shovel to make a level railway grade.

Step 2:
Powdermen or stumpblowers blow up stumps obstructing future track.

Creek

Step 7:
Locomotive with centre-dump gravel car dumps gravel onto ties to hold them and steel secure.

Step 5:
Steel gang bring ties and steel rails, lay steel and tamp ties with spikes.

Step 3:
Marion steam shovel crew dig out stumps and push marketable logs to the side.

Step 1:
Fallers & buckers clear 80 ft right of way. Logs are left on right of way for cherry picker.

100 feet

125 feet

| 0 | | 200 feet |
| 0 | | 40 metres |

Building a logging railway into a skidder setting.

Hughie Stevens, Surveyor

Hughie Stevens was born in Maidenhead, England, in 1884, and came to Canada as a boy. He grew up at Rat Portage at the head of Lake Ontario, and he and his brother both worked as engineers on the Kettle Valley line of the CPR. Hughie left there because, he told a friend, "someone had more letters after his name than I." He worked briefly for the City of Courtenay before Comox Logging hired him as chief engineer in 1919. "Comox Logging was all railroad then so it was logical that they'd hire Stevens," Bruce King said.

"Bob Filberg had been engineer before he got the superintendent job," Stevens' chainman Wallace Baikie wrote, "and although Bob was the best man for running an outfit, Stevens was the best engineer especially for getting out plans and maps." Like all surveyors, Stevens had a distinctive corner post blaze: a dollar sign (the $ was a clever combination of an H and an S).

Stevens, according to Baikie, was "noted for being an authority on almost any subject. . . . Hughie Stevens was a very capable person but could become overbearing to some people. He and I got along very well because I had gotten used to him always knowing more than I did. Tilleard and Drewery when they were on the crew, resented being outclassed in every conversation. These two hung a title on the boss. They called him H. E. Bloody Stevens I.K.E. (I know everything)."

Hughie Stevens was transferred in 1936 to become Comox Logging's chief engineer of the new Ladysmith division. He retired in 1951, and died in 1957.

Hughie Stevens and his transit, c. 1938. Bob Filberg photo.
—FILBERG LODGE & PARK ASSOCIATION

advance crew of about twenty-five men had many skills: their ranks included fallers and buckers as well as powdermen, who blew the stumps from the right-of-way. At first, the grading crew graded and levelled with picks, shovels, wheelbarrows, and blasting powder, as Bob Filberg recalled. "There were no [steam] shovels; no power equipment was used at all. Horses weren't even used in the construction of railroads."

In 1920 a Swede named John Nylander was in charge of a grading crew in Block 28 beyond Oyster River, as Wallace Baikie recorded: "John Nylander was the grading foreman and he and his eleven man crew were on contract, all hand grading, and the contract price was thirty-five dollars per one hundred feet. For that price they would have to fall and buck, blow the stumps and grade three hundred feet a day, to earn eight dollars per day per man, less the cost of the powder. They were all Swedes and hard workers, snoose chewers and big eaters."

Grading became easier in the mid-1920s when Comox Logging bought two electric-powered Marion shovels. These were manned by Ernie Cowie, Tom McQuillan, Arthur "Spit" Quinn, Pinky Davis, Davey Janes, and Bill Wilson. Mat-hookers (swampers) included Bill Nairn, Malcolm Carwithen, and Mose (Moses) Quinn. Foreman of the grading crew in the 1930s was Jimmy Sheasgreen, and Charlie Olson was the resident expert on Marion shovel repair.

The grading crew produced a "felled right-of-way": a graded path through the forest ready for the steel gang to come in with wooden ties, steel rails, and finally gravel. The ties and rails were recycled, taken up from logged-out spur lines.

The culturally diverse steel gang was known as the "League of Nations." Twenty-three-year-old Henry Schulz, a Mennonite from Black Creek, had this to say about the crew:

We picked up railway steel from old tracks or put down steel on new tracks. After a fair length of track was laid, we had to tamp gravel under the cross ties with short handled shovels. The pay at that time was three dollars per day. A full crew consisted of twenty-two men. The crew was an assortment of nationalities. There was a runaway husband from Italy, a Finnish bootlegger from Vancouver, a horse trader from Yugoslavia, an estate manager from Germany, a farmer from Alberta, a man who had worked in a shoe factory in Ontario, as well as an Englishman with only one eye. One man said he came from Russia, but he couldn't speak Russian worth a hoot. There were also some genuine railway men. I had often sweated while working, but never as hard as I sweated when I worked on the steel gang. It was not because the boss was urging the men to work so hard—it was the men themselves who were pushing for fear they might lose their job. They meant to keep up, or exceed the next man. It was nothing unusual to see several men fired in one day and for no obvious reason.

Neil Brady-Browne, who worked on a steel gang lifting ties on the north branch of the Tsolum, recalled that the steel gang was a proving ground. If new people made an impression for their hard work, they might be selected for the skidder crew. Often, the woods foreman would lurk in the forest watching to see which men were working hard. If you "passed the grade" you'd be selected for another job, but it helped to have an "in"—which often meant having a Homeguard connection.

～

Bridges were essential to railway logging. "With a railroad show it has to be level," said Ron Bowen. Logging locies could handle a gradient of no more than five per cent, which meant that the grade had to follow the contours where possible. Rivers, creeks, and gulleys all had to be bridged.

By the time the bridge-builders arrived, the steel gang had laid the rails right to the start of the bridge site to allow the transport of steam donkeys and other heavy bridge-building equipment. As Baikie described:

> Bill Eastman and his bridge building crew, including Tim Paterson, made periodic stays at the different camps when there was something to build. . . . Bill was with the Comox Logging when I started with the company in 1920. Bill's job was pile driver and bridge building superintendent. He usually had six men on his crew; Joe Cliffe, Dunc Thompson, Lyle McKenzie, and Tim Paterson worked for him. They had to be good men and were the highest paid men on the claim. I remember when they were getting one dollar an hour back in the 20s. That was good pay. Bill was a hard boss, but the men respected him. I don't know how many years he worked for the Comox Logging Company but he must have built miles of trestles and bridges; at least three bridges across the Oyster, and they rebuilt the trestles and log dump at Royston several times.

Eastman, according to Ron Bowen, was a "professional bridge man" from Ontario who had worked his way west with a transcontinental railway. When bridge builders like Eastman reached the Vancouver terminus they often found work on the coast with railway logging shows. "At that time," Bowen said, "the bridge men were pretty well all from Vancouver—they'd worked on the CPR and CNR across Canada. . . . All the logging camps of any size had trains, and they all needed bridge crews to build logging railroad bridges." Eastman's bridge crew included an interesting assortment of local men: Joe Cliffe was a Homeguard and well-known rigger; Dunc Thompson was a Nanaimo coal miner's son later known as "Boomstick Thompson"; and Lyle McKenzie of Courtenay was a nephew of Comox Logging blacksmith Hughie McKenzie.

"All you had to do with Bill Eastman or Dunc Thompson," surveyor Tony Turner recalled, "was point and say, 'there's where we want [the bridge] to be' and they'd fell timber and yard them in there. They didn't square their timber: they peeled the log first and then flattened the top with an adze. After peeling, they took a string covered with lamp-black and made a straight line down the tree and hewed to that line. On the bridges they used only two such timbers and put the ties right on top."

~

The final step before falling was to send a cherry picker along the newly opened logging railway. The cherry picker was a small wood-burning donkey mounted on skids on a flatcar and rigged specifically for yarding and loading trackside timber. Its job was to collect the marketable logs felled by the grading crew that had cleared the right-of-way. The crew put out guylines and raised a yarding and loading boom on the cherry picker; then, using tongs, they loaded one flatcar at a time. The train came along regularly to take away the full flatcar, shove the cherry picker into a new location down the track, and leave an empty flatcar. On average, the cherry picker's crew of five or six men yarded and loaded six to eight flatcars of timber each day.

With the settings laid out, logging plans drawn up, railways and bridges built, and right-of-ways picked over, the way was now clear for fallers and buckers to begin levelling the ancient forests.

Johnny Duncan, Engineer

Johnny Duncan (born 1896) was the son of Sandwick farmers William and Mary Duncan and the nephew of Comox Valley historian Eric Duncan. His brother Robbie and his cousin Charlie Duncan were killed in France in 1918. As a boy he went overseas with the RCHA (Royal Canadian Horse Artillery), known as the "Ragged, Cold, Hungry, and Angry."

Opting not to take over the family farm at the foot of Ryan Road in Sandwick, Duncan started as Hughie Stevens and Wallace Baikie's helper in 1925. He took engineering courses by correspondence and was the last engineer in British Columbia to qualify without having to attend university.

In about 1940, Duncan married Marion McPherson. They had no children. He worked for a few years in the Comox Valley before being transferred to Ladysmith, where he died in 1976.

People who worked with Duncan remember him with the greatest respect and affection. He inspired confidence, and was mentor to engineers Tony Turner and Bruce King and to many members of his survey crews. Bruce King said simply, "The finest man I was ever around: Johnny Duncan." Swamper Malcolm Carwithen agreed. "Everybody liked John Duncan. The quality of the guys: Tony Turner, Johnny Duncan—they were the greatest people in the world. They always had time to chat and pass the time of day."

Bill Wilson, Spit Quinn, and Quinn's dog Toby, c. 1935, working in the Cariboo (Woodhus) Creek area. Note the "mat" or wooden platform in the background, upon which the big machine worked and rode for traction. Mats were made of timbers ten inches thick and twelve feet long. Quinn operated the shovel and Wilson was mat-hooker. Bill hooked the mats to a chain suspended from the bucket of the Marion and doubled as an oiler and general helper for Quinn. The shovel crew cleared the tangle of logs, slash, and stumps that had been felled, bucked, and blown along the right-of-way. They pushed the marketable logs to the side and left a level grade behind for the steel gang.—BILL WILSON

A Marion shovel crossing the Oyster River on the way to clear railway grades, 1927. According to Malcolm Carwithen, who worked with the machines between 1937 and 1939, the Marions weighed thirty-five tons, carried a three-quarter-yard bucket, and were electric powered with an alternating current, like a streetcar. Walter Montgomery photo.
—BRITISH COLUMBIA ARCHIVES, F-08667

Bill Wilson on his Marion electric shovel building railway grades at Cariboo (Woodhus) Creek, a tributary of Oyster River, c. 1935. Colton Haggarty, who saw the Marions at work in the early 1930s, recalled, "They ride on cat-mats, three in number, each to keep from sinking in the freshly excavated fill. Each cat-mat had a large ring in the centre. The gas shovels worked on two mats while the third mat could be placed in front or at back depending what direction the gas shovel was to move. The large ring was to pick up the mat for placement."—BILL WILSON

Comox Logging's grade camp at Cariboo (Woodhus) Creek, c. 1935. Note the motley collection of mobile bunkhouses of different eras and the improvised flatbed truck in the foreground. Logging was then taking place in the Quinsam River area.—BILL WILSON

French Canadian Joe Asselin (shown here c. 1943) was foreman of the steel gang based at Headquarters between the wars. He was an unpopular boss—so much so that men frequently quit his crew. Perhaps predictably, some workers referred to him using a vulgarism that closely resembled his surname. Joe Asselin cajoled and wheedled his crews to work harder, and when that failed he threw pebbles at them. He was also known for his stubborn, bull-headed personality. Eddie Murtsell told the story of the time they needed some shakes, so Asselin took a couple of guys into the felled timber. He said, "That one there, cut it off!" One of the guys said, "But it's a hemlock!" And Asselin said, "Cut it off anyway!" To his credit, however, Asselin was kind to the children at Headquarters. "He'd run into us kids in town and buy us ice cream and sodas," Neil Martin recalled. Bob Filberg photo.
—FILBERG LODGE & PARK ASSOCIATION

Bill Wilson:
From Butter Maker to Gandy Dancer

One of seven children, Bill Wilson was born in 1912 at his mother's family's cattle ranch near Keremeos. He went to work as a boy when his father was badly injured while inspecting airbrakes on the Kettle Valley Railway. Bill delivered milk, cut wood, washed windows, and made butter and ice cream for fifty cents a day in the Penticton Creamery.

In 1932, Bill's parents left Penticton for a ten-acre farm on Little River Road in Comox, intending to live off the land during the lean Depression years. Luckily, Camp 3 foreman Jack McQuinn's off-season farm was right across the road, and Bill asked him for a job. "I went to Jack McQuinn and asked for a job—for a job on the steel gang laying steel, laying railroad grades, for twenty-five cents an hour."

McQuinn sent Bill Wilson out in the spring of 1933 laying steel north of Camp 3. "I was with the gang that grabbed the ties and laid them out. This was called 'laying steel'" (also known as "tamping ties" and "gandy dancing").

Between 1934 and 1936 Bill went swamping (mat-hooking) on the railway grade for shovel operators Pinky Davis and Tom McQuillan. He worked at the northern edge of Comox Logging's property on the Oyster and Quinsam rivers, and lived at a temporary grade camp on Cariboo Creek. Once, Bill took a hot bath after a long day and was lying on his bunk in his clean clothes when fellow swamper Spit Quinn came in from work and flopped right on top of him with his dirty clothes on. "Next time," Pinky Davis said, "pull his nose into your chest!" Bill took his advice. "I did so—and the shouts! Spit had a broken nose and found this very painful!"

In 1936 Bill moved to Ladysmith, where he became grade foreman. Eventually he was placed in charge of construction along the whole coast of BC for Comox Logging's successor, Crown Zellerbach. Bill Wilson is now retired and still lives in Ladysmith.

Jimmy Sheasgreen in the timber near Oyster River, 1927. Sheasgreen was a Vancouver boy, son of a doctor whose next-door neighbour was J. D. McCormack. "He wanted to be a doctor," wrote a journalist from *The Timberman* magazine, and meant to finance his years in medical school by working in a bank. What got him off track was a remark by a good friend of the Sheasgreen family. "Loggers," Bob Filberg told him, "make more money than bank clerks." Sheasgreen started as a whistlepunk at Camp 2 in about 1920 before moving to Camp 3 as timekeeper, postmaster, and grade foreman. He moved to Ladysmith as superintendent in the late 1930s—and never did become a doctor. Walter Montgomery photo.
—FILBERG LODGE & PARK ASSOCIATION, JACK CARTHEW DONATION

A logging railway grade in the southern portion of Block 29, c. 1912. Left to right: Jim McGuigan (logging superintendent), Mr. Hogg (railway section foreman, in shadows), and Arthur Hilton. The grade at the right is now the road to Bates Beach. Leonard Frank photo.—BRITISH COLUMBIA ARCHIVES, 90185

Charlie Olson, Shovel Mechanic

Born in Stockholm in 1885, Charlie (Carl) Olson moved with his family to Michigan when he was three and then to Washington, where his family founded the farming community of Malo. He qualified as an electrician as a young man and went to work in about 1905 for the Granby copper mine at Phoenix, BC. There, he met and married Hilma Brusk, who was from the same province in Sweden. The demands of the First World War exhausted the Phoenix copper, and the Olsons then moved to the other Granby mine at Cassidy, just south of Nanaimo. Dave Stafford, master mechanic at Headquarters, remembered his former colleague at the copper mines and in 1929 hired Charlie as electrician.

Olson became Comox Logging's Marion shovel expert. His daughter Mabel Cliffe (born 1916) said that they called him to many places to repair Marions. If she asked him something when he was absorbed in his work, he would say "Quiet! I'm tinking!" in a mock Swedish accent.

A man who apprenticed under Olson remembered him as self-absorbed to the point of being secretive. One day, exasperated, the man said to him, "Jesus Christ, Charlie, you're a son of a bitch!" You could hear a pin drop—everyone stopped working. Then Charlie said, "Crabby old bugger, am I?" He laughed, and opened up after this.

A colleague recalled that when Charlie was told he'd have to retire, "he pretty well broke up; his whole life was the company." His daughter Mabel agreed, adding that he always referred to his retirement as "when I was fired." But, she said, "he was seventy! He couldn't accept it at all! He worked so hard—he worked overtime every night, and by the weekend he was exhausted."

Another Olson daughter, Florence Cooper (born 1910), taught at the Headquarters school in 1929 and 1930.

Mike Majerovich: From Croatia to Comox

Comox steel gang worker Mike Majerovich was born in 1907 in the Croatian town of Gospic, near Zagreb. His father, a labourer, was killed in an accident in Germany when Mike was an infant, and as a young boy Mike packed water and carried drills in tunnel construction. Later, for two or three years, he apprenticed to a shoemaker in Gospic. He learned to make leather shoes all by hand, but the shop went out of business when the Bata shoe people flooded the market with cheap machine-made shoes.

When his twin older brothers, both of whom worked for Comox Logging, heard that Mike was working as a labourer, they bought him a ticket to Canada. Unfortunately, he arrived at the start of the Depression. He lived in a house on Keefer Street in Vancouver with six other Croatians, completely unable to find work for three years. For fuel, they borrowed a truck, went out to Burnaby, and chopped old-growth stumps into firewood. Once, they were warming up in the bus depot when the police came along and evicted them, saying, "Move along, boys!"

Finally Mike's older brothers found an opening for him at Comox Logging, and in the 1930s he worked as a spike driver on the steel gang. "That was hard work. Every five or six minutes we drove fifteen spikes—a spike every twenty or twenty-five seconds. You had to be careful, boy—a spike was like a bullet if you missed it—like a bullet!"

In 1940, Mike married Mary Svetich, daughter of an Elk River Timber track worker who also came from Gospic. Among Mike's Comox Logging friends—all from Gospic—were Emil Dawson (Dosen), George and Joe Saban, George Super, George Cosovic, and George Semak.

After the war, Mike worked as a boom man at Royston. He retired in 1972 and now lives in Courtenay.

Malcolm Carwithen, Mat-Hooker

Born in 1920, Malcolm Carwithen worked on Comox Logging's railway grades as a mat-hooker from 1937 to 1939.

A descendant of the bishops of Bath, Exeter, and Winchester, and grandson of Oxford-educated Reginald Carwithen, who arrived in the Comox Valley in 1862, Malcolm grew up on the family farm on Lower Prairie (later Headquarters) Road.

By the time he was a teenager, Malcolm wanted to work for Comox Logging. His brother Bud was already a rigger, and Malcolm was anxious to be a part of the company that employed so many of his friends and relations.

In 1937, he rode his bike from the farm out to Headquarters every day for three weeks in search of work. Finally Len Harding said, "Well, Carwithen, I'm sick of looking at you around here every morning. You go into the commissary and get yourself a pair of caulk boots and get to work!"

That very day Malcolm caught the train from Headquarters out to Tsolum, where the company was then logging. Larry Lehtonen started work on the same day.

Malcolm was mat-hooker along Constitution Hill and north of the hill for two or three miles. "It's all grown up now," he said in 1996. "There was beautiful timber in there—very long but not very big."

He joined the Canadian Forestry Corps in the Second World War, and after the war ran a crane at the Elk Falls pulp mill. He now lives in retirement in Courtenay.

In the fall of 1934, Wilmer Gold took this picture of a Camp 3 steel gang working in the Oyster River area. The grade has been cleared and levelled by the Marion; marketable logs have been pushed to the side to await the cherry picker; and the surveyors have laid string along the line of the track. The One-Spot is nudging forward flatcars containing steel rails and wooden ties. The men in the foreground include Jimmy Gilmour, William Halbie, Fred Jordt, and Henry Schulz (the last three Russian Mennonites from Black Creek).—WILMER GOLD COLLECTION, IWA CANADA LOCAL 1-80, DUNCAN, BC

A logging railway north of Courtenay, c. 1940. The cherry picker has removed the marketable timber from the right-of-way, leaving a tangle of stumps and slash. The region awaits the fallers' arrival. Bob Filberg photo.
—FILBERG LODGE & PARK ASSOCIATION

One of Bill Eastman's bridges across the lower Oyster River near Camp 2, 1927. Note the solid timber cribbing of this bridge, which gave access to Comox Logging's northern timber blocks. Walter Montgomery photo.—COURTENAY & DISTRICT MUSEUM & ARCHIVES, P200-829B

The Three-Spot and crew pause for a photograph on the large bridge over the upper Oyster River, c. 1938. This bridge was located west of the present Island Highway. The bridge-builders and engineers often managed to combine utility with elegance.—BERNICE JAMES

◄ Comox Logging bridge-building, possibly Oyster River, 1930s. The builders are working during the dry season, with the water at its lowest. The railway has been completed on the far side of the river, allowing a yarding donkey and A-frame to be brought in for bridge construction.—PHYLLIS CURRIE

Tony Turner: From Steel Gang to Surveyor

Tony Turner was born in Oxford, England, in 1908. His mother played with the Lincoln Symphony Orchestra, and his father had a little coal business in Oxford, delivering coal in sacks. One day his father rode his motorcycle to Brighton "and returned with a lot of CPR ads saying how wonderful life was in British Columbia." He came to Canada alone, found a job at the Nanaimo Powderworks, and sent for his wife and Tony, their only child. Tony was four years old when he made the journey to Canada.

After his schooling in Nanaimo, Tony Turner started classes at the University of British Columbia, but left during the Depression. In 1932, while beachcombing on Denman Island, he met a former Comox Logging foreman named Perry Hanson. Hanson got him a job on the steel gang, which paid $2.00 a day. After paying $1.05 for board Tony was left with $.95, out of which he had to buy gloves, overalls, rain clothes, and caulk boots at $14 to $16 a pair.

Tony came to the engineers' attention while rigging on a skidder north of the Oyster River. He was the only man who could determine the length of the hypotenuse on a right-angle triangle. Hughie Stevens and Johnny Duncan hired him to chop brush and test gravel pits for the grading crew, and promoted his career as a logging engineer. He eventually completed his degree.

Tony Turner died in Ladysmith in July 2000.

chapter 8

Falling and Bucking

*I had a top-notch
four-man gang,
And the timber was
falling with a bang.
The trees were good,
the ground was clean,
'Twas the nicest show
I'd ever seen.*

—"The Barber Chair Faller"

FALLERS AND BUCKERS ARRIVED AT A SETTING WITH their work cut out for them—literally. The surveyors had blazed a line of trees down the back and sides of each quarter. "You could see the line clearly," recalled retired faller Sven Ell. Each gang of fallers and buckers was assigned a quarter to cut and buck, and all four quarters were cut at once.

If the ground was reasonably level, the first trees were cut right at the front (or "bottom") of the quarter (near the railway spur), Sven Ell recalled, "and after that we just kept felling trees back and forth across the quarter." They tried to "aim" or "lean" the trees toward the spar tree so that the skidder would be able to yard the trees straight out of the bush by their top ends. If the ground sloped, the fallers started cutting at the lowest side of the quarter and worked their way uphill.

An experienced and diplomatic foreman known as a bull bucker supervised the whole falling operation. He decided who worked with whom and moved fallers from quarter to quarter and setting to setting. "He would tell us where to go next," said former faller Gunnar Jonsson.

Until the early 1930s, fallers worked in four-man gangs consisting of two fallers and two buckers; during the Depression, the company reduced gangs to two fallers and a single overworked bucker. The fallers always worked as a pair, chopping undercuts with razor-sharp, double-bitted axes and then manning the two ends of the falling saw. The buckers, by contrast, worked alone, each with his own single-handled bucking saw. Two fallers could cut a quarter in two to four weeks. They might need a month if the timber was very heavy; small and scattered timber took less time. A three-foot tree could be cut in only ten or fifteen minutes, but a very large Douglas fir measuring nine feet in diameter took four hours to fell: two and a half hours to make the undercut and the rest of the time to make the final cut.

When a quarter was finished, the bull bucker sent the falling gang out

A faller's view. Looking about 150 feet up a Douglas fir tree, c. 1940. This view was encountered thousands of times by fallers in the old-growth forests of Comox District. Few branches interrupt the distance between forest floor and canopy. Bob Filberg photo.
—FILBERG LODGE & PARK ASSOCIATION

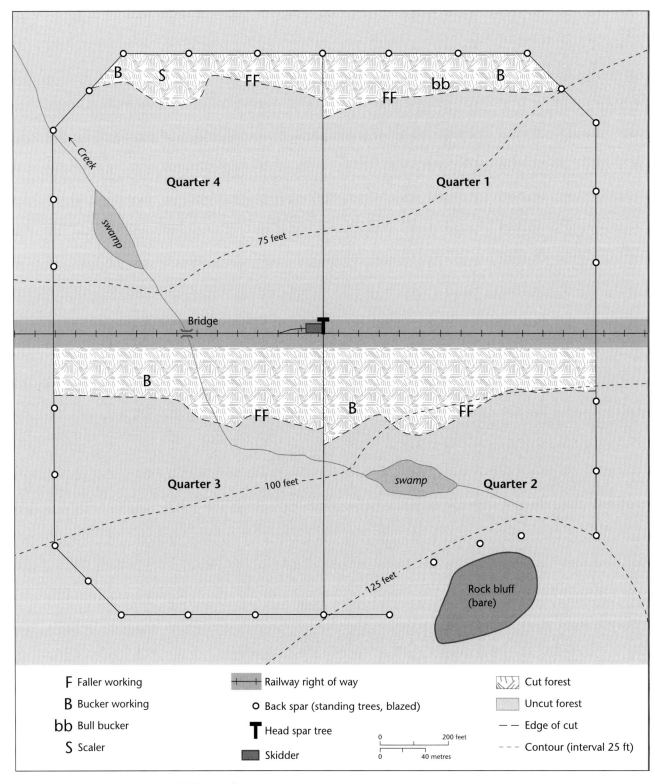

Legend:

F Faller working
B Bucker working
bb Bull bucker
S Scaler

Railway right of way
o Back spar (standing trees, blazed)
T Head spar tree
Skidder

0 — 200 feet
0 — 40 metres

Cut forest
Uncut forest
— — Edge of cut
- - - Contour (interval 25 ft)

Falling and bucking on a typical skidder setting.

Les Marshall, Faller and Bucker

One of the few non-Scandinavian fallers was Les Marshall of Camp 3. According to his daughter Mona Law, Les was "really proud that he kept up with the Finns and the Swedes." One of his close friends was Uno Forsman.

Born in England just before the turn of the century, Les Marshall came to the Comox Valley with most of his family when he was thirteen. His older sister Alice had come earlier, and had married Lu Cliffe.

Les farmed at first, and in about 1925 married Jennie Childs from an old Comox Valley farming family. About the same time, he got work as a faller at Camp 3.

Woods work could be dangerous. Les fell off a springboard and landed on his axe with his buttocks. He wouldn't go to the doctor in his work clothes, so he went home to change first. He found that he was all bloody and that his underwear had stuck to him.

Finally he reached Drs. Straith and Mooney's tiny Courtenay office. After a few minutes a nurse told him to take a seat.

"I can't," Les answered.

"Why not?" the nurse said.

"Because I've sat on an axe!" Les replied.

It took many stitches to close up the wound.

Lin Hunt, Homeguard Bucker

Lin (Lilburn) Hunt was born in Fossil, Oregon, in 1896, and as a young man he worked on the family farm in the Willamette Valley. "He farmed, and logged, and farmed," his son Bob said.

He served in the American army in the First World War, and on his return married Ila "Birdie" McQuinn, sister of Jack McQuinn. It was McQuinn who talked him into working in the woods. "Why don't you go into a logging camp?" he said. "That's where the big money is made."

Lin arrived in the Comox Valley in December 1924, and was a bucker at Camp 3 from 1925 until 1942. In 1933, he moved his family to the old Lewis farm in Courtenay, sixty acres of bottomland that he bought for five thousand dollars. He had beef cattle, Jersey cows, and a milk route of four hundred customers. He credited his wife Birdie with his success. "A wife can either make or break you. I owe my success to her encouragement." Lin died in 1978; Birdie in 1992.

to fell the distant "cold-deck timber" behind their quarter. Such timber was later yarded into the setting from up to 2500 feet away by mobile donkey engines called cold deckers.

In large timber, a faller stood on a springboard, a two-by-six Douglas fir plank up to six feet long inserted in a notch near the base of the tree. Springboards allowed fallers to avoid the swelled and pitch-filled butts of old-growth timber, and gave a good foothold on sloping terrain. In smaller timber on level ground, springboards could be dispensed with. The fallers assessed every tree individually. "It depended on where you had to fall the timber—this might make a springboard necessary," explained Gunnar Jonsson.

It took considerable skill and experience to use a springboard properly. "You had to learn to notch the springboard in so it stayed," continued Jonsson. "[The springboard] had a sharp edge at the top—at the end. You'd make a notch with an axe. You could spring; you could also twist them a little to move." Bull bucker Neil Martin remarked that fallers "got very slick with their springboards." While standing on them, "they'd kick them around behind or in front of them" to find the best angle to the tree. In some camps, fallers made their own springboards and took great care in making them just the right way; in other camps they were mass-produced in the shops.

Two kinds of crosscut saw were used in the bush: falling saws and bucking saws. The standard length of falling saws was seven and a half feet, but saws up to eleven and a half feet long were required for the big timber. Bucking saws usually measured seven feet long and were heavier and more rigid than falling saws.

Fallers and buckers always carried their saws on their shoulders on their way to work—with the sharp teeth facing out, away from the neck. Sven Ell recalled that falling saws were so flexible that "they'd be flopping around on your shoulders as you walked."

All saws had four cutters and a raker grouped on the blade. Cutters were straight, slightly offset teeth, while the raker was a wide double tooth that pulled or pushed the sawdust out with every stroke. Slightly older saws contained three cutters and a raker, while even older saws from the turn of the twentieth century resembled common handsaws: they had teeth but no rakers. Bob Filberg recalled that rakers were introduced into West Coast logging early in the twentieth century, and that they made falling and bucking faster and more efficient.

The pitch in the base of the tree tended to clog and gum the teeth of saws, so fallers and buckers carried a quart bottle of saw oil to reduce friction and help cut through the pitch. Coal oil (kerosene), the original saw oil, gave way to diesel fuel and even turpentine—anything to stop the pitch from sticking to the saw. (Even plain creek water could be used in emergencies.) Oil bottles were hung close at hand on a metal hook in the bark of a tree. Occasionally the men would stop sawing and pour some oil on the blade, sparingly, because each man had only one bottle to last the day. Old photographs show well-oiled falling and bucking saws gleaming in the light—in great contrast to the rusty relics attached to restaurant and pub walls for atmosphere.

The fallers' toolkit consisted of their crosscut saw, oil bottles, two springboards, two double-bitted axes for making the undercut, two or

Two unidentified Comox Logging fallers, c. 1912. Note the scorch marks on this great Douglas fir, indicating that it is a forest fire survivor. The men are wearing caulk boots and standing on springboards to give them access to the tree trunk. Visible at left is a crosscut falling saw and a bottle of coal oil for oiling the saw. Leonard Frank photo.
—BRITISH COLUMBIA ARCHIVES, B-08400

A four-man falling and bucking crew, north of Courtenay (probably in the Oyster River region) in the 1920s. Left to right: W. Beckman, Bill Woods, Austie Blackburn, A. Beckman. Note the coal oil bottle hanging from the undercut, the flexible falling saw glistening with oil, and the thick bark on this magnificent Douglas fir. Retired faller Sven Ell estimated this tree to be seven feet across at the stump.—FRED BLACKBURN

A filer sharpening a bucking saw, possibly in the filing shed at Headquarters, c. 1912. Notice the "raker" tooth between every four cutting teeth. "In the early days of the oxen most trees were felled with an axe," wrote Joe Cliffe. "The reason was possibly because the saws were still crude. All the teeth were made for cutting and there was no means of getting the sawdust out of the cut. Then somebody got the idea to insert a tooth between every four cutting teeth, called a raker which brought the sawdust out every stroke the saw made. This of course was the answer and the cross-cut saw became the main tool in making logs in the logging industry for many years." Leonard Frank photo.
—VANCOUVER PUBLIC LIBRARY, 6060

Arthur "Butch" Grant standing on a springboard oiling his falling saw, in front of a large spruce in the Camp 3 area, c. 1930. "A pitch pocket will stop you dead," said Butch's son Hugh Grant. Despite his nickname, Butch Grant was not especially rugged; in fact he was a slim man. He got his nickname when, as a chubby boy, he resembled the portly butcher in the village of Comox. **Bob Filberg photo.**—HUGH GRANT

A Wonderful Creation

Percy Smith of Comox, brother of timber cruiser Eustace Smith, was an old horse-logger and beachcomber. In 1922, he taught Comox naturalist Mack Laing the art of crosscut saw filing, and Laing was captivated by both Smith's skill and the ingenious design of the saw itself:

A wonderful creation that lance-toothed tool—how greatly it had grown in its evolution since the day, in the form of the backbone of a fish, it caught the eye of acquisitive man! How greatly my respect grew for it when I sat down and looked it over to see why, now that Smith had performed his magic on it, it threw ribbons of wood in showers and went hungrily into its log. How clever—one set of razor-pointed teeth leaning right; the other leaning left; the rakers with their little hooked chisels running between to lift what the teeth cut—all very simple! But a great deal of grey matter had been expended before one such implement had been fashioned. Here in my hand I beheld the thing that had been the means of wrecking with unholy speed these vast forests of the west. From the spine of a fish it had become the backbone of the lumber industry.

167

Six Finnish and Swedish fallers at Camp 3, c. 1933. Among the men are Fred Dahl (bottom right) and Fred Erickson (bottom centre).—HARRY ERICKSON

Seven Finnish and Swedish fallers at Camp 3, c. 1933. Fred (Siegfried) Erickson (bottom left) labelled this photo "Men horsing around." Among the other men are Fred Dahl (bottom right) and Uno Forsman (second from top).—HARRY ERICKSON

Otto Richter slides his saw out as a Douglas fir starts to topple, c. 1930. His partner is doing the same on the other side of the tree. Born in Germany in 1901, Otto Richter arrived in Canada in 1927, farmed in Saskatchewan for a year, and started as a faller for Comox Logging in April 1928. Later he became a high rigger.
—ELEANOR KELLER

The Barber Chair Faller

This anonymous 1920s poem richly evokes the atmosphere of an early Comox Logging operation:

This is a story of long ago,
When I worked for the Comox Logging Co.
The price was seventy-five per M.,
And the quarter to cut was a perfect gem.

I had a top-notch four-man gang,
And the timber was falling with a bang.
The trees were good, the ground was clean,
'Twas the nicest show I'd ever seen.

We were cutting a fir that was tall and thin
When along the track came Jack McQuinn;
Jack was the "Supe" at old Camp Three,
And nothing happened that he didn't see.

As Jack was strolling along the track
The giant fir began to crack;
Crack is right, it did for fair,
And split up a 12-foot barber chair.

There was only a nick for the undercut,
I had no excuse, no if or but;
"Ah ha!" said Jack as he came to a stop,
I see you're starting a barber shop."

The woods is no place for a barber chair,
This is a warning, you'd better beware,
For safety, prevent that splitting butt,
Put in a good deep undercut.

—O'BRENNAN, *Our Branch of the Tree*

Bob Filberg took this photo in about 1938. "The fallers are running back from the falling tree to be safe from chunks or any debris that might be coming down," wrote retired faller Sven Ell. They have already thrown their crosscut saw behind the tree, where it is not visible. Their oil bottle still hangs from the bark of the stump.—FILBERG LODGE & PARK ASSOCIATION

three steel wedges, and a ten-pound sledgehammer for banging in the wedges. Fallers used wedges, which could be over a foot long, when the weight of the tree pinched or threatened to pinch the saw. "The older trees," Sven Ell recalled, "you had to wedge them hard with a long, thin wedge." The fallers left their toolkit in the bush overnight, with the exception of their oil bottles, which they filled each morning, and their saw. "You had two saws," explained Sven Ell. "You took them in and had them sharpened every two days . . . you'd take one in and take a fresh one out."

~

While Homeguard men dominated some parts of Comox Logging's operations, the fallers tended to be Scandinavian, many of them from small farms in northern Sweden. "You had to have Swedes as hand fallers and buckers," said Gunnar Jonsson, "and in all these occupations there were one per cent Canadians." Jonsson, who came from Sweden in 1928, recalled that almost all of the thirty or forty fallers and buckers working out of Camp 3 in the 1930s were Swedes and "Swede Finns"—Finns of Swedish descent. "For a while I worked on the skidder crew," said Jonsson, "and then I started falling timber for seven years like the rest of the Swedes. All the fallers were Swedes and Finns, big husky fellows. I was talked into it by them!"

Among Comox Logging's Swedish and Finnish fallers were Fred Dahl, Sven Ell, Axel Erickson, Fred Erickson, Uno Forsman, Magnus Hoglo, Gunnar Jonsson, Fred Manson (Mansson), Nels Peterson, Carl Sundin, and three sets of brothers: Widen, Beckman, and Hagg (pronounced Haig). Nestor Hagg was a champion bucker at the company's annual loggers' sports. He and his brother Magnus, like many other Swedes, settled in the Dove Creek–Merville area.

Camp life could be difficult for these men. They lived for months on end in the unnatural atmosphere of all-male bunkhouses, eating in the all-male cookhouse and lacking the company of women and children, unlike the Homeguards of Camp 3. Many Swedes met and married local women and moved, like Gunnar Jonsson, out of camp and onto nearby farms and stump ranches. Others were less fortunate. Jimmy Weir, who lived in a Camp 3 bunkhouse from 1926 to 1928, said that "some of the big Scandinavians didn't spend a cent all year, but over the Christmas shut-down they'd go to Vancouver and come home stone broke!"

Fallers had to be fit, resilient, competitive men able to stand the immense physical stresses of standing on a springboard all or part of every day. "Using an eight or ten foot saw was always a tiring occupation, even for the strongest," wrote Joe Cliffe. In the mid-1930s, Bill Wilson was building railway grades in the Oyster River area when the grade crew caught up with the falling crew that was preparing the railway right-of-way. Bill was sent falling for a day with a Finnish partner, but he found it such hard work that "for three days I could hardly walk!" Falling was especially hard on the knees and back. Bill Lyttback, a Finnish faller now over ninety and living in Ladysmith, has arms that seem to stretch down to his knees—the result, he explained, of wielding the "Swedish fiddle" or crosscut falling saw for so many years. Gunnar Jonsson added, "I had to leave the woods in 1944 because I developed a bad nerve in my

Gunnar Jonsson's Lucky Break

Gunnar Jonsson was born in 1909, the son of a Swedish carpenter and small farmer. By the time he was nineteen, he had worked on a farm for two years, and in a small factory making slippers, but he couldn't get any more substantial work.

In 1928 the local paper carried an enticing advertisement about Canada. It showed a team of four horses and a man riding alongside. Gunnar decided to emigrate, though his father promised him twice the price of the ticket if he'd stay.

Gunnar left Sweden in March 1929 bound for Fairlight, Saskatchewan, where he worked for wheat farmer Howard Church until the winter set in. In October, he went to Vancouver, just before the start of the Great Depression. Employment agency notices read "Wanted: a Chokerman," but all sorts of expert help was available.

Six weeks later Gunnar had a lucky break. The proprietor of the Scandinavian Rooms, where he boarded, happened to be a friend of Merville farmer Robert Ault, who hired Gunnar for the winter of 1929–1930 to help with his 1,800 chickens.

Ault, an Englishman, thought highly of Gunnar, as did Ault's son-in-law Eric Flinton, timekeeper at Comox Logging's Camp 3. Flinton spoke to Jack McQuinn, who hired Gunnar on a skidder crew. From 1937 to 1944, Gunnar worked as a faller beyond Camp 3 and past Wolf Lake.

Gunnar Jonsson now lives in retirement in Merville.

leg; it went funny from standing up and holding the heavy falling saw all the time. The weight was always on my feet."

Falling was also technically challenging work. Loggers tried to avoid what was known as a "barber chair," a term that described the appearance of a stump when fallers insufficiently or incorrectly undercut a tree. The tree would then fall before the fallers could cut right through it from the other side. The result of such a premature fall was a stump with large vertical slivers, resembling the back of a chair. The timber nearest the butt of the log then had a reduced market value, which meant loss of face and a smaller paycheque for the unfortunate fallers. Barber chairs were also dangerous: the tree could suddenly fold back toward the fallers instead of falling cleanly in front.

"Hang-ups" presented another challenge and potential hazard. Even though fallers attempted to cut trees so they neatly fell in the same direction, tree crowns sometimes got entangled, or one tree fell against another and refused to drop immediately. A third tree might be felled against the hang-up, but when it too got stuck it was called a "teepee." Sometimes the fallers would just leave a teepee and hope it would blow down overnight, rather than at a time when men were working around it. Similarly, the aptly named "widow-makers" were limbs or parts of trees caught in the canopy that could fall without warning and strike an unsuspecting faller. (Hard hats were not worn until after the Second World War.)

Thick Douglas fir bark also posed a danger to the fallers, who never cut down snags owing to the hazard of falling bark (and to the difficulty of cutting through the rock-hard pitch). Snags and old trees had loose and very heavy bark, as thick as ten inches or a foot. A "split" in the bark high in the tree might go undetected until it was too late, and the bark could come cascading down unpredictably and pile up around the base of the tree, crushing anything it hit. Fallers were killed this way. Gordon Blackburn said that bark was sometimes dynamited off to give the fallers undisturbed access to the tree. A powderman, like Bill Nairn, would hang sticks of powder around the base of the tree, attach a fuse, and blow it up. The bark would tumble down, and only then did the fallers feel safe to move in and work on the tree. Powdermen were also called in after a blowdown to sever the windfall's roots with a small explosion and make it safe for the buckers to move in.

～

After the trees came down, they had to be cut into manageable lengths for yarding and transport. Buckers followed close behind fallers—but not, for safety reasons, right on their heels. "The bucker had to have room to work, so you wouldn't hit him," Sven Ell explained. Bucking, like falling, was a distinct and skilled profession. Buckers carried an eight-foot pole to measure the fallen tree into standard lengths of between 24 and 40 feet—to be precise, into logs 24, 28, 32, 36, or 40 feet long. A flatcar was 40 feet long. If a tree contained, say, 110 feet of good timber, a bucker might cut two 40-foot lengths and one 24-foot length, and they usually left a foot extra for trim.

The bucker determined where to cut first, a decision requiring considerable skill and expertise. The bucker had to consider how and

Gunnar Jonsson's Daily Routine

Gunnar Jonsson described his daily routine north of Courtenay when he was a faller with Comox Logging over sixty years ago. He remembered that the fallers, buckers, and skidder crews rode to work together in a crummy. Everyone got off the train at the skidder landing, but the fallers and buckers put their saws on their shoulders and continued down the track. It could take them fifteen or twenty minutes to walk to where they were working. "The fallers might be three or four settings ahead of the skidder crew," Gunnar explained.

Each gang had two bucking saws and one falling saw. They were company saws, and the men had to be careful not to damage them because the sawfilers were always busy.

At night the fallers and buckers left saw handles, sledgehammers, wedges, springboards, and extra clothes under a log in the woods. Every second night they took the saws, minus the handles, down to Camp 3 to be sharpened by Jabe Day or Herman Carlson. When they got to the crummy they slid the dangerously sharp saws into specially made saw boxes for the men's protection. They used the same saw for two days and then got another from the Camp 3 filing shed.

Every morning the fallers arrived at their quarter with their lunch box and got to work: "Put the handle in the saw, and away you go!"

Comox Logging fallers and buckers with their handiwork north of Courtenay, c. 1912. The logs have all been felled in the same direction for yarding to the skidder landing. Cedar was considered unmarketable and was not felled. "It's all fir," commented retired faller Jim Szasz. "That's all they were after—number one fir."
—BRITISH COLUMBIA ARCHIVES, B-08397

From One Tree to the Next

Fallers were paid by the foot, and speed and efficiency were everything. "Before one tree was halfway to the ground we were on to the next one," recalled Gunnar Jonsson. Similarly, Ruth Masters said of her neighbour John Sandberg, "He never watched a tree fall because he was always running to the next. He was paid by the volume he cut." Sandberg was a Swedish faller who died at the age of forty-eight, "totally spent," he had worked so hard, stripped to the waist, all winter long.

The piece-work system of payment also meant that fallers continually grumbled about scalers' measurements. One of Gunnar Jonsson's scalers was Harold Watkinson, "a nice fellow, but he never gave us anything extra. We'd always complain like hell!"

Jonsson said it wasn't easy to make good money as a faller. "Some days you're up there on the hillside and cut down over a hundred trees a day, and still not make any big scale."

Logging foreman Jack McQuinn shows off two old cedar trees left standing when this land was logged out of Camp 3, c. 1930. Behind McQuinn, the "fell and bucked" Douglas fir has been dropped in the direction of the skidder setting. The end of the skidder's hayrack boom is just visible at the far left. Charles Sillence photo.
—MABEL CLIFFE AND HARRY ERICKSON

◀ A four-man falling and bucking gang working along the Oyster River, three miles west of the present Island Highway, 1927. Left to right: Lilburn Hunt, Waldo Adamson, Gus Hamling, Bill Woods. Notice the gleaming saws and the oil bottle hooked in the bark. "It shows only Douglas fir," Bob Hunt said. "That's all they logged on those days. They didn't even bother with the rest. They've left the cedar standing— it was just junk." Walter Montgomery photo.—BOB HUNT

Scaler Chris Holmes (left) with faller Herman Carlson somewhere north of Courtenay, c. 1930. The scaler's job was to calculate, with the help of an L-Stick (left), the marketable board feet in a log. This was important information in an era when fallers were paid not by the hour but by how much they cut.—JOHN HOLMES

where the tree was lying. Also, a cut in the wrong place would cause the tree to "pinch," that is, to grip the saw so tightly that it could not be pulled out. To help prevent this, buckers drove wedges into the top of the cut. As with fallers, wedges were an important part of the bucker's toolkit. "You got the saw in and started to cut," Neil Martin recalled, "and if it got pinched, you needed to get a wedge in there to stop the pinch." Bucking could continue once the pinch had been eliminated.

Buckers spent little time limbing trees, said Sven Ell. The company wanted only the best, most flawless timber, so the branched treetops were left in the bush. "They only took the bottom log and the second log," recalled retired faller Jim Szasz. "As soon as they got to a limb it was left in the woods. It had to be clear. They left the whole top part. They could only sell number one . . . it could have no knots. They'd leave eighty feet of wood in the woods."

❧

Falling and bucking produced a third profession: saw filing. "Filing was a trade on its own," Neil Martin said. All the camps had filing sheds where the filers plied their trade, like Jabe Day and Herman Carlson at Camp 3 and Bob Larson and Schule Schulson at Headquarters. Sawfilers were important men in the whole operation, and they were particular about how saws were returned at the end of the day. They refused to accept a saw with pitch on it, and if a bucker had hit a rock they'd give him a hard time. By the same token, the men who used the saws preferred the work of some filers over others. "Some guys they liked and some they didn't," as Neil Martin put it.

Fallers and buckers also made work for scalers, who measured the trees after they had been felled and bucked. Scaling allowed the company to monitor productivity in the woods. It also determined payment for the fallers, who received contract wages by the thousand board feet according to the British Columbia Scale Rule (based on a taper of one inch in ten feet). Scalers worked with an "L-Stick"—a ruler shaped like a large L. Once or twice a day, scalers inspected the fallers' work, calculated how much they had cut, and gave the fallers a "scale slip" showing the previous day's scale. To identify themselves, fallers marked with black chalk the butt end of the trees they had cut. Each gang of fallers had its own number sequence.

Fallers were "sometimes happy, sometimes not" with the way their timber had been scaled, according to Neil Martin. Scalers had a high reputation for honesty, but fallers (who liked to call L-Sticks "Gyp-Sticks") questioned their scale out of principle. This kept the scalers on their toes. "The fallers would make jokes about the scalers," Malcolm Carwithen recalled. "They would openly criticize them to their face, but [the scalers] were beyond reproach." Sven Ell agreed, "It was hard to cheat. After you'd felled for years you'd know how much you'd cut."

In the early 1920s, scaler Wallace Baikie worked right on the heels of the Camp 2 fallers and buckers on lower Black Creek. In his memoirs he recalled:

Len Harding took on the responsibility of moving the fallers from one quarter to another. A quarter would have a million feet in it so they did not have to be moved very often. I had six four-man gangs to scale after. Say they were cutting forty thousand per day with each gang, this would require me to scale nearly a quarter of a million feet per

Stumping the Spell-Check

A computer spell-check rejects logging occupations like cherry picker and powderman, not to mention faller and bucker, skidder, cold decker, sparkcatcher, whistlepunk, bunkmaker, car-knocker, and many more.

In Comox Logging terminology, trees were "fell" by "fallers," not felled or fallen by fellers: "One of the Hunt boys fell here for the company"; "That fire burned a hillside of fell and bucked timber."

With dozens of logging occupations and frequent job changes and rotations, loggers developed a kind of shorthand in which "went" and "run" had to do a lot of work. "Went" was a shorthand way of saying "he got a new job," for example: "Pete McLoughlin was fireman on a locie and then he went timekeeping"; "Harry Nordin went skipper on the *Gleeful*." "Run" often referred to operating machinery: "I run yarder for him for 24 years"; "Mack Grant run skidder levers"; "I took his place running skidder when he went camp foreman"; "Austie Blackburn run boat up and down Comox Lake"; "Filberg run the whole outfit."

Comox Loggers also had some favourite expressions, many of which survive today. "Old" refers less to a person's advanced age and more to the special place that a deceased person holds in the speaker's memory. When someone is introduced in conversation as "Old Blowhard Tilleard" or "Old Bill Shevlock," a revealing or affectionate story might follow. "Bullshit" refers to words, talk, or storytelling, not just to lies. "You should talk to Callan—he's a good bullshitter." "All that's left is the bullshit!"

A Greenhorn Bucking

In 1922, Norman Pritchard of Comox taught naturalist Mack Laing the art of bucking, as Laing later described:

In the first couple of days of effort spent in disconnecting these timbers I learned about a cross cut saw. I learned a great deal. I had imagined that a cross cut was just a great tool that you dragged back and forth and cleft the foe asunder by virtue mainly of strength and enthusiasm. I had both these latter, but the saw was a failure until Norman had taken the matter in hand. The implement had not come from the hardware store ready for business. . . . He showed me the tricks of the trade: the use of wedges in preventing locking of the saw—not only by applying wedge to saw-cut, but by applying two wedges at the cut from different angles to "hang" the sections—and how to saw upward from below by use of the notched axe handle, and several other things that went far toward making my path a way of peace rather than despair.

day. It kept me busy and it was quite a lot of responsibility for a nineteen-year-old. It was beautiful fir timber, straight and on level ground. I scaled one tree that the bucker cut five forty-foot logs from. That was the only time in my lifetime that I have seen that happen.

Fallers, buckers, scalers, and skidder crews all rode to work in converted boxcars called "crummies." These utilitarian vehicles had wooden benches, oil drum heaters, and a smokestack through the roof. They also had "sawboxes" on the outside where the fallers and buckers stored their razor-sharp crosscut saws. Neil Brady-Browne, who travelled by crummy with the grading crew daily in the late 1930s, recalled that the "atmosphere in the trains was awful" after a long day's work. Neil remembered seeing guys falling and bucking with wool underwear "and the steam would just rise from them! The atmosphere in the crummy with a barrel stove in the middle was like a sauna. The men had been soaking wet, and there was a very strong body odour—and guys were smoking in there too."

When the fallers and buckers finished their work, the setting was transformed from an ancient forest to a carpet of bucked, scaled, and parallel sections of timber. The woods were now the domain of the yarder and skidder crews.

Crosscut saws dominated the woods until the late 1940s, when power saws became commonplace. In the fall of 1930, Comox Logging employees got a glimpse of the future when this primitive power saw was demonstrated at Headquarters. This unwieldy machine was so massive it had to be mounted on a pair of springboards—a mechanical facsimile of a faller. In effect, it was an attempt to turn a Wee McGregor into a falling saw by turning it on its side and strapping it to a springboard. The tired-looking operator (left) is Headquarters sawfiler Bob Larson. Larson was born in Minnesota in 1885, came to British Columbia in 1910, and became Camp 2 sawfiler in 1918. A champion bucker and inventor of a protective guard for crosscut saws, he died in 1935.—JACK TUKHAM

High rigger Emil "Sailor" Lehtonen, c. 1940. Bob Filberg photo.
—FILBERG LODGE & PARK ASSOCIATION

High rigger Big Jack McKenzie tops a back spar at the back end of a setting north of Camp 3, c. 1930. Back spars were topped to prevent them from blowing over. Viscount Willingdon, the Governor General of Canada, attended this tree-topping. Norman Schwarze photo, Schwarze Photographers, Nanaimo.—MARGARET SMITH

Joe Cliffe rigged and ready to climb a spar tree at the back end of a setting, c. 1930. After serving in the First World War, Cliffe joined Comox Logging as a rigger in 1920; later he became a side push, camp foreman, and noted inventor of logging equipment.—BOB CLIFFE

chapter 9

Strictly Logging

Big Jack McKenzie, High Rigger

Neil Martin remarked that John Alexander (Big Jack) McKenzie (1895–1980) "typifies for me the typical logger." At six-foot-two and 230 pounds (at his slimmest), Big Jack was a big man for high rigging, but he was strong and hard-working, according to his daughter Myrtle Heron. "He climbed those trees—it was difficult for a big man to do this." He and his brother Bill were provincial tug-of-war champions in the 1920s, and he introduced many young loggers to woods work, including Stan Hodgins.

Son of Big Jack McKenzie Sr. and Maude Cliffe, Big Jack married Ella Hawkins of Comox, whose sister Frances married leverman Clifford Janes. When Big Jack got too old for rigging he became a push, and during the Second World War he was a foreman in the Queen Charlotte Islands. He was a master of the logger's practical joke and a great storyteller. Whenever he drove into Camp 3 he would honk his horn gaily. "He was a tease and a card and a lot of fun," Neil Martin said. McKenzie and skidding leverman Harry Shepherd were close friends: "Dad called him 'Old Scissorbill' because he looked like a scissorbill duck with his thin, angular face, and Harry called Dad the 'The Old Clamdigger,'" recalled Myrtle.

NCE THE TREES HAD BEEN FELLED, THE WHOLE logging process was concerned with moving logs. The ultimate purpose of the surveyors, grading crews, steel gangs, falling crews, and scalers was to prepare the way for the men who took the logs out of the bush. The logging crews performed two pivotal jobs for Comox Logging: yarding the massive logs from where they lay in the bush, and loading them onto flatcars for the journey down to the booming grounds.

The first step in readying a cut setting for logging was to prepare the central or main spar tree, known as the "head spar," "skidder tree," or "home tree." Comox Logging used exclusively Douglas fir for its skidder trees—a "sound big fir—a God-darn big fir," as retired bullbucker Neil Martin put it. The head spar was ideally 130 feet high and a minimum of eighteen or twenty inches across at the top. Trees of this size were not always available, and riggers settled for trees as short as 100 feet. When a suitable head spar was not available on site, a tree was brought in from elsewhere by rail. Such trees were called "raised trees" as opposed to "standing trees."

Standing trees were limbed and topped by an acrobatic high rigger like Drew Berkeley, Joe Cliffe, Jack Downey, Norman Janes, Big Jack McKenzie, or Sailor Lehtonen. "Steel spurs made in the blacksmith shop were strapped to a man's legs," Joe Cliffe recalled, "and a wide belt was devised with about 25 feet of inch-thick hemp rope. Attached to the belt was a short-handled axe and other small equipment. A new name was invented and put on the office payroll. This was the arrival of the high rigger."

After topping, spar trees were "rigged," a nautical term that applied with equal accuracy to highlead logging. In the early 1920s Comox Logging created an elite, mobile, five- or six-man crew known as the "flying corps" (also known as the "rigging-ahead crew," "rigging-up

177

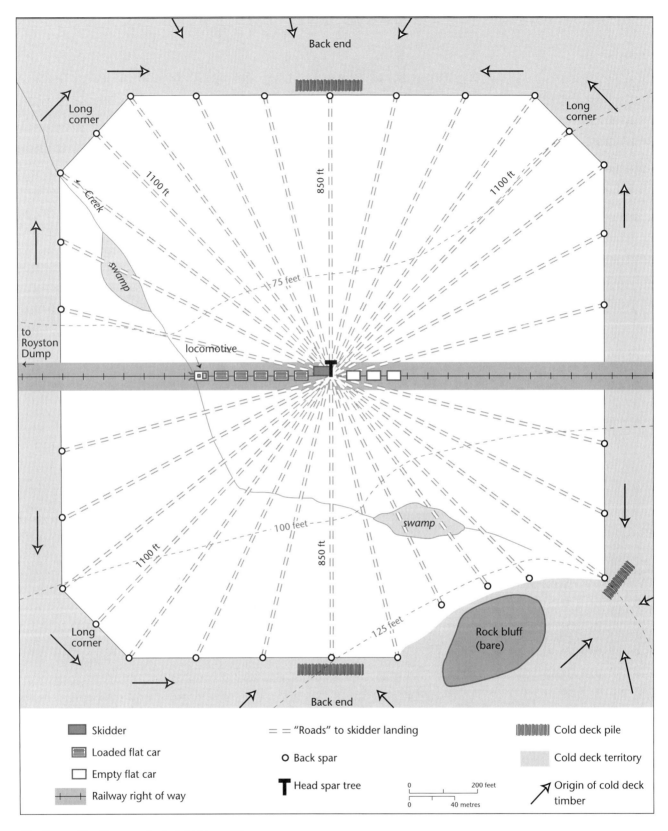

Yarding and loading on a typical skidder setting.

Sailor Lehtonen, High Rigger

Born in Finland in 1893, Emil Lehtonen jumped ship in Vancouver in about 1919 and came to Comox where, already an expert on nautical rigging, he became high rigger at Camp 1 and acquired the nickname "Sailor."

He was soon joined by Saima, his Finnish fiancée, and they were married in Cumberland in 1921. "He married a girl fresh out from Finland that spring," wrote Wallace Baikie. Lehtonen later worked at Camp 2, Bevan, and Comox Lake and finally, Homeguard-style, bought sixty acres at Merville.

"He used to stand on his head on top of a tree," Bill Wilson said. "He'd put on exhibitions. He could climb a tree like a monkey. He'd go up the tree and just sit on top." Sammy Telosky concurred, "He was a good skidder man. When the old quitting whistle would go, Sailor would say, 'I beat you son of a bitch!' He was always in a hurry just before the whistle—trying to get everything done just before the whistle. Every second word was a swear word— Russian, English, Swedish, and Finnish swear words all mixed together." One of Sailor's favourite expressions, according to Bruce King, was "I hear the quiet—the more better I go!" which meant that he worked best when the noisy skidder wasn't working.

Sailor Lehtonen died in 1947.

Laying Out a Skidder Setting

Surveyor Tony Turner described the steps of laying out a skidder setting in the 1930s:

The camp's foreman went around and marked the back spars 200 feet apart around the back boundary, and then one designated fellow chopped the tops of the back spars. The head spar, a choice piece of timber, was rigged on the ground. Guylines were fastened at the top and another set below that, and some more guylines for the hayrack boom. The tree was wheeled in on flatcars above where they wanted it. It was rarely that there was a good enough spar tree where you wanted it, and spar trees were brought in from elsewhere. The chances of finding a standing tree were pretty negligible.

Then the flying corps was brought in: they went around rigging on the ground; they rigged the head spar and set it up and tightened the guylines. If the ground was soft they made a pad out of small trees for a base. It was easier to rig the tree on the ground and then stand it up. This was done with a donkey—a cold decker of some sort—on a flatcar. They didn't use a skidder to raise a spar tree. They used jack spars to raise the spar tree. These trees had been marked with a blaze.

crew," "rigging-up goat," and "rig-up gang"), whose sole job was to unrig head spars at old settings and rig new spars at new settings before logging commenced—a process that took about two weeks. In the 1930s, the flying corps, based at Camp 3, rigged ahead for both Skidder 5 and Skidder 6. "The tree had to be absolutely all rigged for when the skidder came in," Davey Janes said. It took two airborne men to rig a head spar. "There were always two men up there because the shackles were so big it took two men to put them up," Hi Churchill recalled.

The flying corps rigged the raised type of spar tree on the ground ("lying down") with a spider's web of lines and blocks (pulleys) required for yarding and loading. Then they lifted the tree into a vertical position with the help of a donkey engine and two or three small trees known as "gin poles" that had been left standing nearby. Finally, they fastened both standing and raised trees to stumps with guylines, for stability.

With spar trees prepared, the stage was set for the arrival of the mobile, skid-mounted donkey engines called yarders or "cold deckers," which moved distant logs ("the far stuff," "the back end timber," the "cold-deck timber") to within the Lidgerwood skidders' 1100-foot maximum reach. The cold deckers also logged a setting's four "long corners" which stretched to 1200 feet from the skidder tree. According to Hi Churchill, "cold deckers went in first, before the skidder came in, because the setting might have a long corner . . . or a rock bluff or a ravine that the skidder couldn't reach. Then the skidder would yard everything out at once."

Comox Logging preferred Clyde gas yarders—basic 150-horsepower donkey engines mounted on a Douglas fir "sleigh" or "sled" consisting of two skids: hewn fir logs held to the engine by strong bolts. Made of the best timber in the forest, the skids had hardly any taper to them and rarely a knot. Cold deckers actually pulled themselves off the railway flatcar and "walked" up to the back of the setting using lines tied to stumps, resembling a sinister industrial parasite dependent on the remnants of the forest for locomotion.

Filberg recalled:

Cold decking was resorted to in order to better production. Cold decking is when a donkey is used to yard the logs on a given area into a pile. These piles contained from a hundred thousand feet to a million feet or more and were usually located a few hundred feet from the big logging unit [skidder]. The big unit would swing the pre-logged pile of logs to the railway and load the logs on rail cars. The term "Cold Deck" comes from tin horn gamblers who used to get into logging camp poker games on pay day and slip a deck of stacked cards in to the game; this was known as a cold deck.

For highlead, the cold-deck crew rigged one of the back spars, usually the "middle" back spar, which was known as the cold-deck tree. They then yarded the logs into a "cold-deck pile" at the foot of the cold-deck tree, where they were later picked up by the skidder and yarded into the landing. "We'd cold deck it," Sammy Telosky recalled, "bring it into 1200 feet and swing it in on the skyline from there."

Crews of five or six manned the cold deckers. Hi Churchill, who worked on one near Quinsam Lake, remembered that his crew mates were engineer Connie Aitken, rigger and hooker Dave Aitken, and rigging slinger Dennis Currie (who selected logs for yarding). There were also two chokermen, one of whom was Eddy Boyd, and the chaser

A cold decker coming out of the shop at Headquarters, having been serviced and mounted on a new set of skids, c. 1935. Movement was hard on the skids, which were replaced periodically in the Headquarters shop by the company's sleigh-builders, including Fred Erickson. "There were guys who made a *living* building skids," Neil Martin said. Sturdy inlaid bolts held the two pieces of the sled together. "They always used fir for sleigh logs," John Holmes said; "in fact you can see the pitch ring." Cedar wasn't strong enough. **Chris Holmes photo.**—JOHN HOLMES

The Flying Corps

Wallace Baikie described the rigging-up gang of the early 1920s:

When I came to Camp Two in 1921 Bob Grant was the head rigger on the rigging-up crew which went from camp to camp rigging the spar trees for the skidder settings. They called his crew the flying corps; Norman Janes, second rigger, Bob Piercy ran donkey, Jack Downey, Drew Berkeley and one or two more made up the crew.

They had a steam donkey and a couple of flat cars to keep their rigging on. They would move in when a setting was logged, unrig the tree, move it to a new setting and rig or raise a new tree so that when the logging crew arrived with the skidder all they had to do was to set up the skidder, string their lines and be logging in half a day. The company adopted this rigging ahead idea a couple of years earlier when Jack McQuinn first came to run Camp Three.

A self-propelled, gas-powered Clyde yarder in the Black Creek area, out of Camp 3, c. 1927. Mack Grant and Dave Aitken are the two men at the far left. The ill-tempered rigger Dave Aitken was known as "Davo the Ravo." "He was a tough old bugger—real tough," said Sammy Telosky. This yarder and crew are travelling over logging slash to a new yarder setting. **Walter Montgomery photo.**—INEZ CLIFFE

One of Comox Logging's three-drum Clyde yarders with a seven-man crew, 1934. The crew consisted of an engineer, a rigger, a hooker, and three chokermen. Left to right: Dennis Currie, unknown, Dave Aitken (rigger), Eddy Boyd, unknown, unknown, Connie Aitken. These men have yarded logs from afar and placed them in a cold-deck pile (left) ready to be yarded to the skidder landing. The lines go up to the back spar. **Wilmer Gold photo.**—WILMER GOLD COLLECTION, IWA CANADA LOCAL 1-80, DUNCAN, BC

The back-rigging crew standing on a cold-deck pile at the back of a setting with the back spar at left.—FILBERG LODGE & PARK ASSOCIATION, LAURIE MATHERS DONATION

A 150-horsepower Clyde gasoline yarder with back spar and cold-deck pile behind, north of Courtenay, c. 1927. Left to right: Big Jack McKenzie Jr., unknown, Len Harding, Bobby Cessford. Walter Montgomery photo.
—MYRTLE HERON

Detail of above, showing Len Harding and Bobby Cessford. Walter Montgomery photo.—MYRTLE HERON

Detail of photo opposite, showing Big Jack McKenzie and an unidentified man. Walter Montgomery photo.
—MYRTLE HERON

was Hi, who unhooked the logs as they came into the cold-deck pile. "We used a lot of ground lead, and Dave Aitken usually went ahead and fought the hang-ups and kept things going."

When the cold decker had made all its cold-deck piles, "we'd come along with the skidder and take 'em out," recalled loader Dick Bailey. The cold decker would then move ahead to the next setting.

Comox Logging pioneered the use of Lidgerwood skidders in British Columbia in 1911, and used them faithfully until the 1940s. Lidgerwoods went hand-in-glove with railway logging. At seventy-five tons, these "flying machines" were bolted right onto flatcars and were wheeled from setting to setting. At each setting, the skidders were parked on "a little spur that turned real sharp off the main line," rigger Walt Edwards explained. The railway section crew prepared what was called the skidder landing. They cleared the stumps, levelled the ground, built the spur for the skidder, and then "swung the skidder into the head tree," according to Bill Wilson. The spur was constructed so that the skidder was right up against the spar tree and the lines went right up to it. The skidder was then lifted off its wheels with steam jacks and stabilized underneath with large timbers. "The skidders had jacks on all four corners; they were part of the skidder frame on Lidgerwoods," recalled surveyor Tony Turner.

Once it was set up, the skidder landing became the focal point for all logging operations. Logs were loaded there, the crews had lunch there, and they met the crummy there at the end of the day. When the setting was logged out, the skidder was jacked up again, the timbers taken out

Part of the crew of Skidder 5 and guests, taken north of Camp 3, c. 1938. Front row, left to right: Eddy Hayward, Dick Bailey, Joe Stewart, Mack Grant, Butch Grant. Back row, left to right: Stan Woods, Stan Jackson, Wilfred "Skinny" Collins, Ronnie Muir, Henry Mackin (President, Canadian Western Lumber Company), Norman Janes, Bob Grant (logging foreman). Note the skidder's "weight log" hanging behind—a counterbalance to the hayrack boom. Bob Filberg photo.
—FILBERG LODGE & PARK ASSOCIATION

Skidder 5 in the Oyster River area north of Camp 3, 1934. Back row, left to right: hooker Anselm "Hooker" Johnson, Ott (Otto) Richter, chaser Dick Bailey, Mike Goudich, Ernie Pickard, Ronnie Muir, back rigger Gunnar Jonsson, loading leverman George Cliffe, head loader Wilfred "Skinny" Collins, Ted Helmcke, George Super, Tom Clifford, Nick Helm, Johnny Crockett, Alf Bailey, yarding leverman Butch Grant, Jack Clifford, fireman Eddy Hawkins. Front row, left to right: second loader Eric Gray, Stan Woods, head rigger Norman Janes. Wilmer Gold photo.—ELEANOR KELLER

Skidder 6, out of camp 3, c. 1927. Top row: fourth from left, loading leverman Reid Good; fifth from left (in vest), Johnny Batten; sixth from left, second loader Skinny Collins; eighth from left (on drum), rigger Jack Downey; third from right, Fritz Passman; far right, yarding leverman Clifford Janes. Bottom row, left to right: bunkmaker Leonard Pearce from Merville, Harry de Hod, and two unknown. Sitting on cribbing: head loader Eric Gray. Walter Montgomery photo.—INEZ CLIFFE

from under it, and the machine pulled by locie to the next setting or hauled by rail to Headquarters for maintenance.

According to Filberg, skidder "loading engines are ten by ten with four drums. The skidding engines are twelve by twelve with four drums. The boiler is sixty-six inches with a seven-foot-high firebox." Joe Cliffe recalled that "the skidders were built with a fifty-foot steel frame with two separate engines on them." These two powerful steam engines (which produced 180 pounds of pressure—enough to lift the skidder right off the ground) allowed the machine to yard logs of any size from the bush and load them onto waiting flatcars.

Like donkey engines, skidders were at first wood-fired; photographs from before about 1925 show wood split and stacked behind the skidder ready to be thrown into the firebox. Engineers went to work early to fire up the boilers. Joe Cliffe described the transition to crude oil:

In the first half of the steam log yarding period, wood was used for making steam. Logs were sawed into blocks by hand and later by steam using a large steel blade rocked back and forth by a steam cylinder which operated a crank on a shaft. This was a great success, sawing the day's wood in a couple of hours. It never became tired and the steam saw of course eliminated at least one man. It was a strange thing that the best grade log always seemed to make the most steam, and making enough steam with wood was always a problem. Around 1920 all railway logging companies started converting their skidders and yarders to burning bunker fuel oil. This gave a constant, hot, even fire eliminating ninety per cent of fire hazard.

Later photos show a large oil tank on one side of the skidder unit. Even after the conversion to oil, firemen like Eddy Hawkins of Skidder 5 kindled the firebox with firewood before turning on the crude oil tap.

～

Most rigging, yarder, and skidder crews were local men from farming families, though famous skidder boss Jack McQuinn of Camp 3 was from Oregon. Skidder jobs, said Croatian immigrant Mike Majerovich, were largely "reserved for the Homeguard." One newcomer who "made the grade" was Willie Adamscheck, a German. He had been the smallest man on the grading crew, his friend Neil Brady-Browne said, "but they needed a fireman on a skidder. This was a desirable job—you had a roof over your head." Whatever their background, all had considerable woods experience, as Sammy Telosky recalled: "You couldn't put a greenhorn on a skidder—they were highball."

In the 1930s, skidder and yarder crews lived for the most part at Camp 3, but those who lived in Courtenay were picked up first thing in the morning by the main-line train returning from Royston. It picked up the woods crews at the company's siding below the Native Sons' Hall, next to Courtenay Crossing, and took them out to work in the boxcar crummies. If the skidder and rigging bosses needed extra men, they might poach them from a cold-deck crew or, in the Depression era, go to the Courtenay Crossing siding where men gathered every morning in search of work. "If the boss needed you he'd take you," recalled Mike Majerovich; "the other fellows would go home." From Courtenay Crossing the crummies went on to Headquarters, and then to the bush. Everyone got off the train at the skidder landing.

The daily shift started at 8:00 a.m. "You were where you were meant to be at eight when work started," Hi Churchill recalled, "and you worked right through until noon. No coffee breaks in them days!"

Joe Cliffe, High Rigger

In 1980, Joe Cliffe reflected on his career as a high rigger:

I worked, actually, dragging those tongs, what they called hooking, out in the woods for about a year. Then they insisted I start learning to rig, to go high rigging. In 1921, that's when I started to climb trees. I thought I was going to die climbing trees! I think I climbed trees fifteen years. That was quite a long time especially with skidders—you are up in the air so much. . . .

Oh, there was more to do with skidders . . . so many lines on a tree and so many blocks on a tree. Later on I had to rig all the trees and that's all I did was rig, for many years, just sort of up in the air every day for hours and hours. . . .

With six skidders it took a lot of rigging. I also had to take it down. Of course it didn't take too long to take it down, not near as long as to put it up. Later on, when the big trees got scarcer we used to haul out trees. We'd get them where we could, good big trees, then we'd haul them to the place where we wanted to put them up. Then we could put the logging jewellery on the tree down on the ground before we raised it. Then we raised it up—all it meant was a little adjusting here and there, tighten the guy lines and all that. You never knew it was raised, of course, unless you looked. That way you got away from the swelled butts and you got them exactly where you wanted them close to the track.

Skidding by Skyline

Joe Cliffe explained the fundamentals of the skidder skyline system:

Simply explained it was a large cable hung on a spar tree at the track and also hung in a tree at the back of the felled timber. These back spars were spaced approximately 200 feet apart all around the setting. The skyline was threaded through a carriage. When the skyline was tightened the carriage travelled back and forth. Logs were lifted up clear of all stumps and landed at the track without any hang-up trouble. This system was especially suited to rough ground with ravines and side hills. These machines . . . required an immense amount of steel cable as well as a well-trained crew of about twenty men.

Comox Logging's Skidder 5, 1930. Skidders like this one, Davey Janes recalled, were parked beside the track "on wheels on a little wee tiny spur" before being jacked up and blocked with timbers, visible here. Top row, left to right: second loader Jasper Hawkins, fireman Mack Grant, loading leverman George Cliffe, rigger Arvo Eckland, hooker Nick Helm, mat-hooker Davey Janes, loader Skinny Collins, and a Finnish rigger named Oscar. Bottom row, left to right: shovel operator Spit Quinn, chokerman Hi Churchill, second hooker Tom Clifford, chokerman Alfred Bailey, chaser Dick Bailey, chokerman Tom Bailey, bunkmaker Jack Clifford, high rigger Norman Janes. Spit Quinn and Davey Janes were running a grading shovel at the time. "We just happened to be walking home!" Davey Janes said of their inclusion in the photo. They were not part of the skidder crew. Walter Montgomery photo.—DICK AND EVA BAILEY

Lunch was the highlight of the day, Churchill continued. "The food was not bad. For lunch, they had a thing called the coffin, a big wooden box with a handle at each end to take the sandwiches out to the woods." The coffin would be filled up with yesterday's grub from Camp 3. "If you had boiled eggs one day you got them in sandwiches the next," Bill Wilson remembered. Whistlepunk Davey Janes and bunkmaker Jack Clifford got an extra two bits a day for carrying the coffin, and it was the bunkmaker's job to provide hot coffee for lunch. "For coffee," Hi described wryly, "they put the water and coffee into a metal bucket and stuck the steam hose from the skidder into it, and turned the steam on. You'd sweat it all out!" Davey Janes added, "There would be crude oil floating around in it."

Each skidder had a twenty-two man crew divided into a yarding (or "skidding") crew and a landing (or "loading") crew. A fierce rivalry sometimes existed between these two halves of the skidder crews.

The yarding crew was divided, in turn, into a back-rigging crew and a front-end yarding crew. The back-rigging crew consisted of a head rigger, a second rigger, and two, three, or four riggers who helped rig the back spars, which were all standing trees. Head riggers were always up a back spar, according to back rigger Hi Churchill; "they went up most of

187

A Skookum Son of a Gun

Born in Sweden in 1903, Anselm Per "Hooker" Johnson started working for Comox Logging in 1922. Between the wars he hooked on Skidder 6 out of Camp 3 and later rigged on a yarder with Stan Hodgins. Hooker Johnson was famous for his astonishing feats of strength. "He's the guy I started with," Dick Bailey recalled, "a Swede. That goddamn guy could take a forty-five-gallon gas drum and put it on a flatcar." This drum weighed about four hundred pounds. "He was a skookum son of a gun," declared his colleague Stan Hodgins. "He's the strongest man I've ever known!"

Hooker Johnson was long-splicing one day, and in his hurry he put the marlinspike right through his hand. Fortunately he missed the bone. He pulled out his handkerchief, staunched the blood, put his hand right back in the glove, and finished the long splice, which was crucial to the whole logging operation. Only then did he seek medical help.

Hooker Johnson died in Comox in 1996 at the age of 93 years.

Big Jack McKenzie Jr. with tongs, c. 1925.—MYRTLE HERON

Skidder 6 and crew north of Camp 3 at the Diamond, Quinsam, 1934. Standing top row, left to right: loading leverman Bill McKenzie, hooker Anselm "Hooker" Johnson, Joe O'Connor, Carl Widen, chokerman Edwin Linder, chaser Ernie Adamscheck, Andy Nurmi, Dave Pattison, rigger George Super, Ed Boomer, Blackie McAllister, Andy Flawse, Max Adamscheck. Bottom row, left to right: George Stemak, Jasper Hawkins, second loader Harold Brazier, fireman Willie Adamscheck, Axel Erickson, yarding leverman Clifford Janes, high rigger Jack Downey, head loader Ali Helm. Wilmer Gold photo.—WILMER GOLD COLLECTION, IWA CANADA LOCAL 1-80, DUNCAN, BC

Pulling from a cold-deck pile, near Constitution Hill, c. 1935. A skidder (out of the picture to the right) is yarding six logs from the cold-deck pile at the left, while three chokermen and a hooker stand by below. Above the turn of logs is the "bicycle" block from which the choker lines descend. The "road" to the skidder, caused by dragging the butt ends of hundreds of logs, is visible to the right, beneath the mainline.—DAVEY JANES

A hooker and three chokermen near Headquarters, 1941. Left to right: Bill Masters (age 19), Dale Kirby, Norman Hammond, Malcolm MacAulay.—RUTH MASTERS

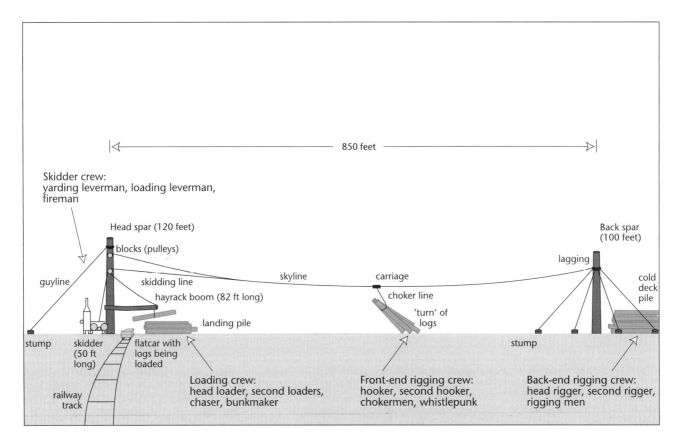

850 feet

Skidder crew:
yarding leverman, loading leverman, fireman

Head spar (120 feet)

blocks (pulleys)

guyline

skidding line

hayrack boom (82 ft long)

skyline

carriage

Back spar
(100 feet)

lagging

cold
deck
pile

choker line

'turn' of
logs

landing pile

stump

skidder
(50 ft
long)

flatcar with
logs being
loaded

stump

railway
track

Loading crew:
head loader, second loaders,
chaser, bunkmaker

Front-end rigging crew:
hooker, second hooker,
chokermen, whistlepunk

Back-end rigging crew:
head rigger, second rigger,
rigging men

Yarding logs from a cold deck pile and loading them onto a flatcar.

the time unless they could BS someone else into it!" The rigging crew was kept constantly at work, rigging, unrigging, falling, and bucking back spars as the skidder crew logged its way around the perimeter of the setting.

Skidders yarded logs by means of lines strung up to blocks on spar trees overhead. The 1¾ inch-thick mainline, or skyline, was attached to shackles on the spar trees, not directly to the skidder itself. Head riggers like Norman Janes and Joe Cliffe (initially part of the flying corps but later assigned to individual skidders) started by "hanging a block" on the back spar. Then they put a rope into the block, pulled it up, and the rigger—up on the tree on spurs—would start rigging. "They were up there for hours and hours standing on spurs," Hi Churchill recalled. On a back spar, one of the first things a rigger would do was put a strip of lagging around the tree. Lagging was a six-inch sheath of a hard wood (usually yew but sometimes crabapple, hemlock, or maple), which was cut into four-foot lengths, wrapped around the spar a hundred feet from the ground, and spiked to the spar to prevent the skyline from cutting the tree through friction.

The rigging crews also had to "notch all those big stumps," Hi Churchill said. "Everyone was handy with an axe. They had to make a notch in the stumps that was six to eight inches wide so they could take

Clearing the Skidder Landing

Old Bill Shevlock, railway section boss, was called to Camp 2 in 1921 to clear stumps from a skidder landing. Wallace Baikie recorded what happened:

Len Harding sent out Bill Shevlock one Sunday with some of his section hands to blow a big stump in a skidder landing. Len said, "You better put a whole box under it because I want it out of there so there won't be any hold up when we move the skidder in tomorrow." Bill spent half the day digging a hole under it and decided he too wanted it out of there, so to make sure he used two boxes of powder and let her go. Well, he blew that stump clear off the claim and spent the next two days with his whole crew filling in the hole.

Another time Len sent him out to blow a root that was sticking out from an unrigged spar tree so as they could lay the track to bring in the skidder. Again Bill got overgenerous with the powder. He toppled the spar tree.

190

Jimmy Weir, Chokerman

Born in Lancashire, England, in 1902, Jimmy Weir came to Cumberland as a boy and joined his father underground in June 1918, when he was fifteen. He worked for Canadian Collieries for eight years. "I had no time for rest or to eat lunch," he remembered. "The job was turning me into a zombie." In 1926 his future brother-in-law Slats Robertson got him a job as a chokerman with Comox Logging out of Camp 3.

The chokers, he recalled, were twenty-one feet long, long enough to encircle a six-foot log, but the first-growth logs were so big that sometimes they had to "bridle" a choker: that is, hook one choker onto another to get it around a log.

Soon he was promoted to second loader on a skidder. He married in 1928 and moved out of the bunkhouse into a house at Camp 3. In 1929, he applied for a job as chokerman on a cold decker, but Jack McQuinn hired Homeguard Eddy Boyd instead. "The boss said, 'I already have someone for that job.' I asked who, and he said, 'Eddy Boyd.' It was a family outfit! And I said, 'If that's the way you look at it, I'm wasting my time,' and I quit on the spot." It was a Saturday, so Jimmy hired a truck driver to move him and his wife back to Cumberland the next day. "That was a pretty wild weekend!"

Jimmy Weir eventually became a foreman with Canadian Collieries. He died in 1996 at the age of 94.

two wraps with the guyline, and then they would spike the lines to the stumps with railway spikes. The first step was to spike it up with three guylines to get it straight; the other guylines came later. It was a lot of work."

Rigging was "dropped" (taken down) and new back spars rigged as quarters were emptied of their logs and cold-deck piles yarded in. The rigging crew always had two sets of back-spar rigging with them, and to save time they would rig a second tree while the first was still being used for yarding. When they finished with a back spar they moved with their second set of rigging to the next tree, two hundred feet away. Two men were dispatched with a crosscut saw to fell a back spar as soon as it had done its job; they bucked it into forty-foot lengths to be yarded down to the skidder. "They wouldn't waste the back spars," Churchill said. "They were some of the best trees!"

Once a back spar had been rigged, and the skyline was operational, the front-end crew would start moving logs. This crew consisted of a hooker (or "hooktender"), second hooker, three or four chokermen, and one or two whistlepunks who signalled the skidder crew when a turn of logs was ready to be yarded in.

Yarding, like everything else to do with skidder operations, rotated clockwise with the skidder at the centre. Overhead, suspended in the air, the skyline stretched between the head spar and the back spar. "They'd go around in a big circle," John Grant explained. The skyline worked something like a clothesline. A block known as a bicycle ran back and forth on it. Suspended from the bicycle was a line, at the end of which a skidding tong picked up logs. Skidding tongs, which were eighty-pound pincers, went out of use in about 1925—to the relief of the chokermen, who had to lug the colossal piece of cast iron around the bush. Skidding tongs were replaced with lightweight cable slings known as chokers: loops of cable with a hook on one end, one for every four chokermen. Chokermen "set their chokers" and then they got right out of the way. The skidder then yarded in four logs at a time. Each cluster of logs was known as a "trip" or a "turn."

Logs were yarded to the skidder along rough avenues called "roads." There were as many roads as there were back spars on a setting. "Once you hooked your logs on the line and picked them up in the air they just came wheeling in without using very much steam, unless it was uphill," Joe Cliffe wrote. They were hardly roads in the conventional sense, but rather flyways surrounded by felled and bucked timber, stumps, and logging slash. They were roads in the sense that you wanted to avoid them when a turn of logs was coming through.

To retrieve distant logs, chokermen pulled their choker lines seventy-five or eighty feet out from each side of the road. They took a turn of logs from one side of the road, then a turn from the other side, until they reached the cold-deck pile at the back end of the setting. Transferring the contents of the cold-deck pile to the skidder was known as "pulling from a cold-deck pile." It usually took an entire day or more to pull a big cold-deck pile down a road, but two or three roads could be done in a day if there were not a lot of logs.

≈

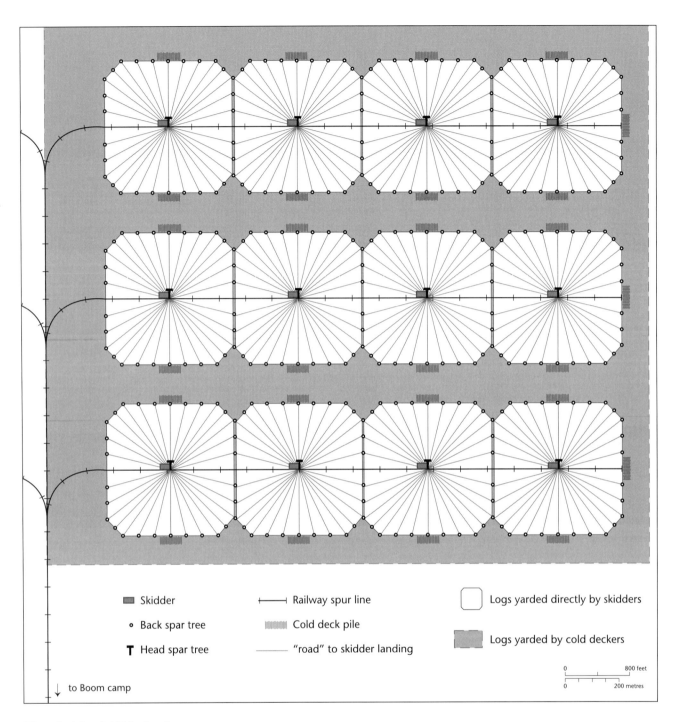

The principle of skidder logging.

Skidder

Back spar tree

Head spar tree

Railway spur line

Cold deck pile

"road" to skidder landing

Logs yarded directly by skidders

Logs yarded by cold deckers

0   800 feet

0   200 metres

to Boom camp

**The practice of skidder logging: Comox ▶
Logging's master logging plan, south of Oyster
River, c. 1921, redrawn from a map at the
TimberWest office, Courtenay.**

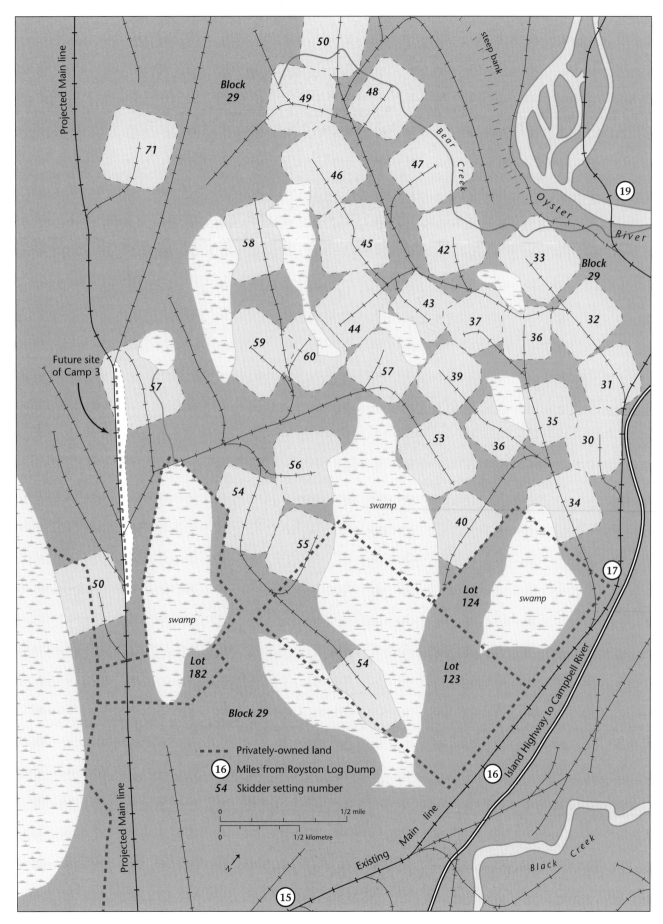

Block 29

50

49

48

71

46

47

Bear Creek

steep bank

Oyster River

19

58

45

42

33

Block 29

32

Future site
of Camp 3

57

59

60

44

43

57

37

36

39

31

35

53

36

30

swamp

40

34

50

56

54

swamp

55

Lot 124

swamp

17

Lot 182

54

Lot 123

Block 29

Privately-owned land

16 Miles from Royston Log Dump

54 Skidder setting number

0   1/2 mile

0   1/2 kilometre

N

Existing Main line

16

Island Highway to Campbell River

Black Creek

15

Projected Main line

Projected Main line

193

Differences in the lie of the land meant that no two settings could be logged in exactly the same way. "Nothing was really fixed," commented retired forester Darrell McQuillan. "Nothing was really the same from one setting to another." Survey, cold-deck, and skidder crews were well known for their creativity and ingenuity. Creeks and rivers meandered southerly and easterly from the Vancouver Island mountains to the Strait of Georgia, and the ground was uneven. As a result, logging railways and skidder settings had to be accommodated between rivers, creeks, beaver swamps, hills, ravines, rock bluffs, and other natural obstacles in the forest north of Courtenay. If, for example, a quarter contained a swamp or a bluff, a back spar might be selected only 200 or 300 feet from the spar tree, instead of the usual 850 to 1100 feet. In hilly country, a back spar might be dispensed with altogether in favour of anchoring the skyline to a big stump on the hillside. Some settings required two or three cold deck piles; some none. Property lines, where they existed, also had to be taken into account. An orderly, checkerboard progression was not possible, and no two logging shows were alike.

A variety of hazards further complicated work in the woods. In those days, settings were not clear-cut; rather, only the best timber was taken. Saplings and snags—the young and the old—were left standing. Some such trees were useful; the whistlepunks used saplings to string their thousand-foot lines out to the back of the setting. The standing trees were, however, hazardous to cold-decker and skidder crews and the cause of many fatal accidents. Such trees could get in the way of lines, and a line bent around a sapling could suddenly snap straight like a giant rubber band—with dire consequences for anything in its bight. "You shouldn't stand in the bight," warned 1920s chokerman Jimmy Weir.

Accidents also resulted from falling objects on these settings crowded with airborne blocks, booms, and logs. Neil Martin recalled that he was blowing whistles when Cyril Hodgins was killed just south of Camp 3 in the late 1930s. Hodgins was falling a back spar with one of his brothers when a single piece of the lagging fell and killed him instantly. "One of those came loose, and bingo." This was before the days of helmets. After Hodgins' death it became customary to remove the lagging before falling back spars.

Once skidder crews managed, in spite of topographical complications and accidents, to yard logs to the landing, the logs became the concern of the loading crew. This crew consisted of two engineers who operated the controls ("levers") of the Lidgerwood skidder: the yarding leverman and the loading leverman. They, along with a fireman, were the only three men to work on the machine itself. The loading leverman, who ran the machine, always stood at the front of the skidder closest to the spar tree; the yarding leverman stood behind him. Some of the well-known yarding and loading levermen were George Cliffe, Reid Good, Arthur "Butch" Grant, Clifford "Mary" Janes, Bill McKenzie, and Harry Shepherd.

Waiting at the track were a head loader, two second loaders, a chaser, and a bunkmaker (who made wooden "bunks" to support long logs— mainly boomsticks—as the flatcars went around corners). The yarding leverman brought in turns of logs from the chokermen. When a turn of

The Whistlepunks

In skidder logging, contact between the yarding leverman and the front-end yarding crew was maintained by means of a wire stretched between the chokerman and the skidder. A bell rang in the skidder when the wire was pulled. The intermediary was the whistlepunk, often a boy or a disabled man. When the chokerman had prepared a turn of logs, the hooker yelled to the whistlepunk, who pulled on the "whistle wire" to warn the leverman that the way was clear to yard the turn to the skidder. Joe Cliffe described this development:

When steam yarding machines were introduced to the logging business it soon became evident that some sort of communication must be arranged between the engineer and the men in the woods. So a small whistle was made and attached to the boiler just above the engineer's head. Steel springs were attached to each side of the whistle lever with some tension on them.

Then a wire was attached to the whistle lever and strung out to the woods close to the area where the loggers were working. The wire was suspended from saplings at various points about the height of a man. To operate the whistle the operator [whistlepunk] would stand under the wire. By pulling it down over his shoulder with his two hands close together he could make any length of whistle he desired. The signal system was based somewhat after the Morse code. For safety and efficiency the two most important signals were the shortest, one short toot to stop and one to start. There were many signals all based on various lengths of whistles which the hooktender would relay to the whistle punk.

In about 1920 an electric whistle system was introduced that greatly reduced the risk of accidents.

One whistlepunk was Bill Nairn, born in Scotland in 1912, the son of the greenskeeper at the St. Andrews golf course. Nairn came to Canada as a boy and started working for Comox Logging in 1929. "My boss was Bob Grant," he recalled. "I was whistlepunk on a big skidder. I had a thousand feet of whistle wire and headed into the woods. The boss would holler for the signal to take the log in. I was aged about seventeen when I started."

Black Humour

Dick Bailey remembered that they pumped crude oil up from the big tank to the skidder a bit at a time, but one time a skidder tank sprang a leak and dumped its contents on Carl Sundin. "Carl Sundin was standing in the slash when three hundred gallons of crude oil hit him! . . . Carl Sundin, a big blond Swede, got hit by the crude oil and he was black as tar. He was a black Swede!"

Hi Churchill recalled an incident that happened to Gunnar Jonsson (later known as "Turkey John" for his farm at Merville) in about 1930. Fresh from Sweden, Gunnar was still learning both English and the logging vocabulary when they sent him from the back rigging to get some grease from the skidder engineer. "He was 1500 feet out. All along the way he kept repeating 'Grease! Grease!' so that he wouldn't forget. Then along comes second loader Skinny Collins, who says, 'How are you doing, my friend John?' Gunnar stops to chat, and then says, 'Goddamn it—I forget!' And he had to walk all the way back again."

Get Me a Sky Hook

Big Jack McKenzie's daughter Myrtle Heron recalled the range of humiliating practical jokes played on greenhorns by older men of the skidder crews. At the back rigging, the rigger might say, "Run down and get me a sky hook" or "Go and get me a choker hole." The kid would run down 1100 feet through the bush to the skidder to have his question met with gales of laughter: there's no such thing as a sky hook or a choker hole. Another favourite was "run down and get me a left-handed monkey wrench." The leverman would say, "I just loaned it to so and so." The kid would go from place to place asking for the fabled left-handed monkey wrench until the joke was revealed. A bunkhouse favourite was nailing a rookie's boots to the floor while he slept.

At lunch the men would speculate that they could hit a block with an axe. They'd say, "I'll bet I could hit it." The banter would go on until someone said, "I'll bet I could hit it blindfolded!" The kid would then say, "I could hit it blindfolded too." Then they'd say, "Well, okay, let's see you do it," and they'd blindfold the kid. Then they'd put his brand new pair of working gloves on the block and the kid would cut them in half. "That's the initiation."

Jokes from the bush extended into the domestic sphere at Camp 3. Once, Myrtle's mother Ella McKenzie unpacked Big Jack's lunch box to find a large green snake curled up inside.

logs arrived at the landing, the chaser unhooked the logs. "There was always a pile of logs waiting there," Walt Edwards recalled, but they didn't have to wait long before being loaded onto flatcars. "When logs got to the landing the chaser signalled to the engineer to drop them down, and then he ran up on top of the pile and undid the hook," recalled Gunnar Jonsson. "When he was done he gave a signal to the engineer and got out of there." Joe Cliffe observed that "chasers were generally kind of heavy-set fellows who didn't like jumping around out in the brush, over logs and one thing and another. As long as they could get at it and unhook the logs fast enough then anybody could do the chasing. Lots of fellows did that who were fairly along in age, you know."

Train crews then brought in about seven empty flatcars at a time to the setting. They were pulled by a small locie, usually a Shay or Heisler. The number of flatcars depended on the grade. The locie backed the line of flatcars up to the skidder for loading and shunted them ahead as needed. If the locie was needed somewhere else, the loading engineer could attach a line from the skidder engine and move the flatcars around himself.

The loading levermen loaded logs onto the waiting flatcars. Between 1911, when Comox got its first skidders, and 1925, the loading leverman used a set of tongs suspended from a single line attached high up in the spar tree. It took great skill to lift a large log held by tongs, drag it, and lower it into exactly the right place on the flatcar. Many flatcars were broken when levermen dropped logs onto them from too great a height. "Reid Good was an expert on the single line loading but some of the loading levermen had trouble placing the logs on the load," Wallace Baikie wrote.

In 1925, Jack McQuinn invented a new loading device known as a hayrack boom. This was an eighty-two-foot (later it was shorter) double boom attached to the spar tree thirty feet above the railway track so that it could rotate, if necessary, right over a skidder if the skidder lowered its smokestack. Suspended beneath the hayrack was a pair of loading tongs. The boom gave the loading leverman many advantages over single tong loading: it allowed logs to be yarded and loaded precisely; it prevented breakage of flatcars; and it speeded up loading. But loading was a still a skilled and delicate job. "The weight on the flatcar had to be even," said Jimmy Weir, who second-loaded in the late 1920s, and loading levermen had to make sure that logs with wide and pitch-heavy butts were not all at the same end of a flatcar.

In the hayrack era, the loading leverman's job was known as "swinging the boom," while the head loader "did a lot of running around," as Hi Churchill put it. One head loader was Eric Gray; another was Skinny Collins. "Skinny Collins was always on top of the car placing logs," Gunnar Jonsson recalled. "The two second loaders would grab a tong, and Collins would say, 'I want the small one next,' and so on." The second loaders, standing on the landing pile, hooked their tongs onto the required log and then got out of the way while the leverman swung the hayrack around to the flatcar. They stayed out of the way when the hayrack returned with the tongs swinging menacingly beneath it, and then they ran back up onto the landing pile to hook another log. "It was

A Camp 2 crew loads old-growth timber onto flatcars with a wood-fired Lidgerwood skidder, c. 1921. The skidder crew, at left, watch the camera while the loading crew pause from work at right. On the forest floor beside the flatcar, to the right, brow logs have been placed to help the loading leverman position the logs. Logs are held in place on the flatcar with cheese blocks.
—PHYLLIS CURRIE

Detail of above. Hot and dry on a wet day: the fireman has one hand on the door of the firebox, which he stoked with the three-foot firewood stacked below. Above him is a sign reading "Logging Operations. Prevention of Forest Fires. Province of British Columbia."—PHYLLIS CURRIE

The skidder crew, left to right: fireman (unidentified), yarding leverman Harry "Shep" Shepherd, loading leverman George Cliffe. Note the stack of firewood for the boiler furnace. Skidders were converted to burn crude oil soon after this photo was taken.—PHYLLIS CURRIE

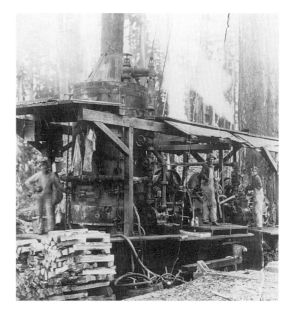

Detail of top right. A loader waits for the cameraman to finish his work.—PHYLLIS CURRIE

Detail of page 196, top right. A loader watches the camera while a large cedar log hangs behind him. Loaders had to be "catty" to work at this most dangerous location.—PHYLLIS CURRIE

◀ Detail of page 196, top left. The engineers: yarding leverman Harry "Shep" Shepherd (left) and loading leverman George Cliffe, with the spar tree behind. A water bucket with tin cup for drinking hangs from the timber below. Cliffe was a Homeguard, and Shepherd came to Canada from the south of England at the age of nineteen. He married Rosalie Williams of the Williams Beach family.—PHYLLIS CURRIE

Detail of the rigger sitting on the skyline carriage and threading a line that descends to the flatcar. "You'd think they'd lower it down, for God's sake!" remarked Davey Janes, who started on the skidders in the late 1920s. In Davey's day no one ever did a stunt like this on the skyline; they'd always lower it.
—MABEL CLIFFE AND HARRY ERICKSON

Skidder logging a few miles north of Courtenay, c. 1921. Both yarding and loading have come to a stop while the rigger (above) fixes the tackle while sitting on a carriage on the skyline. The loading crew sits below while the rigger does his work.—MABEL CLIFFE AND HARRY ERICKSON

Detail of the loading crew watching the high rigger at work. The loader is standing on a brow log, which helped the leverman guide logs into place on the flatcar. Note the minimal taper of these logs.—MABEL CLIFFE AND HARRY ERICKSON

Panorama of skidder logging a few miles north of Courtenay, c. 1921. A skidder (centre) tong-loads a "peaker" log onto the flatcar at right. The head loader and chaser look at the camera. At the same time, two second loaders (centre) watch as a log is yarded into the pile at left. A donkey engine (left) is helping with the yarding. Comox Logging took only the best, the biggest, and the straightest timber before it embarked on pulp manufacture in the 1940s. Davey Janes recalled that the logs were so good in those days, "you didn't know which end was the small end." Head loader Dick Bailey once loaded fifty-one cars a day for seven days straight. "They were beautiful logs!"—MARGARET SMITH

Detail of above. The head loader and chaser pause for the unknown photographer.—MARGARET SMITH

Detail of above. The second loaders watch as a log is yarded into the pile at the skidder landing, and prepare to run up and unhook the choker line.—MARGARET SMITH

A view down a flatcar of the entire yarding and loading procedure of Skidder 6, c. 1930. A turn of four logs is being yarded in at the far right; the horizontal log suspended from the hayrack will be swung onto a flatcar; and a locie (probably the Seven-Spot) waits in the middle distance to take away the loaded flatcars. Jack McQuinn is standing under the hayrack, and Jack Downey is among the other figures. Charles Sillence photo.—CUMBERLAND MUSEUM, C150-5

Comox Logging's Skidder 6 working the landing with a hayrack boom, north of Courtenay, 1934. At left, the skidder is yarding in a turn of logs while at the same time loading a log onto the waiting flatcar (centre). Note that the spar tree has been completely shorn of bark. "You had to get it all off or it could kill someone," recalled Eddy Berkeley. This photo appeared in *Maclean's* in June 1935. Wilmer Gold photo.—WILMER GOLD COLLECTION, IWA CANADA LOCAL 1-80, DUNCAN, BC

A turn arrives at the landing, a skidder toils, and a man runs down a flatcar. To the left of the flatcars is the "coffin" holding the skidder crew's lunches. Walter Montgomery photo, 1927.
—COURTENAY & DISTRICT MUSEUM & ARCHIVES, P200-1001N

Camp 3–based Skidder 5 toils eight or nine miles past Black Creek, beyond McBain's Swamp, in the fall of 1938. Ash from the recent 1938 fire covers everything. In the foreground, head loader Eric Gray supervises the loading of flatcars from the log pile at left. The loading leverman (on machine at left) is Butch Grant; the fireman at the far right is Eddy Hawkins. The skidder smokestack has been taken off to let the hayrack swivel. This photo was taken by Eva Bailey when Jack McQuinn took some women out from Camp 3 to see their husbands at work. On the tracks at the far left are Bessy Collins and Verna Albright. Eva Bailey photo.
—DICK AND EVA BAILEY

Loading with tongs and hayrack boom. The loaders, chaser, and other members of Skidder 6 pose on a log beneath the boom, Oyster River area, c. 1928. The big man at the left is most likely head loader Bill McKenzie, the three-hundred-pound former heavyweight fighter. Jimmy Weir photo.
—CUMBERLAND MUSEUM, C150-58

How Greasy McQuinn Got His Name

Jack McQuinn (1892–1963) knew everything about Lidgerwood skidders. Comox Logging had six of the machines, but production was below potential, and McQuinn, who had been working with them in Washington State, was brought in as a specialist in 1919. "He came with the skidders," Tony Turner said.

His hands-on approach earned him his nickname. "He was always up to his arms in oil," Don McIver remembered, and Davey Janes, who started working for McQuinn in 1925 or 1926, said that he was called "Greasy" not because of his hair or manners but "because he was always laying in oil doing something." His daughter Sybil Sutton remembered McQuinn as "a workaholic. He never asked anyone to do anything he wouldn't do." Wallace Baikie, who knew McQuinn at Camp 3 in the early 1920s, recalled:

I don't know if it was his idea or not, but when one of his skidders was moving, he would be right in there handling greasy ties and speeding everybody up to get logging again. Jack was always in the middle of any breakdown getting all greased up; that's how he got the nickname of "Greasy McQuinn." . . . Some of the old timers used to say that when Jack took over he boosted the production from fourteen to sixteen loads a day to twenty or twenty-two per skidder.

The Fate of the Skidders

Comox Logging's Lidgerwood skidders were carefully updated and overhauled at the Headquarters shops for thirty years after their purchase, but when Comox opened its Ladysmith operation in 1936, it did so with trucks. Skidders and railway logging were gradually abandoned in the Comox Valley. Economical gas-powered cold deckers helped render the big machines obsolete, and the skidders were last used in about 1945, when truck logging took over in the woods of central Vancouver Island. The Lidgerwoods were eventually scrapped altogether.

"It breaks my heart," said high rigger Walt Edwards. "They should still have some of those set up so we could look at them!"

not too safe to stand on a pile of logs," recalled loader Jimmy Weir; "they might start rolling." Meanwhile, the yarding leverman replenished the landing pile.

Yarding and loading put a great strain on the spar tree and accidents did happen. Wallace Baikie recorded one such accident in the late 1920s at Bevan near Courtenay:

The fully rigged spar tree on the skidder setting at the Comox Logging camp at Bevan snapped off at the receding block and everything above that point came rattling down on top of the boom and skidder. Everyone ducked for cover and luckily no one was injured. When things stopped dropping, the rigger—"Sailor" by name and excitable—came running out from behind the skidder yelling to the chaser to bring the pass line for him to go up the tree. Of course the pass line had come down along with everything else. The fireman was busy behind the boiler when all this happened. As the boiler began blowing off, he came out from behind the fire-box wanting to know why they weren't skidding logs!

⁓

Before each log left the forest, the chaser stamped both ends with the "Circle F" log stamp and with another stamp bearing the raised number of the skidder that had produced the log. A log stamp was a heavy hammer, on the face of which was imprinted the company's insignia. "He hit the end of the log with a big whack," said Jimmy Weir. The chaser stamped logs when they were on the flatcar—only occasionally, because it was dangerous, when they were still on the log pile at the landing. "He stamped the logs whenever he had the chance," said Hi Churchill. "He'd go down the track—he'd sneak down the track when he was waiting for a turn to come in—to stamp the logs." In principle a log stamp was the same as a branding iron: it denoted property ownership. It identified the owner of the log for the long and hazardous journey across the Strait of Georgia to Fraser Mills. Such logging stamps actually compressed the grain for at least three feet up the log, so that the "Circle F" motif would be visible even if the ends of the log were cut off illegally by a beachcomber.

When full, the flatcars were pulled by the Shay or Heisler locie to a siding, from where they were gathered up for transport to the log dump and booming grounds at Royston.

Cherry pickers returned at the very end of the show to clean up the setting and remove any trackside timber that the skidder crew had missed. These rail-bound donkeys yarded logs from "nuisance areas" where it was not handy or economical to put up a skidder, for example between the railway tracks and an adjacent swamp or lake. They also, according to Neil Martin, picked up old head spars from logged-off settings.

This is not, however, the end of the story—though historians of coastal logging have focused largely on the central role of rigging, yarding, and loading crews. While these crews certainly performed much of the most dangerous—and glamorous—work in the whole logging operation, they were not alone. Other Comox Logging crews, no less important, would oversee the logs' final transit from the depths of the forest to the mill.

Flooding the Landing

A personality clash on Skidder 4 set new levels of productivity in the 1920s, as head loader Harper Baikie explained:

The skidder operator and the loading engineer were continually feuding with one another and not speaking to each other. If the loading engineer needed a wrench out of the skidding engineer's tool box he would not walk around the other man to get it. He would ask me to get it for him, which I would do. I was a friend to both men. They worked about six feet apart but never spoke to each other.

This situation created a very competitive spirit between the two crews. If the skidding crew were in a good show they would flood the landing with logs and make it tough for the loading crew. . . . One setting we moved into had several big cold deck piles. They had rigged the skyline over one of these cold decks, which had about 4000 logs in it. The night before we moved into this new setting the skidder engineer, the hooker of the skidding crew and myself went down to the beer parlour in Courtenay for a few beers. These two guys started to kid me saying they were going to flood the landing and work the ass off the loading crew. I told them they better go home to get some sleep as they would never flood us with logs. Well, the battle was on.

A few days later Baikie and his crew loaded a total of 512 logs in one day, smashing the old figure of 390. Comox Logging's skidder loading record eventually reached 750 logs in one day.

The "Circle F" Log Stamp

To his delight, retired rigger Walt Edwards of Courtenay recently found an old "Circle F" log stamp on the beach at Comox Lake when the water was low.

Tools sometimes fell from log booms into the lake, and divers have found perfectly preserved axes, peaveys, and other tools beneath freshwater boom locations, their handles rising vertically from the mud.

An original "Circle F" log stamp is still being used by TimberWest in the second-growth north of Courtenay.

Yarding on the Skyline Cable

Journalist Bruce Hutchison of the *Victoria Times* visited Comox Logging's operations early in 1933. His vivid account of yarding and loading was reprinted in the *Comox Argus*, April 20, 1933:

A two-hundred-foot spar tree stands up beside the track and at its base, the puffing, groaning skidder is at work, grimly harvesting the green crop of the valley. On the cable skyline, which runs from the spar tree to another, 1,200 feet away up the hillside, a great steel carriage rides back and forth and from it hangs four huge logs, with cables choked around them. As the wheels and gears of the skidder turn and roar, the logs come trundling across the valley like living monsters, heads up, tails on the ground, leaping over fallen timber, knocking down small trees, bounding off stumps, plunging with a splash of white foam into a small stream, surging on as if by their own efforts towards the great spar tree.

There, of a sudden, they are dropped with a hollow thud, and, quick as a flash, two youngsters leap upon them, release the cables from about their necks and sink a pair of great ice tongs into their sides. The gears and wheels groan again, and a log forty feet long, four feet thick, is lifted bodily, swung around sideways and dropped upon a flat car as neatly as you would put down a cigarette on a table. Back the carriage flies along the sky-line, on the hillside yonder we can see the tiny figures of men putting cables around more logs, and soon they are surging across the waste.

From Tong to Hayrack

Harper Baikie, who worked as head loader at Camps 2 and 3 from 1925 to 1928, witnessed the transition from tongs to hayrack boom:

I want to explain the loading system Comox Logging used with these skidders. When they first got skidders the single tong system was all they used. It was a single line with a tong rigged through the jack on a buckle guy. The idea was to hook onto the log somewhere near the centre and bounce it off the brow logs onto the car. It was hard work for everyone involved, besides being hard on the flatcars and holding up production.

In the summer of 1925, about the time I started at Camp 3, Jack McQuinn invented what we called the hayrack boom. It was two long logs about boom stick size, 82 feet long, made into a frame using cross logs and rods to bolt it all together. At the outer end it would be about six feet wide so the tongs would hang straight with the railcars. This was suspended by a point guy and hung against the spar tree about 30 feet off the ground. There were two tongs hung about 20 feet apart. These tong lines went through two blocks and hooked into the loading line that came to the loader. This boom was swung across the cars, pulled one way with the haul back and the other by a counterweight that was rigged to a guy line. The reason this boom was 82 feet long was so they could load the logs in front of the skidder, which was set at right angles to the track and stayed there for the whole setting. The system worked very well once everyone became accustomed to the working of it.

Jack Clifford, Bunkmaker

Hi Churchill recalled that Jack Clifford was quite an elderly man who had lost a son (also Jack) in the Merville fire of 1922. Every skidder had a bunkmaker, and Jack Clifford was bunkmaker on Skidder 5 in the 1930s:

When they hauled boomsticks or swifters out of the bush they would need a bunk on the second flatcar. Jack would cut a two-foot chunk of wood the width of the car, and notch it on both sides. Then they would cut the long ends of the logs on the bunk so they could swing around corners.

He made the bunks out of fir mostly—he made them in the bush right where they were loading. He'd look over all the flatcars and decide which needed a bunk. . . .

Clifford's other job was to keep the water tank full on the skidder. He'd have to pump water, which might have to come from a mile away. He was a handy man—that's what he was. He had a son Tom Clifford who worked in the bush at Camp 3 for about as long as I did.

Bunkmakers also piled up large pieces of Douglas fir bark that fell off the logs as they were loaded, and one of the locies came up from Camp 3 on the weekend to pick up the bark for delivery to the married men's houses. They also kept the flatcars clean, swept the bark and debris off them, and helped whenever needed. Bunkmaker Jim Sedgewick, for example, was very handy with an axe and helped the riggers notch stumps to hold guylines from spar trees.

From Whistlepunk to Head Loader

Dick Bailey's parents Alf (an agricultural labourer) and Ada came to Canada in 1904 from Staffordshire, England. One of seven children, Dick was born on a Saskatchewan farm in 1913 and moved to Terrace at the age of four when his father got a job packing ties for the Grand Trunk Pacific Railway.

A few years later the Baileys moved to a farm at Grantham. "We lived in the bush like coyotes. Dad pushed a few logs together and put a shake roof on." Dick went to work for Comox Logging when his mother died of cancer. "Dad told me to go to work—I was fourteen."

Dick said he "started in 1928 blowing whistles for Anselm Johnson." How did he get the job? "Oh, BS a little bit. I asked for a job. They didn't ask my age! They never asked no questions. I told Jack McQuinn I was seventeen. Well, McQuinn didn't know, or didn't care—whatever. Him and I got along great."

Head loader Bill McKenzie took Dick under his wing—almost literally. "He was an ex-boxer, a big heavy-set guy—he used to pack me under his bloody arm!" At the age of sixteen, Dick was promoted to chaser on Skidder 5, and later he became head loader. In 1936 Dick married Eva Manson, daughter of Swedish faller Fred Manson of Camp 3.

Dick and Eva Bailey now live in retirement in Duncan, BC.

chapter 10

Out of the Forest, Across the Strait

*When the storms came
—the waves! Why, the
logs would be jumpin'
up and down!*

—RAY STOCKAND,
interviewed by Rick James,
1993

 OGS WERE NOW READY FOR THEIR JOURNEY BY land and sea to the mill. They made a spectacular steam-powered exit from the forest: steam locies hauled the flatcars to the log dump at Royston, where they were tipped into Comox Harbour by a steam-powered unloader. After being sorted into log booms, they were towed by a small, steam-propelled tug from Royston to Comox Spit. There they were picked up by big ocean-going steam tugs and taken across the Strait of Georgia to Fraser Mills, to be sawn into lumber.

The first stage of the journey—from the bush to the boom camp at Royston ("from hill to spill," "from stump to dump")—took place on the Comox Logging main line. Each year between the wars the company tore up and recycled old spur lines and built about twenty-seven miles of new railway. In 1925, the company operated seven locomotives over fifty-five miles of track, and in 1938, nine locies over sixty-six miles. This transport pattern would end in the 1940s, when logging trucks began to replace trains in the woods.

Shays and Heislers, workhorse locies, were central to the rail network. They gathered loaded flatcars from settings, coupled them, and stored them at isolated sidings. Seventy or more flatcars were picked up at once by the powerful main-line locies, the One-Spot and Three-Spot, from large sidings adjacent to the main line, and hauled down to the log dump. The One-Spot and Three-Spot were "travelling engines, not too good on the hills," Ralph Harmston said, suitable for escorting heavy loads down the gentle main-line grade to Royston.

One aspect of Comox Logging's rail operations that set it apart from other coastal logging outfits was that the company "didn't like skeleton cars," as Eddy Berkeley put it. "They liked decks," that is, full-deck flatcars, of which the company had a fleet of 212. Logs were secured not with vertical steel stakes, as in skeleton cars, but with four small steel wedges known as cheese blocks, two on each side of the flatcar.

In the 1930s, Comox Logging's railway ran north to within a stone's throw of Forbes Landing on lower Campbell Lake, some thirty miles from the Royston log dump and in a region known as "the Diamond." The company's northern timber blocks met those of the Elk River Timber Company just east of Block 27 near Quinsam River, and their main lines crossed in one place. The boundary between the companies' properties was "like a sawtooth," Ralph Harmston said, making necessary a railway crossing near the Quinsam River. This crossing gave the area its nickname, because of the diamond shape produced when one set of railway tracks crossed another. From the Diamond, the Elk River main line departed for the log dump at the mouth of the Campbell River, while the Comox Logging main line headed for Royston.

The entire length of the railway was maintained and repaired by section crews or section gangs, each of which was in charge of its own stretch of track. In the 1930s, southern regions of track were maintained by a four-man crew based at Headquarters, and northern regions of the track were maintained by an additional two gangs based at Camp 3. The traditional railway workforce manned these section gangs: mostly young, recent immigrants from Ireland, Italy, and eastern Europe.

Boss of the Headquarters section gang was an Irishman named Fred Griffith. His territory stretched from Headquarters to Dove Creek and halfway up the main line to Camp 3. Two of his men carried ties, the other two tamped them with spikes, and Griffiths supervised and checked the work. They travelled the line in "handcars," small vehicles with two handles that were pumped up and down, providing power. They were about seven feet square, with room for six men to ride and pump together, three on each side. Handcars were light enough to be lifted off the track and out of the way of approaching trains. They were later replaced by "speeders"—motorized units with hand-cranked Ford car engines.

Every day, two log-laden trains made their way from Headquarters, south through the farm settlements of Dove Creek, over the Puntledge River, through Courtenay, and down to Royston. Farmers sometimes brought claims against Comox Logging for killing their cattle on unfenced railway land north of Courtenay. It was impossible to get away from Comox Logging, even in Courtenay, because the main line went through the heart of town, right beneath the Riverside Hotel and the Bickle Theatre. Long trains would make their way slowly through the town during theatre performances. "When the play was on in the theatre you'd just have to halt," Rene Harding recalled. "It went on forever! Sometimes they'd have countless flatcars behind, all making a noise." Historian Isabelle Stubbs had similar memories: "Passing trains, with long bursts of train whistles and the loud rumbling of heavily laden wheels, disrupted meetings, church, speeches, movies, plays, lodge events and all talk."

Everyone in the valley had to endure the sound of the train hauling flatcars to and from the bush. Mavis Blackburn (*née* Harrison) lived near the tracks. "Every time a train went by my mother would take us out on the porch to watch the train, and our whole house would shake and rumble for a few minutes while the train went past." Walt Edwards,

From Stump to Dump
with the Main-Line Locie

Brakeman Hi Churchill hauled "from stump to dump" on the main-line locie in 1940. His colleagues were engineer Jack Carthew, fireman Jock Nairn, and conductor Norman Battersby. "The engineer and fireman were in the cab at all times," Hi recalled. He explained that the engineer ran the locie while the fireman kept the supply of fuel going:

They had all these gauges to watch and make sure the steam was in the right place. The fireman had to make sure the water didn't get too low. The brakeman was out on the front end. He threw switches so the train wouldn't have to stop—he'd get out and stand on the front end of the train, then he'd run like hell and throw a switch and then jump back on. Brakemen tended to be young men!

The conductor was in the caboose at the back end. As you're going around curves he could see if anything was wrong, and he could stop the train. At night he could see sparks flying if anything was wrong. The brakeman and the conductor hooked the train up at a siding by giving signals to the engineer, and when it was all hooked up, the brakeman and conductor walked the whole length of the train, checked all the cars, released the brakes, and then walked all the way back and double checked that all the brakes were released properly. It took a long time to get to Royston because you had to go really slowly with sixty loads of logs. We could dump twenty-five loads at a time in one spot, then switch and shove more out. Most nights from fifty to seventy-five flatcar loads went down there.

Closing up shop, *c.* 1917. Flatcars of logs about to leave a skidder setting along with the skidder itself, which the crew prepares to roll onto the spur line. This skidder was attached to Camp 4 in what became the Merville settlement. Note the surveyors' prominent blaze on the spar tree—a mark to prevent fallers from cutting it. —AUDREY MENZIES

The Six-Spot, a geared Shay locie, pulls three flatcars away from a skidder setting, *c.* 1920, with the head spar tree and skidder smokestack in the background. Both locies and skidders wore sparkcatchers on their smokestacks in summer.—MONA LAW

Here, the same Shay locie pulls the flatcars out of the bush and towards a siding for amalgamation into a much larger train of flatcars destined for Royston. Note the guylines coming down from the head spar to stumps in the foreground.—MONA LAW

Four men including George Cliffe (top right) posing on a full flatcar, c. 1914. In the bush, logs were bucked into sections measuring 24, 28, 32, 36, or 40 feet. This flatcar contains several 40-foot logs.—PHYLLIS CURRIE

who grew up in Courtenay, remembered the slow and laborious *chug-chug-chug-chug* made by the engine hauling a hundred empty flatcars back to Camp 3. Sometimes they took fifty flatcars at a time to make it easier on the locie.

Jack Hawthorne, formerly a brakeman with Comox Logging's train crew, was a signalman for many years at Courtenay Crossing, a block above (west of) the Courtenay River. Hawthorne's presence was in part a safety measure: in 1928 a boy named Pat Fairbairn, watching the passing trains at Courtenay Crossing, was killed when a log rolled off and struck him. Also, according to Rene Harding, "at least half the cars in Courtenay then had no brakes and that was a steep hill, so the people would go down the hill with their wheels locked against the sidewalk so they wouldn't run into the train." Hawthorne lived in a little house above the track and walked down to stop traffic on Union Street (Fifth) when trains passed. He waved his warning flag when the trains made their way south and when locies pulled empty flatcars back to the bush.

Beneath the Riverside Hotel and Native Sons' Hall, Comox Logging had a siding and platform which served as distribution point for that most valuable and sought-after fuel—old-growth Douglas fir bark. The people of Courtenay and nearby farms valued this precious fuel as much as the residents of Headquarters and the woods camps. Skidder and section crews collaborated to bring slabs of bark down to Courtenay on a flatcar, and Dick Creech hauled it for everyone by truck. Bob Filberg arranged for Creech to deliver free firewood and bark to the widows of men who had been killed in the woods.

~

It was a short three-mile trip from Courtenay to the Royston log dump and boom camp. At the boom camp, logs were delivered from the woods, dumped into the water, sorted, stowed, and then made into rafting booms for towing to Comox and ultimately Fraser Mills. The camp was a vital link in the overall operation of Comox Logging. It was where raw material from the forest—the handiwork of falling, bucking, skidding, and loading crews—was readied for ocean transport. In 1935, the Royston booming grounds processed ten million feet of timber a month.

The office, cookhouse, and bunkhouse were right on the beach. Married men's houses were unnecessary at this camp, a short distance from both Royston and Courtenay, though a few company houses occupied by Hughie Cliffe, Ab Stewart, and their families were nearby.

The office was the domain of the foremen, timekeepers, and scalers. An American named Pete Donnelly was the first foreman of the boom camp in 1911, replaced in 1928 by the legendary Hughie Cliffe, who remained in charge of the camp until 1948. Ab Stewart, Cliffe's boom foreman, would drown in the early 1940s while hunting brant at Royston.

The cookhouse was run, in the 1930s, by Bob Bowen and his wife. Bowen, from Haliburton, Ontario, came to Royston via a homestead near Lloydminster. "Dad drove logs on the rivers of Ontario for nine springs," said his son Ron Bowen (born 1909). "They hauled logs out with a sleigh and horses; it was a seasonal thing." Bob's familiarity with

A Pie for the Section Gang

Neil Martin recounted the story of the time Hazel Stevens, the surveyor's wife, cooked two pies at her house at Headquarters. In those days before refrigerators, she put the pies out on the porch to cool. Train boss Clay Walsh, who happened to walk past, smelled the delicious aroma, stole one of the pies, and took it up to the section gang.

He told the crew that Mrs. Stevens had baked it for them. After they'd devoured it he said, "Since she's been so kind maybe one of you boys wouldn't mind returning Mrs. Stevens' plate!"

A Rake and a Ride

Trains returning to Headquarters from Royston were often covered with precious Douglas fir bark. Bob Martin, brakeman on the main line, used to tip a load of bark off a flatcar for his old friend Walter Rigler as he passed Rigler's house on the outskirts of Courtenay. "Rigler never forgot that—that was a big deal," Bob's son Neil remarked.

Railway historians Cummings, Oliver, and Anderson described the bark free-for-all in downtown Courtenay:

A northbound, or Headquarters bound, train would sometimes stop in up-town Courtenay to pick up oil or supplies. This was a moment eagerly awaited by the majority of property owners along the right-of-way who, armed with rakes, would descend on the train and rake off the bark. The long line of cars would reach from town nearly to the city limits and in the feverish activity some souls would climb on the cars to push off their bark.

At the sound of the locomotive switching or whistling the flats would suddenly clear, as if by magic. However, one old lady did distinguish herself by delaying her departure a little too long with the result that she rode the flat cars through town and all the way to Headquarters. None of this, except possibly the latter incident, was known to railway officials.

The perfect load. When Comox Logging first logged on the "logger's Eden" north of Courtenay, a flatcar load often consisted of one large tree cut into three, four, or even five forty-foot logs. In this 1912 photo, photographer Leonard Frank posed head loader Dickie Downes and his young assistant beside a flatcar containing three logs. Notice the oozing pitch. Wallace Baikie recorded a story from one of Frank's visits: "Well, the foreman personally picked out 'the perfect load,' three logs across the bunk, two more on the second tier, and the peaker on top of all of the logs scaled, about 3,000 [board feet] apiece which was quite a load for a flat car. Leonard Frank got the picture and it is still displayed in some boss's office. The load was left at the back end of the landing over the weekend and when the crew came out Monday morning it was gone. The brakes had come off the load and the logs were all 100 feet back in the woods."—VANCOUVER PUBLIC LIBRARY, 6055

The Three-Spot backing a long load onto the Royston wharf, 1927. Crew members shown here are engineer Jack Carthew; fireman Jack Armstrong; conductor Bob Martin; and brakeman Harry Winders. Comox Logging's bridge crew, headed by Bill Eastman, was kept busy maintaining the pilings, trestles, and wharves. "They were always changing pilings because of teredos," said Bill Wilson. The crew rebuilt the trestles and log dump several times—a considerable job, for the camp had as much as a mile of trestle. Walter Montgomery photo.
—BRITISH COLUMBIA ARCHIVES, F-02347

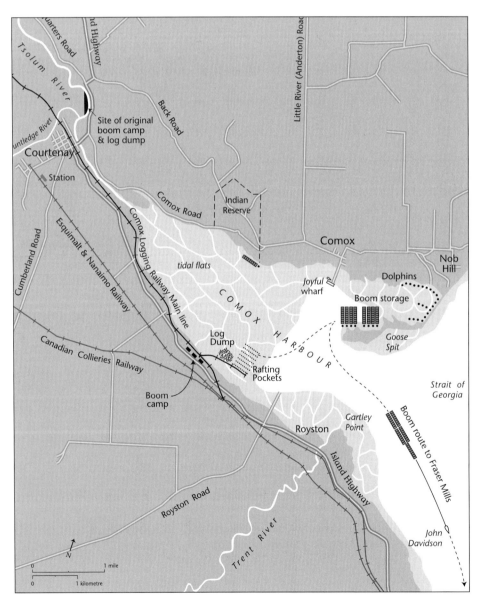

Booming grounds and boom storage, Comox Harbour, c. 1935. Redrawn from a 1924 Geological Survey of Canada map with information supplied by Charlie Nordin Jr.

The One-Spot approaches on a trestle near Courtenay, c. 1914.—BRITISH COLUMBIA ARCHIVES, A-04525

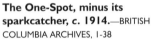

The One-Spot, minus its sparkcatcher, c. 1914.—BRITISH COLUMBIA ARCHIVES, 1-38

Boom camp foreman Samuel Hughes Cliffe, known as "Big Hughie Cliffe" or "High Pockets" for his size, strength, and immensely long legs. He was about six-foot-six. Hughie regularly broke wooden pike poles and eventually had them custom made from one-and-a-half-inch pipe. Wallace Baikie recalled that when Cliffe "got to pushing on logs he would move about half a section at a time." He was also known to stride across a boom with six or eight chains thrown over his shoulders. Boom man Donnie Haas said that Cliffe was a "good boss, good to the crew," paying them for an eight-hour day even if the low tide meant they could work only four or five hours. Cliffe died in 1964 at the age of 75. He learned of an incurable heart condition at the same time his friend Jack Mitchell learned he had cancer. They had a bet: whoever died first had to buy the other a case of Scotch. Bruce King, a pallbearer at High Pocket's funeral, said that his coffin was so heavy "we figured he'd put a couple of boom chains in there!" Note the snoose around Cliffe's mouth. **Bob Filberg photo, 1943.**—FILBERG LODGE & PARK ASSOCIATION

214

Tricks of the Track

Comox Logging railway historians Cummings, Oliver, and Anderson described the route to Royston and an odd part of the line where an eerie silence reigned:

From Headquarters the railway ran south through bush and farming country to Courtenay, then through the heart of the city (though not a city at this time) and onward through a large tract of land known as Campbell Ranch (after its pioneer owners) where it ran close to the tide flats (Campbell Flats) and finally arrived at the boom camp where the logs were dumped.

By a strange trick of acoustics there was a section of wooded area on the railway where a train could be present without being heard. You could hear a train enter this area, then silence until it emerged. One day some section men were returning to Courtenay from the boom camp on a hand car when, rounding a curve in this area, they came face to face with a train. The men jumped for their lives and all escaped injury, except for minor bruises and scratches, but the hand car came off second best. . . .

pike poles and peaveys landed him a job as a boom man at Royston in the early 1920s; he took over the cookhouse when he grew too old for boom work.

Conditions in the Royston bunkhouse were spartan, with orange crates serving as dressers, cupboards, and tables. A bell rang in the morning and the men went over to the cookhouse for breakfast. Theft was unheard of and the bunkhouse was left unlocked during the day. The men left their money and other belongings on their orange crates when they went to work, and the only thing that was ever stolen was a pocket knife, which was traced to the cook's helper, and "he was gone pretty quick!" said Donnie Haas. Between the wars, up to forty men lodged at the bunkhouse, among whom were cookhouse staff, boat builders, pile driving crews, train crews, and others (as well as bed bugs, a common scourge of logging camps). Bullcook in the double-ended bunkhouse was a French-Canadian from Ontario known as "Old Louis Ranger," who made the beds and swept the floors. Years before, Ranger had been working at the log dump, knocking logs off the train, when he fell beneath a moving flatcar and mangled his leg so badly that it had to be amputated. Thus disabled, he was made bullcook at the boom camp—an early form of worker's compensation.

In the 1930s, single men from the boom camp patronized Joe and Elsie Idiens' celebrated Royston Pavilion, a dance hall with a sprung floor that attracted Comox Logging employees from every point on the main line. "There was lots of dancing when the loggers were not up in the woods," said Doris Walker (*née* Marvin), whose parents owned the Royston Beach Auto Court.

~

The main-line locie crew (which in the 1920s comprised engineer Jack Carthew, fireman Jack Armstrong, conductor Bob Martin, and brakeman Harry Winders) backed the full flatcars onto the wharf for unloading into the water. The logs were scaled before they were dumped. Ron Bowen, who started working at the boom camp in 1929, recalled that head scaler Pete Donnelly assessed all the trains that came to Royston and turned in a report every day.

Dumping was assisted by an unloading rig known as the "humdirgen." The first humdirgen, a wood-fired donkey engine grafted onto the chassis of an old locie, was made in the shop at Headquarters. It ran until about 1928. Later models, built by master mechanic Dave Stafford, were oil-fired. Walter Pritchard (1890–1979), son of early logger Archie Pritchard, was one of the first operators of the humdirgen, followed by George Hudson and George Brown. The origin of its unusual name is lost in obscurity. The only explanation around is that a Swede, on seeing the new machine, exclaimed, "She's a real humdirgen!" meaning "humdinger."

According to Ron Bowen, the trestle had room for the main-line train to dump about twenty-three cars at a time. "They dumped on the dry ground when the tide was out," he said; "it was a dry dump." The humdirgen operator, George Hudson, blew his steam whistle to let Jack Carthew, the locie engineer, know when he was ready for another twenty-three cars. Carthew then pulled out the empty flatcars, shunted

215

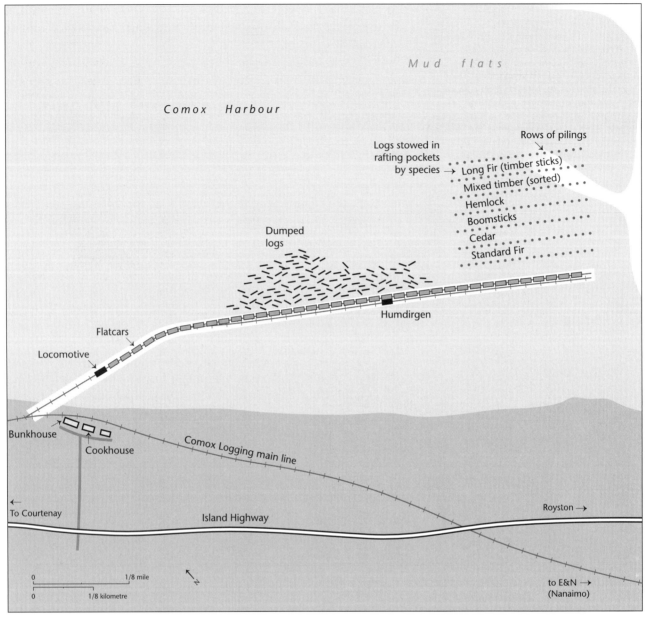

Mud flats

Comox Harbour

Rows of pilings

Logs stowed in
rafting pockets
by species → Long Fir (timber sticks)
Mixed timber (sorted)
Hemlock
Boomsticks
Cedar
Standard Fir

Dumped
logs

Humdirgen

Flatcars

Locomotive

Bunkhouse

Cookhouse

Comox Logging main line

← To Courtenay

Island Highway

Royston →

0   1/8 mile

0   1/8 kilometre

N

to E&N →
(Nanaimo)

The log dump at Royston, c. 1924.

A dramatic baptism of ancient trees. The humdirgen at work on the Royston wharf, c. 1914; view to south. In this photograph the Three-Spot is shunting the humdirgen down the inside track while it tips logs into Comox Harbour with its "kicker" or "arm." (The tracks on the wharf were canted, and gravity allowed logs to roll into the water.) At right are empty flatcars on the canted track. The logs lie in disarray in the water, but soon they will be sorted by species and stowed in the rafting pockets in the distance. **Vincent Russell photo.**—BRITISH COLUMBIA ARCHIVES, E-004746

The main-line **Three-Spot** locie, the **humdirgen** (right), and their crews prepare to tip logs into **Comox Harbour** at **Royston**, *c.* 1914. **The Royston wharf carried double railway tracks, side by side. The log train sat on the outer one while the humdirgen ran up and down on the inside track, dumping the logs into the water by means of a line and swamp hook. The two men at the far right are Walter Pritchard, who operated the humdirgen, and conductor Bob Martin, who set the line for Pritchard. Vincent Russell photo.**—ALLAN PRITCHARD

Royston boom camp foreman Pete Donnelly and his son Fred on the office porch, *c.* 1927. Fred later recalled that he had spent twenty years at Royston "rafting timber, sorting, breaking jackpots, and assembling log booms with the aid of caulked boots, pike pole, auger, peavey, chains and so forth." In the late 1940s, Fred moved to Hollywood. Under the name Don Frederic, he acted in TV commercials and movies.—ED DONNELLY

The main-line Three-Spot and crew at Royston, c. 1914. Standing on the train in overalls is engineer Pa Dixon; standing at bottom right is conductor Bob Martin. Vincent Russell photo.—ALLAN PRITCHARD

The humdirgen tipping a flatcar load of logs over the splintered pilings and into the harbour, Royston, c. 1920.
—JACK TUKHAM

◀ The humdirgen, operated by George Hudson, tips a load of logs from the Royston wharf, c. 1927; view to north. A member of the boom crew went along knocking the cheese blocks (also called "dogs") off the flatcars, and the logs rolled off. Those that wouldn't roll on their own were "kicked off" by the humdirgen. Walter Montgomery photo.
—FILBERG LODGE & PARK ASSOCIATION, JACK CARTHEW DONATION

them onto the tail track, and backed another twenty-three loads down the trestle. These were dumped right on top of the previous load so that the whole lot would rise and float evenly as the tide came in. At the end of the day there might be three, four, or five loads of logs piled right on top of each other in the chuck. Inevitably, logs got stuck or jammed together with the rising tide, and these log tangles were known as "jackpots," "pots of logs," or simply "pots." "A crew always had to go down and break the jackpots," Bowen said. Some boom men, like Jimmy McKay and Skinny Thompson, specialized in breaking jackpots with peaveys. At times, when greater force was needed to break a jackpot, a line was hooked between the humdirgen and a snarled log. This was known as "rigging the jackpots." "You'd flatten them out at night," explained Bowen, who worked on the night shift for two years in the 1930s, "straighten them up. You'd put a line on the humdirgen to straighten them. . . . They'd break them so the dump was free the next day . . . then the day crew came in and stowed the logs up and sorted them."

Long-time residents of Comox, two miles across the bay, remember the roar of falling logs at the booming grounds. The thunder was loudest when the tide was out and the mud flats resounded with the impact. Sometimes the wolves howled in the woods behind Royston, adding to the din.

Comox Logging boom crew, Royston, October 1940. Front row, left to right: Bill Franklyn, Bernie Blakeley, Uno Saari, Jim McKay, Ed Clayton, Jack "Skinny" Thompson, Hughie Cliffe, Joe "Curly" Bergsma, Andy Wood, Donnie Haas, John Larson, Tommy Cessford, Nate MacElwayne, Efe Desroche, Captain Charles Nordin, Bob Bowen, Ab Stewart. Standing, upper left (left to right): Charlie Stockand, Charlie Vaughan, John Blomgren, Clarence Hansen. Standing, upper right (left to right): Julius Lindberg, Bobby Smith, Jack Wiart. Bob Filberg photo.
—FILBERG LODGE & PARK ASSOCIATION

Pete Donnelly and the Open Range

Born in rural Wisconsin in 1857, Pete Donnelly moved to the logging camps of Washington as a young man and was hired to run the boom camp at Royston in 1911.

His grandson Ed Donnelly of Seattle visited him at Royston every summer during the 1920s. "Grandfather was generalissimo at the boom camp—he did just about everything but weddings, and people went to see him to resolve disputes." Ed Donnelly recalled that his grandfather's first car was no match for the rural forces of the Comox Valley:

He'd been to Victoria and bought a car, a Star automobile, and had it delivered to Royston. The guy who delivered it said, "I want to teach you how to drive it," but Grandfather said, "No, I'll take care of it!" So Grandfather gets in and drives off. An hour and a half later he's towed in by a team of horses. He'd hit a cow! He gave up driving. It was open range—cows went any place.

Pete Donnelly also worked as a water scaler at Royston. He died in 1930, at the age of 73.

The Royston boom crew, *c.* 1914. Boom camp foreman Pete Donnelly is sitting at right front, while his son Jack Donnelly is standing in the middle of the photo wearing a dark shirt and light braces. Cooks like those at the right were replaced by Chinese cooks in 1921. Vincent Russell photo.—CUMBERLAND MUSEUM, C150-31

Once the logs were dumped and untangled, the boom crew took over, sorting and storing the logs before they were towed to Fraser Mills. This crew contained an interesting mix of nationalities and backgrounds. Among the cast of characters were Homeguards Hughie Cliffe and Harold Cliffe (uncle and nephew), as well as farm boys Andy Radford of Comox and Tommy Cessford of Dove Creek. Cessford ran the gasoline jitney known as "the Canary," a contraption used on the rails for switching oil cars at Royston. The Canary also served as the crew bus, conveying men from the boom camp down to the booming grounds. Cessford was also skipper of the camp boat *Caroline*. Other local men included Charlie Stockand from Cumberland, Ed Clayton from a stump ranch near Headquarters, and Ron Bowen of Royston.

Others came from the Strait of Georgia and up the coast. From Nanaimo came foreman Ab Stewart and Jack "Skinny" Thompson, uncle of the bridge crew's Dunc Thompson. Stewart brought his friends Bobby Smith and Clarence Hanson along as boom men. Bill Walker from Union Bay worked on the boom, as did the McKay brothers of Deep Bay—Jimmy, Bob, and Bill, who had worked previously at the Robert Dollar Company's boom camp at Union Bay. From north of Campbell River came Andy Wood, boom foreman in 1929, who had been a gyppo logger at Ocean Falls, as well as two men who had worked at the Menzies Bay boom camp for Bloedel, Stewart & Welch: Bernie Blakeley, a boom foreman, and Uno Saari, a Finn and a "very nice fellow," according to Donnie Haas. Haas (1912–1999) was the son of Shorty Haas, an American-born donkey and locie engineer with Merrill & Ring, Hastings Mill, and Bloedel, Stewart & Welsh.

Much of Canada was represented on the boom crew. From the Maritimes came Charlie Vaughan, who arrived during the Depression, found a job on the boom, and married a local girl. Other easterners were Louis Ranger, the French-Ontarian bullcook; Nate MacElwayne, an Irish-Ontarian bachelor and long-term resident of the Royston bunkhouse; and Sandy Bishop, "an old Frenchman" (French-Canadian) and straw boss on the boom in 1929. Bill and Joe Muckle came from The Pas, Manitoba, as did Efe Desroche, formerly sawyer at Dan Kilpatrick's (Pidcock's) water-powered steam sawmill on the Courtenay River.

From Europe came three Swedes: boom men John Larson and "Big John" Blomgren, as well as shipwright Julius Lindberg. France was represented by Jack Wiart, who claimed to be related to Charles de Gaulle, and Holland by Joe "Curly" Bergsma, who had poled barges on Dutch canals. He got a boom job on the strength of his previous experience with canal barges, and proved his commitment to the place by marrying George Hudson's sister.

These men, like many Comox Logging employees, were hired not through the Vancouver hiring halls but through personal and family connections. Donnie Haas, for example, had always wanted to work on a boom, and in 1935, at the age of twenty-two, he gave Hughie Cliffe his name, expecting a long wait before hearing from him. Only a week later, Cliffe phoned from the Royston office and offered him a job. Haas spent his first night in the Royston bunkhouse, which was then infested with bed bugs.

Even those from overseas were often hired by word of mouth. Many

The Howl of the Logging Train

Farmer-poet Eric Duncan, living in pastoral Sandwick, suddenly found himself only half a mile from Comox Logging's busy main line. In an interwar poem he reflected on the mournful sounds he had heard since arriving in the Comox Valley from Shetland in 1877:

I have heard all night the doleful plaint
  Of the cow bereft of young—
At the Indian grave I have heard the song
  By the ancient Klootchman sung.

I have heard the voice of the wandering wolf
  Afar on the snowy plain—
But for long-drawn misery give to me
  The howl of the logging train.

—ISENOR ET AL., *Land of Plenty*

such employees of Comox Logging had worked for other companies along the coast, and a man's reputation as a good (or bad) worker preceded him.

The boom crew used pike poles and peaveys to sort and stow logs. The original pike poles were made of a hardwood (often ash), and came from Ontario. When Ron Bowen started working at Royston, all the pike poles had ash handles, but aluminum poles appeared during the Second World War, and the wooden variety soon became obsolete. The standard length of a pike pole was sixteen feet, but if the tips broke they would be rehung at twelve or fourteen feet. Peaveys measured a standard six feet in length, and had a hardwood handle.

Logs were sorted by species and then stowed in one of the large "pockets," or corral-like enclosures fenced by pilings. The pockets were narrower at one end than the other, Ron Bowen said, "so that the booms would go out easy." Stowing, according to Charlie Nordin Jr., involved "shoving logs tight into the booms. You'd push them in one behind the other." Men on the boom crew had to be versatile; indeed most moved around the camp a good deal depending on the season and the changing timber demands of Fraser Mills. "Sometimes you'd do two or three jobs—sort, stow, and I scaled too," said Donnie Haas.

Depending on what was in demand at the mill, the pockets might contain Douglas fir, cedar, hemlock, boomsticks and swifter logs, timber sticks, or peelers. Timber sticks, also known as "long fir," were straight and extra-long Douglas fir intended for long structural timbers. "Peelers" were high-quality, flawless Douglas fir destined to be peeled, literally, into plywood at Fraser Mills' plywood plant. The aim was always to have a variety of timber available. For example, the mill manager might phone Hughie Cliffe to say that the demand for cedar shingles and shakes on the Vancouver market had unexpectedly risen. If no completed cedar booms were available, Cliffe would then order the crew to make some booms from the contents of the cedar pocket.

One pocket held the boomsticks and swifters, which were the long logs used for holding booms together. Boomsticks were seventy-two-foot Douglas fir logs that had been bucked specially at the skidder settings and hauled down to the log dump along with the timber destined for the mill. Swifters were much the same as boomsticks but slightly shorter. Their standard length was sixty-six feet with a minimum twelve-inch top end, but they varied between sixty-five and seventy-two feet to allow for a boom's taper. The swifters rode on top of a log boom and held it secure. Boomsticks and swifters stretched over two flatcars and created a special job on the skidder crew—the bunkmaker, whose flatcar bunks allowed the long sticks to swivel as the train rounded bends on the way to the dump. Eighteen sticks were required for every boom in addition to seven swifters and nine "rider logs" of swifter length, which crossed the boom and held it secure. Every log boom, therefore, had a framework consisting of thirty-four specially formed poles holding it together.

Boomsticks and swifter logs needed holes drilled in their ends so that they could be chained together. Thus was born another distinct Comox Logging occupation: the boomstick borer. Ed Clayton, Curly Bergsma, Fred Donnelly, and Donnie Haas specialized in boring the four-inch

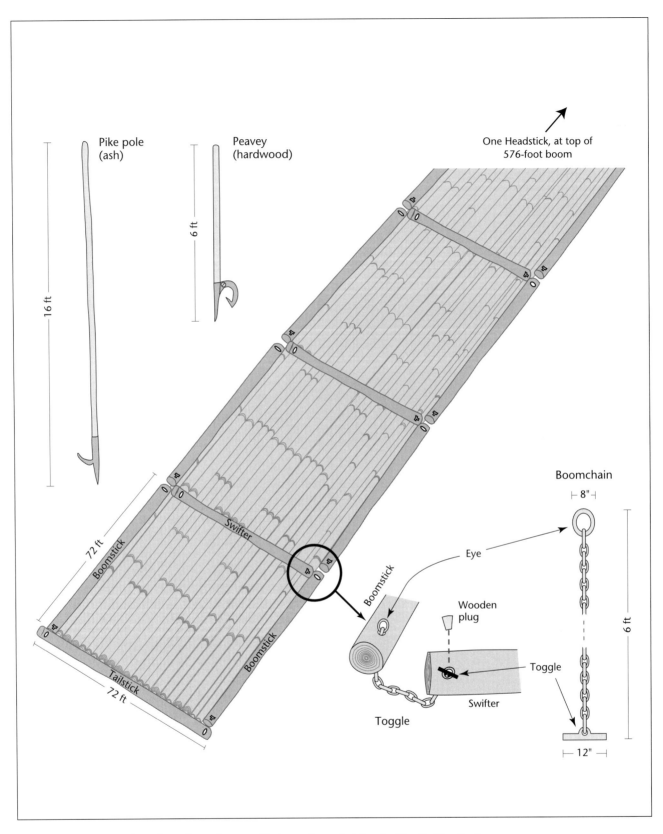

Pike pole (ash)

Peavey (hardwood)

16 ft

6 ft

One Headstick, at top of 576-foot boom

Boomchain

8"

Eye

Boomstick

Wooden plug

Toggle

Swifter

Toggle

6 ft

12"

Swifter

72 ft

Boomstick

Boomstick

Tailstick

72 ft

A log boom, boom chains, pike pole, and peavey. Redrawn from sketches by Charlie Nordin, Jr.

Sorting logs inside the Royston wharf, c. 1914. These twelve boom men, armed with pike poles, are assembling a line of boomsticks in the shallow water. The wharf is on the right, and the village of Royston is in the distance. Vincent Russell photo.—COURTENAY & DISTRICT MUSEUM & ARCHIVES, P200-25

In this photograph, taken from the Royston wharf c. 1930, the boom crew have stowed the logs tight into three boom pockets behind them separated by pilings, and they are in the middle of chaining up the nearest boom. They have not yet started swiftering the logs. Hughie Cliffe is at bottom left.—MARGARET SMITH

Swiftering a boom, c. 1930. Here, the boom crew are pulling swifter logs across the boom, chaining them to the boomsticks, and cutting the swifter logs to the desired length. The two men at the right are Dunc Thompson (holding the saw) and Hughie Cliffe. —LORNA CLIFFE

Pete Donnelly, water scaler for Comox Logging, in his watery element at Royston, 1927. He is holding his clipboard and L-stick.
—FILBERG LODGE & PARK ASSOCIATION

Alec Tilleard, chief scaler at Royston, c. 1935, with his L-stick—the device used to calculate the board measure of timber. Bob Filberg photo.—COURTENAY & DISTRICT MUSEUM & ARCHIVES, P225-864

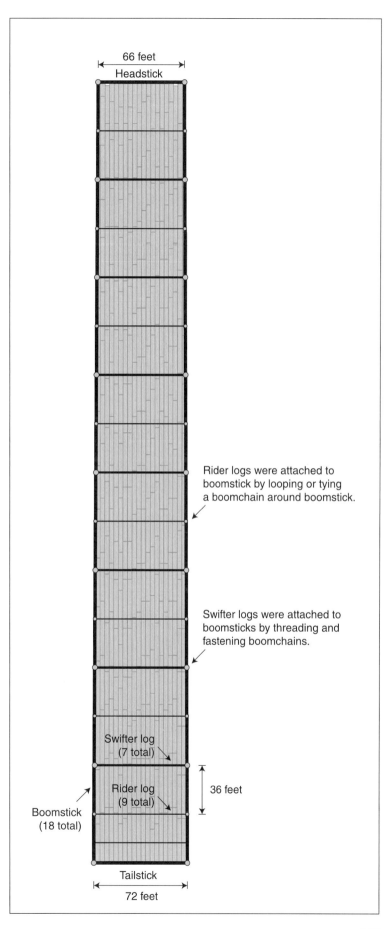

66 feet

Headstick

Rider logs were attached to boomstick by looping or tying a boomchain around boomstick.

Swifter logs were attached to boomsticks by threading and fastening boomchains.

Swifter log (7 total)

Rider log (9 total)

36 feet

Boomstick (18 total)

Tailstick

72 feet

An eight-section boom. Each eight-section boom contained about 300,000 board feet of timber.

holes, which was usually done on the mud flats when the tide was out. At first they used a hand auger, but in the 1930s Comox Logging obtained two electric augers. It took two men to operate these giant drills: each took an end of the auger handle (a big horizontal iron pipe) and held fast while the auger drilled through the top and butt ends of the log. If the boomstick had a swelled butt they'd chop it narrow and flatten it with an axe. But the electric augers had problems, as Haas explained. They tended to hang up when the hole was just about bored, and "if they hung up in the hole, they would throw you overboard, right off the sticks!" To prevent this, the stick borers learned to hang back a little at the last stage of boring.

Once bored, the sticks were pushed into the boomstick pocket. They were taken out as needed, chained, and hung. "You'd have nine or ten strings of boomsticks all ready to go," said Ron Bowen. "You'd go there with the boat and tow one out."

Boomsticks and swifter logs were held together with boom chains, sturdy chains eight feet long with a big ring at one end and a long link and toggle at the other (upon which the "Circle F" motif was stamped). Linking boomsticks together was known as "chaining up" and "hanging sticks." "You dropped the toggle through the hole and pulled it up through the other stick, and crossed it," explained Ron Bowen. These sturdy chains gave the boom the strength and flexibility needed to withstand the stresses of towing, particularly in foul weather. Newer boom chains, called "big chains," weighed forty pounds and the links were an inch thick. They tended to wear with salt and strain until they were only fit for use as "swifter chains." Only big chains were used to join the boomsticks together, while swifter chains held swifters to the boomsticks beneath.

After chaining up, the humdirgen pulled the swifter logs across the boom. This was known as "swiftering" or "pulling swifters." Swifter logs were pulled out of the water, guided into place on the boom, and secured to the boomsticks with chains. Two swifter chains were needed to hook each end of a swifter to the adjacent boomsticks.

Before the boom went out to sea, water scalers went out onto it—now stored snugly in its pocket—and carefully tallied its contents. Mill managers later used this information to determine how much timber had been lost in the Strait of Georgia. In the 1920s, water scalers included Pete Donnelly and later Alec Tilleard, Alec's fellow Englishman Fred Storr, and Fred Thatcher, a woods scaler who worked at the boom once in a while when woods work was slow. Donnie Haas worked as a tallyman for Tilleard and Storr. They stood at opposite ends of the boom and shouted "So-many-feet to this log," to Donnie, who stood in the middle making notes in a waterproof book.

A finished log boom tapered gently from one end to the other. The top (seaward) end might be sixty-five or sixty-six feet wide while the bottom was seventy-two—indeed, a boomstick at that end determined the width. The booms' taper, Ron Bowen said, "gave them the freedom to get out of the boom pocket," and tapered booms were also more seaworthy.

≈

Greenhorns and Boom Chains

Like other aspects of logging operations, boom work could be both humorous and hazardous. Wallace Baikie related the following stories:

They tell about a time a green horn was confused about which direction he should be pushing the logs. Hughie [Cliffe], who was about four sections away, started giving him verbal instructions and realizing that the green horn didn't know east from west or any of the local geography started yelling at him to push the logs towards V-I-C-T-O-R-I-A. Of course everyone within a mile could hear him.

Another time they were swiftering a boom and Hughie sent a young tall fellow (Harrison Piket) across the boom to get a boom chain. Piket was hurrying back across the stowed logs with this chain around his shoulders. He tripped and fell and disappeared down a hole in the boom. Hughie ran over to the spot and spent a few anxious moments waiting for Piket to appear. When he came up Hughie grabbed him by the scruff of the neck, stood him on a log, and with his dry humour asked the kid what he did with the chain.

Such black humour helped men cope with the reality that boom accidents could be fatal. Doris Walker (née Marvin), whose husband Bill worked on the Royston boom, told a story about a boy who fell off a boom while carrying heavy boom chains. "He's down there still. They searched and searched and never found him. . . . He wasn't very old. It was very sad, but then that's logging."

Comox Logging stored its log booms temporarily in the shelter of Goose Spit, Comox. The tug *Joyful*, a sixty-foot, coal-burning steamship built for Canadian Western in New Westminster in 1912, towed between Royston and Goose Spit from 1912 to 1948. Designed as a towing boat for eight-section log booms, the *Joyful* often pulled double her capacity. For almost her entire Comox Logging career she was manned by Captain Charles Nordin and engineer Jock Smith, who could be seen walking together down to the Comox wharf at all times of year, working with the tides. They never had a deckhand.

The camp at Royston specialized in boom construction. There was no room for boom storage, so when a boom was ready, and the tide was high, George Hudson blew the humdirgen whistle four times for the *Joyful* to come and latch onto a boom. The *Joyful* was always moored at the end of the Comox wharf, waiting for orders, and Nordin and Smith worked constantly because a boom left in a pocket could hold up the whole operation. "The pressure was on," wrote Charlie Nordin. "'Get those booms out of the pockets!' they'd say. 'They're holding up the whole industry!'" The *Joyful* would dart over to Royston and pick up, say, an eight-section boom of fir, cedar, or hemlock. Often, the *Joyful* was still on its way to Goose Spit with a boom when the four whistles blew again.

Emptying a pocket of its boom was known as "kicking it out." Nordin kicked out a boom by putting a line around a piling and pulling the boom out. Before he took it to Comox, however, he usually tied it up for a few minutes while he ran to the boomstick pocket for a new set of sticks which he put in the empty pocket to start another boom. Tommy Cessford and the camp boat *Caroline* also performed this task.

The *Joyful* then towed the booms across Comox Harbour to Goose Spit where, for storage and protection from the weather, they were tied by wire straps to rows of pilings and dolphins that circled much of the inner spit, on both sides of the Royal Canadian Navy's wharf. Dolphins consisted of four or five pilings driven in a circle one next to another and strapped tightly at the top with wire. They were used for boom tie-ups where extra strength was required. Booms of timber most in demand at the mill—fir and cedar—were moored at the outer or west end of the naval wharf, while those that were not of urgent use, mainly hemlock, were tied up for storage on the mud flats at the foot of Midden Road, where they were left aground at low tide. The inner spit could hold at least forty booms—twenty at the top for ready shipment and twenty on the flats. Booms were always linked to each other by boom chains.

Captain Nordin was ever alert at his home in Comox for telephone calls from Fraser Mills, informing him that a certain outside tug was on her way from the Fraser River and would require so many sections of Douglas fir, hemlock, cedar, or balsam. Because there were no radio telephones aboard the tugs at that time, the outside tug would alert Nordin of her arrival with a long blast from her steam whistle. This signal meant that the yarding of booms could begin. It might take several hours for Nordin and the skipper of the outside tug to "pull out" the required booms from the Goose Spit shelter.

Nordin's son, Captain Charlie Nordin Jr. (born 1923), spent his whole career on coastal tugs. He recalled the flurry of activity around the spit when the tugs arrived from Fraser Mills:

A Tumble in the Humdirgen

Lorna Cliffe related the following incident involving Comox Logging's humdirgen. Mary Darling, who lived in Royston, went out to feed her cat one night in the 1930s when she heard a voice calling "Help!" from the direction of the boom camp. She phoned Hughie Cliffe, who with Dunc Thompson helped rescue George Hudson from the humdirgen, which had toppled off the wharf into Comox Harbour.

Donnie Haas witnessed the same incident. He was scaling when he noticed an electrical flash from the direction of the wharf, and he looked up in time to see the humdirgen tip over. The machine had broken an axle and gone off the wharf backwards, hitting an electrical line as it fell. It landed in the mud, fortunately in about two feet of water at low tide. "She was laying half on her back in the mud."

First on the scene was Hudson's helper Bud Carwithen, who had been knocking cheese blocks off the flatcars on the wharf with a sledgehammer. He jumped down into the mud and jammed his sledgehammer handle into the gears to shut the engine down, and then he got Hudson out. Hudson had often been asked what he would do if the humdirgen fell off the wharf, and he'd answered that he'd shut down the drum. But when it happened he had no time to do anything; fortunately he avoided falling into the machinery.

Cliffe and Thompson gave Hudson a hot bath and "a few shots of booze," and within days both he and the humdirgen were back on the job.

The *Joyful* docked at Comox wharf, *c.* 1920. Seated in the stern is Captain Charles Nordin and standing next to him is his engineer, Jock Smith. While Smith manned the engine room, Nordin skippered the tug and acted as deckhand, walking on booms and tying up in all kinds of weather. "Other crews were amazed at this," recalled Charlie Nordin Jr. "For an engine room–controlled, two-man tug, this operation was a seventh wonder to fellow marine men. Dad refused a deckhand because . . . the responsibility of those booms was in his hands."—GLORIA DRAPER

John Tukham, who took this photo in about 1925, captioned it "*Joyful* in Comox most every Sunday during summer." Sunday was the only holiday in the week. Courtenay people swam in the Courtenay River, but Comox people favoured the wharf. "You could go and swim at Comox wharf," Barbara Marriott recalled. "It was a dandy place to swim."—JACK TUKHAM

Captain Charles Nordin with a big chinook salmon on the deck of the *Joyful*, c. 1925. Nordin was a member of the Tyee Club of Comox.—GLORIA DRAPER

The tug *Joyful* tows a boom away from the Royston wharf and towards the shelter of Comox Spit. Canadian Collieries' wharf is at the right. Vincent Russell photo, c. 1914.—GLORIA DRAPER

Eight-section booms stored in front of the Comox Indian Reserve on the Dyke Road, Comox, c. 1940. The tip of Comox Spit is at left and Baynes Sound and Royston are in the distance. Local children turned such booms into a playground. Sue Mouat (*née* Greig) recalled rowing over to Comox Spit from Royston with her brother Jim and running along the logs. She said she will never forget how the huge, buoyant cedar logs "bobbed gently underfoot." Bob Filberg photo.—FILBERG LODGE & PARK ASSOCIATION

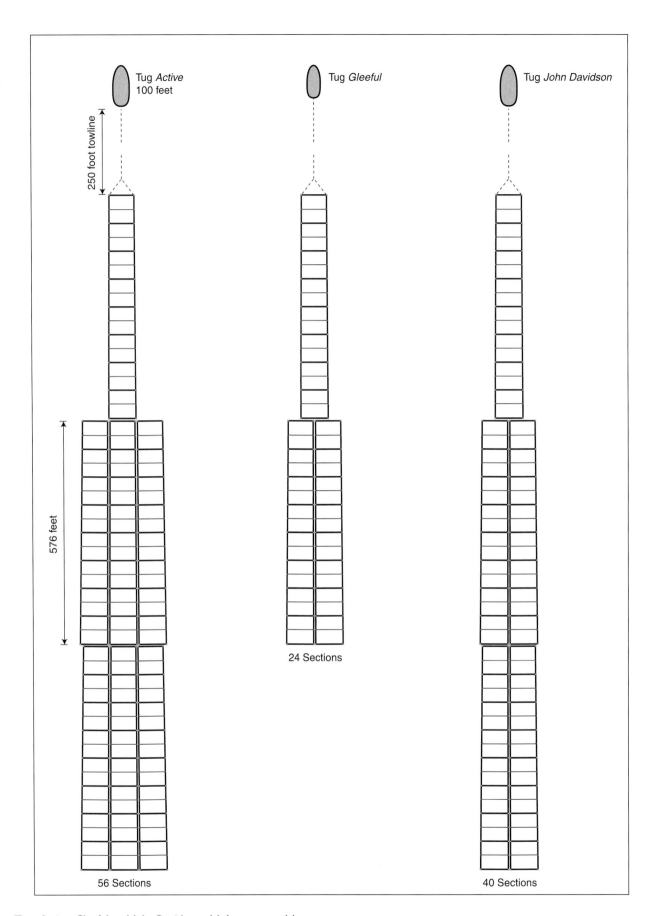

Tug *Active*
100 feet

250 foot towline

576 feet

Tug *Gleeful*

Tug *John Davidson*

24 Sections

56 Sections

40 Sections

Tugs *Active*, *Gleeful* and *John Davidson* with boom capacities.

232

The *Joyful* and an eight-section boom leaving
the Royston wharf, c. 1914. Vincent Russell
photo.—COURTENAY & DISTRICT MUSEUM & ARCHIVES

Skipper Tommy Cessford and the Royston camp boat *Caroline*, c. 1940.
This boat, with its strong hull and reinforced bow for pushing log
booms, was a forerunner of Comox Logging's revolutionary boom boats
of the 1940s. Bob Filberg photo.—FILBERG LODGE & PARK ASSOCIATION

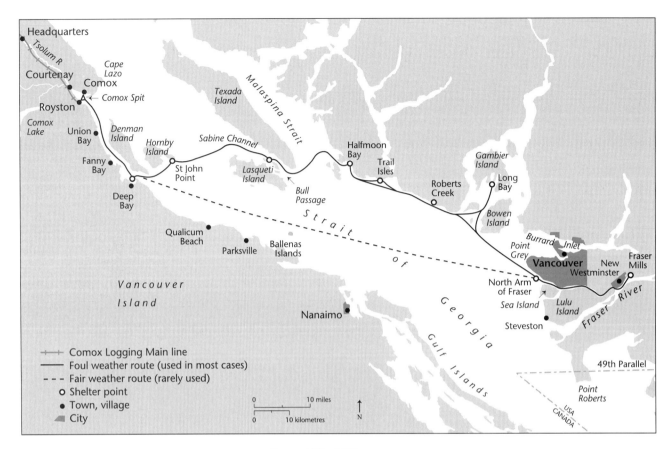

Comox Logging's tug and boom route, Royston to Fraser Mills, 1938.
Based on maps and information from Harry Nordin and Charlie Nordin Jr.

The shipping wharf at Fraser Mills, c. 1920. A spur line from the Canadian Pacific
Railway spiralled right through the mill.—BRITISH COLUMBIA ARCHIVES, B-08337

Rarely did the loggers of Comox Logging visit the destination of all their activity: Fraser Mills. "It was a whole different world at Fraser Mills," said Gerry Grant. "Never the twain shall meet!" The log slip and jackladder are shown here, c. 1920. Leonard Frank photo.—VANCOUVER PUBLIC LIBRARY, 5766

Logs booms, safe from the teredo worms of the Strait of Georgia, were stored in the Fraser's fresh water or in Pitt River, up from the mill. Here, the *Gleeful* is tied up alongside an eight-section boom near Fraser Mills, c. 1925. The company liked to get its booms to the mill early in the spring to avoid the freshet on the Fraser River. The *Gleeful*, a seventy-three-foot tug, was built in Vancouver in 1913 for the Canadian Western Lumber Company and towed logs across the Strait of Georgia until the 1960s. Leonard Frank photo.—VANCOUVER PUBLIC LIBRARY, 3149

When the outside tugs came in for their standing order of booms required by the mill it was like a regatta at the inner Goose Spit tie-up. Some of the eight section booms had to be towed out of their inner pockets. From the wharf at Comox one could hear the manoeuvring bells given to the engine room. "Bong" for slow ahead. "Jing-a-ling bong" for half ahead. "Jing-a-ling" for full ahead. "Bong" for stop. "Bong-bong" for slow astern. "Jing-a-ling bong" for half astern. "Jing-a-ling" for full astern, then "bong" for stop. Yarding for outside tows would take hours as booms had to be taken out of the inner pocket to suit the tow according to log category—cedar, hemlock, Douglas fir, peelers, etc.; and by the time the yarding was finished, often heavy winds would appear, and when the wind reached up to gale force, the outside tugs would push against the heavy congestion of booms with their deck line boat hook attached . . . to prevent the boom from breaking from its tie-up. Their strong search lights at night could be seen scanning the booms from end to end.

Nordin Sr. was also in charge of the safety of the booms tied up at the spit. Charlie Jr. remarked that during the high winds of winter his father spent "many a worrisome night thinking that the booms at the Comox Spit booming ground tie-up might break up," but his vigilance was rewarded: he never in forty-four years lost a single boom, either in towing to the Comox shelter or storing them there.

The outside tugs belonged to Canadian Western's subsidiary, the Canadian Tugboat Company of New Westminster, but carried the "Circle F" logo on their funnels. In the 1930s, the *Active* was flagship of the fleet while the *John Davidson*, *Gleeful*, and *Petrel* were slightly smaller. Among their crew were Captain Jim Goodwin, skipper of the *Gleeful*, Captain Dan Fiddler, and Captain Nordin's son Harry (1918–1999), who started as a crew member on the *Active* before the war.

The tugs had different capacities. The flagship *Active* could tow fifty-six sections at once (seven booms). The *John Davidson* could tow forty sections (five booms) and the *Gleeful* and *Petrel* could manage twenty-four sections each (three booms). The big tugs towed the booms three wide. The length of the tow line (a wire cable) varied according to the weather, Charlie Nordin Jr. explained, but about 250 feet of line was required "so the propeller wash wouldn't hit against the headstick— they'd lose power." The tow line was attached to the headstick by a boat hook and shackle, and the boom chains linked all the booms together snugly.

In fine weather, tugs could make the journey from Royston to the Fraser River in fifteen hours. Their "fair weather route" took them directly across the Strait of Georgia, from Deep Bay to the Ballenas Islands and the Fraser. The weather, however, rarely allowed a continuous journey between Comox and the Fraser, and in most cases tugs took the "foul weather route" around Hornby Island, between Texada and Lasqueti islands, and past Howe Sound. There were several points of shelter and tie-up places on the way across the Strait. "If the weather was really good they just kept going," said Charlie Nordin, "but if the weather was uncertain they'd have to decide if it was worth the risk or not. They had a decision to make. Sometimes they'd go by the smell of it: there was no radio or anything. It was a ticklish deal." In unsettled weather and at a maximum speed of three or four knots, it often took a week to get from Royston to New Westminster, and in very rough weather it could take a month to get to the mill and back. Harry Nordin recalled the route taken by the *Active* in the 1930s:

As shipmate aboard the SS *Active*, upon leaving with tow from Comox, having forty sections of logs in tow, the first shelter point was Deep Bay. With weather permitting,

Captain Nordin

Charles Emil Nordin was born in 1887 on a farm in Finland and, at fourteen, went to sea on a sailing ship. In 1905 he arrived in New Brunswick, where he worked briefly as a teamster in a logging camp. He came to the West Coast in 1911, got his master's towboat ticket the next year, and joined the crew of the *Fearful* in January 1913. That spring he moved to Comox as master of the *Joyful*.

Given a day off for his wedding, Nordin married Alvina Sanderson (1892–1972) in July 1913 at the Port Augusta Hotel, Comox. She had also come from a farm in Finland, but they met at a dance in Vancouver.

Charlie Nordin was a "great old man," according to Donnie Haas. A keen inventor and an ardent fisherman, Nordin conceived the idea of a self-dumping log carrier and designed his own salmon spoons, including the famous "Big Bertha."

Ever faithful to his rural roots, Nordin was a member of a Comox club called the "Burbankers," named after a famous potato. His son Charlie related that the Burbank Club met every year between Christmas and New Year's to tell stories, eat clams, smoke, and drink. Among the members were Hughie, Joe, and Ted Cliffe, Eugene Croteau, Jock Smith, Captain Alex Brackett, and chicken farmer Harry Rossiter.

Nordin died in 1976, leaving six children.

upon leaving Deep Bay the next point for shelter in a westerly was in the lee of Hornby Island, anchoring at St. Johns Point. Otherwise we would continue to Sabine Channel, and if a southeast would come up we would tie up at Bull Pass. If the weather was suitable we would go to Halfmoon Bay. With weather clearing up we would continue to Trail Isles, suitable for a southeasterly but not for a westerly. Next we would travel down to Howe Sound and go to Long Bay, Gambier Island.

The SS *Active* would then run light to Vancouver Harbour for provisions and a day off. If the weather was suitable, instead of going into the Long Bay tie-up, the SS *Active* would head to the mouth of the North Arm of the Fraser, where the smaller tugs would relieve her of the tow on account of the shallow draft in the North Arm.

Deep Bay was the main point of shelter on the Vancouver Island side of the Strait, and the *Active* sometimes tied up there for three weeks in winter. Sometimes they'd tie their tow up at Deep Bay and go back to Comox for another to relieve the pressure on the booming grounds. Companies logging far up Johnstone Strait also sheltered at Deep Bay, and rival captains competed to see who could reach the Lower Mainland first. It was the law to have a lantern at the end of the boom, but sometimes tugs pulled out of Deep Bay secretly at night with no lantern. "You'd wake up in the morning and they'd be gone!" said Harry.

Some captains took more risks than others. Charlie Nordin related that one captain from far up the coast stopped in Deep Bay on his way to Vancouver, delivered the booms to his mill on Burrard Inlet, and on his return found the *Active* still anchored at Deep Bay, awaiting a break in the weather. This caution contributed to a popular misconception that Comox Logging's tugs actually wintered at Deep Bay. "I imagine my brother played a lot of cards there," Charlie Nordin remarked.

The weather made for perilous diversions on the Strait. "Sometimes they'd come back after Hornby Island if the weather was bad," said Ron Bowen. "It was a cat and mouse deal. The skipper had to know the tricks. . . . When the weather was good they'd make a dash across. The hard part was getting into the lee of Texada Island. There was a fair amount of shelter on the inside." Howe Sound was the "worst stretch of water," crew member Bob Cliffe recalled. "It could be scary as hell—there was no protection." Log losses came with rough water; in particular, lowland hemlock was heavy and tended to sink right out of the boom or form deadheads. "There are probably thousands and thousands of hemlock logs at the bottom of the sea up and down the coast," Gord Blackburn said. These were routine losses, but some were far more dramatic. Donnie Haas recalled the time the *Active* left Royston with forty sections in tow, got caught in a southeaster past the Trail Isles, and lost every single log. The tug reached Gambier Island with nothing but the boomsticks in tow. The logs were scattered all along the shoreline at Roberts Creek. To make matters worse, beachcombers found the logs before the company's own agents, bucked off the ends with their "Circle F" identification, and stole the logs, leaving only the tops and stamped butts bobbing behind.

Fraser Mills, twelve miles up the Fraser River, was the final destination. Log booms were tied to pilings and dolphins at the mill's many storage places upriver from the mill, safe from the ravages of the saltwater teredo. When needed, tugs towed booms down to the mill for sawing, while the boomsticks, boom chains, and swifters were towed back to Royston for re-use. A chain conveyer, called a "jackladder," hauled the logs up into the mill, which was "geared up only for big logs," as Eddy Berkeley put it. Nothing entered the mill that was less than two and a half feet across at the top.

Meanwhile, back in the Comox Valley, far from the industrial complex at Fraser Mills, rural life continued its traditional course. The Homeguards and other Comox Logging employees arranged their lives around the seasonal demands of farm and forest.

The Royston Wrecks

As protection from the weather, old donkey sleds and boomsticks were at first strung around the booming grounds, but this was not enough.

Starting in 1937, Comox Logging enclosed its exposed booming grounds at Royston with a breakwater made of the beached hulks of fifteen ships, most of which were filled with rock ballast after being sunk: five sailing ships, *Laurel Whalen*, *Melanope*, *Riversdale*, *Comet*, and *Forest Friend*; two whalers, *Blue* and *Black*; two CPR tugs, *Nanoose* and *Qualicum*; and six naval vessels, HMCS *Gatineau* (formerly HMS *Express*), HMCS *Dunver*, HMCS *Prince Rupert*, HMCS *Eastview*, USS *Tatnall*, and the tug *Salvage King* (formerly US Navy tug ATR-13).

The first ship sunk was the *Laurel Whalen*, as Charlie Nordin Jr. recalled. Then a boy, Charlie was with his father on the *Joyful* when the ship was brought in and sunk. "Hughie Cliffe had a pretty good temper," he said. "There was lots of hy-y-ying and ky-y-ying going on as he tried to get it into the exact position he wanted it. It was not a very pleasant thing for me to hear!" The oldest ship was the *Melanope*, a five-masted barquentine launched at Liverpool in 1876.

Sawn lumber, timbers, and South Asian workers on the sorting platform at Fraser Mills, c. 1920.
—BRITISH COLUMBIA ARCHIVES, B-08359

238

The motors used to drive the planers at Fraser Mills, c. 1920. In 1931, the mill employed 495 men: 16 managers, 7 clerks, 68 tradesmen, and 404 semi-skilled and unskilled workers. In 1936, the mill's door factory produced between 2,000 and 2,500 doors a day, and the plywood mill produced 50,000 square feet a day. Bullen and Lamb photo.—BRITISH COLUMBIA ARCHIVES, B-08377

chapter 11

Homeguard Seasons

When the woods were closed you'd catch up on your farming. If the woods were closed for months, you'd have the chance to get a little land cleared up.

—STAN HODGINS,
January, 1996

IKE FARMING, LOGGING WAS A SEASONAL ACTIVITY. "It all depended on the weather," said Hi Churchill. Cool or wet weather provided the safest conditions for wood- and oil-fired locies, skidders, and yarders. The best time to work was "when everything was nice and damp," as Ralph Harmston put it.

The prime working months were February through June, and September through November. Climate varied from year to year, and market conditions also influenced when the woods were open, but a typical year between the wars generally saw seven or eight months of logging and four or five months without. The woods might be closed for two, three, or four months in the slack winter season, when snow was present or lumber demand low, or both, and closed again for two or three months during the fire season. "We were always laid off for two months in the winter and two in the summer," recalled Hi Churchill, "but in some years, we might have three months of snow and three months of heat, and only work six months."

After the winter layoff, logging usually started again in February or March. Hi Churchill can remember starting work as a brakeman early in the spring, "and you'd be shovelling snow on the railway tracks and chipping ice off the rails." However, by the end of March the woods would usually be in full swing and would remain so until the fire season began in June or early July. The camps emptied when the summer layoff was announced. "The woods were always closed in the summers on account of fire," said Ralph Harmston; "everything was steam and flames and sparks." Some Homeguard families went to Williams Beach, but most men returned to their farms in the valley. At the start of the fire season Bert Marriott, who owned a gravel pit on Cumberland Road, used to say to his wife Barbara, "You watch—we'll be getting calls!" Loggers came home and needed gravel for concrete foundations and driveways, and for other building projects.

Farming in Retreat

Between the wars, Comox Logging provided a huge infusion of money into the valley, but high wages drew men away from the farming economy.

In August 1929, Sandwick farmer and rural apologist Eric Duncan was scathing in his denunciation of logging:

The Cumberland collieries, while active, were an unmixed benefit to the district, but then logging is not so. Formerly good farm help could be got for $25 a month with room and lodging, but the ridiculous wages paid in the camps has stopped all that and a good man wants at least $60. Very few farmers can afford to pay this and the bulk of them must get on as best they can alone. Nor is the big money of much real use to those who get it, for it is largely spent on autos, which the roads are cluttered up—often with unfit drivers—and Sunday peace is a thing of the past. However, this is only a transition period, the big timber will soon be cleared away, things will settle down and agriculture will come into its own again.

Mack Laing cutting a Douglas fir with a Wee McGregor, a mechanical bucker, on the Comox waterfront, September 1925. To hold the saw down, the operator lifted the two arms of the Wee McGregor's A-frame and spiked them down to the log. Mack Laing photo.
—BRITISH COLUMBIA ARCHIVES, I-51808

Mack Laing of Comox splitting cedar shakes from salvaged driftwood, January 1934. Laing is holding a froe—a wedge-shaped splitting tool which was driven into a log with a sledgehammer (far right) to produce a shake. The tools behind include a bucking saw, a peavey, and a double-bitted axe. Mack Laing photo.
—BRITISH COLUMBIA ARCHIVES, I-51811

Mack Laing "stump-wangling" at Comox, March 1938. "Forcing a tunnel under the monster," Laing wrote of this photo. "This passage is large enough to admit entry of the workman and ends below the seat of the stump in a cavity large enough to hold 100 sticks of powder." **Mack Laing photo.**—BRITISH COLUMBIA ARCHIVES, I-51818

The final moment of the same stump. "Going up,'" Laing wrote. "The same stump snapped the instant after the 100 stick shot went off." Mack Laing photo.
—BRITISH COLUMBIA ARCHIVES, G-03318

"The strategy in stump wangling is 'divide the enemy,'" Laing wrote of this self-portrait, taken in 1929. "Here a big one is nicely quartered by about 50 sticks of powder. One section has been blown clear. More powder would have made a better job."
—BRITISH COLUMBIA ARCHIVES, I-51819

A Homeguard's Progress

Hi (Hiram) Churchill was born in Yarmouth, Nova Scotia, in 1912. His father, who made a living cutting lumber for lobster pots, died in the 1919 Spanish flu epidemic. A year later, Hi's mother moved to Vancouver with her children, and in 1922, Hi's older brother Bernard, aged fourteen, got a job with Comox Logging.

Hi started working in 1928, aged sixteen, when he rode a freight train to Calgary. It was too early for the harvest, so he slept under a railway bridge for five days with nothing but fifty cents in his pocket. Soon he joined a "harvest excursion" near Strathmore, Alberta:

I got a job with a farmer stooking grain. They gave me a team of horses and a bundle-wagon. I was up at four-thirty harnessing and feeding the horses. I collected sheaves to take them in and get them thrashed. This was 1928. . . . I never worked so hard in my life. They were goddamn big fields! As far as you could see were bundles laying on the ground waiting to be stooked up.

Hi returned to Vancouver at the end of the harvest and worked there until 1930, when his brother Bernard contacted him. "He sent word over that there was a job here if I wanted it. That was wintertime. It was colder than hell. I said to myself, 'I'll go till the weather warms up.' But I've been here ever since!" Hi Churchill started setting chokers for Comox Logging for $2.30 a day in 1930, at the age of eighteen, and stayed in the bush until 1940, when he went braking on the main-line locie.

Churchill and his wife Mavis (née Janes) bought a farm in Grantham, where they brought up their daughter and two sons. The farm was a blessing when the woods were closed. "I had thirty-five acres down here with a few cows and pigs—you had to have that to live. I grew hay for the cattle I had. We usually killed a steer every fall and butchered a pig or two, and it kept things going. I had about ten acres of hay. Usually I cut it myself—I had an old tractor here, and I raked it and dried it and stacked it in the barn."

He also sold potatoes to the marketing board in Courtenay or bootlegged them to whoever wanted them. "I shipped a bit of milk to the dairy—not a lot—but every bit counted." Like other farmers, he'd leave his milk beside the Island Highway and Art Brazier would pick it up and take it to the Comox Creamery. "Pretty near everybody did these things."

Hi and Mavis Churchill still live on their farm beside the Island Highway in Grantham.

Hi Churchill described the start of logging in the fall, which was usually about September 15. "I always remember that! When it started to rain enough they'd call you out. They'd phone you up, or pass around the word to different people, and everybody soon got to know. Comox Logging was right here in the valley and everybody that worked here found out. If I heard, I'd phone you." It didn't matter how much it rained in the winter, Stan Hodgins remembered; they never shut the woods down for the rain. "The rain didn't bother you, but sometimes the wind would force the people in." At first, loggers wore rubber clothes when it rained heavily; later they switched to heavy, waxed canvas pants. "They'd stand up in a corner by themselves!" joked Hi Churchill. Larry Lehtonen recalled that the only seasonal difference noticeable in Dick Bailey's outfit was that in the summer he undid the top button in his shirt and in winter he did it up.

Lives and routines of the Homeguards were also seasonal. When the woods shut down, "you'd have no money at all, but if you had a little farm, you had something to do," Stan Hodgins said. The fire season provided an opportunity to grow and harvest hay and other crops. Homeguards also spent part of the off-season falling, bucking, and splitting the next winter's supply of wood from their own land. They usually cut trees a whole year in advance and allowed the split firewood to dry for a summer before using it. A bucker's best friend was a mechanical bucking machine known as a "Wee McGregor," a one-cylinder gas engine attached to a two-armed A-frame that slowly sawed its way through the largest fallen timber with a steady *putt-putt-putt*. Those who bought land in the Block 29 region devoted part of the off-season to blowing up large stumps the logging company had left behind.

Many Homeguards, especially in the 1920s, took part in late summer "harvest excursions" to the Prairies. By 1916, the annual wheat harvest in Canada stood at about four hundred million bushels, requiring tens of thousands of temporary workers every fall. Many loggers laid off in the summer took advantage of the CPR's cheap travel rates (half a cent a mile) and harvested on the Prairies, where they could earn higher wages than on Comox Valley farms. "They paid a lot better out there— you worked longer hours and got paid more for it," remarked Hi Churchill, who went on a harvest excursion to Alberta in 1928, when he was sixteen. "A lot of guys went back to the Prairies," Neil Martin said, including his cousin Carl. Harvesting was barely mechanized, and the excursions involved a lot of hard work. "They pitched stooks of hay. It was very labour intensive," Neil added.

～

After 1928, when they were moved to Courtenay from Oyster River, Comox Logging's annual Loggers' Sports were held on Dominion Day (July 1) and at the Courtenay Fall Fair in late September. Loggers competed in bucking, log chopping, axe throwing, log rolling, tree climbing, long splicing, and eye splicing. Their families took part in the tug-of-war, the boys' pie-eating competition, and other events.

Bucking was the most popular event. A large Douglas fir log about thirty inches in diameter would be "dogged" in place with a spiked bar

The boys' pie-eating contest, Lewis Park, Courtenay, c. 1928. "I think boys were the only ones who'd go in for a pie-eating contest!" said Barbara Marriott, and Neil Martin agreed, adding that sometimes the pies were made from molasses "because they didn't want to make it too easy."—JACK TUKHAM

The Homeguard and His Axe

Bob Gordon of Campbell River related the story of the time Bob Filberg met a new boy at a Comox Logging camp. He asked, "Have you got your company axe yet?" The self-conscious kid didn't know what to say, so Filberg said, "No? Then you'd better take one home with you—everyone else who works here has one!" The boy hadn't been with the company long enough to know that everyone helped himself to at least one company axe. Most company employees lived on rural lots and split their own wood for their stoves and fireplaces.

Beatty Davis remembered the time a locie came into the shop at Headquarters after fire season and someone happened to comment that half the tools were missing. Filberg said, "One day, you know, these farmers are going to have all the tools they need and then we'll be able to keep our fire tools!"

The Camp 3 women's tug-of-war team, c. 1928. "They used to pull on ladders," Neil Martin said. The woman at the front is Lil Grant (née Woods), wife of Comox Logging foreman Bob Grant. She is wearing a "middy," a fashionable item in the 1920s, modelled after a sailor's blouse. Jack McQuinn supervises in the background.—JACK TUKHAM

Boy on roundabout, Courtenay Fall Fair, 1930.—JACK TUKHAM

Bucking contest, Lewis Park, Courtenay, c. 1930. A bucking saw was much thicker and less flexible than a falling saw, reflecting the heavier job for which it was designed.—BERNICE JAMES

Winner of the bucking contest, Lewis Park, c. 1928. Champion Mack Grant is holding a big crosscut bucking saw. Next to him is Jabe Day, Comox Logging sawfiler; the woman presenting the trophy is unidentified.—JACK TUKHAM

Esther Forsman, world champion women's log bucker, in action at Lewis Park, Courtenay, 1940. Bob Filberg photo.—FILBERG LODGE & PARK ASSOCIATION

Champion long splicers of the Pacific Coast: Jack "Greasy" McQuinn (left) and Jack Downey, c. 1927. McQuinn, from Oregon, and Downey, a Comox Homeguard descended from the Andertons of Comox, fathered nineteen children between them. McQuinn was "short but very powerful" and "walked almost like a gorilla," said an acquaintance. Note the equipment: marlinspikes, sledgehammer, and double-bitted axe with a short handle. Walter Montgomery photo.—EVIS DOWNEY

on the contest platform, and Comox Logging employees competed for the fastest time in bucking off a round of wood. The skilled sawfiler equally shared the platform. Among the champion buckers of the 1920s were Axel Erickson, Bill McKenzie, Mack Grant, and Frank Helman. Their sawfilers included Jabe Day of Camp 3 and Bob Larson of Headquarters.

Some loggers' wives competed in the "Ladies' Bucking Contest." For many years Esther Forsman, wife of Finnish faller Uno Forsman of Camp 3, was Pacific Coast Ladies' Bucking Champion. In 1939 she became Women's Log Bucking Champion of the World after winning a championship in Tacoma, Washington. "Courtenay has its own world's champion in Mrs. Esther Forsman of Sandwick," wrote the *Comox Argus* in March 1939. "She met all comers of her own sex in bucking a 21½ inch log in 2 min. and 17 sec. Mrs. Forsman is the wife of a Camp 3 faller and she has been seen in action at the First of July sports in Courtenay several times. This is the first time she has tried her prowess in a wider field. Her rival at Tacoma was twice her size; Mrs. Forsman weighs only 135 lbs and is in her early thirties. Mrs. Forsman is not only the world's bucking champion but she will challenge any man of her weight at 'pulling fingers.'"

Cable-splicing competitions were also popular. Cable, often called "line" and sometimes "wire rope," was important in every aspect of logging, from the back rigging to the boom camp; in a sense, line tied it all together. When cable frayed or broke, loggers had to know how to join or "splice" it back together. They used two kinds of splicing: the eye splice and the long splice, as the authors of *Land of Plenty* explained: "The 'eye-splicing' competition saw a heavy cable bent to form an 'eye,' the end strands separated and laced between the cable strands to form a secure loop. This was often completed by one man in less than two minutes. The 'long splice,' where two cables were joined by separating and weaving together the strands, was a two-man event." Among Comox Logging's champions were Jack Downey, Jack McQuinn, Joe Cliffe, Alex Kapela, Skinny Collins, and three of the Grant brothers: Butch, Bob, and Mack.

Champion log rollers included Bob Martin, Jack McQuinn, and brothers Wallace and Harper Baikie. "It was a big deal to watch the log rolling contest," Wallace Baikie recalled. "Bob Martin was the champion for years and I got the inspiration to learn to log roll." In 1925, Baikie beat his mentor at the Fall Fair on the Courtenay River. "Bob never rolled again. He was near forty and I was twenty-three. That was my day!"

⁓

The summer layoff period also provided an opportunity for leisure activities. In the Comox Valley, logging and baseball went hand in glove. Victoria had its rugby, rowing, and cricket; Nanaimo had its soccer; and Courtenay and Cumberland adopted baseball with a passion. The first teams were the Courtenay Cubs and the Herringbones (the latter sponsored by the Elk Hotel, Comox). Soon, however, Comox Logging got a team of its own: the "Circle F." Bob Filberg, an avid baseball fan, sponsored the team, and Pa Dixon, an American locie engineer and

Harvest Excursions to the Prairies

In the 1920s, the great "harvest excursions" to the Canadian Prairies attracted many men from the Comox Valley. Les Marshall, a bucker with Comox Logging, went haying near Prince Albert, and Fred White of Dove Creek worked at Rosetown and Weyburn in Saskatchewan. Another summer, White—who began his life as an agricultural labourer in rural Wiltshire—worked with Bert Harris at Okotoks, Alberta.

Edward Hodgins (born 1902) went to the Prairies on a harvest excursion and returned to Comox early in December 1925. It was a few weeks before Christmas, so he and an older brother decided to work for a week or two at Menzies Bay for Bloedel, Stewart & Welch. "Edward was a greenhorn; he'd never worked in the woods," recalled his younger brother Stan Hodgins. Edward was killed on the day the job ended, aged twenty-three, and was buried at St. Andrew's Anglican Church, Sandwick, on December 16, 1925.

Eighteen-year-old Harper Baikie also went east in the fall of 1925, leaving his job as a chaser on Skidder 5 behind him. In his book *A Boy and His Axe*, Baikie recalled his trip:

I stayed on chasing until the first week of August, 1925. It was getting very hot and dry in the woods, and there was talk of closing down until it rained. About six of us young fellows decided to go back to the prairies to get in on the harvest. There was a harvest special from Vancouver to Moose Jaw for $11 by train. I got a job on a big farm out of Rosetown stooking wheat. After about three weeks on that farm I moved to another farm about 26 miles north of Rosetown, where I worked for a Danish farmer. He was a very good farmer and had a heavy crop about 35 to 40 bushels to the acre. . . .

Along about the middle of October the threshing was pretty well over. It was getting very cold on those windswept prairies so I quit my job, caught the train to Rosetown and headed home. Going to the Prairies we had travelled through Banff, Calgary, Medicine Hat to Moose Jaw. On the return trip we caught the CNR train from Rosetown to Edmonton, Jasper, Kamloops and then to Vancouver. When we got to the CNR station in Vancouver it was so foggy you could not see across the street.

A week later Harper was back on a skidder crew at Camp 2.

Jack Downey (left) and Jack "Greasy" McQuinn demonstrate their skill, c. 1927. Downey and McQuinn became champions through a fearsome combination of brawn and speed. They could splice and reconstitute a completely severed cable in just over five minutes, a task that might take an experienced rigger, working alone, almost an hour to complete. To speed things up, Downey used his shoulder as a hammer. Walter Montgomery photo.
—EVIS DOWNEY

Long-splice partners and Pacific Coast champions Jack Downey (left) and Jack McQuinn, Lewis Park, Courtenay, c. 1928. Long splicing contributed to McQuinn's famous appetite. Once, after a hunting trip, he and Wallace Baikie ate four dozen fried eggs between them—a ten-pound lard pail full.—JACK TUKHAM

Baseball at Lewis Park, c. 1925. Baseball was played very seriously by some employees of the Comox Logging Company. The large building at right is the Courtenay Hotel; among the buildings at left are the Orangemen's hall and the agricultural hall.—JACK TUKHAM

Two players for the Cumberland Cubs, Arthur "Spit" Quinn (left) and Joe Ducca, c. 1933. The boy is Wally Churchill. A Courtenay boy, Spit Quinn became a famous pitcher for the "Circle F" team. His habit of spitting tobacco juice while on the mound gave him his nickname. Both men worked for Comox Logging: Quinn ran a Marion shovel on the railway grade and Ducca was engineer on a cherry picker.—WALLY CHURCHILL

Naming the Homeguards

Most boys born to Comox Logging fathers received names inspired by kings of England and Scotland: Alexander, Alfred, Andrew, Arthur, Charles, Donald, Edward, George, Harold, Henry, James, John, Kenneth, Malcolm, Richard, Robert, William. These were soon shortened to Al, Alec, Alex, Sandy, Alf, Andy, Art, Charlie, Don, Donny, Ed, Eddy, Ted, Teddy, Harry, Jim, Jimmy, Jack, Jackie, Ken, Kenny, Malc, Dick, Bob, Bobby, Bill, Billy, and Willie. Two out of three Comox Loggers bore such names, and Bill and Jack were the most common Homeguard names.

Others received traditional British or Biblical names: Allan, Ambrose, Cecil, Clive, Clyde, Cyril, Daniel, David, Edwin, Ernest, Eustace, Frederick, Gerald, Gordon, Herbert, Howard, Hubert, Hugh, Joseph, Leonard, Michael, Norman, Percival, Raymond, Reginald, Ronald, Samuel, Stanley, Thomas, Victor, Walter, Wilfrid. These became Al, Cece, Cy, Dan, Danny, Dave, Davy, Ed, Eddy, Ernie, Fred, Freddie, Gerry, Gord, Gordie, Herb, Herbie, Bert, Bertie, Howie, Hughie, Joe, Len, Lenny, Mike, Norm, Percy, Ray, Reg, Reggie, Ron, Ronnie, Sam, Sammy, Stan, Tom, Tommy, Vic, Wally, Wilf.

A bewildering number of women's names ended in "a," a repetitive assortment of Victorian revivals, invented names, Celtic (especially Scottish), Scandinavian, and German names: Ada, Adela, Aida, Aleda, Aleta, Alma, Alva, Alvina, Alweena, Amelia, Armelda, Aura, Beda, Bertha, Clara, Cora, Danetta, Decima, Della, Dola, Dolena, Dolina, Dona, Donna, Dora, Dorothea, Drina, Edna, Elfrida, Ella, Elma, Elnora, Elva, Elvina, Elvira, Emilia, Emma, Ena, Erna, Estella, Eva, Flora, Gayla, Hilda, Ida, Ila, Ina, Inga, Iona, Lavina, Leila, Lena, Leona, Lola, Lorna, Maida, Maria, Melba, Melda, Melinda, Melva, Melvina, Meta, Mona, Myna, Myra, Myrna, Nana, Neta, Nina, Nola, Nora, Ora, Ramona, Reba, Rena, Reta, Rhoda, Rita, Rodina, Rona, Rosa, Rosella, Rosetta, Rosina, Selena, Stella, Theda, Thelma, Thora, Una, Urma, Velma, Verna, Vera, Vina, Viola, and Wilma.

later owner of the Riverside Hotel in Courtenay, managed it. Dixon brought in capable players and gave them temporary jobs serving beer in the bar. Filberg also gave several of them jobs, including Sam and Andy Telosky from Haney, who arrived in 1936, and machinist Jimmy Pettigrew from Victoria. Sammy Telosky recalled that the team was semi-professional; it sent several players to the big leagues, and did very well against touring teams from the United States. "I don't think you'd see a better ball team anywhere than the one in Courtenay," Sammy declared. A favourite pitcher was Arthur "Spit" Quinn.

Fire season was a time for courtship, marriages, dances, and social visits. One happy event was the 1937 marriage of Harold Cliffe, youngest of the Cliffe family, to Mabel Olson, daughter of Headquarters mechanic Charlie Olson. Dances were popular at Headquarters, Merville Hall, the Native Sons' Hall in Courtenay, and Joe and Elsie Idiens' Royston Pavilion. Among the dances were the Circassian Reel, the Schottische, the Lambeth Walk, and all the usual favourites (waltzes, polkas, foxtrots).

Loggers' fights often added some excitement to Saturday night dances, and the Merville Hall became known as the "Bucket of Blood" as a result. Davey Janes recalled that Comox Logging guys fought guys from northern outfits, including Elk River Timber and Bloedel, Stewart & Welch, at the Bucket of Blood. Guys from Cumberland tended to work for the northern logging outfits, and they'd come down to Merville to fight the Camp 3 men. The fights always took place outside, so "you didn't have to engage in it," according to Beatty Davis. "One night there was a fight between Fred Dahl—who was a pretty good fighter—and Oliver Doucette, but Doucette beat him. You could hear those fists smacking. But if two guys got in a fight, nine times out of ten they'd shake hands. There were no grudges." No weapons were used; it was all fisticuffs. "Loggers were in such good shape that when they did hit each other it was terrible," said Mauno Pelto. "I was never in a fight. I learned early in the game that nobody wins."

The off-seasons gave loggers time to heal from injuries sustained in the woods (or dance halls), and time to grieve men who had been killed. Skidder settings were dangerous places, partly because men were expected to run from one place to another. Speed was everything; as Filberg wrote, "Every man in a logging crew is a potential bottle[neck]. They must all be agile, skillful, experienced, and hit the ball." If the men valued their jobs, they complied. Jobs were scarce, and laziness was considered sinful, as Neil Martin remarked: "In those days the worst thing that could be said of you was that you were lazy." Men had to run eight hours a day, six days a week. "You couldn't walk; you had to run, and there were men around who were willing to run if you didn't want to," said Stan Rennison, who worked briefly for Comox Logging in 1937. Hi Churchill said that when his crew worked on the rigging in the early 1930s, they might be 1500 feet from the skidder landing when it was time for lunch, but they'd have to run down to the skidder, eat their lunch from the communal "coffin," and run back—all in half an hour. Some men quit Comox Logging because of the pace and the associated danger.

The fighting woodsmen, c. 1925. Left to right: **Bill McKenzie, Dode Bowcott, Roy Cliffe. Cold-deck engineer Bill McKenzie (1902–1988) stood at least six-foot-one and weighed 272 pounds when he was boxing. He entered the ring as a heavyweight in about 1924, won three of his first five fights by knockouts, and lost for the first time in San Diego in 1926. Bill Wilson recalls that McKenzie "was too good-natured to be a boxer." Roy Cliffe (1903–1992), McKenzie's first cousin, had once worked as a loader on a Comox Logging skidder. For three years in the 1920s, Cliffe held both the Canadian and Pacific Northwest Light Heavyweight titles, and he was ranked fourth in the world. In 1928, at the age of twenty-five, his career was cut short owing to a hereditary "high first knuckle" on the middle finger of his right hand. This knuckle took a battering, and the doctor told him he'd better take two years off to let it heal. He had fought sixty-four professional fights. In the meantime he married "schoolmarm" Ethel Knight in 1927, went back to the family farm, and never returned to boxing. Bowcott was a game warden on Whidbey Island, Washington State. Hartsook photo, Seattle.**—BOB CLIFFE

"Off with Their Doojiggers"

Wilma McKenzie told the story about her cousins Bob Cliffe (son of Roy Cliffe the boxer) and Harvey Walsh, son of Edith Cliffe and Comox Logging railway foreman Clay Walsh. Harvey, who died young, was what was then called "simple"—"he was very slow mentally." After his mother's early death, Harvey lived with his uncle and aunt, Big Jack Sr. and Maude McKenzie, at their farm in Comox.

One day, Big Jack and another man were castrating pigs in the barn. "They'd hang the pigs up, cut their doojiggers off, and let them go. The pigs would run off squealing, as though to say, 'What did you do that for?'"

Bob and Harvey were standing in the barn watching this operation, captivated and horrified. When all the pigs were finished, Big Jack turned around to the boys and asked "Who's next?" Harvey jumped straight in the air, crying "Not me! Not me!" Bob and Harvey tore out of the barn and back to Maude McKenzie, who gave her husband hell when she found out.

The ex-boxer Roy Cliffe at his farm at Mission Hill, 1943.
Bob Filberg photo.—FILBERG LODGE & PARK ASSOCIATION

Bill McKenzie, Homeguard

Son of Maude Cliffe and Big Jack McKenzie Sr., Bill McKenzie was born in 1902 in the "Ladies and Escorts" beer parlour at the Lorne Hotel, Comox. There was no hospital at the time, and his mother's family owned the hotel. Bill would later take his friends into the Lorne and say, "That's where I was born!"

Bill McKenzie and his brother Jack grew up on the family farm in Comox, and in 1927 Bill married Rose Baikie, schoolteacher at Camp 3. Teachers were supposed to resign when they got married, but Rose neglected to tell the authorities and kept working until the birth of her daughter Wilma in 1930. For twenty-seven years Bill McKenzie worked for Comox Logging, most of the time on a cold decker. He was also a fine all-round athlete, excelling in boxing, log bucking, log rolling, tug-of-war, and other sports.

A Homeguard's wedding, 1937. Left to right: Johnny Duncan (best man), Valerie Cliffe (flower girl), Harold Cliffe, Mabel Olson, and Grace Martin (bridesmaid). Charles Sillence photo.—LORNA CLIFFE

Bill McKenzie with his daughter Wilma (born 1930) at Camp 3. "He had hands like meat hooks," Wilma McKenzie said of her father; "they were three times the size of normal." McKenzie's cousin Myrna McTaggart remembered his "wonderful personality: he was a great big, loveable guy."—NANCY BROWN

Before 1920, Comox Logging's safety reputation was as bad as any. The company had an abysmal accident record, along with poor working and living conditions at its camps. In his memoirs, Hilton claimed that accidents were infrequent in the early days of Comox Logging, "but when they did occur, it was nearly always on the weekend—or on Mondays, when the men were getting over a binge." But Hilton's own records show that, in fact, very few deaths occurred on Mondays. Most accidents happened at the end of the long six-day week—on Thursdays, Fridays, or Saturday mornings, when the men were exhausted. When there was a fatality in the woods, the train would sound its mournful whistle as it went through Courtenay on its way to Royston.

Those who were fortunate enough to survive accidents found that medical aid was primitive, if a priority at all. For instance, Joe (Poika) Moelanen broke his leg and had to wait for a train to take him down to Headquarters. He was then lifted onto an empty flatcar and conveyed, log-like, down to civilization. Another story concerns a manager at Headquarters who insisted on finishing his lunch before arranging for an injured man to be sent to hospital. Oscar Davies, timekeeper from 1911 to 1912, recalled that "I had no medical kit but the loggers chewed herbs from the bush for their physic."

When the company was formed, Comox District still lacked a hospital. As Joe Cliffe wrote, "a hospital was really needed because so many employees would be injured in logging accidents." Instead, however, "a little bit of money was taken off each worker's wages to pay for [a] medical service." Loggers were persuaded to pay one dollar a month for regular medical visits from Dr. Harrison Millard of Courtenay, remembered by Major Hilton as a "real horse-and-buggy doctor" who rendered excellent service. Of course, this arrangement was no substitute for emergency medical aid.

Finally, in 1912, J. D. McCormack, vice-president of the Canadian Western Lumber Company, became concerned about the lack of medical attention for men injured in the woods. He asked the Sisters of St. Joseph of Toronto to establish a hospital at Comox. In February 1914, they opened St. Joseph's Hospital in a converted eight-room farmhouse at the top of Comox Hill.

In spite of such improvements, working conditions were far from perfect and the company soon found itself embroiled in union conflicts. The first union encountered by Comox Logging was the radical IWW (Industrial Workers of the World, or "Wobblies"), which arrived in British Columbia in 1907. The company, like all others on the coast, kept the union out by firing or blacklisting anyone who sought union recognition or who showed socialist sympathies. Wartime conditions put a great strain on relations between capital and labour; the Russian Revolution of 1917 encouraged working people to seek revolutionary alternatives to capitalist rule, and the federal government banned the militant Wobblies under the War Measures Act in September 1918.

In the next year, 150,000 Canadian soldiers returned home from the First World War to be met with unemployment, the Spanish flu epidemic, and a general postwar malaise. At Comox, some complained that jobs had been taken by Finnish, Swedish, and Russian workers, many of them hired in neutral wartime United States.

A Cold Dip for a Foreman

Timekeeper Oscar Davies recorded his impressions of an Australian socialist's sojourn at Camp 9 in 1911:

Somehow, I smelled trouble the day that big, muscular Australian hit our camp, looking for work. We had nothing to offer him but a job with the railway gang at $2.50 a day. I was astonished when he took it but he was apparently desperate. When he had been with us for ten days the foreman came to my office demanding that I fire the Aussie. "He's a socialist! He talks too much."

By coincidence the big man dropped in to see me that afternoon to ask if he could work a day in the cookhouse which would allow him time enough to write some letters. I told him his foreman was dissatisfied with him and he grinned. "The old ———— hasn't the guts to fire me." But he did ask me to make out his time sheet so that he could leave in the morning.

Shortly after 5 o'clock that afternoon the foreman came in with his gang and went to the bunkhouse. You can imagine my astonishment when I saw the Aussie come out with the foreman struggling in his arms. The powerful man lifted the much smaller man high in the air then crashed him down through the ice coat of the rain tub and into the icy water, where he held him a few moments, finally releasing the enraged foreman. . . . The victor carried the vanquished to his bunk and dropped him on it and the fight was over.

254

The End of Two Lives and a Career

Harper Baikie was head loader on Skidder 4 out of Camp 3 from 1925 until 1928. In his autobiography *A Boy and His Axe*, he recalled that he left Comox Logging after two friends were killed in the same week:

I stayed on this head loading job until the late summer of 1928. It was very dry and we were working a very early morning shift, which meant we started work at daybreak. Where we were working there were some big snags left standing. Our hook tender, Skinky Boyd, who was a very good pal of mine, hooked on a turn of logs, then ran over and got on a big stump about 100 feet away. When the turn started it pulled the skyline over and hit the top of the snag knocking it over. The top flew off, hitting Skinky, killing him instantly. He never knew what hit him. That was the first turn of the morning.

About four days later when the first turn came into the landing, the chaser, another pal of mine, ran out to unhook the turn. He jumped on a log, it rolled and crushed him against another log. We managed to get the log off of him but he died two days later. This was a great shock to all of us, especially me as I was such a good friend to both men. It got me to the point where I went into the office and quit before I would be the next one to be killed. They tried to talk me out of quitting but I had to get away from it all. Besides I was getting pretty stakey, as they say in the woods, and needed a change.

Poor working conditions, combined with high accident rates, sparked the formation of the British Columbia Loggers' Union (BCLU) in January 1919. Workers at Comox Logging were the first to take part in the massive BCLU strikes of that year. Three hundred men at Headquarters and the outer camps struck on May 1, 1919. Major Hilton and logging superintendent Jim McGuigan spent much of the next two months finding replacement workers. "To Courtenay this afternoon trying to round up crews for work tomorrow," Hilton wrote in his diary on May 8. "Several seem to want to start but don't like to be thought or called strike breakers." Two days later: "Starting work with men towards a settlement by ousting Finns which seems to appeal strongly." He also recruited men in Cumberland, Campbell River, and Port Alberni, and in June and July he brought in many scabs from Vancouver, but the strike continued. The strike at Comox corresponded with the Winnipeg General Strike of May–June 1919; indeed, the BCLU was the largest member of the One Big Union, which organized the Winnipeg strike. In July, the BCLU changed its name to the Lumber Workers' Industrial Union (LWIU).

Hilton met with strike committees to try to improve wage, sanitation, food, and school conditions, and the loggers went back to work briefly. On September 1, 1919, however, the company's entire workforce of 429 men went back on strike. The local LWIU strike committee submitted a total of twenty-seven demands, including a minimum wage of five dollars a day; an eight-hour (rather than ten-hour) work day; hot and cold water and a reading room at all camps; "antiseptic soap and towels to be furnished free"; and licenced first-aid workers at all camps. The strike ended on September 20, after the company raised wages slightly and promised to meet some of the union's sanitation and health concerns. (Such concerns were certainly justified; the Royston boom camp, for example, was riddled with rats and lice, and a government inspector had rebuked the company for conditions there.)

The strike had both short-term and long-term effects. In the short term, McGuigan quit, Hilton was fired, and Filberg took over. Filberg had played an important role as a mediator. His friend Kay Pollock of Comox said that Filberg became superintendent during the "big strike" in the following way: "He phoned his father-in-law J. D. McCormack and said he could straighten it out. He did straighten it out."

In the long term, coastal logging companies took measures that kept unions out of their camps until the 1940s. In the fall of 1919, the timber owners formed the BC Loggers' Association and the Loggers' Employment Agency, an employment office on Carrall Street in Vancouver that kept track of men who had taken part in the 1919 strike. According to historian Gordon Hak, by 1922 about 1,500 members of the LWIU had been blacklisted by the agency.

At the same time, Filberg (encouraged by Jack McQuinn) embarked on his policy of hiring from local farms—from the Comox Homeguard, few of whom at first sympathized with the union movement. Harper Baikie captured the Homeguards' anti-union sentiments of the interwar era. "I can remember in the mid-twenties when I started in the woods," he wrote, "if you mentioned union in a camp, the men—not the operators—would run you out of camp. This condition went on for about twenty years."

A positive result of the 1919 strike was that Comox Logging decided to teach first aid to its employees. "The government said to Filberg, 'You're killing too many men,'" Arne Anderson said, "so he had to start a first-aid course." "Safety First" became the company's official workplace motto. The company had by this time hired its own doctor, Tillman Briggs, who instituted a safety program in the early 1920s to which "all foremen, scalers, and timekeepers were particularly asked to attend," as Wallace Baikie wrote. Within months the course had proved its worth. Foreman Len Harding of Camp 2 was driving back from Courtenay in the fog one night with the fireman of the Two-Spot, Gordon McEntee, when he drove off the road and into a stump. McEntee cut his throat when he went through the windshield, and Baikie recorded that "Len, remembering what Dr. Briggs had taught him, pounced onto the lad and held his thumbs on his throat until help came." The *Comox Argus* reported the same incident: "Sitting for two hours with his finger on the jugular vein of Gordon McEntee, a young logger of Camp 2 of Comox Logging, Mr. Len Harding, foreman at the same camp undoubtedly saved the man's life."

Even after the first-aid innovation, Comox Logging's safety record was not perfect, but as Stan Hodgins said, they were "the best of the lot." In 1927, there was not a single fatality, and *West Coast Lumberman* noted the following spring that "Comox Logging has the enviable record for the last year of having had no fatal accidents nor any one permanently injured. Four hundred men were employed." Improved safety resulted as well from the Homeguards' rise to prominence between the wars: men who worked with their cousins, brothers-in-law, or old school friends tended to be more safety conscious than if they worked with strangers.

Still, there was no union at Comox Logging and company foremen, though respected as loggers, continued to rule dictatorially and ruthlessly. "If you happened to look at the foreman sideways, by God you were sent down the road!" Stan Hodgins recalled. "They could fire you if they didn't like the look of your face," said another logger. But, by and large, the Homeguards were satisfied with Filberg's brand of relatively safety-conscious paternalism.

⌇

In spite of the blacklisting, the unions persisted. They made a small step forward in January 1934, when the Vancouver-based LWIU called strikes at Bloedel, Stewart & Welch camps at Menzies Bay. The nearby camps of Campbell River Timber, Merrill & Ring, and several smaller outfits also struck in the next couple of months. They protested "autocratic treatment" by their employers and unsafe living and working conditions, and demanded a new minimum wage, a wage increase, a recognition of camp union committees, and an end to Sunday work. Strikers from Campbell River visited Camp 3 in March, recruited men, and prepared to strike. Hi Churchill recalled that "a bunch of guys from the up-island camps . . . marched into Camp 3 one morning and shut her down. That's when the union started." Thelma Reid (*née* Miner),

Sick Leave

Perhaps the most respected and feared Comox Logging foreman was Jack McQuinn, who was in charge of hiring and firing at Camp 3. Gunnar Jonsson described McQuinn's policies during the work-starved Depression:

They laid some of the men off, and if you were sick for one day you were out: they had another man to put in your place. We worked from March to October when I was living at Mrs. Patterson's, and I was sick for one day. I was sick all night so I couldn't go to work the next morning. There was a bit of snow so I couldn't go in, but I was up all night. The boss, Jack McQuinn, got me as I got off the crummy the next day and said, "Gunnar, we don't need you any more." He laid me off. The next spring, after the woods were shut down, I went up and asked McQuinn for more work, and McQuinn said, "I'll take you back on, but I don't want anybody staying home for a little bit of snow!"

One fellow, Reg Taylor, was cutting laggings from crab apple or some hard wood, to be nailed or spiked on a spar tree to hold the cable, when the axe slipped and he cut his leg. He had to get home, and he was off work for a few days to heal the cut. He had to go to the doctor to have it sewn up. When he went back to work he was laid off by Jack McQuinn. McQuinn had men ready to go in.

who was then a child at Camp 3, recalled hearing "heavy loggers' boots clunking over the ties on the railway . . . the sound of metal against metal when they hit the rails." She was scared, and wondered why the men were striking. "I figured life was great!" she said.

Gunnar Jonsson remembered that the striking men gathered in front of the bunkhouses:

> There was a big fight one morning. We were waiting for the locie, and the big boss [McQuinn] called in Filberg, and [Filberg] came up and he went to hit one of the Swedes. But he was held back. . . . Filberg came up to see what the devil was going on—to lay the law down—and a bunch of twenty or more fallers, big Swedes, had a hell of an argument. Filberg went to hit one of them, and two bosses from Camp 3 went up to Filberg and said, "Don't do that, or you'll get the worst of it!"

Filberg's response was to shut down Camp 3 to prevent the strike from continuing; or, as the *Comox Argus* put it, to prevent "a battle in which there might have been broken heads." Men returned to work when the government intervened and raised the minimum wage to $3.20 a day, which is what the strikers had demanded. Filberg also countered by blacklisting the strikers, many of whom were Swedish and Finnish fallers and buckers. "They wouldn't get into the main camps because they had their names down," said Gunnar Jonsson. "They were blacklisted all over BC. Ragnar Lidberg from Courtenay, a single man—he was blacklisted. . . . It took a long time before Ragnar got a job back; no matter where he went they wouldn't have him. He got in with a few small gyppo outfits but . . . if you said too much, boy, you were out!" Despite this, Jonsson recalled, "it was a little start towards a union."

Another blacklisted striker was Jock Nairn, who, according to Bob Cliffe, tried repeatedly to get a job with Comox Logging in the following years. One day in 1936 Bob Filberg picked him up hitchhiking and Nairn told him about his search for work. Filberg said, "You were in that goddamn strike, weren't you?" But at the end of the ride Filberg said, "You go into the office tomorrow and see what they can do for you." The next morning Jock was hired.

As with the 1919 strike, the 1934 strike brought about an improvement in conditions. The company made an agreement with the Comox hospital so that, for a fee, employees got complete medical coverage for themselves and their families, except for dental and "ocular" needs. Married employees paid three dollars a month and unmarried men two dollars, and the company also contributed to the program. "Our first daughter was born January 10, 1935," recalled Gunnar Jonsson, "and I had money to pay the doctor, but the doctor said, 'It won't cost a nickel.' The agreement had gone into effect on January 1! So instead I bought some brand-new linoleum and laid the floor."

By the 1930s, deaths were infrequent at Comox Logging and are even now remembered in detail—morality stories about carelessness, misfortune, managers' negligence, or just plain "shithouse luck." Many recall the death of back rigger Cyril Hodgins, who was hit by lagging while felling a backspar, and that of Charlie Churchill, who was killed by a log in 1938 when he was chasing on a skidder out of Camp 3.

Men involved in any way with deaths or injuries felt a tremendous sense of guilt and responsibility. Hallie Dixon was running the log loader on Comox Lake in 1936 when the loading boom got away and crushed chaser Davey Janes' leg, which had to be amputated above the

Gunnar Jonsson, Swedish Homeguard

Gunnar Jonsson arrived in Merville from Sweden in 1930 and three years later married Jennie Goodsell, the daughter of his neighbours:

> You got only one day off to get married, or you were gone; you'd get married on a Saturday, and back to work on a Monday! There was so much unemployment—people were running around looking for work. The company had no trouble getting men. . . .
>
> Jennie Goodsell is my wife. Her parents came from England. Her father was in the war and got gassed. He went all to pieces. His memory went; he didn't know what he was doing half the time. Two or three times a week he would come around and ask me to look at his medals. He might have been fifty years old. . . . He died in June 1933 and we were married in December 1933.
>
> Our first two kids were born in the shack, and then I built an eighteen-by-twenty addition and put a new roof over the whole thing. More kids were coming, and the neighbours would say, "He's hammering again: there must be another kid coming!" And the house is still there—the old floor of the chicken house is still there! We had eight kids, four boys and four girls. Four were born when we were living in that place, and then we bought forty-seven acres nearby. It was another Land Settlement Board place, but there was a real two-bedroom house on that place. I put in a bid for it and got it. They accepted my offer!
>
> So we sold where we were and moved five or six hundred feet down the road to the other place, and four more youngsters were born there. All our children were born between 1935 and 1955. We got a piece of land, got a cow, got some chickens, got a few pigs. We churned butter and raised turkeys.

Safety signs were placed at all the camps, including this one in front of the warehouse at Headquarters, which reads, "It's hell to be a cripple. Be careful. Safety first." Don McIver recalled that this sign was "what the men saw when they got off the train" before transferring to the crummy to take them to the bush. The two men are British shareholders in Canadian Western. The small sign behind reads, "Visitors are prohibited to carry firearms on this train"—a warning to hunters. Bob Filberg photo, 1938.
—FILBERG LODGE & PARK ASSOCIATION

Skidder Accidents: The Front Line

Skidder jobs were the most glamorous jobs in the whole logging operation, but they were also the most dangerous. "Lots of guys got banged up" on the skidder, said Bill Woods. "It was terrible hard work."

When asked how Stan Woods was killed on Skidder 5, Dick Bailey answered simply, "He couldn't jump fast enough." Neil Martin related a story about Tommy Gray of Dove Creek, who was working on the rigging out of Camp 3 when he got thrown in the air by a rogue line. "He said, 'I was flying through the air like the flying nun, and hoping I was going to land on something soft!'" But he landed on something hard and among other injuries dislocated his hip. He was in considerable pain. On his way to the hospital they were met by Dr. Straith at the crossing at Headquarters. "Tommy said to the doctor, 'Are you going to give me anything to fix this leg up?' and the doctor said, 'Yes,' and Tommy said, 'Well, why the hell don't you give it to me right now!'"

At the hospital, they had to get the hip back in its joint again, and Straith was pulling at his leg with no success. Harold Mooney, a young doctor at the time, asked Dr. Straith if he could have a go. "He pulled and pulled and suddenly the leg went back into the joint and kicked old Mooney right across the room!"

◀ **Comox Logging's first-aid team with provincial and national trophies, 1936. The company hired instructor Percy La Mare, and later Jack Taylor, to teach first aid to hundreds of men. Back row, left to right: John Pritchard, Eric Gray, Wilfred "Skinny" Collins. Front row, left to right: Percy La Mare, Jim "Slats" Robertson, Harold Brazier. Pritchard was a scaler, while Collins, Robertson, and Brazier were members of skidder crews, where accidents were common. Gray and Collins had been affected personally by accidents; Gray himself was injured, and Collins' brother killed. "Skinny Collins and Eric Gray were always studying the first-aid book," recalled Davey Janes. Charles Sillence photo.**—COURTENAY & DISTRICT MUSEUM & ARCHIVES, P315-994

knee. Davey, who was twenty-four at the time, would see Hallie at dances in Merville and Hallie would break down and cry about what had happened.

But at the best of times such incidents seemed unavoidable, and everyone could tell of many accidents or near-accidents. Stan Hodgins, who worked in the woods for forty-one years, "nearly got it once" when the haulback line flipped over and he needed twenty stitches under his ear and on the side of his face. In the late 1930s Eddy Murtsell, machinist at Headquarters, was making piston rings when a tool broke and hit him in the eye. He was taken to the hospital. Dr. Mooney told him he'd lose the eye and that he'd be flown to Vancouver to have it removed, but a storm stopped the plane from leaving. In the meantime, the nurses put hot and cold presses on his eye all night, and in the morning it was much better and it didn't need to be taken out.

Doris Walker recalled that her husband Bill, of the Royston boom crew, "nearly got it once on a Sunday." The foreman had called and asked if he could come out for a couple of hours. Doris and her mother were waiting for Bill to come home for supper, when her mother, Mrs. Marvin, looked out the window and said, "Come and look at Bill!" He was coming down the path and was weaving from side to side. Mrs. Marvin, a strict teetotaller, suspected Bill was drunk. In fact, the men had been moving a large piece of equipment down the railway line and needed Bill to hold up the electric wires with a pole and wire contraption. It started to rain. Bill slipped while he was standing in a ditch beside the track holding up the wires, and his wire pole made contact with the live electric wires. "He went right up in the air and came down again. He had burns to his hands and inside his caulk boots. They took him to the boom camp, put him in bed, and phoned the company doctor and told him about it. He said, 'Oh, it's all right, just give him a strong drink of gin.' That's the way company doctors were. Bill couldn't keep anything in his stomach for weeks."

Injured men stayed with the company and, depending on the severity of the injury, were given menial, downgraded, or less physical jobs. Some became whistlepunks and sparkcatchers. Louis Ranger, who lost a leg while dumping logs off the Royston wharf, became bullcook at Royston; Warren Bannerman, who had his leg amputated after getting it twisted in some line, became a mechanic at Headquarters. Davey Janes drove grade shovels, Caterpillars, and later trucks (he was known to everyone as "Peg Leg" for his wooden leg). Loader Eric Gray "got smashed up pretty bad when a line broke," said Hi Churchill. His right arm was permanently twisted, but he kept his job as head loader until early arthritis set in.

≈

Even with a hospital, safety committee, and health coverage in place, an increasing number of Comox Logging employees became unsatisfied with harsh foremen, paternalistic policies, low pay, long hours, and bed bugs. Their concerns were allayed somewhat because the company, under superintendent Bob Filberg, was known for its excellent safety record and was regarded by many as the finest logging company on the coast. Other companies on the Island had atrocious records by

Comox Logging superintendent Bob Filberg, c. 1940. He came to favour hiring Homeguards and encouraged newcomers to buy little plots of land to sustain them in the off-seasons. Jimmy Sheasgreen photo.—FILBERG LODGE & PARK ASSOCIATION

Major Arthur Hilton in 1940, aged seventy-five, at his house at Royston. Hilton arranged funerals for loggers killed in the woods between 1911 and 1920.—HUGH HILTON

Outside the Homeguard: Jack Fossum

Born in Norway in 1905, Jack Fossum came to Canada in 1925. In his book *Mancatcher* he described how he went to Major Black's Loggers' Employment Agency on Carrall Street, Vancouver, and worked as a faller for Merrill & Ring at Theodosia Arm; for Bloedel, Stewart, & Welch at Myrtle Point near Powell River and Menzies Bay near Campbell River; and for the Robert Dollar Company at Deep Bay south of Courtenay.

When asked if he had worked for Comox Logging, Fossum said no, he hadn't, but he had worked all around the edges of the Comox District, and as far south as Cowichan Lake. He never bothered to apply for a job with Comox Logging because the Homeguards had all the jobs tied up. "I was told it was hopeless—I just didn't bother. People stayed there for life: it was one hell of a good company to work for. People didn't budge."

Part of its reputation was its safety record. "Comox Logging had a good reputation for safety—for companies in those days," he said. "It was a good outfit to work for, no doubt about that."

Jack Fossum now lives in retirement at Miracle Beach, north of Courtenay.

comparison. "When guys got hurt in the bush further up-island, they'd lean 'em up against a stump until the train went in," recalled Beatty Davis, who worked for Campbell River Timber in the 1930s. Also, Filberg himself was known to some as "King of Comox" for his immense power over local jobs and careers. "Bob Filberg was big Daddy Warbucks in this town," said Neil Martin. "Guys like my dad [Bob Martin] and [Jack] Carthew thought the world of him—and he thought the world of them."

Filberg's days as benign dictator were, however, numbered by the late 1930s. "You won't always have Bob Filberg looking after you," warned visiting union organizers. Comox Logging became the last large company on the coast to be organized by the IWA (International Woodworkers of America), a union formed in 1937 from the remnants of the LWIU. The Courtenay local of the IWA was formed in 1942.

Filberg, who had fought the unions for years, later remarked, "Oh, it was just evolution that was coming."

Fatalities in 1918

Major Hilton's curt 1918 diary entries recorded notable events such as the deaths of Comox Logging men (and the occasional non-human bystander):

January 1. "F. Johnson killed at Camp 1 by falling tree."
January 2. "Inquest on F. Johnson at 2.30 p.m. Verdict accidental death."
April 16. "3 Spot killed calf."
May 10. "To Courtenay with J. McGuigan re death of C. Lehto."
August 13. "J. McBeth killed in overturn of 3 Spot near HQs. To inquest at Courtenay 8 p.m."
August 18. "To funeral of J. McBeth this afternoon."
November 11. "Germany fell to pieces. Allied victory assured. Armistice signed 11 a.m. 11th day 11th month."
November 12. "Claude Stewart died this p.m."
November 15. "To Courtenay at funeral of C. Stewart."
November 16. "To Courtenay at funeral of S. Smith and E. Hilvanen."
November 28. "Courtenay funeral Kendall."
December 30. "At HQ. J. McGraw [of the] Steel Crew killed this morning."

chapter 12

The Aftermath

All along the way, where the deep green forest used to stand, lies a waste of mangled trunks and branches, enough wood to keep your fires burning for a thousand years or so.

—BILL HUTCHISON, journalist, at Comox Lake, April 1933

COMOX LOGGING DELIVERED ONLY THE VERY BEST old-growth timber to the sawmill on the far side of the Strait of Georgia. The rest was left behind: tall stumps of trees; snags; billowy, shaggy treetops and thick branches; and timber with knots, twists, or any other imperfection. Collectively, this tangled debris was known as slash.

"The slash was impenetrable!" Neil Brady-Browne recalled. "It was all criss-crossed with stuff. . . . They creamed the crop in such a hurry, and we were left with the leavings." Norman Sprout concurred, "Boy, they were extravagant! They'd long-butt the logs and if there was any kind of twist in them they'd leave it. Talk about high-grading!" Environmentalist Melda Buchanan (*née* McCulloch) said bluntly, "It was an unholy situation. No human or animal could get through the slash."

Comox Logging embarked on pulp and paper manufacturing only in the late 1940s, and until that time, anything less than Grade A timber was regarded as waste. Sometimes even old-growth cedar containing the best shingle material in the world was simply cut and left on the ground, depending on the market value of cedar. "If the price of cedar was too low they'd just leave it in the bush, even though it was all fell and bucked," Eddy Berkeley recalled. Sustainable forestry practices were still in the distant future.

Logging companies customarily burned slash because it constituted a major fire hazard, especially during the bone-dry summer months. A huge inferno could result if hundreds or thousands of acres of slash caught fire. The companies tried to reduce the risk of such a conflagration by eliminating their slash using controlled seasonal burns. Slash burning started at the beginning of the cool and rainy season, in September or October, and went on for several weeks, with dozens of men overseeing the burn and containing it if necessary.

◄ The head spar of an abandoned skidder setting at the foot of Constitution Hill, December 1934. Thirty feet up this fine old Douglas fir is the notch for the hayrack boom, while below are piles of unburned logging debris and long grass that colonized the former forest floor. The standing figure is Comox naturalist Mack Laing. Mack Laing photo.

—BRITISH COLUMBIA ARCHIVES, I-51828

September was considered an ideal time for burning slash because the logging debris was still dry from the summer, yet there was dew at night and often mist during the day. Slash burning had the added advantage of promoting the growth of Douglas fir seedlings, which thrive in sunny, open areas.

Slash burning was controversial in the nearby communities, as valley historian Eric Duncan wrote in December 1936. "Mountain views were clear until the 28th [of] September," he wrote, "and then the smoke from the burning woods came down and obscured everything. We suppose that logging waste must be got rid of in this way till some more useful means is found for its disposal, but it always makes a mean ending to a glorious month." Others agreed. "Fires were set when thought safe," historian Rene Harding recorded, "the air being full of smoke during fine weather as a result. At night the sky would often be illuminated by their glow, and sometimes slash fires got out of hand and had to be fought."

Many people still remember these great slash fires. Tom Barnett, former lumber worker and later Member of Parliament, described the view of Vancouver Island from the University of British Columbia on Point Grey, where he studied in the 1920s: "It looked like the whole island was on fire because of the smoke! Sometimes you could even see the glow." The sun itself was often blotted out by the fires' thick smoke. "A whole month of the year could be totally spoiled," remarked Melda Buchanan, who grew up in Comox between the wars. "They used to slash and burn so much that you couldn't see the sun in September. For three weeks you might not see the sun for a single day." The severity of the smoke depended, of course, on weather conditions, and residents always hoped for a big southeaster to blow the smoke to the north.

Comox Logging had a choice with its logged and burned timberland. The land was sometimes sold to potential settlers, if it was at least marginally suitable for agriculture. In 1919, the company sold thousands of acres at Merville to the Soldier Settlement Board, but settlers had to contend with massive stumps and rocky soil. Most often, therefore, the land was simply left to regenerate a timber crop on its own, among the fire-blackened remains of the original forest. Replanting was not yet considered: the company did not plant a single tree before 1943.

Such transitional forests offered a temporary bonanza for local residents. The wholesale removal of the trees, followed by controlled slash burning, resulted in a period of remarkable natural abundance on the old clear-cuts. Residents of the Comox Valley, especially those who lived in the logging camps, were quick to take advantage. They saw clear-cut lands as providing an important supplement to their logging and farming livelihood, and much hunting and gathering took place in the logged and burned areas. Many logging families survived the Depression by exploiting the transformed natural resources of Block 29. "We never wanted but it was certainly work getting it," commented Thelma Reid (*née* Miner) of Camp 3. "God helps those who help themselves!"

For twenty years after a burn, according to forest ecologist John Parminter, a second-growth forest enters "a highly diverse shrub stage which supports much wildlife. Shrub and herb cover later decline as the

Bruce Hutchison Ponders Progress

In the big woods the snow still lies two feet deep and it makes you a little melancholy to think that these cool green depths will shortly be reduced to ruin by monsters of machinery. The towering logger with the movie-star face, who stands beside us on the flat car admits a pang of remorse at the prospect of denuding this green valley, but what can you do about it? No logging, no work for loggers. No work for loggers, no money for merchants in town, no taxes for the government, no prosperity for any of us.

Yes, more trees will grow, the valley will be green again some day, but it will never see giants like these. They are a thousand years old, these trees beside the little railway, five and six feet through at the butt, and over a hundred feet to their lowest branches. It will take ten centuries to replace them, and men will not wait that long again. Their successors will be cut in a tenth of that time—small sticks which today are bowled over in the harvest of the big trees and left to rot on the ground. The logger knows this only too well, because he has time and silence in the woods to think, that we have been living recklessly on our capital in British Columbia and are living on it now, and that the best will be gone during our lifetime. The progress of the little locomotive up this narrow valley is the progress of man, most destructive of all animals, into the vanishing storehouse of nature.

—Comox Argus, April 20, 1933

tree canopy develops and closes." As Eva Bailey of Camp 3 recalled, "They'd burn the slash, and the next year you'd never know there'd been a fire gone over it!" It was covered in purple fireweed which was "absolutely gorgeous. And the next year, you'd see the young trees growing up—they'd seed themselves."

Blackberries were among the wild foods favoured by families at the logging camps. These were not the big, introduced, European blackberries known as "Himalayas" but the native trailing blackberries—the "small ones that crawled along the ground," as Dick Bailey put it. (Devotees of wild blackberries consider Himalayas excessively seedy and watery.)

Everyone in the valley seemed to pick these native blackberries for pies and winter jam. "It was one of the big treats of our life," Melda Buchanan remarked fondly. Most blackberry gathering took place on weekends in the fall. Walter Anderson took his son Arne out to gather blackberries with a twelve-gallon milk bucket; engineer Shorty Miner took a locie up the tracks after the berries; Butch Grant took his whole family on a speeder out from Camp 3 to the logging slash around Oyster River. The only drawback to blackberry picking, Myrtle Heron (*née* McKenzie) noted, was that the pickers shared the clear-cuts with huge (but harmless) garter snakes.

A number of indigenous birds and mammals, most notably blue grouse ("hooters"), ruffed grouse ("drummers," also called willow grouse), and black-tailed deer, multiplied in the lush new growth of ferns, fireweed, shrubs, and young deciduous trees. Joe Cliffe recalled in 1980:

> Our present forest wasn't always as we knew it. None of these things can live in the shade, the complete shade, and that's the way the forest gets to be. That is why when they fall the forest the sun increases so much there is more feed per acre. You know—in a big forest a deer couldn't find anything to eat. It would take twenty acres or more just to feed one deer. The same thing happened with the grouse—I mean the blue grouse. They lived in the forest; they were scarcer than the devil years ago when the forest was here, but as soon as we cut the forest there were tens of thousands. The salal came back, and the berries, and bits of grass. . . .

Grouse provided meals for many grateful logging families. "There was a grouse on every stump," recalled several former residents of Camp 2 and Camp 3. Blue grouse flourished on the abundant insect and plant life of the deforested land; they were so numerous they sometimes flew into open windows at the camps. These docile birds could be hit with a slingshot and even snagged with a noose tied to the end of a stick. At Oyster River, Herbert Pidcock excelled at shooting grouse. His mother would say, "Go out and get some willow grouse," and Herbert would go to the swamps where the willow grouse roosted in crabapple trees. Blue grouse liked it out in the open where it had been logged, but willow grouse preferred the security of canopy cover left around the swamps.

Other birds, such as pheasants, also found congenial homes in the logging slash. Introduced from Britain, pheasants had colonized Vancouver Island as far north as Comox by 1905 and subsequently spread into the clear-cuts, where they thrived along with the grouse until the coniferous forest re-established itself. Ducks, geese, and other waterfowl flocked to the newly opened swamps and lakes. Eva Bailey recalled the time in the 1930s when her brother Fred Manson shot a fine

Foraging the Clear-cut

Emma Churchill (*née* Ducca, born 1907), moved to Camp 3 from Courtenay in the 1920s. Like many women in the Depression, she gathered berries, fished, and preserved grouse and deer shot on the extensive slash around the camp. She described her collecting and preserving methods during a 1998 interview:

The wild blackberries are different: the seed is smaller. Some of them were big, and you can still get them, but only after a fire goes through. We picked blackberries after that fire in washtubs; we got sugar sacks full of berries. They loaned Nick Helm a speeder, and you could pick a water bucket full in one stop!

We put grouse and deer in jars, and in the winter we went to the lakes and cut a hole for fish. These were for eating, not preserving.

A lot of people canned grouse. We also did deer meat: we put it inside jars. You had to process deer and grouse meat for four hours in jars. There were no pressure cookers then.

Logging slash at the south end of Constitution Hill, December 1930, consisting of snags, saplings, stumps, and tangled treetops, limbs, and branches left by the skidder crews. This slash had not yet been burned. **Mack Laing photo.**—BRITISH COLUMBIA ARCHIVES, I-51822

Ideal grouse and deer habitat. Naturalist and hunter Mack Laing of Comox took this self-portrait somewhere in the Comox Valley in September 1932. His caption reads, "The burned over lands Blue Grouse Country Comox BC." Note the bracken fern at bottom right and the clumps of willows coming up around the scorched stumps.—BRITISH COLUMBIA ARCHIVES, I-51804

◀ A view from the Comox waterfront, 1923, looking southwest to a forest fire near Royston, with the Beaufort Range in the background. The origin of this forest fire is unknown, but slash burnings regularly got out of control. Mack Laing photo.—BRITISH COLUMBIA ARCHIVES, I-51801

A blue grouse on a scorched stump, Comox Valley, 1936. Right in the middle of the stump is a springboard notch. Mack Laing photo.—BRITISH COLUMBIA ARCHIVES, I-51802

Mack Laing with a brace of blue grouse, Comox, September 1924. Behind Laing is a second-growth forest. **Mack Laing photo.**—BRITISH COLUMBIA ARCHIVES, 96656

Mack Laing called this "a mixed bag." His shooting excursion near Comox resulted in (left to right) a pheasant, two mallard ducks, and two ruffed grouse. Mack Laing photo, 1931.—BRITISH COLUMBIA ARCHIVES, I-51805

Headquarters machinist Walter Anderson with a coastal black-tailed deer, *c.* 1925, near Headquarters. Note the dense mass of bracken fern on the burned-over clear-cut behind him. "Deer have to get out into the open," Eddy Berkeley said. "They can't live in tall timber because there's nothing to eat. They need brush." John Tukham photo.—JACK AND DOROTHY TUKHAM

John Pritchard (1891–1972) of Comox packing a black-tailed deer from the forest, 1939. Pritchard scaled at Camp 3 for Comox Logging. Mack Laing photo.
—BRITISH COLUMBIA ARCHIVES, I-51793

Cecil "Cougar" Smith of Comox adopted many orphaned cubs of cougars he had shot and later gave them to zoos in Canada and the United States. Here, in about 1930, Smith carries a pet cub on each shoulder.—MARGARET DUNN

Cecil Smith at Comox, November 1929, with his dog Prince and the hide of a bear that killed many sheep at Little River. Mack Laing photo.
—MARGARET DUNN

goose near Camp 3 in what he thought was the restricted hunting season. He plucked the goose quickly and shovelled the feathers into the wood stove to destroy the evidence. His brother-in-law Dick Bailey found a carpet of telltale white feathers all over the black paper roof. "They went up the draft and all over the roof!" Fred needn't have worried; it hadn't been the restricted season after all.

Elk also foraged in the clear-cuts. Eddy Berkeley remembered seeing herds of fifteen or twenty elk near Camp 3 feeding on lichen that grew in the downed treetops. Ordinarily the lichen and moss came down with the wind or in a heavy snowfall, but logging provided this food in abundance. The elk would still be there at the crack of dawn when the skidder crews arrived for work. "They came down at night to feed on the fell and bucked timber," Berkeley said. "They'd feed on the tops of the trees, and then they'd head up the hill in the morning."

Black-tailed deer were so numerous that they moved through the clear-cuts like herds of caribou. "As long as there were deer running around in the bush," recalled Gladys Thulin (*née* Dawson) of Campbell River, "we didn't have to go hungry." Austin Blackburn used to go to McPhee's swamp across from the Merville store and pick out whatever deer he wanted, Davey Janes recalled, and Old Man Charlie Williams of Williams Beach took orders from families in Cumberland as to what size of deer they wanted: a two-spike, three-spike, four-spike, etc. Charlie delivered the deer to the mining town every week. But this was not indiscriminate slaughter: hunters shot bucks only, according to Dick Bailey. "I never shot a doe. I preferred the two-spikes."

"We ate a lot of deer meat in those days!" remarked Helen Parkin (*née* Babcock), who arrived at Headquarters in 1921. "It was a necessity. We did everything imaginable with it—canned it, fried it, baked it, bottled it." Women in Camp 3 also braised, broiled, and bottled the venison for winter use (often adding a single onion to each jar), and some sent it far afield. Finnish immigrant Emilia Erickson of Merville sent haunches of deer to friends in Vancouver during the Depression. Her son Harry recalled that she'd "bundle it up" and ship it over to Vancouver on the CPR boat. Venison also entered the Depression-era barter economy: Jackie Gray noted that her grandfather Fred White of Dove Creek paid Dr. Briggs a "haunch of venison" on the birth of his son Robert in 1934.

Deer, in turn, became prey to cougars, for which the government offered a handsome bounty until the 1950s. Local hunters capitalized on this source of income. The most notable of them was Cecil "Cougar" Smith (1878–1961) of Oyster River and Comox, who shot at least one thousand cougars between 1900 and 1940. Smith made use of many parts of the cougar. He always packed out the tail for his favourite cat-tail soup, and he was fond of cougar tenderloin, as were some people at Camp 3. If Smith was near Cumberland he took the carcass into Chinatown where, in 1925, he got $7.50 for a big male cougar. "They wanted the gall bladder and the paws particularly," his daughter Margaret Dunn recalled. Smith also (in 1925), collected a forty-dollar bounty per cat, sold adult cougar skins to taxidermists for ten dollars, and sold the occasional skull to museum collectors for a further ten dollars. Many pelts, including the head with fangs bared, became hearth rugs. Scores of big game hunters came to the Comox Valley to shoot a

Collecting the Cat Bounty

Cougar were numerous between the wars owing to the large deer populations in the logging slash. Cougar sightings were common, and two Comox Logging Marion shovel operators—Tom McQuillan and Ernie Cowie—were also keen cougar hunters; both men built railway grades. Another hunter was Aubrey "Skate" Hames. The cougar bounty ranged from a high of forty dollars in the 1920s to a low of ten dollars during the Depression.

One day in the 1930s Bill Wilson was quietly eating his lunch when a cougar, not seeing him, jumped right over top of him. The cougar hissed and snarled, and walked away, but Bill never moved. The only weapon he had was a hand axe.

Malcolm Carwithen recalled the time in the late 1930s when he and Ernie Cowie were coming down the main line on a speeder. It was a summer night at 8:30 when all of a sudden a cougar jumped across the track a couple of miles north of Headquarters. Ernie threw the speeder out of gear, jumped down and shouted at the cougar so that it ran right up a tree. Then he turned to Malcolm and said, "Malcie, you stay here and I'll go and get Bonzo [Ernie's cougar dog]. I'll be back in a couple of hours."

"What do I do if the cougar comes down?" asked Malcolm. Ernie gave him an old red fire bucket and threw a few rocks into it. "If it tries to come down, you rattle the bucket!"

Ernie came back after two hours with his rifle and Bonzo and shot the treed cougar. The ten-dollar bounty "was a lot of money in those days."

cougar with Cougar Smith; they were almost guaranteed to add a trophy to their study wall back in Brighton, Berlin, or Boston.

Smith and other guides took the same hunters out after bear and elk, which fed seasonally on berries and browse in the clear-cuts. Men at Camps 1, 2, and 3 had unofficial traplines laid out along the swamps, lakes, rivers, and logging slash in Block 29. Among them were filer Jabe Day, scalers Alec Tilleard and Wallace Baikie, head loader Eric Gray, and rigger Jack Downey. "There was lots of beaver on Black Creek near Camp Three," Baikie recorded.

Fire-season foraging extended right to the intertidal zone of the Strait of Georgia and beyond. Many families made trips to the sea to fish for salmon and to collect clams and mussels. As the Depression-era motto went, "When the tide is out the table is set." For some, the fire season layoff at Williams Beach presented a commercial opportunity. In the 1930s, Bernard Churchill and his brother-in-law Joe Ducca, both of Camp 3, fished and sold salmon to cannery packers at Cape Mudge.

Residents harvested nature's bounty for other materials, too. They gathered old-growth Douglas fir bark for fuel; salvaged honey from beehives in old cedar snags; and harvested and sold some medicinal plants. In July and August, many residents of clear-cut areas, especially those around Headquarters and Camp 3, peeled the medicinal bark of the small cascara tree (known to several logging families as "barberry"). They would dry the strips on their roofs or on their fences, pack them into burlap sacks, and take them to a second-hand dealer in Courtenay named William Douglas. He in turn sold the bark to local and Mainland manufacturers, who made this "cascara sagrada" (Spanish, 'sacred bark') into a powerful laxative in the form of tablets or syrup; it is still sold as a laxative today. Indeed, cascara is such a powerful purgative that modern foresters have to wear gloves when handling the tree to avoid feeling its effects.

Ron Dalziel of Denman Island recalled that Mr. Douglas always paid in cash from his thick wallet. He was not fooled by a girl from Hornby Island who weighed down her sacks of cascara with stones. Dick and Eva Bailey remembered how Mr. Douglas would inspect their haul in the 1930s: "To see if it was dry he'd step on the sack, and it'd crackle if it was dry."

Logging families also gathered pine cones for Christmas decorations. These were six-inch pine cones—"the long ones"—from the white pine (sometimes called balsam). They sold the cones either to Mr. Douglas or to an outfit based in Ladysmith, which would paint them in festive colours and sell them. "Anything you could find out in the bush" was fair game, Dick Bailey recalled—"cascara bark, pine cones, anything! Took 'em to Douglas—he would buy anything if he could make a nickel out of it." Douglas also dealt in empty beer bottles.

≈

These Depression-era strategies of subsistence and survival—and the burgeoning second-growth on which they depended—were devastated by the forest fire of July 1938. The fire—known variously as the Great Fire, the Fire of '38, the Comox Valley Fire, the Sayward Fire, and the Bloedel Fire—started on July 5 on the Bloedel, Stewart & Welch

Scavenging the Bee Trees

The authors of the Comox Valley history *Land of Plenty* recorded that logging yielded a sweet dividend in the form of honey:

The cedar tree was often an unwanted species in the early half of the century. Cedar swamps were left unlogged by companies eager for the strong, straight Douglas fir. These cedars sometimes provided settlers with a source of honey. Loggers or hunters would spot a "bee tree," usually a hollow cedar in which an escaped swarm of bees had made their hive. A bee tree could be identified by bear claw scratches on the trunk. When fallen across an appropriate stump, the cedar tree would then split allowing the honeycomb, with some hazard, to be collected in washtubs.

"They'd find a hollow tree or a cedar tree and they'd bust it open," recalled John Grant of Camp 3. "There were all kinds of bee trees then." He remembered his father Butch Grant coming home with buckets of honey.

Once, faller Fred Manson of Camp 3 brought home a washtub of honeycomb and left it outside overnight and, his daughter Eva Bailey related, the honeybees belonging to neighbouring farmer Mr. Leighton "came and cleaned the washtub right out!"

**Tablets and syrup of cascara sagrada
—powerful purgatives. Comox, 1940. Mack Laing
photo.**—BRITISH COLUMBIA ARCHIVES, I-51825

**Cecil Smith stripping the
bark from a cascara tree near
Comox, 1940. Behind are a
large rotting Douglas fir log
and young cedars, suggesting
that this is second-growth.
Mack Laing photo.**—BRITISH
COLUMBIA ARCHIVES, I-51827

**Cecil Smith drying "barberry
bark" (cascara) at his house in
Comox, 1940. Mack Laing
photo.**—BRITISH COLUMBIA
ARCHIVES, I-51826

operations near Gosling Lake, just north of Campbell Lake and fifteen miles inland from Campbell River. It was a hot and dry summer, and Bloedel, Stewart & Welch had broken Forest Service rules to stop logging until the fire hazard had passed.

The immediate cause of the fire was a spark from the Bloedel company's Two-Spot locie that ignited a large cold-deck pile and produced an intense, uncontainable blaze. Flames jumped into the timber limits of the Elk River Timber Company and spread south along Campbell Lake, destroying Forbes Landing and coming within a mile of Campbell River. It then tore into stands of timber owned by Comox Logging. Before it finally ran its course on August 1, the fire had ripped across the Quinsam and Oyster rivers, Black Creek, the Tsolum River, Constitution Hill, Wolf Lake, and south towards Courtenay.

The fire was fuelled by successive patches of seasoned felled timber, cold-deck piles, and huge areas of tinder-dry slash from all three major companies—Bloedel, Stewart & Welch, Elk River Timber, and Comox Logging. It torched old pitch-filled snags, which erupted into spectacular vertical blazes like giant Roman candles. Violent updrafts tore the ancient burning branches right off snags and threw them far in advance of the fire, endangering the lives of men battling the blaze. Ferocious gusts of wind drove balls of fire through the treetops. This was known as "crowning"—a term that described a fast-burning, wind-propelled fire as it devoured the dry needles of the forest canopy.

When the fire reached Constitution Hill it "crowned" and afforded a spectacular sight. Eva Bailey was at a relative's house at Merville, watching the fire from the window. She remarked that "the flames rolled over Constitution Hill—the fire went three miles in twenty minutes." Forester John Hatfield further commented, "You could hear a roar like a freight train. That fire went around the hill in an hour or two."

The fire finally petered out at Browns River, five miles from Courtenay, when the wind changed. Heavy rains, high humidity, and the efforts of over 1,500 men helped douse the inferno.

Both Camp 3 and Headquarters were spared, though a small camp at Tsolum was consumed. Comox Logging put seven locies to work fighting the fire and lost two or three donkeys and cold deckers, as well as other equipment.

The blaze destroyed almost 75,000 acres (30,184 hectares—1,878 in Sayward Land District and 28,306 in Comox Land District). Ninety per cent of the timber destroyed belonged to Comox Logging. It was and is the biggest forest fire in recorded history on the coast of British Columbia, laying waste to a swath thirty miles long and up to eight miles wide. Great clouds of smoke and ash rolled down the east coast of Vancouver Island and into the Strait of Georgia. Comox and Courtenay were blanketed with ash, which also fell in Nanaimo, Vancouver, Seattle (where people had to sweep it off their cars), and as far away as the Prairies. Curiously, Campbell River was free of smoke and ash for much of the fire, thanks to a northwest wind.

Hi Churchill recalled that the wind changed just before the fire reached Camp 3. They had locies and Caterpillars fighting it, making good wide trails, but their efforts were defeated by back fires when fir

Last Train over the Oyster River Bridge

During the 1938 fire, brakeman Hi Churchill was sent out on the Two-Spot to retrieve a donkey engine used for raising spar trees on the far side of the Oyster River. He got the donkey—which was on a flatcar—and made it back over the Oyster River just before the bridge burned. He recalled:

When the fire came though from Elk River it took a couple of weeks to work its way through, and finally they took a hundred men out to the Oyster River bridge. They had a pump in the river keeping the bridge soaked down. I was sent out in the Two-Spot—Joe Ducca was firing and Bert Woodruff was the engineer—they sent the three of us out to bring the machine down to Headquarters.

When we were gone the pump broke down and the bridge was starting to burn. We got over it OK: we got to the Oyster River siding OK and left the machine there, which is where they'd sent the Three-Spot, but on the way out the phone line was down and the railway ties were on fire! We couldn't phone to see if the line was OK, so we hooked all the locies together and all the crummies. We sprayed the men with water, and away we went for Headquarters!

snags with a hundred feet of dry bark exploded behind them. "The wind would hit a burning snag and the pieces would fly!" Snags were thus a major cause of the fire's rapid spread. "That is why they started falling all snags," Hi said. "They were dead, and they had lots of loose bark, and the fire got up inside the bark and lasted for a long time and it could start another fire."

One of many serious incidents during the fire happened at quitting time one day, when a locie was bringing a crew out from the upper Tsolum River. A section of ties had burned out and two crummies went off the track. "The men jumped out and ran into the swamp with the fire coming through," recalled Hi Churchill. "They stayed in the swamp, which saved them." One of the men was Otto Richter, whose daughter, Eleanor Keller, said that he got stuck in a swamp behind Black Creek. The men's wives were not told what was happening; they believed their husbands were fighting the fire. Then a man from Merville dropped into the Oyster River beer parlour and word spread about the stranded men. Not without reason, at least one of the men's wives panicked. It was several days before the men could be rescued.

Headquarters, threatened during the fire, had been fully prepared for evacuation. Train crews showered the dry houses with water from tank cars, in an attempt to protect the houses from hot embers. "They were up on the roofs putting out spot fires," recalled Neil Martin. According to Bill Wilson, "The draft from the fire tore the roofing paper off the roundhouse at Headquarters. The fire came sweeping down. It came so fast that it only singed some trees." Gunnar Jonsson recalled, "I was working at Camp 3, and we saw it coming for two days before it came. We fought the fire for several days—we surrounded it with fire trenches, and the fire came damned close to Headquarters and the machine shops, and they fought it with water." Fortunately, the town was saved at the eleventh hour. As Jonsson explained, "The wind changed and it headed for Dove Creek and some of the Dove Creek people had to leave."

The fire remains seared in the minds of those who witnessed it. At night the glow could be seen for miles. Eleanor Keller remembered an inch of ash left on the front steps of her parents' house in Merville. "The sky turned plum purple as thick clouds of smoke blanketed the heavens," wrote Rene Harding. "Cars travelling the highway north had to turn their lights on at four in the afternoon—and this was July! The day became known as 'Black Friday.' The outlook appeared so alarming that guests at the Elk Hotel in Comox, seeing ashes and scorched leaves falling around them, packed their bags and left." Brian Bayly recalled the surreal spectacle of whole charred maple leaves falling on his parents' farm at Happy Valley, south of Courtenay. John Hatfield, then a teenager, "worked to exhaustion" during the fire: "The smoke was so searing that your lungs pained during the day. It was like a fog but a dry fog; searing heat; biting smoke in your lungs and mouth—like the eruption of Vesuvius. You couldn't see the sun for two weeks. It was just an orange glow. The grass was white like straw everywhere. I can still see the great big maple leaves, all white. Ashes landed as far away as Manitoba."

Fighting the Fire of '38

Dozens of Comox Logging employees returned from Ladysmith, where the company had opened a branch in 1936, to fight the 1938 fire. Clive Davis and Bill Wilson brought their Caterpillar up to Courtenay on the E & N railway as the fire approached Oyster River. "The ash was flying in Courtenay when we arrived," said Bill Wilson, "and at Black Creek the fire went overhead like thunder—it swept overhead!" They built fire trails and a fire guard around the Oyster River bridge, but the bridge burned out anyway.

Another Ladysmith man, Mauno Pelto (born 1918), had arrived at Youbou from his native Finland in 1929. He joined Comox Logging at Ladysmith in 1937 after blowing whistles at Caycuse. A year later Pelto and his cold decker were sent north to help salvage the burned and scorched timber "before the bugs got it." He worked first at Constitution Hill and then in the Quinsam region. "Campbell River was just below us," Pelto recalled. "We could hear the [Cape Mudge] foghorn."

In 1938 Mauno met carpenter's daughter Babs (Marguerite) Burnett while roller skating at the Native Sons' Hall, Courtenay. "It took me four months to realize that his eyebrows weren't black!" she laughed. They were married two years later.

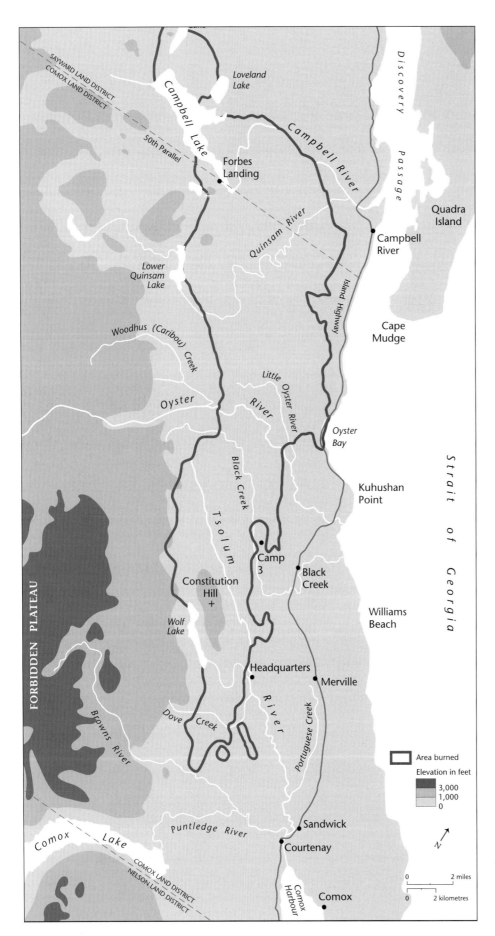

Area burned by the fire of 1938. Redrawn from a BC Forest Service map, c. 1939, provided by John Parminter, BC Ministry of Forests.

The Comox Peninsula and Royston wharf pictured from Major Arthur Hilton's house at Royston during the fire of 1938. A great cloud of smoke fills the sky overhead and a Royal Navy ship rides at anchor in Comox Harbour. In the foreground is the hulk *Laurel Whalen*, sunk the previous year by Comox Logging as a breakwater for its booming grounds (at left). Ash had not yet started to fall on the Hiltons' garden (foreground).—HUGH HILTON

Major Hilton's house at Royston during the great fire of 1938. The driveway is covered with white ash, and a cloud of smoke billows above.—HUGH HILTON

The cottage and hotel resort at Forbes Landing, Campbell Lake, on the fiftieth parallel, was destroyed in the 1938 fire. Comox Logging's northern timber property reached almost as far as this popular holiday and fishing destination for families from the Comox Valley. Shown here are Evelyn Blackburn, her mother Marjorie Blackburn (*née* Janes), and an unidentified woman behind, c. 1924.—FRED BLACKBURN

The smouldering remains of a skidder setting soon after the 1938 fire, probably near Oyster River. The felled timber in the foreground had been bucked into forty-foot lengths for yarding to the skidder when the setting was evacuated. In the distance is an eerie forest of snags and burned timber. **Bob Filberg photo.**—FILBERG LODGE & PARK ASSOCIATION

Comox Logging superintendent Bob Filberg took this photo of a fully rigged head spar destroyed in the fire of July 1938, probably near Oyster River. Note the collapsed hayrack boom and the burned-out tank of crude oil behind it. Thousands of acres of logging slash fuelled the great fire.—FILBERG LODGE & PARK ASSOCIATION

The Oyster River bridge after the fire of 1938. Bob Filberg photo.
—FILBERG LODGE & PARK ASSOCIATION

Ruth Masters of Courtenay climbed up to the Forbidden Plateau during the fire of 1938. Her caption reads, "July 22, 1938. From Mt. Elma—Comox Valley fire—14 miles away." P. Tait photo.—RUTH MASTERS

Looking west across the Oyster River bridge, July 1938, immediately after the fire. A water tank for filling the locie boilers is at right. Bob Filberg photo.—FILBERG LODGE & PARK ASSOCIATION

The "Oyster Barrens" just north of Oyster River, 1939, a year after the great fire. The view is east toward Quadra, Cortes, and Hernando islands, the Strait of Georgia, and the mainland coast. A Cat road has been built to salvage the timber. Patches of bracken fern have sprung up amidst the burned slash.—BRITISH COLUMBIA ARCHIVES, I-51813

◀ The White family of Dove Creek during their evacuation to Lewis Park, Courtenay, in July 1938. Clockwise, from front left: Bob White, Violet White, Dorothy White (*née* Lampard), Muriel White, Ralph White.—JACKIE GRAY

The 1938 fire swept quickly across Constitution Hill, killing many of the smaller trees but merely scorching the mature fire-resistant Douglas fir for twenty feet up their trunks. Two years after the fire, when this photo was taken, the damage was still evident. Mack Laing is standing in a large patch of fireweed. Mack Laing photo.—BRITISH COLUMBIA ARCHIVES, I-51815

In 1939, naturalist Mack Laing took this photo of a burned area near Oyster River, with snow-covered Mount Alexandra and Mount Adrian in the distance. "Prairies of bracken trying to hide miles of black stumpage," stated Laing's caption, "and the slashings creeping up the distant hills to the skyline—timber-mined." Bracken fern like this came up in abundance during the first year after a big fire.—BRITISH COLUMBIA ARCHIVES, I-51814

Pete Harms, a Mennonite farmer from Black Creek, replanting in Block 28 north of Oyster River in the spring of 1949. Note his canvas bag containing Douglas fir seedlings. Don McIver, who supervised the operation, recalled that the Mennonites each planted 1265 seedlings a day; returned soldiers planted only 400. Don McIver photo.—DON McIVER

Evacuating Headquarters

Sam Telosky helped prepare Headquarters for evacuation during the fire of 1938:

We were working ten miles out of Headquarters. The wind was blowing and the fire was chasing us. The locie came and blew its whistle lots of longs and shorts and took us into Headquarters. Filberg was there. We had to move everything onto flatcars, and between 4:00 and 9:00 p.m. we moved everything out of Headquarters. We moved everything out—they figured the fire would take the town out. We filled fifty or sixty flatcars.

You could hear the fire roar. It went over Constitution Hill just roaring. Half an hour later everything was quiet.

At 9:00 p.m. Filberg was out there and he had a smorgasbord laid out on a flatcar, and it was something! This was in case we'd be there all night.

A week later we got rain and that just about finished the fire. I worked on the fire for five weeks.

◀ Ten years after the 1938 fire, much of Comox Logging's Block 28 was still a sterile wasteland with only patches of willow to break the monotony. The fire was especially fierce on this hilly country, and no seed trees survived the conflagration. Block 28 was located between the Quinsam and Oyster rivers, eight miles inland from Oyster Bay. Here, a crew of Mennonites from Black Creek plant Douglas fir seedlings—second-growth trees that, fifty years later, are large enough to be cut. Don McIver photo, 1949.—DON McIVER

Many people hiked up to Forbidden Plateau to escape the low-lying smoke and watch the progress of the fire. "The sun was purple," Don McIver recalled. "You could look right at it. It was just a purple smudge in the sky . . . and you could see the smoke come up in waves, in clouds." Sandy Strachan from Courtenay also remembered the scene at Forbidden Plateau. "I can still see that smoke from the big fire coming over the mountain. Boy, was it scary! You couldn't see Courtenay—all you could see was boughs of fir and tree skeletons sticking up through the smoke."

Residents were evacuated from the communities of Black Creek, Merville, Grantham, and Dove Creek as hot embers rained on the houses. Men stayed behind to spray the roofs with water and look after the livestock, and evacuate them if necessary. Women and children were sent to Lewis Park in Courtenay, where a tent camp of refugees was set up. "Auntie Sylvia White remembers taking beds to the Agricultural Hall, now called the Lewis Centre," wrote Jackie Gray (*née* Gullett). "She remembers sleeping in the hall with her sisters Muriel and Violet, but said they had a tent as well. It was a lot of fun for the girls, as it was like a big pajama party. Uncle Bob remembers the story that his Dad was fighting the fire up by the Oyster River, and at the end of the day, he returned to the house to find the family all gone to the agricultural hall. The Navy had checked the house in the family's absence and eaten the stew that Grandma had left on the stove for Grandpa's supper." The wind swung around at the last moment and saved the farms on lower Dove Creek from destruction.

～

The great fire of 1938 produced enormous devastation. Almost thirty years of logging by Comox Logging and the northern companies had created, in the thousands of acres of logged-over land and logging slash, the potential for an inferno of this magnitude. Over a hundred square miles of land was razed. Everything was burned out: cold-deck piles, skidder settings, spar trees, fell and bucked timber, new second-growth, and much of the remaining original forest. Wallace Baikie described the view from a hill near the John Hart Dam on Campbell River after the fire. Looking south, he recorded, all you could see was "black stumps for twenty-five miles." The journalist Renny Englebert noted much the same bleakness in 1947. "Stand on a hillock anywhere in Vancouver Island's forest regions," he wrote, "and you will see below you a dense mass of the world's tallest trees. Their branches whisper in the wind. Look in another direction, and you will see thousands of acres of land, cut bare and burned bare. Here there is silence and an eerie feeling of desolation."

The original forest was now a thing of the past on most of the level plain between Courtenay and Campbell River. According to Eleanor Keller of Merville, this had the effect of "opening up the land." At Merville, for example, the sunlight could be seen reflecting from house windows on the other side of the Strait of Georgia, twenty-five miles away: "After the devastation we could see the sun setting in the windows east of Powell River, and we could see Constitution Hill to the west. The first growth was all gone by then."

Comox Logging acted quickly to salvage timber from its properties burned in the 1938 fire. Here, near Helldiver Lake and Constitution Hill, timber has been cold decked to a spar tree. Mack Laing photo, 1940.—BRITISH COLUMBIA ARCHIVES, I-51816

The fire had other results. With its northern timber gone through cutting and fire, Comox Logging closed Camp 3 in 1942 and moved its personnel and machinery south to the uncut and unburned timber at Comox Lake and Ladysmith. At these places, the company would abandon skidder logging and begin truck logging. Camp 3 became an army camp for the remainder of the war.

The fire also brought with it the possibility of renewal. Like the smaller slash fires of previous years, the fire of 1938 produced an ideal habitat for many plant and animal species. Within a year, the burned regions produced immense crops of bracken fern and trailing blackberries, which in turn attracted grouse, deer, and cougar. "Fireweed came in," recalled John Hatfield. "There were deer everywhere.... The game that resulted was unbelievable; the grouse and deer exploded. In the early 1940s you could get forty to sixty blue grouse a day." Oscar Kreutziger, whose family farmed near Camp 3 in its last years, said that every car coming from the camp had a deer tied to its fender.

The barren tracts of land were also ideal beds for reforestation, which finally began on Comox Logging's scorched property in 1943. The first tree planters were Mennonite men from Black Creek, who knew how to make things grow in unlikely areas. "As farmers they wanted everything to grow," reasoned their supervisor Don McIver. Loggers were also hired as tree planters in the fire season, but most of them were too impatient. "They thought it was a joke," McIver recalled. "The ex-loggers would plant five or seven seedlings in a hole and say, 'plywood!'"

The seedlings planted by Mennonite farmers have become second-growth forests, which are now managed by Comox Logging's successor, New Zealand–based TimberWest. But they bear little relation to the original forests. These professionally managed tree farms are being cut already—some say far too soon—and long before the trees grow to maturity. In some places a second replanting has already taken place.

But among the new seedlings and the small second-growth stumps persist many enormous and seemingly indestructible old-growth stumps, their pitch-filled bases providing a hard veneer against the passage of time. And while modern foresters look ahead to a third cutting, a few venerable men who helped remove the first forest remain rooted to their family farms in the Comox Valley. Now aged about ninety, men like Hi Churchill, Davey Janes, and Gunnar Jonsson have witnessed the passage or planting of three generations of forest.

The original forest may have been replaced with quick-yield tree farms, but at the start of the twenty-first century, much farmland in the Comox Valley remains in the possession of the district's original settler families. Farming, while important, was rarely enough to provide a living, and the Homeguard owe their persistence to the payroll of the Comox Logging and Railway Company and its successors. The Homeguard adapted to the arrival of this colossal industrial concern by combining farming with employment in the woods, on the railway, at Headquarters, at the outer camps, at the boom camp, and on the tugboats. Men worked for the company seasonally, and their wages allowed them to marry and bring up families in the valley. Their successful strategies were followed by newcomers from Britain, Scandinavia, and elsewhere, who worked for Comox Logging, bought land, married local women, and became part of the Homeguard. What sustained both the Comox Homeguard and the Comox Valley for much of the twentieth century—through war, depression, and fire—was Island timber.

Hi (Hiram) Churchill (left) and Davey Janes at Hi's house in Grantham, April 2000. The youngest of the Homeguard Janes boys, Davey was born in Comox in 1912, started working as a whistlepunk for Comox Logging in 1925 or 1926, and lost a leg in a logging accident in 1936. He left Comox Logging in 1949 and worked as a gyppo truck logger and beachcomber. His brother-in-law Hi Churchill, also born in 1912, came to the coast from Nova Scotia at the age of eight, started setting chokers for Comox Logging in 1930, and married Mavis Janes a few years later. These men retain a comprehensive memory of logging in the era of skidders and steam. Len Todd photo.

glossary

Note: These terms are defined as they were used in Comox Logging between 1910 and 1940. Some terms have evolved over time with modern logging methods.

Back end   the part of a skidder setting farthest from the track, containing the back spars.

Back rigger   a rigger who helps rig the back spars. *See also* Rigger.

Back spar   a tree rigged up at the back end of a setting to provide lift (highlead) for yarding logs.

Barber chair   a tree stump with a large splintered piece of wood left sticking up (like the back of a chair), as a result of an inadequate undercut.

Bicycle   a carriage apparatus that runs along the skyline in skidder logging; it brings logs in to the landing and takes chokers back out to the chokermen.

Bight   the dangerous area in the curve of a yarding line, which is under tension and may suddenly straighten out; a common cause of logging accidents and loggers are frequently admonished to "Keep out of the bight!" *See also* Siwash.

Blaze   an axe mark made on a tree to indicate surveyors' boundaries and spar trees.

Block   a metal shell encasing pulley sheaves, used to guide cables (*see also* Carriage); or a section of a bucked log suitable to be split into firewood (also called a round).

Blowdown   a tree or stand of trees felled by the wind.

Blue butt   the lowest log cut from a large fir tree, usually pitchy.

Board foot   the standard unit of volume for timber during the railway logging era, measuring one foot by one foot by one inch (144 cubic inches); also called foot board measure (ft.b.m.).

Boilermaker   a machine shop worker in charge of building and maintaining locie, skidder, and donkey boilers.

Boom (Log boom)   a 576-foot raft of timber for water towing, enclosed by a boomstick frame and held together with boom chains.

Boom chain   a stout chain, generally six feet long, used to link boomsticks together.

Booming   making log booms by sorting, stowing, and moving logs in the water.

Booming grounds   a protected bay, often a tidal estuary, where logs are boomed and stored.

Boomstick   one of the logs that surround a boom to hold it together. Usually 72 feet long, boomsticks have four-inch holes at the ends so they may be joined together with boomchains. *See also* Rider, Swifter, Headstick, Tailstick.

Brow logs   large logs placed on each side of the track to help the loading leverman guide logs into place on the flatcar.

Buck   to cut or saw a tree into log lengths for yarding or for firewood.

Bucker   a logger whose job is to follow the fallers and saw the felled trees into standard log lengths.

Bucking saw   a sturdy crosscut saw, generally seven feet long, used by a single bucker for cutting felled trees into lengths. *See also* Crosscut saw, Falling saw.

Bull bucker   the supervisor of fallers, buckers, and scalers.

Bullcook   a man (usually an old or maimed logger) who performs various odd jobs in a logging camp, such as sweeping out bunkhouses, making beds, cutting firewood, etc.

Bull of the woods   *see* Push.

Bunk   a wooden platform, usually made of Douglas fir, set at one or both ends of a flatcar to support boomsticks and timber sticks.

Bunkmaker   skidder crew member who makes flatcar bunks, sweeps debris from flatcars, and performs other odd jobs at the landing.

Butt   the lower trunk of a tree, often flaring ("swelled butt") and so avoided by loggers when falling a tree (*see also* Springboard); can also refer to the large end of a log.

Cable   *see* Line.

Car-knocker   man who maintains and repairs flatcars.

Car shop   a building for the repair and maintenance of flatcars.

Carriage   a block suspended from the skyline and from which the choker lines descend.

Caulk boots   boots with spikes on the soles for better grip when walking on logs and slash (pronounced "cork").

Chainman   survey crew member who holds the measuring chain, carries the compass, and performs minor jobs.

Chaser   member of a skidder (or cold decker) crew who unhooks the chokers from the logs after they have been yarded to the landing pile.

Cheese blocks   steel wedges placed on the decks of flatcars to hold the logs in place; also called dogs.

Cherry picker   a small donkey engine fitted with a loading boom, secured to a flatcar, and taken along the track to retrieve timber from trackside nuisance areas, and to pick up logs that have fallen from flatcars.

Choke   to pass a line or choker around a log and pull it tight, like a noose.

Choker   a short loop of cable with a hook at one end, attached to the skyline carriage and used to pull logs.

Chokerman   member of a skidder or cold decker crew who "sets chokers," i.e., straps chokers around logs for yarding to the landing.

Chuck (or **Saltchuck**)   the ocean (Chinook trade jargon).

Coffin   portable two-handled box for transporting lunches from the cookhouse to the skidder landing.

Cold decker   a mobile donkey engine mounted on a sled, used to yard distant logs and stack them within reach of the skidder; also called yarder.

Cold deck pile   in skidder logging, a pile of logs (as many as 4,000) yarded from a distance and stacked by a cold decker beneath a back spar for transport to the landing by the skidder.

Cold deck timber   timber beyond a skidder's 1100-foot reach, yarded to a back spar by a cold decker.

Cribbing   a framework of logs, square timber, or railway ties used for supporting bridges and portable skidders, schoolhouses, and camp houses.

Crosscut saw   a saw for cutting across the grain of wood. These were long, flat, steel saws with two types of sharp teeth (cutters and rakers). *See also* Bucking saw and Falling saw.

Cruiser   *see* Timber cruiser.

Crummy   an old boxcar with benches and perhaps a stove added, used as a log train caboose to carry loggers to and from work.

Deadhead   in towing, waterlogged timber that sinks out of the boom and can present a hazard to shipping.

Dogs   U-shaped spikes used to fasten logs together for transport in skid road logging. *See also* Cheese blocks.

Dolphin   several pilings driven together in the water and bound with cable, to which log booms are tied for storage or safety. *See also* Pilings.

Donkey engine   a steam engine with an upright boiler and two drums, mounted on a heavy log sled and used for power in yarding logs; also called steam pot.

Donkey puncher   the engineer on a donkey engine, yarder, or skidder.

Donkey sled   *see* Sled.

Double-bitted axe   a hand axe with two cutting blades, used for chopping undercuts, firewood, guyline notches, etc.; also called double-bladed axe.

Dump (**Log dump**)   place where logs are literally "dumped" from the end of the railway into the ocean. Logs are generally pushed or rolled from a trestle built out over the water.

Engineer   used two ways: 1) any man operating a steam engine (thus for yarding and loading levermen as well as locomotive engineers); 2) any man on the survey crew, whether or not a civil engineer.

Eye splice   to make a secure loop of cable by bending the cable back and splicing it into itself. *See also* Splice, Long splice.

Faller   a woods worker who cuts down (fells) trees, usually by chopping and sawing with a partner.

Falling gang   gang of two fallers and one or two buckers responsible for falling and bucking trees, under the direction of a bull bucker.

Falling saw   a flexible crosscut saw generally between 7.5 and 11.5 feet in length, used by a pair of fallers for cutting down trees. *See also* Crosscut saw, Bucking saw.

Farmer   a derogatory term for a new worker or one who is slow or clumsy.

Farm timber   timber growing on farms or pre-emptions, often sold to a logging company.

Filer (**Sawfiler**)   man who sharpens crosscut saws with files.

Fireman   man who keeps the steam up on a skidder or locomotive by stoking it with firewood or monitoring the flow of crude oil.

Flatcar   a wooden-framed rail car usually forty feet long, used for hauling logs from the skidder landing to the dump.

Flying corps   *see* Rigging crew.

Flying machine   *see* Skidder.

Gandy dancer   member of steel gang or section crew who pounds spikes into wooden ties to hold down steel rails; also called tie tamper.

Gilchrist jack   a portable but hazardous hand-jack used to roll logs for short distances and to tip logs from the end of a skid road into the water; also known as "Killchrist jack."

Gin pole   a small pole (resembling a telephone pole) used as a spar in parbuckle loading or in raising a spar tree.

Grading (**grade**) **crew**   workers who prepare railway grades by falling trees and digging and blasting out rock, earth, and stumps.

Ground yarding   any yarding system in which logs are pulled over skids or simply over the ground, as opposed to highlead yarding.

Guylines   strong cables running from the top and centre of a spar tree to surrounding stumps, to hold the spar firmly in place.

Gyppo   a small, minor, or fly-by-night logging outfit.

Gyp-stick   *see* Scale stick.

Handcar   a small, hand-pumped vehicle used by the section crew to patrol the railway track and monitor repairs. *See also* Speeder.

Handlogger   a logger who logs by hand adjacent to rivers or inlets, using such tools as an axe, crosscut saw, peavey, and Gilchrist jack.

Hang-up   a tree that refuses to fall because it is caught in the canopy of nearby trees; or a turn of logs caught behind a stump, root, snag, or other obstruction when yarding; or fouled-up rigging; or any kind of problem in a logging show.

Haulback line   a line on a yarder or skidder that draws the mainline and chokers back out into the woods to pick up a new turn of logs.

Hayburner   horse.

Hayrack boom   in skidder logging, a device for loading logs onto flatcars, consisting of two timbers (originally eighty-two feet long) fastened together and attached to the head spar horizontally above the skidder. The hayrack boom rotates around the spar tree to allow logs to be picked up and loaded.

Head loader   member of skidder crew in charge of loading at the landing.

Head rigger   *see* High rigger.

Head spar   *see* Spar.

Headstick   the boomstick at the top end of a log boom; generally sixty-six feet long. *See also* Tailstick.

Highball   to move quickly; or a fast and efficient logging operation.

Highlead logging   logging method in which spar trees—in combination with donkeys or skidders—are used to lift one end of the logs during yarding for easier transport; also called overhead or aerial logging.

High rigger   the high rigger or head rigger, along with his rigging crew, is in charge of rigging up the spar trees and determining how the lines run out in the setting. He climbs, limbs, tops, and rigs up spar trees. *See also* Rigger.

Homeguard   has been defined as "a man who works for the same company and never leaves his job" (Swanson, *Bunkhouse Ballads*); used here in a specific sense to refer to workers with strong family ties to the Comox Valley and often lifelong employment with Comox Logging—a "family company."

Home spar   *see* Spar.

Hooker (Hooktender)   the yarding crew boss, in charge of the whole operation of hauling logs from where they are cut to the landing, and in charge of the chokermen and whistlepunk. Sometimes referred to as the "side-push."

Humdirgen   a steam-powered log unloader at the boom camp.

Inside tug   a small tug used for towing log booms from the booming grounds to the sheltered log storage area. *See also* Outside tug.

Jackladder   a chain conveyance at a sawmill by means of which logs are moved from the water into the mill.

Jackpot (Pot)   a snarl of criss-crossed logs, often occurring when logs are dumped on top of one another in shallow water.

Jam (Log jam)   a tangle of logs in a river drive.

L-Stick   *see* Scale stick.

Lagging   a strip of hardwood nailed or spiked to a back spar one hundred feet from the ground to prevent the skyline from cutting the tree through friction.

Landing   used two ways: 1) any level ground to which logs are yarded for sorting or loading; 2) a cleared area near the skidder (skidder landing) where logs are piled (the landing pile) before being loaded on flatcars.

Leverman, Loading   the skidder engineer who "swings the boom"—who loads logs onto flatcars with tongs and hayrack boom.

Leverman, Yarding/Skidder   the engineer who yards logs from every corner of the setting to the skidder landing.

Lidgerwood   a brand of skidder engine made in Washington State, used on the coast of British Columbia from 1911 until about 1950. *See also* Skidder.

Line   the cable or "wire rope" used extensively in yarding, skidding, and rigging; or a blazed survey line or boundary.

Line horse   a horse employed in early donkey engine logging before haulback lines were devised, to drag the line out into the woods.

Loader   member of skidder crew whose job is to load logs from the landing to the flatcars; normally a crew of three can keep pace with the logs brought in by the yarding leverman. *See also* Head loader, Second loader, Skidder crew.

Loading and skidder levermen   *see* under Leverman.

Loading crew   *see* Skidder crew.

Locie logging locomotive, also called engine. Logging locies were of two types: heavy rod engines (Baldwins) used for main-line hauling, and lighter but versatile geared engines (Heislers, Shays, Climaxes) used on steep grades and for hauling flatcars in and out of skidder settings.

Log boom *see* Boom.

Log dump *see* Dump.

Log jam *see* Jam.

Log stamp large hammer imprinted with a logging company's insignia for stamping both ends of a log at the skidder landing.

Long-butt in bucking, to leave the swelled or pitch-filled butt of a tree in the woods.

Long corner a distant corner of a skidder setting, inaccessible to skidders, where logs are retrieved by cold deckers or cherry pickers.

Long splice to join two cables by weaving together the separated cable stands at the end of each cable. *See also* Splice, Eye splice.

Main line the main stretch of a logging railway.

Mainline the heavy main cable used in yarding and to which chokers are attached.

Marion shovel an American-made brand of electric shovel used for building railway grades.

Marlinspike an iron spike that tapers to a flat point, used in splicing wire rope.

Mat a portable set of logs fastened together, upon which a grade shovel rests when making grades; or a set of logs placed beneath a spar tree on swampy or unstable ground.

Mat-hooker shovel crew member who hooks and unhooks the shovel mat and oils the shovel. *See also* Swamper.

Outside tug a powerful deep-sea tug used for towing log booms from the sheltered log storage area to the mill (in this case, across the Strait of Georgia). *See also* Inside tug.

Parbuckle a line slung around a log causing it to roll onto a skid road or flatcar when one end of the line is pulled by a donkey.

Peaker log the top log on a flatcar load.

Peavey a six-foot tool with a metal spike and hinged cant-hook at one end, used for rolling and positioning logs and for breaking up jackpots.

Peeler a flawless Douglas fir log ideal for peeling into plywood.

Pike pole a pole about sixteen feet long, with a sharp point and hook, used by boom men to sort and stow floating logs.

Pilings (**Piles**) heavy poles, usually of Douglas fir, driven into the seabed or mud flats to form the support of a logging wharf or trestle. *See also* Dolphin.

Pinch the tendency for a tree, by its weight, to squeeze a saw during falling or bucking, corrected by driving a wedge into the saw cut.

Pocket a corral-like enclosure, fenced by pilings, in which log booms are made up and stored; also called rafting pocket.

Powdermen men whose job is to blow up stumps from rights-of-way, to blow up roots from blowdowns, and to blow bark off snags for safety.

Push camp foreman or logging superintendent; also known as "bull of the woods."

Quarter section of a setting.

Raise a tree set up a spar tree.

Raised tree a spar tree that is brought into a setting by rail and raised in the absence of a suitable standing tree. *See also* Standing tree, Spar.

Ride the natural lie or balance of a log used in skid road construction. To "find the ride" means to find the best position for such a log.

Rider log a swifter, with or without bore holes, tied to the top of a boom to secure floating timber.

Right-of-way a graded path through the forest, sixty or eighty feet wide, containing a logging railway.

Rig (**Rig up**) set up a spar tree for logging by attaching guylines, skyline, and mainline.

Rigger depending on context, may refer to 1) a high rigger, or 2) a back rigger (member of a skidder or yarder crew who helps rig the back spars).

Rigging the lines, blocks, carriages, and other gear used in highlead logging systems (also called tackle or jewellery); or working on rigging jobs.

Rigging crew the woods crew involved with rigging spar trees in advance of skidder crews; also called rigging-ahead crew, rig-up gang, flying corps.

Rigging slinger the supervisor of a rigging crew, who chooses the logs to be yarded, untangles rigging, etc., and directs the chokermen and whistlepunk.

Rigging-up goat a donkey engine used by the rigging crew in raising and rigging spar trees; also called goat.

Road in highlead logging, the path or avenue along which logs are yarded.

Roundhouse building used for repair and maintenance of locomotives.

Sand house shed at a logging camp used to store sand for locie traction.

Sawfiler *see* Filer.

Scaler   man who scales timber; that is, assesses grade and measures bucked logs to estimate board footage, using scale stick or calipers and steel tape. *See also* Water scaler.

Scale stick   a measure for calculating board footage; also called L-stick and gyp-stick.

Second hooker   skidder crewman second in command to hooker.

Second loader   skidder crewman who helps transfer logs from the landing to the flatcar.

Section   a stretch of logging railway; or a seventy-two-foot length of a log boom.

Section boss   foreman in charge of a railway section gang.

Section gang, crew or hands   crew in charge of maintaining the ties, steel, and grade on a section of railway.

Setting   the roughly sixty-six-acre area logged from a single central spar tree: the work site of falling and skidder crews.

Show   a logging operation or outfit; or the area being logged.

Side-push   an assistant foreman. *See also* Hooker.

Siwash   Chinook jargon for a line that has been diverted by getting bent around a stump, tree, or log. *See also* Bight.

Skid   used two ways: 1) a partially sunk, barked, and greased log upon which logs are dragged by horses or oxen (*see also* Skid road); 2) a hewn Douglas fir timber attached to the bottom of a donkey or yarder to enable it to move through the bush and over felled timber (*see also* Sled).

Skid greaser   a junior member of a horse or oxen logging crew whose job is to grease the skid road with oil or fat to facilitate movement of logs.

Skid road   in the days of horse and oxen logging, a road formed of skids along which logs were yarded. *See also* Road.

Skidder   the powerhouse of highlead logging: a glorified donkey engine mounted on a flatcar and able to yard logs with one engine and load them with another by means of highlead and hayrack boom. Also called flying machine, overhead rig, cable-way skidder. *See also* Lidgerwood.

Skidder crew   a crew of about twenty-two men divided into two groups: a "skidding" or "yarding" crew (consisting of head rigger, back riggers, hooker, second hooker, chokermen, whistlepunk, and yarding leverman); and a "loading" or "landing" crew, consisting of loading leverman, fireman, head loader, second loader, chaser, and bunkmaker.

Skidder landing   *see* Landing.

Skidder spar or tree   *see* Spar tree.

Skidder spur   a small spur line at the landing where the skidder is parked.

Skidding   the process of yarding logs from where they are felled to where they are loaded; in ground yarding this takes place on a skid road, in highlead yarding, on a "road."

Skookum   strong, powerful, well-made, solid (Chinook jargon).

Skyline   an overhead cable stretched taut between head spar and back spar along which logs are yarded into the skidder landing, by means of choker cables suspended from a travelling carriage.

Slash   debris resulting from logging; or a logged-off area strewn with such debris.

Slash fire or burn   a controlled fire set in logging slash, usually in fall, to remove debris, reduce risk of forest fire, and promote growth of Douglas fir.

Sled   two hewn Douglas fir skids bolted to the bottom of a donkey or yarder to enable locomotion; also called sleigh.

Sleighmaker   man who makes sleds for donkeys or yarders.

Snipe   to bevel the end of a log so it will ride smoothly over a skid road during ground yarding.

Spar (Spar tree)   a topped and limbed Douglas fir tree (either standing or raised) to which cables are attached for yarding and loading logs in skidder logging. Most spar trees are about 120 feet high and at least four feet in diameter at the base. Also called head spar, home spar, skidder spar.

Sparkcatcher   used two ways: 1) a cap resembling a chef's hat that is placed on top of locomotive, donkey, and skidder smokestacks to reduce the chance of fire (also called a spark arrestor); 2) a boy or elderly man hired by a logging company to douse sparks produced by locomotives, donkeys, or skidders, using a hose attached to a water tank on his back.

Speeder   a four-wheeled, gas-engined vehicle running on railway tracks. Transports logging and camp personnel, and the section gang to repair the grade; took the place of the handcar.

Splice   to join together two cables, or ends of the same cable, by unravelling and tying the individual strands. *See also* Eye splice, Long splice.

Springboard   a Douglas fir plank five or six feet long and two inches thick, inserted into a notch in a tree as high as twelve feet from the ground. A faller stands on a springboard to avoid a swelled butt and large amounts of pitch; also for a foothold on sloping ground. Also called chopping board or falling board.

Spud   a steel bar with a spoon-shaped blade for removing bark from timber.

Spur line   subsidiary line on a railway; also called feeder line.

Stakey   used to describe a logger who had made a "stake." To get stakey meant to get the urge to quit and collect his paycheque, get out of camp, and go to town to spend his money, often with binge consequences.

Standing tree   a tree selected in its original position as a spar. *See also* Raised tree, Spar.

Steam pot   *see* Donkey engine.

Steel gang or crew   the crew concerned with laying down steel rails, tamping ties, and dumping gravel for the logging railway.

Stow   to push logs into pockets at booming grounds.

Straw boss   an assistant foreman.

Stump ranch   a subsistence farm on logged-over land, often bought from a logging company.

Surveyors   the crew that works with the civil engineer to survey logged areas, lay out railways and campsites, and generally plan a logging operation. Used by loggers interchangeably with "engineers."

Swamper   an apprentice or assistant to a teamster on a horse or oxen logging show; later, an assistant on a steam shovel or Caterpillar. *See also* Mat-hooker.

Swedish fiddle   a crosscut falling or bucking saw.

Swifter   bored boomstick between sixty-six and seventy-two feet long, placed across the top of a log boom, and for stability linked to the boom with boom chains. *See also* Rider log.

Swiftering   the act of pulling swifter logs across a boom and securing them by boom chains, usually with the help of a humdirgen. Also called "pulling swifters."

Tailstick   the boomstick at the bottom end of a log boom; generally seventy-two feet long.

Teepee   a hang-up consisting of three or more trees that refuse to fall.

Timber cruiser (Cruiser)   man who initially surveys a forest stand and estimates the volume of timber therein. After his field work he submits a map showing the contours and physical features of the land as well as the volume and type of timber.

Timber sticks   flawless logs, destined for use as structural timber, that are cut in long lengths, extending over more than one flatcar and requiring bunks for transport.

Timekeeper   a logging camp official who keeps track of men's working hours and wages.

Top (a tree)   in skidder logging, to remove the heavily branched top section of a spar tree in preparation for rigging.

Trip   *see* Turn.

Turn   a load of logs yarded to the landing pile in one trip; also called a trip.

Undercut   a notch chopped in a tree trunk to direct its fall when the tree is sawed from the other side.

Water scaler   a scaler at the booming grounds.

Wee McGregor   a portable bucking saw powered by a one-cylinder gas engine; precursor to chainsaw.

Weight log   a log suspended from one end of a hayrack boom as a counterweight to the boom's load.

Whistlepunk   signalman on the skidder crew who relays to the yarding leverman the hooktender's signal that the logs have been secured with chokers and may be hauled away. Whistlepunks are usually boys starting out in the woods.

Widow-maker   a loose branch or piece of bark that may fall on a logger below.

Yarder   *see* Cold decker.

Yarding   the process of moving logs, whether on land (skidding), or in the water (pulling log booms out of their pockets for towing to the mill).

Yarding crew   *see* Skidder crew.

METRIC CONVERSION CHART

1 in. = 2.5 cm

1 ft. = 30.5 cm

1 mi. = 1.6 km

1 sq. ft. = 0.09 m^2

1 acre = 4047 m^2 or 0.4 ha

1 sq. mi. = 2.6 km^2 or 259 ha

1000 ft.b.m. = 2.358 m^3

1 lb. = 0.45 kg

1 ton = 907 kg

1 mph = 1.6 km/hr

1°F = $\frac{5}{9}$°C

bibliography

INTERVIEWS CONDUCTED BY THE AUTHOR

Anderson, Arne, 28 December 1997

Anderson, Walter, 7 February 1999

Annand, Gordon, 2 October 1996

Appleby, Madge (*née* Shepherd), 24 February 2000

Bailey, Dick and Eva (*née* Manson), 21 November 1998

Bailey, Lloyd and Thora, 1 December 1996

Barnett, Tom, 27 January 1997

Bayly, Brian, 2 October 1996

Beadnell, Jack, 23 January 1996

Berkeley, Eddy, 25 and 28 November 1996

Biss, Frank and Ruth (*née* Christenson),
    16 and 17 November 1998

Blackburn, Fred and Mavis (*née* Harrison),
    30 October 1996, 10 and 15 December 1996

Blackburn, Gord, 30 October 1996

Bowdler, Lucy, 17 April 1998

Bowen, Ron, 14 and 16 October 1999

Brady-Browne, Neil, 18 November 1998

Brooks, Allan and Betty (*née* Hatfield), 9 November 1995,
    29 January 1996, 30 November 1996, 19 April 1998,
    25 December 1998

Brown, Nancy (*née* Thomson), 9 December 1998,
    6 February 1999

Buchanan, Melda (*née* McCulloch), 22 January 1996,
    17 March 2000

Bullen, Alice, 1 December 1996, 17 October 1997

Carwithen, Malcolm, October 1996

Churchill, Emma (*née* Ducca), 16 November 1998

Churchill, Hiram and Mavis (*née* Janes),
    7 September 1998, 27 and 28 March 1999, 13 May 1999,
    6 and 24 June 1999

Churchill, Wallace, 16 November 1998, 4 February 1999,
    24 June 1999

Cliffe, Bob and Lil (*née* Willis), 6 February 1998,
    18 April 1998, 2 February 1999

Cliffe, Inez (*née* Ledgerwood), 11 October 1996

Cliffe, Lorna, 9 December 1998, 31 March 1999

Cliffe, Mabel (*née* Olson), 23 November 1997,
    16 November 1998, 24 February 2000

Cooper, Florence (*née* Olson), 23 and 24 February 2000

Coulter, Ida (*née* Grant), 29 March 1997

Currie, Phyllis (*née* Radford), 5 September 1998

Dalby, Ralph, 5 September 1998, 8 December 1998,
    28 August 1999

Davis, Beatty and Penny (*née* Bailey),
    10 and 13 November 1996, 23 November 1999

Davison, Frank and Kay (*née* Blakely), 5 and 7 October
    1996, 22 October 1999, 23 February 2000

Defty, Bill, 29 September 1996

Denny, Roy, 22 February 1997

Donnelly, Ed, 13 April 1999

Downey, Dick, 10, 13, 29 October 1996, 20 November 1996

Downey, Evis (*née* Slaughter), 30 October 1996

Draper, Gloria (*née* Nordin), 2 February 1999, 8 March 1999

Dunn, Margaret (*née* Smith), 5 September 1997,
    2 August 1998, 9 December 1998

Edwards, Walt, 19 January 1996, 26 February 1998,
    22 October 1999, 29 February 2000

Ell, Sven, 8 December 1998, 15 and 17 October 1999,
    22 March 2000

Erickson, Harry and Margaret, 6 and 8 December 1998,
    21 and 30 March 1999, 24 April 1999

Fossum, Jack, 20 November 1997

Gallagher, Lilian, 14 November 1996

Gordon, Bob, May 1996

Grant, Gerry, June 1996

Grant, Hugh and Allison (*née* Williams), 10 January 1998

Grant, John and Lu (*née* Carwithen), 29 December 1997

Grant, Mack, 5 November 1995

Gray, Jackie (*née* Gullett), 20 January 1996,
    29 December 1997

Griffiths, Bus, 14 December 1997

Haas, Donnie, 12 and 17 June 1999

Hanham, Stan and Betty, 1 October 1995, 3 June 1996

Hansen, Cora (*née* Cliffe), 1 October 1995

Harding, Bob and Rene, 29 January 1996, 21 May 1996

Harmston, Ralph and Thelma, 23 January 1996

Hatfield, John and Phyllis (*née* Janes),
    7 and 15 October 1996

Hembroff, Bill, 18 January 1996

Hemmingsen, John, 1 December 1996

Heron, Myrtle (*née* McKenzie), 24 and 25 February 1996, February 1998, 9 and 23 August 1998, 25 November 1998, 27 December 1998, 6 February 1999

Hilton, Hugh, 5 November 1997

Hind, Babs, 31 October 1995

Hodgins, Stan, 2 October 1995, 26 January 1996

Holmes, John and Jackie (*née* Harding), 19 and 21 January 1996, June 1996, 30 September 1996, 1 and 31 October 1996, 1 November 1996

Hopwood, Allen, October 1996

Hunt, Bob, 1 October 1996, 26 November 1996

James, Bernice (*née* Baker), 4 January 1996, 20 December 1996

Janes, Bert, 7 September 1998

Janes, Davey, 5 November 1995, 2 and 6 June 1996

Jennings, Bob, 14 December 1999

Jonsson, Gunnar, 11 and 13 October 1996

Keller, Eleanor (*née* Richter), May 1996

Kennedy, Sheila (*née* Haggarty), 18 December 1997

King, Bruce, 9 November 1996, 30 January 1999

Kitto, Richie, 20 November 1996

Kreutziger, Oscar, 19 April 1998, 29 June 1998

Lancashire, Helen (*née* Johnson), 24 February 2000

Law, George and Mona (*née* Marshall), 9 February 1998

Lehtonen, Larry, 31 January 1996, 3 June 1996

Lyttback, Bill, 14 November 1996

McIver, Don and Joan, 8 October 1996, 7 November 1996, 14 and 23 February 2000

McKay, Tom, 23 February 1996

McKenzie, Wilma, 21 January 1996

McNish, Edith (*née* Crockett), 1 February 1996

McPhee, Bob, 16 and 18 December 1997

McPhee, Bruce and Nanette (*née* Grant), 19 December 1994

McQuillan, Darrell and Patricia, 31 January 1996, 12 June 1996, 5 March 2000

McQuinn, Howard, 26 September 1995

McTaggart, Myrna (*née* Cliffe), 23 November 1997

McWilliam, Allen, 9 October 1996

Majerovich, Mike and Mary (*née* Svetich), 3 November 1996

Marriott, Barbara (*née* Duncan), 20 December 1994, 17 January 1996, 4 and 13 October 1996, 17 November 1996, 17 and 23 February 2000

Martin, Neil and Eleanor (*née* Burritt), 13 and 19 January 1996, 2 and 4 February 1996, 19 November 1996, 30 December 1997, 20 February 1998, 2 June 1999, 23 February 2000

Masters, Ruth, 10 March 1994, 17 and 18 November 1996, 28 November 1996, 1 December 1996, 17 June 1999, 22 January 2000

Menzies, Audrey (*née* Grieve), 11 February 1996, 3 June 1996

Mouat, Ivan and Sue (*née* Grieg), 10 March 1998

Muckle, Jim, 29 January 1996

Murtsell, Eddy, 6 February 1999, 23 February 2000

Nairn, Bill and Joan (*née* Bridges), 7 September 1998

Nordin, Charlie and Eleanor (*née* Bridges), 1, 4, 7 February 1999, 1 March 1999, 24 October 1999

Pagan, Tommy, 28 November 1996

Parkin, Avril (*née* Grieve), 27 December 1997

Parkin, Helen (*née* Babcock), 29 December 1997

Pelto, Mauno and Babs (*née* Burnett), 11 November 1996

Pidcock, Dick, 22 March 1999

Pidcock, Herbert, 24 and 25 October 1998, 23 and 29 March 1999, 20 June 1999

Pidcock, Les, 15 April 1996

Planedin, Jenny (*née* Whittall), 1 October 1998

Pollock, Kay (*née* Piercy), 4 June 1983

Pritchard, Allan, 22 September 1998, 21 February 1999, April 1999

Pritchard, Gordon, 25 and 29 November 1996

Quinn, Cora (*née* Bowen), 27 December 1998, 5 April 1999

Rafter, Doug and Shirley (*née* Thompson), 24 January 1996

Reid, Thelma (*née* Miner), 2 August 1998, 23 February 2000

Rennison, Stan and Betty, 24 October 1995, 28 May 1996

Ross, Brian, 2 March 1997

Shilton, Pat (*née* Burgess), 28 December 1997

Smith, Sid and Margaret (*née* Cliffe), 19 April 1998, 6 September 1998

Sprout, Norman and Eleanor (*née* Kravik), 16 and 23 November 1997

Stewart, Allan and Suzanne (*née* Hadwen), 4 November 1983

Stockand, Ray, 13 October 1996, 29 June 1998, 6 September 1998

Strachan, Sandy and Betty, 1 March 1999

Stubbs, Isabelle (*née* Moncrieff), 28 January 1996

Surgenor, Tyke, 14 December 1997

Sutton, Sybil (*née* McQuinn), 24 February 2000

Svetich, Grace (*née* Downey), 10 October 1996

Szasz, Jim and Lorraine (*née* Ingram), 17 November 1998

Szasz, Rod, 19 December 1999

Taylor, Jeanette, 21 January 1999

Telosky, Sammy, 31 December 1997, 18 March 1998

Thatcher, Fred, 14 October 1999

Tobacco, Tchuna, 23 February 1996

Tukham, Jack and Dorothy, 9 November 1996

Turner, Tony and Mary, 9 November 1996, 20 April 1998, 22 June 1998, 29 February 2000

Walker, Doris (*née* Marvin), 8 December 1997

Watson, Walter, 28 November 1996

Weaver, Robert and Marg, 9 November 1996

Weir, Jimmy, 23 February 1996

Williams, Pat (*née* Holmes), 23 June 1997, 30 July 1998, 22 January 2000

Williamson, Ron, 24 February 1996

Willis, Ken, 30 September 1996

Wilson, Bill and Betty, 10 November 1996, 18 April 1998, 17 November 1998

Wilson, Walter, 28 November 1996

Woods, Bill and Rita, 7 September 1998, 11 January 2000

Woods, Bob, 4 October 1996

Yates, George and Amelia (*née* Williams), 8 October 1996, 30 November 1996, 11 December 1996

LETTERS TO AUTHOR

Anderson, Walter, 9 October 1999, November 1999, 11 December 1999

Bailey, Eva, 9 December 1998

Barnett, Ruth, 19 April 1995, 20 August 1995

Bell, Florence, 11 May 1998

Biss, Frank, 24 March 1999, 23 June 1999, 1 and 27 January 2000

Cliffe, Lorna, 21 March 1999

Dady, Art, March 1998

Davison, Frank, June 1999, December 1999

Donnelly, Ed, 14 April 1999, 26 May 1999, 16 June 1999, 17 July 1999

Downey, Dick, March 1999

Ell, Sven, 27 March 1999, 11 January 2000

Erickson, Fred, March 1999

Gray, Jackie, 16 March 1998

Haggarty, Colton, 11 December 1997

Heron, Myrtle, 2 February 1998, 1 December 1998

Jennings, Bob, 16 December 1999

Jonsson, Gunnar, 25 May 1999

McIver, Don, 25 March 1998, 7 March 1999, December 1999, January 2000, 23 March 2000

McPhee, Bruce and Nan, 22 December 1997

Martin, Neil, 16 and 29 January 1998, 10 March 1999, October 1999, 20 October 1999

Masters, Ruth, 31 January 1996, 5 June 1999

Muckle, Jim, 24 October 1999

Nordin, Charlie Jr., May 1999, October 1999

Nordin, Charlie and Harry, May 1999

Parkin, Helen, 12 February 1999

Pidcock, Herbert, June 1999

Pritchard, Allan, 25 March 1995, 27 June 1995, 28 August 1995, 28 December 1995, 14 June 1996, 4 November 1998, 31 March 1999

Rippingdale, Janet, 18 December 1997

Rogers, Fred, 5 May 1996, 31 May 1996

Shopland, Lois, March 1999

Smith, Margaret, July 1998

Sprout, Norman, November 1997

Stewart, Alan, 1 November 1995

Stubbs, Isabelle, 20 February 1999

Szasz, Rod, 29 August 1995, 3 February 2000

Taylor, Jeanette, 21 January 1999

Wade, Jill, 4 April 1995

Williams, Pat, 11 October 1996, 1 and 24 November 1996, 6 December 1996, 23 February 1997, 30 January 2000

Williamson, Ron, 26 November 1997

OTHER UNPUBLISHED SOURCES

Aldred, Robert William. "The Public Career of Major-General Alexander D. McRae," Master's thesis, University of Western Ontario, 1970

Anderton, Leo. Interview by Ben Hughes, 26 April 1956, TS (Typescript), Courtenay Museum

Baikie, Wallace. "Seven Years with the Comox Logging Company," TS, Campbell River Museum

Berkeley, Eddy. Papers, private collection

Buckham, Alexander Fraser. Papers, British Columbia Archives

Cartwright, Helena. "An Outline of Logging in the Comox Valley," in Isenor, "The Comox Valley"

Cash, Gwen. Scrapbook, British Columbia Archives

Cliffe, Joe. "Data on Steam Locomotives," 22 September 1980, TS, Courtenay Museum

———. "Evolution of Logging or One Man's Life in Logging on the West Coast," November 1976, TS, Courtenay Museum

———. "The Filberg I knew," c. 1980, TS, Courtenay Museum

———. Interview by Lyn Henderson, 31 July 1980, Courtenay Museum

Cliffe, Samuel Jackson. Diary, 1862–1870s, Courtenay Museum

Comox Logging and Railway Company. "Comox Lake Camp" [guestbook kept by Chris Holmes at Comox Lake Camp, 1933-44], Courtenay Museum

———. Company Records, TimberWest Office, Courtenay

———. Company Records, Courtenay Museum

Cox, Donna. "Research Notes—Logging Camps," June 1994, TS, Campbell River Museum

Davison, Frank. Papers, private collection

Donnelly, Fred. Papers, private collection

Downey, Mrs P. (née Mary Anderton). "A Settler in the Early Eighties," in Isenor, "The Comox Valley"

Drabble, George Fawcett. Field Books, 1873–1901, Drabble Papers, Campbell River Museum

Draper, Gloria. Papers, private collection

Duncan, Eric. Newspaper Cuttings and Scrapbook, c. 1927–1936, family collection

———. Draft Description and History of the Comox Valley, 1916, family collection

Filberg, Bob. Interview by C. D. Orchard, 14 June 1960, University of British Columbia Special Collections

Filberg Lodge and Park Association, Comox. Notes and photographs relating to the Comox Logging and Railway Company

Grant, Bob. Interview by Tom Menzies, 23 November 1956, Courtenay Museum

Harding, Rene. "The Story of Logging in the Comox Valley," in Isenor, "The Comox Valley"

Hembroff, Bill. Papers, private collection

Hemmingsen, John. "Matt Hemmingsen. Career Background," 1996, TS, private collection

Henderson, Lyn McClintock (née Hilton). "Arthur Mansfield Hilton," n.d., TS, British Columbia Archives

Hilton, Arthur Mansfield. 1908–1919 diaries, British Columbia Archives

———. "The Story of the Comox Logging Company," 1954 (as told to Rene Harding), in Isenor, "The Comox Valley"

Hilton, Hugh. Papers, private collection

Holmes, John. Papers, private collection

Humbird family. Papers, University of British Columbia Special Collections

Isenor, D. E., ed. "The Comox Valley: Its Pioneers. Parts 1-8," 1962, TS in Buckham Collection, British Columbia Archives

Jennings, Bob. Papers, private collection

Keller, Eleanor. Papers, private collection

Laing, Hamilton Mack. Papers, British Columbia Archives

McKelvie, B. A. "The 'S' Sign. A Biographical Sketch of Eustace Smith, Logger, Timber Cruiser and Forest Engineer," n.d., TS, Courtenay Museum

McLoughlin, Peter. Interview by Ben Hughes, c. 1958, TS, Courtenay Museum

McNish, Edith. "Livery Stables in the Comox Valley," in Isenor, "The Comox Valley"

———. "St. Joseph's General Hospital, Comox, B.C. A Summarized History for Hospital Day, May 1956," in Isenor, "The Comox Valley"

McPhee, Margaret (née Urquhart). Interview by George Bates, 1956, Courtenay Museum

McQuillan, Darrell. Papers, private collection

Martin, Neil. Papers, private collection

Menzies, Audrey. "George Grieve," in Isenor, "The Comox Valley"

Nordin, Charlie Jr. Papers, private collection

Parkin, Norm. Interview notes made by Martin Hagarty, c. 1984, Filberg Lodge and Park Association

Pidcock, Harry. Papers. British Columbia Archives

Pidcock, Herbert. Papers, private collection

———. "William Thomas Pidcock, 1874–1942," private collection

Pidcock, Les. Papers, private collection

Pidcock, Reg. Interview notes made by Martin Hagarty, c. 1984, Filberg Lodge and Park Association

Pidcock, Robert H. "Record of Teachers at Oyster River School, 1922–1933," n.d., MS, private collection

Rogers, Fred. Papers, private collection

Spielman, Phyllis, ed. "The Filbergs. A History of Four Filberg Brothers and a Nephew, All from Sweden, Who Came to the U.S.A. in the 1880s . . ." TS, May 1993, Courtenay Museum

Stewart, Florence M. J. "The History of the Cliffe Family in the Comox Valley (1862-1979), TS, private collection

Weir, James. "James Weir, January 1991" [Reminiscences], TS, private collection

SELECTED NEWSPAPERS AND PERIODICALS

Comox Argus, 1919–1955

Comox District Free Press, 1958

Crown Zellerbach News, 1964

Victoria Daily Colonist, 1905

Nanaimo Daily Free Press, 1958

Vancouver Province, 1948

West Coast Lumberman, 1925, 1940

Western Lumberman, 1908–1910

PUBLISHED SOURCES

Agnes, Sister Mary. *The Congregation of the Sisters of St. Joseph* (Toronto: St. Joseph's Convent, 1951)

Andrews, Ralph W. "This Was Logging!" *Selected Photographs of Darius Kinsey* (Seattle: Superior Publishing Company, 1954)

———. *Glory Days of Logging* (Seattle: Superior Publishing Company, 1956)

———. *Timber: Toil and Trouble in the Big Woods* (Seattle: Superior Publishing Company, 1968)

Anon. "Comox, The Island Favoured District," *Telephone Talk* 3:6 (June 1913), 5-9

———. "The Evolution of Yarding Methods at the Coast," *Western Lumberman* (April 1919), reprinted in *Whistle Punk 1:3* (Summer 1985), 23-29

Arnett, Chris and Maywell Wickheim. *4,000 Years: A History of the Rainforest of Vancouver Island's Southwest Coast* (Sooke: Sooke Regional Museum and Archives, 1989)

Baikie, Harper. *A Boy and His Axe* (Campbell River: Harper Baikie, 1991)

Baikie, Wallace. *Rolling with the Times* (Campbell River: Kask Graphics, 1985)

Baptie, Sue. *First Growth: The Story of British Columbia Forest Products Limited* (Vancouver: British Columbia Forest Products, 1975)

Barman, Jean. *The West Beyond the West: A History of British Columbia* (Toronto: University of Toronto Press, 1991)

Bergren, Myrtle. *Tough Timber: the Loggers of British Columbia—Their Story* (Vancouver: Elgin Publications, 1979)

Biscoe, F. R. Fraser. *Comox Valley Farm Lands* (Courtenay: 1921) [pamphlet]

Blythe, Ronald. *Akenfield: Portrait of an English Village* (Harmondsworth, UK: Penguin, 1969)

Bowen, Lynne. *Those Lake People: Stories of Lake Cowichan* (Vancouver: Douglas & McIntyre, 1995)

Canadian Western Lumber Company. *Report of the Boards of Directors of Canadian Western Lumber Company, Limited, and the Columbia River Lumber Company, Limited, as at December 31st, 1911* (London: Waterlow & Sons, 1912)

Carney, Pat. "Bob Filberg—A Smiling, Swearing Logger," *Vancouver Sun, 3* November 1967

Carroll, Leila. *Wild Roses and Rail Fences* (Courtenay: E. W. Bickle Ltd., 1975)

Cliffe, Joe. "Early Methods of Logging," in Isenor, *Land of Plenty*, 184-87

Coulson, Barry. *The Logger's Digest Vol. 1: From Horses to Helicopters* (Victoria: Orca Books, 1992)

Courtenay Board of Trade. *Courtenay, Comox District* (*c.* 1913) [pamphlet]

Crawford, Dora. "First Prize Article," *Union Weekly News*, 21 September 1897, 1

Cummings, Doug, Gary Oliver and Keith Anderson. "Comox Logging and Railway Company. Railway History," *The Steamchest 5:6* (August 1962), 1-11

Dalziel, Ron. *It Was Quite a Performance: The Memoirs of Ron Dalziel* (Victoria: Classic Memoirs, 1997)

Davies, Oscar (as told to Lucy Bowdler). "Flashback on Logging," *Victoria Daily Colonist*, 9 March 1969, 12-13

Day, David. "Eustace Smith: The Last Authority," in Howard White, ed., *Raincoast Chronicles Six/Ten* (Madeira Park: Harbour Publishing, 1983), 272-75

———, ed. "Men of the Forest," *Sound Heritage 6:3* (Victoria: Provincial Archives of British Columbia, 1977)

Day, J. H., L. Farstad and D. G. Laird. *Soil Survey of Southeast Vancouver Island and Gulf Islands, British Columbia* (Ottawa: The Queen's Printer, 1959)

Drushka, Ken. *Against Wind and Weather: The History of Towboating in British Columbia* (Vancouver: Douglas & McIntyre, 1991)

———. *HR: A Biography of HR MacMillan* (Madeira Park: Harbour Publishing, 1995)

———. *Working in the Woods: A History of Logging on the West Coast* (Madeira Park: Harbour Publishing, 1992)

Duncan, Eric. *From Shetland to Vancouver Island: Recollections of Seventy-Eight Years* (Edinburgh: Oliver and Boyd, 1934)

———. *The Rich Fisherman and Other Tales* (London: The Century Press, 1910)

———. *Rural Rhymes and the Sheep Thief* (Toronto: William Briggs, 1896)

———. "The Tsolum River," *Gems of Poetry 2:4* (14 June 1881), 188-89

———. "Vancouver Island from a Farmer's Standpoint," *Chambers's Journal* (June 1903), 366-68

Egan, Brian. *The Ecology of the Coastal Douglas-fir Zone* (Victoria: Ministry of Forests, n.d.)

Englebert, Renny. "Hunt's Fine Dairy Farm," *Forest and Mill* (10 November 1947), 3

———. "Sixty-One Years in the Forests of British Columbia: The Story of Eustace Smith, Timber Cruiser," *Forest and Mill* (13 April 1948), 3

Evans, Patrick M. O. *The Pritchards and Related Families* (Ottawa: The Descendants of James and Judith Pritchard, Inc., *c.* 1980)

Feely, Jean and Margery Corrigall. *A History of 'Tle-tla-tay' (Royston)* (Royston, BC: Royston Centennial Committee, *c.* 1967)

Filberg, R. J. "In My Time: Filberg Recalls His Early Days in Logging on Coast," *The Truck Logger* (January 1968)

Fossum, Jack. *Mancatcher: An Immigrant's Story of Logging Policing and Pioneering in the Canadian West* (Comox: Lindsay Press, 1990)

Galloway, F. W. "The Call of Oyster River in the Backwoods of Vancouver Island," *The Field* (22 August 1936), 450

Galois, Robert M. Plate 22 of Donald Kerr, ed., *Historical Atlas of Canada, Volume 3: Addressing the Twentieth Century* (Toronto: University of Toronto Press, 1990)

Garner, Joe. *Never Chop Your Rope* (Nanaimo: Cinnabar Press, 1988)

Glover-Geidt, Janette. *The Friendly Port: A History of Union Bay, 1880–1960* (Campbell River: Kask Graphics, 1990)

Gold, Wilmer. *Logging As It Was: A Pictorial History of Logging on Vancouver Island* (Victoria: Morriss Publishing, 1985)

Gormely, Marc. "From Cruisers to Foresters: Background to a Profession," *Whistle Punk 1:1* (Spring 1984), 3-7

Gould, Ed. *Logging: British Columbia's Logging History* (Saanichton: Hancock House, 1975)

Green, Mervyn T. *British Columbia Industrial Locomotives* (Richmond: M. T. Green, 1986)

Griffiths, Bus. *Now You're Logging* (Madeira Park: Harbour Publishing, 1978)

Haig-Brown, Roderick. *Timber* (Toronto: William Collins, 1946)

Hak, Gordon. "British Columbia Loggers and the Lumber Workers' Industrial Union, 1919–1922," *Labour/Le Travail 23* (Spring 1989), 67-90

———. "Red Wages: Communists and the 1934 Vancouver Island Loggers Strike," *Pacific Northwest Quarterly 80:3* (1989), 82-90

Hames, Jack. *Field Notes: An Environmental History* (Courtenay: Gertrude Hames, 1990)

Harding, Rene. "'Black Friday' a Scare," *Comox District Free Press*, 18 August 1976

———. "History of Lumbering in the Comox Valley," *Comox Argus*, 9 February 1955, 10

———. "Valley Logging Started in 1872," *Comox District Free Press*, 25 October 1967, 10

Heltzel, Muriel Gabriel and Marjorie Gabriel Neilson, comps. *The Gabriel-Hitt Family* (Beaverton, OR: Copies Plus, 1986)

Hodgins, Jack. *Broken Ground* (Toronto: McClelland & Stewart, 1998)

———. *Spit Delaney's Island* (Toronto: Macmillan, 1981)

Hodgins, Reta Blakely, ed. *Merville and Its Early Settlers 1919–1985* (Campbell River: Kask Graphics, 1985)

Hughes, Ben. *History of the Comox Valley, 1862–1945* (Nanaimo: Evergreen Press, *c.* 1962)

Hutchison, Bruce. *The Unknown Country: Canada and Her People* (Toronto: Longmans, Green, 1942)

International Woodworkers of America. *I.W.A. Annual 1976* (Vancouver: Brent G. Naylor Publications, 1976)

Isenor, D. E., Margaret McGill and Donna Watson, eds. *"For Our Children": A History of Comox Valley Schools* (Courtenay: School Board District #71, *c.* 1980)

———, W. N. McInnis, E. G. Stephens and D. E. Watson, eds. *Land of Plenty: A History of the Comox District* (Campbell River: Ptarmigan Press, 1987)

———, E. G. Stephens and D. E. Watson, eds. *Edge of Discovery: A History of the Campbell River District* (Campbell River: Ptarmigan Press, 1989)

James, Rick. "Logging Saga," *Victoria Times Colonist Islander*, 20 July 1997

———. "Over 1,000 Miles of Railroad Logging Tracks Laid in Region," *North Island News*, 12 December 1993, 34

———. "Schooner Saga," *Victoria Times Colonist Islander*, 26 October 1994

Jungen, John. *Soils of South Vancouver Island* (Victoria: Ministry of the Environment, 1985)

Keenleyside, Hugh. *Memoirs of Hugh L. Keenleyside, Vol. 1: Hammer the Golden Day* (Toronto: McClelland & Stewart, 1981)

Lachocki, Michael. "Early Logging Methods in the Campbell River Area," Campbell River Museum and Archives, *Museum Note 4* (1983), 1-4

Laing, Hamilton M. *Allan Brooks: Artist-Naturalist* (Victoria: British Columbia Provincial Museum, 1979)

Laroque, Colin P. and Dan J. Smith. "Tree-ring Analysis of Yellow-cedar (*Chamaecyparis nootkatensis*) on Vancouver Island, British Columbia," *Canadian Journal of Forest Research 29:1* (1999), 115-23

Lembcke, Jerry and William M. Tattam. *One Union in Wood: A Political History of the International Woodworkers of America* (Madeira Park: Harbour Publishing, 1984)

Leonoff, Cyril E. *An Enterprising Life: Leonard Frank Photographs 1895–1944* (Vancouver: Talonbooks, 1990)

Loomis, Ruth, with Merv Wilkinson. *Wildwood: A Forest for the Future* (Gabriola: Reflections, 1990)

McArthur, Craig J. and Frank Waters. *B.C. Centennial of Logging: A Century of Photographs* (Vancouver: The Truck Logger and Gordon Black Publications, 1966)

MacKay, Donald. *Empire of Wood: The MacMillan Bloedel Story* (Vancouver: Douglas & McIntyre, 1983)

Mackie, Richard Somerset. "Farmers to Loggers: The Comox Logging Company in the Twentieth Century," *British Columbia Forest History Newsletter 46* (April 1996), 7-8

———. *Hamilton Mack Laing: Hunter-Naturalist* (Victoria: Sono Nis Press, 1985)

———. *The Wilderness Profound: Victorian Life on the Gulf of Georgia* (Victoria: Sono Nis Press, 1995)

McLeod Gould, L. *From B.C. to Baisieux, Being the Narrative History of the 102nd Canadian Infantry Battalion* (Victoria: Thos. R. Cusack Presses, 1919)

Macoun, John. "Professor Macoun's Impression of Comox District," *Courtenay Weekly News*, 5 July 1893

Mayse, Arthur. *My Father, My Friend* (Madeira Park: Harbour Publishing, 1993)

Mitchell, Helen A. *Diamond in the Rough: A History of Campbell River* (Campbell River: The Upper Islander, 1966)

———. "A Mountain Named Myra," *Victoria Daily Colonist Islander*, 13 February 1972, 3

Mulholland, F. D. *The Forest Resources of British Columbia* (Victoria: King's Printer, 1937)

Myers, Jeanne. "Class and Community in the Fraser Mills Strike, 1931," in Rennie Warburton and David Coburn, eds., *Workers, Capital, and the State in British Columbia: Selected Papers* (Vancouver: UBC Press, 1988), 141-57

O'Brennan, Thomas. *Our Branch of the Tree* (Vancouver: privately printed, 1989) [McQuinn family history]

Olsen, W. H. *Water over the Wheel: A Story of the Chemainus Valley* (Chemainus: Chemainus Crofton Chamber of Commerce, 1981)

Ormsby, Margaret. *British Columbia: A History* (Toronto: Macmillan of Canada, 1958)

Parminter, John. "Fire History and Effects on Vegetation in Three Biogeoclimatic Zones of British Columbia," in *Fire and the Environment: Ecological and Cultural Perspectives* (Knoxville, TN: United States Department of the Interior, Parks Service, 1990), 263-72

Paterson, T. W. "Half Century of Logging History Comes to an End," *Victoria Daily Colonist*, 25 June 1978

Pemberton, J. Despard. *Facts and Figures Relating to Vancouver Island and British Columbia, Showing What to Expect and How to Get There* (London: Longman, Green, Longman, and Roberts, 1860)

Phillips, Paul. *No Power Greater: A Century of Labour in British Columbia* (Vancouver: BC Federation of Labour, 1967)

Piercy, Archie. *Thomas Piercy, Jane Speedy Married March 11, 1867* ([Courtenay]: *c.* 1967)

Pierre, Joseph H. *When Timber Stood Tall* (Seattle: Superior Publishing Company, 1979)

Pojar, J., K. Klinka and D. A. Demarchi. "Coastal Western Hemlock Zone," in Del Meidinger and Jim Pojar, eds., *Ecosystems of British Columbia* (Victoria: Ministry of Forests, 1991), 95-111

Pritchard, Allan. "Jack Hodgins's Island: A Big Enough Country," *University of Toronto Quarterly 55:1* (Fall, 1985), 21-44

———. "West of the Great Divide: Man and Nature in the Literature of British Columbia," *Canadian Literature 102* (Autumn 1984), 35-53

Prouty, Andrew Mason. *More Deadly than War: Pacific Coast Logging, 1827–1981* (New York: Garland Publishing, 1985)

Rajala, Richard A. *Clearcutting the Pacific Rain Forest: Production, Science, and Regulation* (Vancouver: UBC Press, 1998)

———. "'A Dandy Bunch of Wobblies,' Pacific Coast Loggers and the Industrial Workers of the World," *Labor History 37* (Spring 1996), 205-34

Reksten, Terry. *The Dunsmuir Saga* (Vancouver: Douglas & McIntyre, 1991)

Richardson, James. "Report on the Coal Fields of the East Coast of Vancouver Island," in *Geological Survey of Canada, Reports of Explorations and Surveys 1871-72* (Montreal: Dawson Brothers, 1872), 73-100

Schmidt, R. L. "Factors Controlling the Distribution of Douglas-fir in Coastal British Columbia," *Quarterly Journal of Forestry* 54:2 (April 1960), 156-60

———. *The Silvics and Plant Geography of the Genus Abies in the Coastal Forests of British Columbia* (Victoria: Queen's Printer, 1957)

Schulz, Henry. *A New Frontier: The Canadian Chronicles of Henry Schulz* (Campbell River: Ptarmigan Press, 1984)

Stubbs, Dorothy I. *"All About Us": A History of the City of Courtenay* (Courtenay: *c.* 1965)

———. "Logging Trains Huffed Through City Centre," *Courtenay Record*, 7 April 1995

Swanson, Robert E. *Book 3, Bunkhouse Ballads* (Toronto: Thomas Allen, 1945)

———. *Rhymes of a Western Logger: A Book of Verse* (Vancouver: The Lumberman Printing Company, 1942)

———. "A Saga of the Tsolum River," *Forest and Mill 2:7* (13 April 1948), 2

Taylor, G. W. *Builders of British Columbia: An Industrial History* (Victoria: Morriss Publishing, 1982)

———. *Timber: History of the Forest Industry in B.C.* (Vancouver: J. J. Douglas, 1975)

Taylor, Jeanette. *River City: A History of Campbell River and the Discovery Islands* (Madeira Park: Harbour Publishing, 1999)

Turner, Robert D. *Logging by Rail: The British Columbia Story* (Victoria: Sono Nis Press, 1990)

———. "Logging Railroads and Locomotives in British Columbia: A Background Summary and the Preservation Record," *Material History Bulletin* (Fall 1981), 3-20

———. "Pacific Coast Logging: Comox Log Unloader," *Railroad Model Craftsman 52:8* (January 1984), 88-94

———. *Vancouver Island Railroads* (Victoria: Sono Nis Press, 1997)

Twigg, Rubina. "Shipwrecked at Oyster River," *The Rural Shopper 3:1* (May 1998), 1, 4

———. "Stan Hanham," *The Rural Shopper* (June 1998), 8

University of British Columbia. *Record of Service, 1914–1918* (Vancouver: 1924)

Vessey, Bessie. *My Little Comox Shack* (Toronto: W. R. Draper, 1927) [musical score]

Whitford, H. N. and R. D. Craig. *Forests of British Columbia* (Ottawa: 1918)

Wild, Paula. "The Graveyard of Ships," *In Focus Magazine 6:4* (September 1998), 9-11

Willemar, J. X. Letter to the editor, *Banner of Faith,* reprinted in *Columbia Mission Annual Reports,* 24th Report, for 1884–1885

Wong, Daryl. "The Pacific Coast Logging Industry in the 1930s," *British Columbia Historical News, 29:3* (Summer 1996), 26-30

Workers' Compensation Board of British Columbia. *Yarding and Loading Handbook* (Vancouver: Workers' Compensation Board of British Columbia, 1980)

index